D1796901

The Jews as a Chosen People

The concept of the Jews as a chosen people is a key element of the Jewish faith and identity. This book explores the idea of chosenness from the ancient world, through modernity and into the post-Holocaust era.

Analysing a vast corpus of biblical, ancient, rabbinic and modern Jewish literature, the author seeks to give a better understanding of this central doctrine of the Jewish religion. She shows that although the idea of chosenness has been central to Judaism and Jewish self-definition, it has not been carried to the present day in the same form. Instead it has gone through constant change, depending on who is employing it, against what sort of background, and for what purpose. Surveying the different and sometimes conflicting interpretations of the doctrine of chosenness that appear in ancient, modern, and post-Holocaust periods, the dominant themes of 'holiness', 'mission', and 'survival' are identified in each respective period. The theological, philosophical, and sociological dimensions of the question of Jewish chosenness are thus examined in their historical context, as responses to the challenges of Christianity, Modernity, and the Holocaust in particular.

This book will be of interest to scholars and students of Jewish Studies, the Holocaust, religion and theology.

S. Leyla Gürkan is a research fellow in the Department of History of Religions for the Centre for Islamic Studies (ISAM), Istanbul. Her research interests include Jewish theology and comparative approaches to Jewish and Islamic concepts. She is the author of a Turkish book on Judaism.

Routledge Jewish studies series

Series Editor: Oliver Leaman
University of Kentucky

Studies, which are interpreted to cover the disciplines of history, sociology, anthropology, culture, politics, philosophy, theology, religion, as they relate to Jewish affairs. The remit includes texts which have as their primary focus, issues, ideas, personalities, and events of relevance to Jews, Jewish life, and the concepts which have characterized Jewish culture both in the past and today. The series is interested in receiving appropriate scripts or proposals.

Medieval Jewish Philosophy
An introduction
Dan Cohn-Sherbok

Facing the Other
The ethics of Emmanuel Levinas
Edited by Seán Hand

Moses Maimonides
Oliver Leaman

A User's Guide to Franz Rosenzweig's Star of Redemption
Norbert M. Samuelson

On Liberty
Jewish philosophical perspectives
Edited by Daniel H. Frank

Referring to God
Jewish and Christian philosophical and theological perspectives
Edited by Paul Helm

Judaism, Philosophy, Culture
Selected studies by E.I.J. Rosenthal
Erwin Rosenthal

Philosophy of the Talmud
Hyam Maccoby

From Synagogue to Church: The Traditional Design
Its beginning, its definition, its end
John Wilkinson

Hidden Philosophy of Hannah Arendt
Margaret Betz Hull

Deconstructing the Bible
Abraham ibn Ezra's introduction to the Torah
Irene Lancaster

Image of the Black in Jewish Culture
A history of the Other
Abraham Melamed

From Falashas to Ethiopian Jews
Daniel Summerfield

Philosophy in a Time of Crisis
Don Isaac Abravanel: defender of the faith
Seymour Feldman

Jews, Muslims and Mass Media
Mediating the 'Other'
Edited by Tudor Parfitt with Yulia Egorova

Jews of Ethiopia
The birth of an elite
Edited by Emanuela Trevisan Semi and Tudor Parfitt

Art in Zion
The genesis of national art in Jewish Palestine
Dalia Manor

Hebrew Language and Jewish Thought
David Patterson

Contemporary Jewish Philosophy
An introduction
Irene Kajon

The Jews as a Chosen People

Tradition and transformation

S. Leyla Gürkan

Routledge
Taylor & Francis Group

LONDON AND NEW YORK

First published 2009
by Routledge
2 Park Square, Milton Park, Abingdon, Oxon OX14 4RN

Simultaneously published in the USA and Canada
by Routledge
270 Madison Ave, New York, NY 10016

Routledge is an imprint of the Taylor & Francis Group, an informa business

Typeset in Times by Wearset Ltd, Boldon, Tyne and Wear
Printed and bound in Great Britain by TJI Digital, Padstow, Cornwall

British Library Cataloguing in Publication Data
A catalogue record for this book is available from the British Library

Library of Congress Cataloging in Publication Data
Gürkan, Salime Leyla.
The Jews as a chosen people: tradition and transformation/S. Leyla
Gürkan.
p. cm. – (Routledge Jewish studies series)
Includes bibliographical references and index.
1. Jews–Election, Doctrine of–History of doctrines. I. Title.

BM613.G87 2008
296.3'1172–dc22
2008026896

ISBN10: 0-415-46607-5 (hbk)
ISBN10: 0-203-88489-2 (ebk)

ISBN13: 978-0-415-46607-3 (hbk)
ISBN13: 978-0-203-88489-8 (ebk)

To the memory of my beloved father,
N. Haldun Gürkan,
to whom I owe everything I have and everything I am.

Contents

Preface

This book, which grew out of a PhD thesis, is the result, on the one hand, of a personal curiosity about the Jewish idea of chosenness, which, I believe, is what makes Judaism what it is, and, on the other hand, of a scholarly interest in examining the process in which the idea has developed until today. I believe the underlying cause of such curiosity and interest has something to do with my Muslim background, which has enabled me to be familiar with many aspects of Jewish and Christian religions throughout my education for all these religions belong to what are known as Semitic religions. This familiarity has provided me with a desire to know more about what is different in them. Moreover, the idea of chosenness is one of the topics which immediately grabbed my attention when I started to study the history of religions in Istanbul, and my interest in the topic intensified during my MA and PhD in the Department of Religious Studies at Lancaster University. I can suggest two reasons for this. First, the idea of chosenness lies at the centre of the Jewish religion and, therefore, is essential to understanding Judaism. Second, I could find some references to the election of the people of Israel in Islamic sources, which increased my interest in the topic. In parallel to this there is one particular personal observation that I would like to share. I find it quite interesting, and also contrary to what is commonly believed, that the idea of chosenness is, in fact, a problem for a Jew, whereas for a non-Jew it is more a matter of curiosity. This is why, while trying to quench my curiosity as an outsider, I have also come to share an intense and sometimes agonizing experience of writing about chosenness. And it is in the hope of making a contribution to a better understanding of the Jewish identity as well as Jewish religion, as shaped around different Jewish interpretations of chosenness over the course of time, that I have written this book.

I would like to thank all the people who have helped make this possible. First of all my sincere and special thanks go to my supervisor, Professor John Sawyer, and my editor, Professor Oliver Leaman, for the encouragement and help in getting it published. I would also like to thank my examiners, Professor Richard Roberts and Professor Nicholas de Lange, for providing very helpful comments on the first draft, and Professor Robert Segal and Professor David Waines for their valuable advice during my PhD. I am also grateful to my friends and colleagues for their constant encouragement and support. Last and most of all I wish to express my profound thanks to my family for their precious love and caring support, without which this book would never have come to existence.

May 2008, Istanbul

Abbreviations

1QM	The War Rule
1QS	The Community Rule
Ab.	Aboth
Abr.	*De Abrahamo*
A.Z.	Abodah Zara
B.B.	Baba Bathra
Ber.	Berakoth
Cant. R.	*Cantata Rabbah*
CD	The Damascus Rule
Cong.	*De Congressu*
Decal.	*De Decalogo*
Dt. R.	*Deuteronomy Rabbah*
Est. R.	*Esther Rabbah*
Ex. R.	*Exodus Rabbah*
Gen. R.	*Genesis Rabbah*
Hag.	Hagigah
Hor.	Horayoth
Hul.	Hullin
Immut.	*Quod Deus immutabilis sit*
JAAR	*Journal of the American Academy of Religion*
JPS	The Jewish Publication Society
Ket.	Ketuboth
Koh. R.	*Koheleth Rabbah*
Leg. All.	*Legum Allegoriarum*
Legat.	*De Legatione ad Gaium*
Lev. R.	*Leviticus Rabbah*
Mek.d.r.Ish	*Mekilta de-Rabbi Ishmael*
Men.	Menahoth
Midr. Ps.	*Midrash to Psalms*
Mig.	*De Migratione Abrahami*
Mos.	*De Vita Mosis*
Mut.	*De Mutatione Nominum*
NRSV	New Revised Standard Version of the Bible

Num. R.	*Numbers Rabbah*
Pesik.	*Pesikta de-Rab Kahana*
Post.	*De Posteritate Caini*
Praem.	*De Praemiis et Poenis*
Quis Her.	*Quis Rerum Divinarum Heres*
RSV	Revised Standard Version of the Bible
Ruth R.	*Ruth Rabbah*
Sab.	Sabbath
Sanh.	Sanhedrin
Som.	*De Somnis*
Sot.	Sotah
Spec. Leg.	*De Specialibus Legibus*
Virt.	*De Virtutibus*

Introduction

The Jewish idea of the chosen people is one of the topics on which a great number of academic as well as non-academic works have been written from theological, philosophical, and psychological perspectives. However, if we put aside Arnold Eisen's *The Chosen People in America* (1983), little has been done concerning the socio-historical aspect of the question of chosenness, and Eisen's excellent work restricts its scope to American Jewish experience from the late nineteenth century to 1980. This present study aims to examine the relation between the development of the idea of chosenness and the shaping of Jewish religion, in particular as it affects notions of Jewish identity down through the ages. The intention is to survey a vast corpus of Jewish literature, biblical, ancient Jewish, rabbinic, and modern, and conduct a descriptive and analytical study designed to contribute to a better understanding of a central doctrine of the Jewish religion and the primary constituent of Jewish identity.

The idea of chosenness, which basically denotes the special relationship between God and the people of Israel, is the *raison d'être* of the Jewish religion as well as Jewish people. In one way the Jewish idea of being chosen refers to a general problem of all monotheistic religions in respect of their claim to exclusive truth; in this Judaism is not alone. However, unlike the Christian notion of chosenness and the Islamic claim to truth, both of which are individualist and faith-centred, the Jewish doctrine of chosenness is based on the physical and collective existence of one people, the Jews. Indeed, what is unique about the Jewish idea of chosenness is related to the fact that it provides Judaism with the elements of religion and nationality at once.[1] This is why the Jewish religion is bound up with the existence and experience of the Jewish people as a physical collective entity. So Judaism does not only shape but is also shaped by its followers, namely the Jewish people, more so than any other religion is.

Despite an apparent traditional Jewish emphasis on being the priestly people of God serving humanity, chosenness is usually understood in terms of 'a covenantal community in which one's primary concern is for his own people'.[2] As a result of this, the Jewish conception of a special relationship between God and Israel also erects a fundamental separation between Jews and other nations, by leaving the latter at the periphery of Jewish history. From a non-Jewish, and particularly Christian, point of view, however, the ongoing Jewish claim to chosenness and uniqueness becomes a reason for the Jewish subjection to otherness, inferiority, and even persecution.[3] Nevertheless, it was, and still is, strongly emphasized by many that the election of Israel among all other peoples was due to its monotheistic commitment in the completely idolatrous world of ancient times. Thus chosenness, it is argued, was granted to serve one God in purity and not for the attainment of any privilege or superiority.[4] However, there have been, and still are, Jews who believe in the holiness and superiority of the Jewish people as an innate and eternal quality. Besides, in the presence of other monotheistic religions, the ongoing Jewish insistence on chosenness and the subsequent claim to having a 'unique' role in the establishment of monotheism in the world seems superfluous. In such circumstances, Judaism could claim at best to undertake 'a' role to help, alongside other monotheistic religions, the establishment of the true worship of one God – as has been advocated by several modern Jewish scholars.

Throughout Jewish tradition there have been two major dimensions of the concept of chosenness: one as a 'quality' and the other as a 'duty'. The history of the doctrine of chosenness has witnessed sometimes an overlap of the two, namely the unconditional/substantial and conditional/relational aspects of chosenness. In rabbinic literature, in particular, these two dimensions of chosenness, quality (holiness) and duty (covenant), can be found side by side. However, according to the majority of ancient rabbis, it is because the people of Israel have been unconditionally chosen by God through his eternal love for them that they are appointed with a duty. It is formulated in Jewish liturgy as 'Blessed are you, O Lord our God, King of the universe, who has chosen us from all peoples and has given us your Law'. For some others like Maimonides, however, Israel is great only for the sake of the Torah. In this way it is believed that the Jewish people incorporated in themselves chosenness on both conditional and unconditional terms. However, the question of how far the physical Israel corresponds to the spiritual Israel has been at the centre of the Jewish religion up to contemporary times. Most of the time the physical Israel as a tangible collective community constituted of the Jews is equated with the spiritual Israel as an abstract utopian entity. Chosenness in this way refers to an eternal and unconditional quality of the Jewish people as well as and even more than an ambition towards and a search for an ideal, which might include other peoples as well. On the other hand, the tension between the 'particularity' of the election of Israel and the 'universality' of the creation of humans in the image of God and of the redemption of humanity, cannot be explained away very easily.[5] The dilemma embedded within the Jewish claim to chosenness for the service of humankind becomes even more problematic in the face of the fact that, in Judaism, humanity is usually understood to be divided into two fundamentally opposite groups: Jews (God's people) and non-Jews (the gentiles). In accordance with changing socio-political circumstances, the attitude of Jews towards non-Jews had different forms in Jewish tradition, ranging from hostility to tolerance and friendship; and often the nature of the non-Jewish attitude determined the shape of the Jewish attitude. However, the fundamental *aggadic* division between Jews and non-Jews was fixed, to a great extent, by the Jewish law, *halakhah*, as being mainly independent of the outside world. In fact, this point leads to another argument that the Jewish claim to chosenness greatly helped create the above-mentioned inner dynamics of Jewish self-understanding, which in turn made the Jewish people subject to either the position of a 'superior' *chosen* or that of an 'inferior' *other*. Jewish self-understanding rules out the option of being 'equal' and 'normal' in the real sense unless one totally gives up chosenness. Equality and normality come with a sense of uniqueness at best. There is also a parallel question to answer, namely whether chosenness, and therefore Jewishness, to use the division made by Rav Joseph Soloveitchik, is a given identity into which a Jew is born (fate) or a faith/responsibility/a way of life that one chooses to embrace (destiny), or a bit of both.

In parallel to these divisions, it is strongly argued in this book that although the idea of chosenness has been central to Judaism and Jewish self-definition in every period, the concept of chosenness has not stayed the same throughout. In other words, the doctrine of chosenness is not a monolithic and homogenous doctrine which retains its original form and content in every period of Jewish history; just as, and perhaps because, Judaism, as Jacob Neusner rightly argues, is not 'a unitary and uniform religion, unfolding in a continuous history from beginning to present'.[6] Accordingly, the doctrine of chosenness, as a dynamic one, has gone through a constant change, depending on who is employing it, against what sort of background, and for what purpose. Despite the fact that a sense of uniqueness, as understood in both religiously given and historically inherited terms, has always been essential to Jewish identity throughout the history of the Jewish people, chosenness was originally understood in terms of holiness (election and covenant) in pre-modern times, and later mission (a unique Jewish vocation) and survival (a unique Jewish existence) in modern times, with an overlap of quality and duty, on the one hand, and of superiority and inferiority on the other.

As regards the structure of the book, although it is broadly historical, tracing the main characteristics of different periods and the forms into which the idea of chosenness has been moulded in those periods, there is an overlap between historical and thematic perspectives. Having surveyed the various different and sometimes conflicting interpretations of the doctrine of chosenness that appear in our three periods, ancient, modern, and post-Holocaust, often at the same time, a dominant theme, i.e. 'holiness', 'mission', and 'survival' respectively, can be identified in each period, and the historical and socio-political developments underlying each are highlighted. The theological, philosophical, and sociological dimensions of the question of Jewish chosenness are thus examined in their historical context, in particular as responses to the challenges of Christianity, modernity, and the Holocaust. This three-fold historical/thematic division leads to the conclusion that, on the one hand, Jewish understanding of chosenness has developed in two directions, one quality-based, the other duty-based, and, on the other hand, the different forms into which it has evolved down the ages have had important implications for the factors that make up Jewish identity. Accordingly, it is possible to survey the changing parameters of Jewish self-understanding from a religious-national category separated from other peoples (pre-modern) to a religious community working towards universal redemption (modern) and an ethnic group striving for survival in both physical (post-Holocaust) and spiritual terms (post-modern).

The first part of the book, 'Chosenness as "holiness"', deals with the foundation of the Jewish idea of chosenness as laid out in the Hebrew Bible, by defining the basic terms and concepts related to it and by indicating certain ambiguities surrounding it, particularly in relation to the reason for and the purpose of chosenness. It also deals with the interpretation of the biblical notion of chosenness in rabbinic (mainly Talmud and Midrash Rabbah) and non-rabbinic literature from the Second Temple period (i.e. Apocrypha, Pseudepigrapha, Qumran Writings, Philo, and Pauline letters). In the formation of the late rabbinic writings, in particular, an emphasis is placed on the rise of Christianity and the Christian version of chosenness as a counter movement to the Jewish religion and Jewish chosenness. This is a process which, it is argued, had a significant influence not only on the growing rabbinic support of the biblical idea of chosenness, but also on the nature of Jewish self-understanding in successive periods, by creating an ambivalent sense of Jewishness, namely that of a socially inferior and religiously superior one. It is also emphasized that the main theme in all biblical, rabbinic, and non-rabbinic writings is the eternal holiness of the people of Israel, as a religious-national category separated from other peoples in this world as well as in the world to come.

The second part, 'Chosenness as "mission"', in which early and late modern Jewish interpretations of chosenness in both Europe and America are discussed, points to a new turning point in the history of the Jewish people and Jewish religion. What is emphasized here is that in the wake of the European Enlightenment and the Jewish Emancipation, the theme of holiness of the pre-modern period was replaced by the theme of mission, creating a new Jewish self-understanding as based on the principles of universalism and progress. German Reform Jewry, in particular, which eventually became the leading voice of the American Jews between the mid-nineteenth and the early twentieth centuries, redefined Judaism as a universal religion based on a mission, instead of an exclusive one based on a nation. The Jews, in the same way, were defined as a religious community striving for a universal goal. They were not only a chosen people awaiting a national redemption to be established by God, but also a choosing people working towards universal redemption. Chosenness thus was considered to refer to something beyond mere status. It was a responsibility as well, a universal/spiritual role which would establish redemption on earth on the basis of justice and equality. In this way, the rabbinic notion of the fundamental difference between Jews and non-Jews, each having totally different attributes and opposite roles to play in this world (i.e. the people of God versus the enemies of God), was fiercely challenged by the enlightened Jews.

The third and final part, 'Chosenness as "survival"', in which the Jewish encounter of chosenness in post-Holocaust Jewish writings is discussed, sheds light on the most recent period in the history of the Jewish people. Here a contrast is made between earlier and more recent Jewish responses to the Holocaust and the influence of the latter on the shape of a Jewish theology and Jewish understanding of chosenness in both America and Israel. What is indicated by the term post-Holocaust is the period that began after the Six Day (1967) and Yom Kippur wars (1973), when the theology of survival with its emphasis on Jewish suffering and victimization (Holocaust theology), as well as Jewish uniqueness and unity, became dominant themes in Jewish self-definition. In this way the post-Holocaust discourse refers to a transformation of Jewish self-definition from a universalist into a particularist basis, through which the modern rhetoric of a unique Jewish contribution to humanity has been replaced by the rhetoric of a unique Jewish survival, with its religious and secular versions. So in relation to this early reaction to the Holocaust, the main emphasis is placed on the condition of survival, which controlled the Jewish agenda in both America and Israel throughout the 1970s and 1980s. As for more recent years, it is argued that it is possible to see it as a beginning of a reorientation, particularly among American Jewry, from a mere survivalism to a search for meaning in being Jewish. This part will also cover some recent interpretations of chosenness, with an emphasis on the points at which they depart from the previous three main interpretations of chosenness, namely holiness, mission, and survival.

Part I

Chosenness as 'holiness'

1   The biblical language of chosenness

The expression 'the chosen people' (*'am hanivhar*), which has been employed more than any other term to designate the Jewish people by both Jewish and non-Jewish scholars in the modern period, is found almost nowhere in the Hebrew Bible.[1] Instead, in the Torah, the term 'holy people' (*'am qadosh* – Dt. 7:6; 14:2, etc.) or 'holy nation' (*goy qadosh* – Ex. 19:6), among others, is often used in association with the people of Israel. The Hebrew word *qadosh*, translated into English as 'holy', comes from the root *qdsh*, which means in its precise sense 'to separate or set apart from common use to the divine purpose',[2] as it is written: 'You shall be holy (*qedushim*) to me; for I the Lord am holy (*qadosh*), and I have separated (*havdil*) you from the other peoples to be mine' (Lev. 20:26).[3] The expression 'You shall be holy for I the Lord am holy' is repeated several times in the book of Leviticus, with some little nuances. And most of the repetition takes place between chapters 17 and 26, what is known as the Holiness Code (11:44–5; 19:2; 20:7; 20:26). A similar expression such as 'You shall be/are a people holy to your God' is also used in several passages throughout Jewish Scripture (Num. 15:40; Dt. 7:6; 2 Chr. 35:3). In this way, Israel's holiness consists in her being set apart for a specific purpose, i.e. the service of God, according to which Israel's entire life is directly regulated by God.[4] In fact, 'holiness' is one of the most distinctive attributes of God in the Hebrew Bible, as it refers to an ultimate separation of God from all other beings: 'Who is like you O Lord, among the gods? Who is like you, majestic in holiness' (Ex. 15:11; also 1 Sam. 2:2; Ps. 29:2). In the same way, the holiness of the people of Israel above other peoples denotes a fundamental separation between Israel and other peoples: 'Who is like your people Israel, one nation on earth' (1 Chr. 17:21; also 2 Sam. 7:23). The meaning of 'chosenness' is also included in the word *qadosh* for 'separation to be holy', when attributed to creatures, is understood to be tantamount to election.

Apart from the 'holy people' some other phrases used in the Hebrew Bible in relation to Israel are the 'treasured possession' (*'am segullah* – Ex. 19:5; Dt. 7:6; 14:2; 26:18; Ps. 135:4), 'God's own portion' (*heleq YHWH* – Dt. 4:20; 9:26; 32:9), and 'a people of inheritance' (*'am nahalah* – Dt. 4:20; Ex. 34:9). The expression 'kingdom of priests' (*mamlekhet qohanim* – Ex. 19:6), on the other hand, appears in one place making a pair with the 'holy nation', which points to the people of Israel as both a political and religious entity.[5] Again, expressions like the 'children of God' (*banim la YHWH* – Dt. 14:1; Ezk. 36:20), 'my people' (*'ammi* – Ex. 3:7, 10; Isa. 1:3; 3:12; Jer. 30:22; Ezk. 37:27; Hos. 11:7; Joel 2:26; Amos 9:14, etc.), 'my servant' (*'avadai* – Lev. 25:55; Isa. 41:8; 42:1, etc.), 'my witnesses' (*edai* – Isa. 43:10; 44:8) and also 'my beloved' (*didi* – Jer. 11:15) are found especially in the prophetic books. Moreover, in the book of Isaiah, there is a unique depiction of Israel as a people created to be a 'covenant people' (*berit 'am* – 42:6) and a 'light of the nations' (*or goyim/'amim* – 42:6; 49:6; 51:4), which would give rise to the idea of a Jewish mission later in Jewish thought.

The Hebrew root *bhr*, which means 'to choose', is also mentioned in the Hebrew Bible in relation to the people of Israel as well as the land of Israel, the Patriarchs, and some other biblical figures. It is used mostly in a verb form, as in the case of 'the Lord your God has chosen (*bahar*) you out of all the peoples' (Dt. 7:6; also 4:37; 10:15; 14:2; Gen. 18:19; Isa. 41:8; 44:1; Ps. 33:12). It appears approximately 39 times in the book of Deuteronomy, and a third of these references is applied to the people of Israel. According to E.W. Nicholson, the deuteronomic use of the verb *bahar* to define God's action on Israel's behalf in history is of a distinctive nature as it is with this usage that 'the doctrine of Yahweh's election of Israel to be his people, though implied in Israel's faith from the beginning, is first defined in Deuteronomy'.[6] Robert H. Pfeiffer, on the other hand, maintains that 'It was ultimately from J the Deuteronomist derived the daring notion that Israel was the chosen people of God'.[7]

As regards the vocabulary of chosenness, Arnold Eisen draws attention to the fact that whereas the term

> 'chosen people' makes chosenness an ascriptive status, a quality inherent in the people as such, the Hebrew reliance on active verbs, such as 'God chose,' 'God loved,' 'God knew,' or 'God called,' describes only what God did and indicates what Israel must to do in response.

Eisen also hastens to add that the biblical expressions such as *'am segullah* and *'am qadosh* place 'chosenness in passive, adjectival voice comparable to "chosen people", thus making of election a status'.[8] In fact, alongside the above-mentioned receptive expressions, there are some other examples in the Hebrew Bible, especially in the book of Isaiah, in which Israel is referred to as 'my chosen/ elected people' (*'ami behiri* – Isa. 43:20) once, and as 'my chosen/elected ones' (*behiri/behirai* – Isa. 42:1; 43:20; 45:5, etc.) or 'his chosen/elected ones' (*behirav* – Ps. 105:6; I Chr. 16:13) several times, with an apparent parallel with the term 'chosen people' (*'am hanivhar*). In addition to this, the original Hebrew vocabulary of chosenness, as used in the Jewish Scripture as well as in rabbinic literature, incorporates a tension between quality-based (receptive) and duty-based (responsive) formulations of chosenness. A statement like 'you are a people holy to your God' (Dt. 7:6; cf. 28:9), which suggests a status and quality on the part of Israel, makes an obvious contrast with 'you shall be holy, for I am holy' (Lev. 11:45; Num. 15:40–1), for the latter does not denote a status of holiness but instead, requires the people of Israel to act in a holy way, by imposing on them a privileged responsibility. As with this, Ronald Clements rightly asserts that in the deuteronomic statement ('you *are* a people holy'), the holiness of Israel is presented as an 'established fact' instead of a 'spiritual ambition', which is rather indicated in the statement of Leviticus and Numbers ('you *shall be* holy').[9] Again, as we have seen, the biblical terminology in respect of God's relation to Israel mostly consists of terms that connote an ownership and sovereignty on God's part and a status on Israel's part, such as 'special possession' (*segullah*), 'portion' (*heleq*), and 'inheritance/heritage' (*nahala*). This vocabulary, which implies a natural bond between God and Israel, draws a contrast, on the surface, with the verbal use mentioned above, i.e. 'God chose'. However, the reason why 'God has chosen' Israel is also given as that they are 'to be his people, his treasured possession' (Dt. 7:6; 14:2; Ps. 135:4) or 'to be his inheritance' (Ps. 33:12), which refers to an apparent association of an active usage with a passive status.[10] The special relationship between Israel and God is also strengthened by another expression which depicts God as the portion of Israel this time: 'The Lord is my allotted portion [*heleqi*]'[11] (Ps. 16:5; also 73:26; Lam. 3:24 – JPS translation).

Election and covenant

Israel is designated in the Hebrew Bible as a people 'established' or 'formed' by God for himself (2 Sam. 7:24; Isa. 43:1, 21), which might point to two different meanings: either that Israel as a nation is uniquely formed by God right at the beginning (eternal election) or that only after entering into a covenant with God at Sinai the tribes of Israel were made into a holy people (historical election). In fact, one can find evidence of both formulations in the Hebrew Bible.

In the book of Deuteronomy we are told that Israel is God's portion right from the beginning:

> When the Most High gave to the nations their inheritance (*nehel*) ... He set the borders of the peoples according to the number of the children of Israel. For the portion (*heleq*) of the Lord is His people, Jacob the lot (*hebel*) of His inheritance (*nahalah*).[12]
>
> (Dt. 32:8–9 – Soncino Chumash translation)

Again, Jeremiah 2:3, where Israel is declared as 'holy to the Lord, the first fruits (*reshith*) of his harvest', implies a primordial existence on the part of Israel and this is the way that the passage has been interpreted in rabbinic literature (*Lev. R.* 36:4). In a parallel passage, in the book of Isaiah, Israel is also designated as the one who is 'chosen' and 'formed in the womb' by God (44:1–2). According to this, some later actions in the history of Israel (i.e. the Exodus and Sinai) are not so much to establish but more to express this already-existing holiness or chosenness of Israel.

On the other hand, the chosenness of Israel is frequently associated with an historical event, namely God's delivering the tribes of Israel from Egyptian bondage in order to make them his own people (Dt. 4:20, 32–4; 9:26–7; Lev. 11:45; 22:33, etc.). It is also written that *if* only the people of Israel 'keep the commandments of the Lord' God *will* establish them as 'his holy people' (Dt. 28:9; 29:13). In Amos, in particular, the notion of an innate or substantial separation of Israel from other peoples is explicitly repudiated, as it is written: 'Are you not like the Ethiopians to me, O people of Israel? Did I not bring Israel up from the land of Egypt, and the Philistines from Caphtor and the Arameans from Kir?' (9:7).

In parallel to this, it is emphasized that the people of Israel, as a people chosen by God, are charged with greater responsibilities: 'You only have I known of all the families of the earth; therefore I will punish you for your iniquities' (3:2). Here the only difference between Israel and other peoples is suggested to be the religious–ethical responsibilities imposed on the former,[13] namely that a proper response was expected from the people of Israel in response to God's choosing them.

In this way, chosenness or holiness of Israel, as an eternal quality, seems to make a contrast with the obligations of the covenant. There are, in fact, three major covenants mentioned in the Torah, namely Noahide, Abrahamic and Sinaitic covenants, of which the last two are particularly essential to the concept of chosenness. The Abrahamic or Patriarchal covenant, being personal and intimate in nature, is formulated as an unconditional 'promise' through which God chooses and blesses Abraham and grants him many children and the possession of the land of Canaan (Gen. 12:1–3; 17:2–14.). The Sinaitic covenant, on the other hand, which is public and formal in nature, is set up as a 'contract' agreement between God and the people of Israel, requiring mutual obligations from both parties (Ex. 19:5–8; Dt. 26:16–19). As a matter of fact, there is quite a complicated relation between the two: one referring to an everlasting promise and a privilege ('I will establish my covenant between me and you, and your offspring after you throughout their generations, for an everlasting covenant') and the other referring to a set of obligations ('the Lord your God is commanding you to observe these statutes and ordinances'). On the one hand, the chosenness of Israel is justified as going back to the unconditional promise made to Abraham and later repeated with Isaac and Jacob (Dt. 4:37; 7:8; 10:15) as well as to God's love for the Patriarchs, which renders election an eternal one (Dt. 4:31). On the other hand, the covenant of contract made at Sinai binds Israel to full obedience to God and his commandments (Torah), as a condition for the continuity of the promises of the covenant, if not the covenant itself (Dt. 8:1; 11:22; 26:16; 28:9). According to some, the covenant made at Sinai indicates that God was not related to Israel by 'physical' or 'natural' ties, like other gods were to their peoples, but, instead, with a 'free act of will' in which both parties, God as an initiator and Israel as a responder, had taken part,[14] as it is written: 'So Moses came and summoned the elders of the people, and set before them all these words that the Lord had commanded him. The people all answered as one: "Everything that the Lord has spoken we will do"' (Ex. 19:7–8).

However, in the renewed covenant agreement at Moab the people of Israel are described as left with no choice but to accept the agreement:

> I call heaven and earth to witness against you today that I have set before you life and death, blessings and curses. Choose life so that you and your descendants may live, loving the Lord your God, obeying him, and holding fast to him...
>
> (Dt. 30:19)

According to the passage, the Torah looks not like something given to Israel, but rather as something forced upon her. Nevertheless, in the time of Joshua the covenant between God and Israel was renewed on the basis of the people's choosing to serve God alone through their own free will (Jos. 24:16–27). Another such renewal of the covenant was also made with later generations under the leadership of David (2 Sam. 7–8) and Ezra (ch. 9). In this way, the apparent arbitrariness of God's election of Israel through Abraham and the imposition of the covenant decrees on the people of Israel are combined with human free will.

Yet chosenness overall retains its eternal and conditional dimensions, on the one hand, and the absolute will of God and human free will, on the other. In this context, it is interesting to point to the metaphors of 'husband and wife' (Isa. 54:5; Jer. 31:31–3; Hos. 2:19–20) and 'father and child' (Dt. 1:31; 8:5; 14:1; Hos. 11:1; Ps. 2:7), as employed in the Hebrew Bible as well as in rabbinic literature in respect to the special relationship between God and Israel.[15] These metaphors draw a parallel with the above-mentioned twofold aspects of Israel's relationship with God, one representing the conditional (the marriage metaphor) and the other the unconditional nature of such a relationship (the fatherhood metaphor). The act of marriage, being of a legal nature, can be nullified due to the disloyalty of either party, as it is written: 'a covenant that they broke, though I was their husband' (Jer. 31:32). Yet the relation between father and child, which is purely organic, lasts forever even when the latter is disobedient and unworthy: 'A faithful God, without deceit, just and upright is he; yet his degenerate children have dealt falsely with him ... Is not he your father, who created you, who made you and established you?' (Dt. 32:4–6). Despite their iniquities Israelites are still called God's 'children', and God their 'father': 'in the place where it was said to them, "You are not my people," it shall be said to them, "children of the living God"' (Hos. 1:10). In the same way, the metaphor of father and child which symbolizes an everlasting relationship is employed in 2 Samuel in relation to the King David: 'I will be a father to him, and he shall be a son to me. When he commits iniquity, I will punish him with a rod such as mortals use. But I will not take my steadfast love from him...' (7:14–16).

So, while Israel, as a disloyal wife or a disobedient child, is condemned, chastised, and even abandoned by God (God's hiding his face – Isa. 54:8; 59:2), God's love for Israel as that of a father/mother for his/her child renders the covenantal connection between God and Israel an eternal one. For the tie between

God and Israel is depicted not merely as a legal but also an emotional one: 'Can a woman forget her nursing child, or show no compassion for the child of her womb? Even these may forget, yet I will not forget you' (Isa. 49:15). Though this love of God is expressed in different ways and with different terms in the Hebrew Bible, the idea of love itself remains permanent. This is why the Sinai covenant, especially as depicted in the book of Deuteronomy, is regarded by some as an 'affair of ritual' or 'kinship', instead of a 'contract' or 'agreement'.[16] In fact, in the deuteronomic account of the election of Israel, there is a constant reference to God's promise to the Patriarchs (29:13; 4:37; also 1:8; 6:10; 9:5, 27; 30:20; 34:4). In this way, the covenant at Sinai works as a medium through which the family union built between God and the Patriarchs is re-established between God and the descendants in terms of the marriage of love with law.[17] Due to this previous union, God calls Israel 'his people' (Ex. 3:7–10; Hos. 11:1) even before the Exodus and covenant takes place. The theme of love is, therefore, understood to change the tone of the relationship between God and Israel from a legal to a moral and emotional union, 'marked by love and affection on the one side, and demanding a corresponding love and affection on the other' (Dt. 10:12–16; 30:5).[18]

In fact, no obvious reason other than 'God's love' is given in the Scripture as regards the election of Israel: 'because He loved your ancestors, He chose their descendants after them' (Dt. 4:37). One can think of Abraham's faith as the starting point for the election of Abraham: 'And he believed the Lord; and the Lord reckoned it to him as righteousness' (Gen. 15:6). Yet Abraham's faith in God appears to be subsequent to God's election of him through an unconditional promise: 'I will make of you a great nation, and I will bless you, and make your name great, so that you will be a blessing' (Gen. 12:2; cf. 26:5). In the case of Jacob, on the other hand, the account of the meeting between Jacob and God in Genesis chapter 32 is particularly worth noting. Here, after wrestling with (the angel of) God, Jacob says, 'I will not let you go, unless you bless me', which suggests the importance of Jacob as the first active party in Israel's encounter with God. The special role attributed to Jacob in election is approved in some other passages as well: 'the Lord's own portion was his people, Jacob his allotted share' (Dt. 32:9; cf. Jer. 10:16). The greatness of Jacob in God's eyes, however, explains only why God chose him over Esau, his twin brother: 'Yet I have loved Jacob but I hated Esau' (Mal. 1:2–3). It falls short, however, in answering the question of why God has chosen Abraham in the first place, as election does not begin with Jacob; it only reaches a high level with him. So the sole reason for the election of Abraham and the lineage of Jacob lies in God's unconditional love for them.

The theme of a love relationship between God and Israel, which is believed to be first introduced by the prophet Hosea ('I will love them freely' – 14:5), runs through the book of Deuteronomy, and the prophetic books, as well as the Psalms and Song of Songs.[19] In the following deuteronomic passage the relation between election and love is explicitly presented:

> It was not because you were more numerous than any other people that the Lord set his heart on you and chose you – for you were the fewest of all

peoples. It was because the Lord loved you and kept the oath that he swore
to your ancestors...

(Dt. 7:6–8)

As regards the giving of the land of Canaan to Israel, on the other hand, a
similar, yet slightly different, explanation is made:

> It is not because of your righteousness or the uprightness of your heart that
> you are going in to occupy their land; but because of the wickedness of
> these nations the Lord your God is dispossessing them before you, in order
> to fulfill the promise that the Lord made an oath to your ancestors, to
> Abraham, to Isaac, and to Jacob.

(Dt. 9:5)

According to this, Israel's election and possession of the land have nothing to do
with any superior physical or moral character on the part of Israel. The question
is here rather God's unconditional and incomprehensible 'love' for Israel as well
as for the Patriarchs, which indicates the strong emotional element involved in
the election. Moreover, in the book of Isaiah, God's ongoing concern with and
protection of Israel is also attributed to God's love for Israel: 'Because you are
precious in my sight, and honoured, and I love you, I give people in return for
you, nations in exchange for your life' (Isa. 43:5).

The tendency to see the relationship between God and Israel in terms of not a
'natural and physical' but an 'adoptive' one implies, by definition, the historical
and conditional nature of election. However, it is a common view that the
covenant responsibilities were mainly the result of election, not a condition of it.
In fact, the conditional nature of the covenant agreement, which is repeatedly
emphasized in the book of Deuteronomy in particular, applies especially to the
hold and rule of the land of Canaan by the Israelites. While the majority of the
commandments in the Torah, to which a full obedience on the part of Israel is
required, are based on living in the land and, therefore, can only be performed in
that land, Israel's disobedience to the Torah and its walking after other gods
result in a severe punishment, including God's giving the Israelites into the
hands of the nations and the expulsion of the former from the land (Lev.
26:14ff.; Dt. 28:15ff.; Jer. 7:21–3; Hos. 8:1ff.; 10:1–4; Amos 5:7–15, 21–4;
Hab. 2:8–12). It is written that if the people of Israel do not observe all the
statutes and ordinances commanded in the Torah, the land will vomit them out
in the same way as it vomited out the other nations (Lev. 20:22). However, the
covenant agreement, broken by Israel (Hos. 8:1), is still kept by God for his own
sake (Isa. 43:25; 48:9, 11; Ezk. 20:44). At this point, it is stated that the 'separateness between the Torah and the story of the conquest of the land expresses
the absoluteness of the covenant and its independence of the land' and also
shows that even outside the land the covenant is 'still binding on the people of
Israel' and a 'precondition for their return to the land'.[20] In parallel to this, the
exile of Israel also becomes of a temporary character, for in the end Israel's

repentance and return to God (Hos. 14:1–7) is anticipated when God will restore them to the land (Amos 9:14–15) by taking revenge on the nations who oppressed Israel (Dt. 30:1–8; Isa. 60: 21; 63:6–9). In the prophetic books, after an account of severe punishments for the transgression of the people, Israel is said to be taken back by God with an everlasting covenant and to 'possess the land forever' (Isa. 60:21; Ezk. 36:28). As a matter of fact, God's love for Israel is presented in the Hebrew Bible not only as the reason for its election by God but also one of the reasons as to why God will not forsake it ultimately (Dt. 4:31; 7:9; Ps. 11:7; Isa. 54:8; 63:7–9; Lam. 3:22, 31–3; Hos. 2:19–20).

What is most interesting in this terminology of reconciliation between God and his people is the idea of a 'renewed covenant', in which God mysteriously transforms Israel's heart. In the book of Deuteronomy, this transformation is likened to the act of circumcision as in the case of the Abrahamic covenant, but this time the reference is to a spiritual, rather than a physical circumcision: 'the Lord your God will circumcize your heart and the heart of your descendants, so that you will love the Lord your God with all your heart and with all your soul' (30:6). A similar theme of a renewed covenant or an eternal covenant also takes place in the books of Isaiah (54:7–10), Jeremiah (31:31–4), and Ezekiel (18:30–1) where 'a new covenant' is declared between God and Israel, a covenant which will not be like the previous ones in which God asks the Israelites to love him with all their hearts and with all their souls but, this time, God himself will make the Israelites love their God: 'I will put my law within them, and I will write it on their hearts; and I will be their God, and they shall be my people' (Jer. 31:33). Indeed, there is an obvious contrast between '*You shall* put these words of mine in your heart and soul' (Dt. 11:18) and '*I will* put my law within them, and *I will* write it on their hearts' (Jer. 31:33). Despite the obligation-bound nature of the covenant, the chosenness of Israel is regarded primarily and ultimately as an eternal and unconditional one.

The idea of a 'remnant of Israel' is also to be understood within the context of an eternal or renewed covenant, as the latter is usually presented alongside the remnant of Israel. Indeed, the continuity of the covenant in the face of a disobedient Israel is justified through the notion of a remnant of Israel, according to which the covenant lasts forever for the sake of a 'repentant' remnant, as it is written: 'A remnant will return, the remnant of Jacob, to the mighty God. For though your people Israel were like the sand of the sea, only a remnant of them will return' (Isa. 10:21–2; see also Jer. 5:9–10; Ezk. 14:22; Amos 3:12; 4:11).

There seems to be a parallel here between Jacob's relation to the descendants of Abraham and the relation of the righteous ones in Israel to the entire people of Israel. An apparent contradiction in the election of all children of Abraham while God rejects Ishmael and Esau is solved through an emphasis laid on Jacob and his descendants. In this way, Jacob is treated as a kind of righteous remnant of Abrahamic offspring. The conflict inherent in the election of all the children of Jacob while many others are destroyed among their descendants due to their wickedness is also overcome by this notion of the remnant of Israel. However, the remnant is not always understood to be a righteous one. Sometimes those who survive of Israel are not a 'chosen random' but an 'accidental random'.[21] The notion of an accidental random can, in fact, be justified by the idea of a renewed covenant. If the remnant were already a righteous one, it would be pointless to say:

> I will sprinkle clean water upon you, and you shall be clean from all your uncleanness, and from all your idols I will cleanse you. A new heart I will give you, and a new spirit I will put within you...
>
> (Ezk. 36:25–6)

According to H.H. Rowley, on the other hand, the prophetic concept of the remnant indicates both the limitation of election on the part of Israel and its expansion in the world through the service of the remnant. At this point, Rowley refers to Isaiah in particular, alongside other post-exilic prophets (e.g. Zech. 2:11), who were engaged more with the 'service of the nations' than the 'glory of Israel', by describing a 'remnant' who is 'first saved and then sent on a mission to the world' (Isa. 66:18–20).

God, Israel, and other nations

The question of to what extent the unique relationship of God with Israel is set against a monotheistic background in the Hebrew Bible is also of special importance as it involves the question of the place of other nations in the theology of chosenness and, therefore, relates to the universal–ethical dimension of it. When one looks at the book of Deuteronomy, whose theology is considered to be closer to monotheism than any other book of the Torah, there appear to be two different theistic stresses. What is pointed out in a statement like 'the Lord your God has chosen you out of all the peoples' (Dt. 7:6) is the belief that God is the god of all peoples and with his free will He chose Israel from among them, which is a statement in complete accord with the apparent monotheistic stress made in several other places in the book of Deuteronomy (4:35, 39). In another deuteronomic passage, however, it is written:

> And when you look up to the heavens and see the sun, the moon, and the stars, all the host of heaven, do not be led astray and bow down to them and serve them, things that the Lord your God has allotted to all the peoples everywhere under heaven. But the Lord has taken you and brought you out of the iron-smelter, out of Egypt, to become a people of his very own possession, as you are now.
>
> (4:19–20; cf. Jud. 11:24)

What is emphasized here is the uniqueness, rather than the oneness, of the God of Israel as a national god or the exclusiveness of his relation to the people of Israel, which in any case stands in an apparent contradiction with pure monotheism. Nevertheless, once the God of Israel is presented in such nationalist or monolatrist[22] terms it makes more sense to speak of a unique relationship between God and Israel. Besides, it was quite a common assumption among ancient Semitic as well as non-Semitic peoples of the Near East that the kings, and therefore the nations represented by them, were chosen by their gods for divine commission. What differentiates the covenant idea of the Israelites from that of other peoples is, however, considered to be the relationship of a family, instead of a vassal, between God and Israel and 'the distinctively ethical and spiritual sense of mission' adopted by Israel later in the post-exilic period.[23] A difficulty arises in explaining the uniqueness of Israel in God's eyes against a monotheistic background. However, it is a view shared by many Jewish scholars that as only a universal God can choose a nation out of others, the doctrine of election is completely compatible with monotheism.

Yet, as seen in the examples above, it is difficult to mark a definite time or period for the establishment of pure monotheism within the tribes of Israel. It is a widely accepted notion that in the early stages of Israel's religion the matter of concern was less about the numbers of gods that really exist than the numbers of gods that Israel should obey. Historical–scientific evidence shows that the monotheistic formula which describes the God of Israel as the one and only true and living God over all the peoples of the earth did not properly develop until the seventh century BCE.[24] Apparently it was the result of a gradual process, and sometimes in the same book of the Hebrew Bible different emphases, corresponding to different stages, are made.

It seems that when different biblical representations of the special relationship between God and Israel are read against an evolutionary background, in which different views of the deity were adopted at different stages in the history of Israel's religion, the presence of both the particularistic–national and universalistic–ethical presentations of chosenness in the Hebrew Bible at the same time becomes less problematic. The real problem arises, in fact, with a view of God, who in terms of his dominion and power is universal but in terms of his favour and self-revelation is particularistic. And this question is partly connected with the issue of the purpose of election. As a matter of fact, there is no systematically pursued purpose of God's election of Israel in the Hebrew Bible, apart from some sporadic implications. However, in the prophetic books, in general, and in the book of Isaiah, in particular, there are certain passages in which, alongside a strong monotheistic emphasis, the people of Israel seems to be appointed with a kind of mission or vocation. And this can be enunciated as setting the example of an ideal people. In Isaiah 43:21, for example, Israel is called 'the people whom I formed for myself so that they might declare my praise'. In some parallel passages God addresses the people of Israel by saying: 'You are my witnesses ... and my servant whom I have chosen, so that you may know and believe me and understand that I am he' (Isa. 43:10), or 'You are my servant, O Israel, in whom I will be glorified' (Isa. 49:3). Furthermore, it is also stated, 'I will give you as a light to the nations, that my salvation may reach to the end of the earth' (Isa. 49:6; cf. 'in you all the families of the earth shall be blessed' – Gen. 12:3),[25] which indicates the idea of a vocation on the part of

Israel. The notion of Israel as 'the light of the nations' is understood by some in terms of 'bringing all mankind into a covenant relation with Jahweh'.[26] In Ezekiel, on the other hand, it is written, 'the nations shall know that I am the Lord ... when through you I display my holiness before their eyes' (36:24; also Isa. 55:4–5). In all these passages the purpose of Israel's chosenness is presented within a universalistic and fully monotheistic context, taking an apparent step further from the nationalist notion of God as presented in the Torah in general. Perhaps one of the few passages in the Pentateuch that display a somewhat similar meaning to the above-mentioned prophetic passages, takes place in Deuteronomy:

> I now teach you statutes and ordinances for you to observe in the land that you are about to enter and occupy. You must observe them diligently, for this will show your wisdom and discernment to the peoples, who, when they hear all these statutes, will say, "surely this great nation is a wise and discerning people!" For what other great nation has a god so near to it as the Lord our God is whenever we call to him? And what other great nation has statutes and ordinances as just as this entire law that I am setting before you today?
>
> (Dt. 4:5–8)

In fact, as the degree of monotheistic emphasis increases, the universalistic tendencies become more frequent, and this is particularly the case in the prophetic books. In contrast to this, however, what is prevalent in the books of Ezra and Nehemiah is a spirit of rigidity and exclusiveness,[27] which was influential on the shape of Judaism in more of a particularistic line.

However, despite a more developed sense of God and the universalistic position adopted by the prophets in general, their attitude towards other nations was also not free of ambiguity. What is even more interesting is that such an attitude can be observed throughout Jewish tradition, as will be seen in the following chapters. On the one hand, there is the notion of God who, despite his special bond with Israel, is the creator of all, and a concomitant expectation that in the end one true God will be a source of worship for all peoples (Isa. 2:3; 51:4; 56:7; 66: 18–19; Jer. 1:5; Amos 9:7). Furthermore, sometimes an ironic tone is used in relation to the people of Israel who forsake their God and follow the idolatrous ways of other nations, while these same nations seek to know the law of the God of Israel and to share Israel's privileges (Isa. 2:2–10). On the other hand, the theme of the ultimate wickedness of the nations and the hatred and oppression of the people of Israel by them and God's judgement of them (Isa. 33:12; 40:17; 63:6; Jer. 46–50; Ezk. 25–30, etc.) runs through the Hebrew Bible, especially in the books attributed to exilic prophets. One might think that the idolatrous nature of the nations at the time was the reason for such a negative view of them, which is partly true. However, the condemnation and judgement of the nations seem to be, for the most part, the result of their actions, i.e., their mistreatment of Israel (Dt. 23:3–6; Isa. 14:2; Joel 3:19; cf. Dt. 23:7–8) and their leading Israel astray, or the abominations attached to their religion (Dt. 12:31; 20:17–18), rather than their idolatrous faith itself.[28] It is mostly Israel who is rebuked for following the idolatrous ways of the nations (Dt. 29:18f.; 31:16–17; Hos. 4:12f.; 8:4f.). In this context, God is usually referred to as the 'Redeemer' and the 'Holy One' of Israel (Isa. 43:14–15; see also Isa. 45:3, 15 46:4; 48:17; 54:5).

Yet, there are some passages indicating that God will not forsake his people by letting the heathen destroy them. And this is so not due to any merit of Israel but, on the contrary, for God's own sake, for the sake of his holy name and of his glory, as it is written:

> It is not for your sake, O house of Israel, that I am about to act, but for the sake of my holy name, which you have profaned among the nations to which you came. I will sanctify my great name … and the nations shall know that I am the Lord…
>
> (Ezk. 36:22–3; also Isa. 43:25; 48:11; 39:7, 25; Ps. 111:9; cf. Dt. 9:26–9)

As a matter of fact, when these passages are perceived under the light of some other passages, which describe the God of Israel as the one and only true God over all the kingdoms of the earth (Dt. 4:35, 39; Isa. 40:28; 44:6), the existence of pure monotheistic concerns behind the destruction of the nations (Jer. 46:28) and the redemption of Israel by God, despite their disobedience, seems obvious. However, there are some other passages in which a kind of servitude is attributed to the nations in a mode of vengeance:

> He said to me: 'You are my son; today I have begotten you. Ask of me, and I will make the nations your heritage, and the ends of the earth your posses-sion. You shall break them with a rod of iron, and dash them in pieces like a potter's vessel.'
>
> (Ps. 2:8–9)

In the same vein, in the book of Isaiah it is written: '[A]nd the house of Israel will possess the nations as male and female slaves in the Lord's hand; they will take captive those who were their captors, and rule over those who oppressed them' (Isa. 14:2; see also 60:12ff.). Taking into consideration these last state-ments, which display some sort of rivalry between the God of Israel and other false gods, on the one side, and between Israel and other peoples, on the other, it becomes difficult to decide whether the question at stake is uprooting polythe-ism and idolatry from the earth as a whole or just from among the people of Israel. Most of the time, other nations are depicted as those by whom Israel is led astray, instead of ones whom Israel is meant to guide to the true worship of God. The God of Israel, as depicted in the Hebrew Bible, is thus of an ambigu-ous character. Perhaps this is mainly related to the fact that the history of Israel's religion as recorded in the Hebrew Bible reveals an 'unfinished' struggle between God who is trying to establish a monotheistic faith within his covenanted people and the Israelites who are constantly disobeying and defying their God. This is why the prophet Isaiah's conception of one God as worshipped by all does not indicate an established reality but an ideal, in which the chosenness of Israel is reduced from an eternal quality into an historical, albeit yet to be fulfilled, mission. In other words, in the minds of the prophets of the Israelites, for the eternal truth to be spread to the world it had first to be settled in the hearts of the people of Israel. Nevertheless, when the Hebrew Bible is looked at as a whole there seems to be a constant shift between the national and universal notions of God, on the one hand, and between the conditional and unconditional understandings of chosenness, on the other; with an unsteady relationship between God and the people of Israel and an unstable view of the nations.

2   Ancient Jewish literature

What we call ancient Jewish literature includes such works as the Apocrypha, Pseudepigrapha, and the Qumran Writings, which do not belong to the Jewish canon, and also the writings of Philo and Paul, of which the latter is hardly considered part of the Jewish legacy.[1] However, as Nicholas de Lange rightly asserts, all those writings (excluding Paul's), written in the period from the end of the second century BCE to the end of the first century CE, 'form part of the Jewish heritage', on the grounds that 'they were written by Jews to be read by Jews, and they bear witness to the life and thought of Jews in bygone times.'[2] As for the writings of Paul, despite the fact that they were written by a Christianized Jewish figure and addressed primarily to Christians of both Jewish and non-Jewish origin, they are of great importance in showing the sort of background against which rabbinic literature evolved. Accordingly, all these non-rabbinic Jewish writings of antiquity present indirect, yet significant, evidence on the nature of the rabbinic understanding of chosenness. It fact, one main purpose of the formation of the post-biblical Jewish literature, both rabbinic and non-rabbinic, was to maintain and further the biblical notion of the 'holiness' of the people of Israel. So what follows will be a discussion of Israel's chosenness as it appears in the ancient Jewish literature – in terms of non-canonical Jewish books as well as the writings of Philo and Paul. Although dealing exhaustively with the whole topic is beyond the reach of a single chapter, some main points will be highlighted in this way.

Apocrypha, Pseudepigrapha, and the Qumran Writings

As observed by many 'the ingathering of the dispersed of Israel into one national entity' and 'the eternal relation between Israel and God' are the themes common to most apocryphal and pseudepigraphical writings.[3] What is emphasized in this way is that 'all Israel', i.e. the descendants of Jacob, are chosen through 'an everlasting covenant'. In fact, reminiscent of certain biblical passages, the people of Israel are frequently referred to as 'holy people' (2 Mac. 15:24; 3 Mac. 2:6; Jub. 22:12; 33:20; Ps. Sol. 17:28; Wis. 10:15; 17:2), 'priestly and royal nation' (Jub. 33:20), 'God's portion/possession' (Sir. 17:17; 24:12; 3 Mac. 6:3; Jub. 16:18; 33:20), 'God's inheritance (for all the ages)'

(Jub. 16:18; 22:9, 10; 33:20; 2 Esd. 8:16, 45; Ps. Sol. 7:2; 2 Bar. 5:1), 'first-born (son)' (Jub. 2:20; Ps. Sol. 13:8; 18:4; 2 Esd. 6:58), 'beloved people' (2 Bar. 21:21; 3 Mac. 6:11), the 'chosen (servant/nation)' of God (Sir. 47:22; 2 Esd. 15:21, 53; 16:73, 74, Jub. 22:9, 12), 'holy seed' (Jub. 16:26; 22:27; 25:18), 'plant of righteousness' (Jub. 16:26; 36:6), and 'blameless race' (Wis. 10:15). In the book of Jubilees, it is also called 'a peculiar people above all peoples' (Jub. 2:22).

Despite an apparent insistence in the book of Jubilees as well as in 2 Esdras (4 Ezra) on righteousness, that is obeying the law as an eternal truth (Jub. 6:14; 2 Esd. 9:30–7), in many places the eternal character of Israel's holiness is attributed to God's endless 'mercy' and 'compassion' for Israel (Tob. 13:5; 14:5; Jdt. 7:30; Sir. 36:11–12; 2 Esd. 2:30–2; 1 Bar. 4:22; Ps. Sol. 7:5; 9:16–19). Israel is the people that God has 'loved' and 'chosen' by taking from all the multitude of peoples for himself (2 Esd. 2:15–17; 4:23; 5:27; Jub. 2:20, 15:31; 2 Bar. 48:20; Ps. Sol. 9:16–17) and the one for whose sake He has 'made the world' (2 Esd. 6:55; 12:46ff.; 2 Bar.14:19). Therefore, even if they sin God will not abandon them forever (Jdt. 7:30; Ps. Sol. 7:8; Jub. 1:18). Instead, He will bestow his mercy upon them and circumcize the foreskin of their heart when they return to him (Jub. 1:23; 1 Bar. 2:31–5). Israel is also provided with an everlasting hope and a promise that the dispersed tribes of Jacob will be gathered together in the end when they return to God (2 Bar. 78:7; Jub. 1:15–17; Sir. 36:11–12; Ps. Sol. 8:34–5). It is important to note that although the chosenness of Israel is considered to go back to the covenant made with Abraham, election and salvation are seen to belong exclusively to the descendants of Jacob, the holy seed. In this way the third patriarch appears as the key figure in the eternal covenant relationship between God and Israel, as it is written:

> And when they were committing iniquity before you, you did choose for yourself one of them, whose name was Abraham; and you did love him.... You did make with him an everlasting covenant, and promise him that you would never forsake his descendants; and you gave to him Isaac, and to Isaac you gave Jacob and Esau. And you did set apart Jacob for yourself, but Esau you did reject...
>
> (2 Esd. 13:6)

Again, in the book of Jubilees, there is a clear account of God's rejection of Ishmael and Esau and his election of Jacob and his descendants eternally to constitute what is known as 'Israel'.

> For Ishmael and his sons and his brothers and Esau, the Lord did not cause to approach Him, and He chose them not because they are the children of Abraham, because He knew them, but He chose Israel to be His people. And He sanctified it, and gathered it from amongst all the children of men...
>
> (15:30f.)

In the rest of the passage just cited the ultimate separation between Israel and other nations is emphasized by declaring that Israel alone is the possessor of divine election and salvation:

> [F]or there are many nations and many peoples, and all are His, and over all has He placed spirits in authority to lead them astray from Him. But over Israel He did not appoint any angel or spirit, for He alone is their ruler ... in order that He may preserve them and bless them, and that they may be His and He may be theirs from henceforth for ever.
>
> (Cf. Dt. 32:9; also Sir. 33:10–12)

Nevertheless, to state that salvation belongs to Israel, who are righteous, does not mean to say that every single Israelite was considered to be saved by the authors of the above-mentioned passages. As E.P. Sanders points out, in principle 'physical descent is the basis of the election, and the election is the basis of salvation'.[4] However, in the book of Jubilees in particular, being a descendant of Jacob is not taken as the sole condition of salvation. While it is a common belief that God's mercy covers Israel's transgressions (1:5, 18), even more so when they repent, disobedience to the covenant, by transgressing one of the 'eternal laws'[5] for which there is no atonement, forfeits their salvation (23:14–24). In other words, salvation is not earned by obedience, but it may be lost by extreme disobedience.[6] At this point, a strong connection is made between the people of Israel, taken by God as his holy people, and the seventh day, sanctified by God as the holy day of Sabbath, which Israel alone is commanded to keep (2:17–21).

However, unlike the writings of the Qumran community, the notion of 'true Israel' as associated with a particular group within the people of Israel does not appear in the apocryphal and pseudepigraphical books. Indeed, the Qumran community, which is usually identified with the Essenes, regard themselves as 'the remnant' of the 'holy people' of Israel, who, out of God's mercy, was not let go astray from his Covenant (1QM 14). They are the 'congregation of men of perfect holiness' who enter a 'New Covenant' with God in the land of Damascus' and, therefore, are the 'redeemed' who alone are 'destined to live for ever' to inherit the world to come while the rest of the children of Jacob perish (CD 3–15). This covenant is also called the 'covenant of the everlasting Community' and there is no remedy for those who do not partake in this new covenant as well as those who backslide from it (1QS 3).[7] In the Gospels, on the other hand, while there is no mention of a remnant of Israel, it is still declared: 'Although many are called, few are chosen' (Matt. 20:16).

Despite an overall emphasis on a combination of obedience, repentance, and God's mercy, leading to salvation for all Israel, the idea of a '(righteous) remnant' arises in the apocryphal and pseudepigraphical writings as well (Tob. 13:16; Sir. 47:22; 2 Bar. 40:2; 2 Esd. 13:48–9). There is an apparent acceptance that not all Israel is righteous or repentant, but rather that some among them are wicked and therefore will share the same fate as the gentiles, namely eternal damnation and destruction (1 En. 45:6; 81:8; Sir. 5:1–7; 21:10; 41:5–11; 2 Esd.

15:24–6). In the book of Jubilees, in a similar way to the qumranian division between the 'children of righteousness' (the sons of light) and the 'children of falsehood' (the sons of darkness), a distinction is made between the 'children of God' and the 'children of destruction' (Jub. 23:23–4), the latter including the gentiles[8] as well as the wicked Israelites. However, the general view stemming from the apocryphal and pseudepigraphical, as well as the Qumran, writings is that, notwithstanding the wicked ones, Israel (or the remnant of Israel), as the chosen and covenanted people of God, is eternal.

Philo's works

Philo, despite his reputation as a Hellenistic Jewish philosopher, whose thought was apparently influenced by Hellenistic Judaism, retained to a great extent the biblical notion of God as a personal deity and the traditional Jewish concept of Israel as the chosen people. In his discussion of the difference of the people of Israel from other peoples, Philo frequently refers to certain deuteronomic passages, such as 4:6f. ('Lo this great nation is a wise and understanding people'), 7:7f. ('did the Lord prefer and choose you out'), 14:1 ('You are sons of the Lord God'), and so on. He uses the term 'to choose' only twice in his work, in one of which he writes 'He chose as of special merit' (*Spec. Leg.* i, 303) and in the other 'the chosen race of Israel' (*Post.* 92).[9] However, he refers to Israel in various other ways, such as 'the race beloved by God' (*Quis Her.* 203), 'a nation destined to be consecrated above all others' (*Mos.* i, 148), 'the nation dearest of all to God' (*Abr.* 98), 'a nation the Sovereign Ruler will draw near' (*Mig.* 165), the 'race endowed with vision' (*Immut.* 144), and 'the best of races' (*Cong.* 51).

Based on Deuteronomy 32:8–9, in particular, which reads, 'When the Most High apportioned the nations … he fixed the boundaries of the peoples according to the number of the gods; the Lord's own portion was his people', Philo arrives at an interesting conclusion as regards the nature of the human soul. What is implied in the above-mentioned deuteronomic passage, for Philo, is a divine separation of 'the nations of the souls' into three categories: 'the children of earth' (sons of Adam), 'the offspring of virtue' (sons of heaven), and 'the chosen race of Israel' (sons of God) (*Post.* 91–2). Philo does not give any explanation as to why God set the boundaries between the nations in this way. He apparently accepts this as a necessary act, which was fixed on divine principles and therefore preceded the creation of the world (*Post.* 89–90). However, it is clear that God's setting apart Israel as his own portion right from the beginning has a lot to do, in Philo's thought, with Israel being the only people who have actually 'seen God';[10] because to be able to 'see God', for Philo, is the most important virtue that no other nation can acquire (*Immut.* 143–4; *Cong.* 51; *Som.* ii, 173; *Legat.* 4; cf. Dt. 5:4; Ex. 24:10). 'Seeing God' means reaching the knowledge of God through himself without the assistance of any other instrument (*Praem.* 43–4) and, therefore, the knowledge by 'sight' surpasses other ways of knowledge, including 'reason'. Thus, due to their being able to see God, which requires a sort of intimacy, the people of Israel gain a superior place over other nations. In response to a possible question as to why the virtue of seeing God is given to Israel instead of any other nation, Philo states that 'to see the best, that is the truly existing, is the lot of the best of races, Israel, for Israel means seeing God' (*Congr.* 51). Philo, in this way, ascribes to Israel a sort of innate character of superiority, by depicting it as the 'best race'.[11]

Nevertheless, there remains a sort of ambiguity in Philo's understanding of Israel. Sometimes he refers to Israel in terms of an abstract type of entity rather than a particular physical group. For example, in his interpretation of Isaiah 5:7, 'For the vineyard of the Lord of hosts is the house of Israel', Philo sees 'Israel' as 'the mind which contemplates God and the world' (*Som.* ii, 172–3). Again, he takes the biblical expression 'the great and wise nation' (Dt. 4:6) to indicate 'all the lovers of wisdom and knowledge' (*Migr.* 163–5). However, in some other places when he speaks of Israel, he has the Jewish people in mind (*Immut.* 147; *Fug.* 208). For example, in *De Legatione ad Gaium* 3–4 what Philo designates as 'the suppliant race', namely Israel, whom God has taken as his portion, is considered by many to refer to the Jewish nation per se.[12] In the same way, when Philo speaks about peculiar characteristics of the Jews and their ancestors in *De Virtutibus* 209 onwards, he uses the terms 'race' (*genos*) and 'nation' (*ethnos*), both implying a particular group which belong to the same ancestral line. Moreover, commenting on Genesis 16:13, which deals with an angel appearing to Hagar, Philo further says, 'being Egyptian by descent she was not qualified to see the Supreme Cause' (*Som.* i, 240). However, as H.A. Wolfson points out, Philo also emphasizes the religion-based relationship, namely the one based on 'the willingness to serve God' as the only tie of affinity for being 'sons of God' (*Spec. Leg.* i, 317–18).[13] And surely the service of God here is understood in accordance with the Law of Moses (*Decal.* 98). So, the blood relationship is the primary, but not the sole, criterion for being the people of Israel; the ultimate goal for Israel is seeking 'the honour of God' through the law.[14] In fact, in this way Philo places a greater emphasis on the kinship of those who honour God than on the one based on blood. He describes the former as a 'kinship of greater dignity and sanctity' (*Spec. Leg.* i, 317–18), which stands in an apparent contrast with the earlier mentioned passages on the importance of the ancestral pedigree.

To better understand the functions of two different types of kinship in Philo's definition of Israel, one might examine the place of the Patriarchs in it. In fact, Philo lays a particular stress on the virtues of the Patriarchs, who are the founders of the Jewish race. In *De Praemiis et Poenis* 166, in particular, while he attributes two of the intermediary elements for the redemption of the Jews to God's mercy and the improvement of the Israelites he also links the one to the holiness of the Patriarchs, as he writes:

> Three intercessors they [Jews] have to plead for their reconciliation with the Father. One is the clemency and kindness of Him.... The second is the holiness of the founders of the race because with souls released from their bodies they show forth in that naked simplicity their devotion to their Ruler

and cease not to make supplications for their sons and daughters ... the Father grants to them the privilege that their prayers should be heard.

Philo's understanding of the Jewish race, Jewish law, and Jewish religion is modelled on, or the embodiment of, the lives of the Patriarchs (*Abr.* 56–8, 275–6). Perhaps, when he wrote, 'to see the best, that is the truly existing [God], is the lot of the best of races, Israel', he was indicating the privileged position of the Jews due to their ancestors. Indeed, he clearly declares that the cause behind God's choosing the people of Israel out of all nations is 'the precious signs of righteousness and virtue shown by the founders of the race' (*Spec. Leg.* iv, 180–1). He also maintains that even if the descendants are sinners, as long as these are curable sins, the virtues of the Patriarchs will bear their imperishable fruits for subsequent generations. Although Philo admits that good lineage is not the only condition for blessing and the latter requires noble actions as well, he underlines the significance of the virtues of the Patriarchs as a primary cause for Israel's separation from other nations to be the portion of God.

What is at stake in Philo's emphasis on the virtues of the Patriarchs is also the question of human free will. As mentioned above, Philo clearly asserts that the distribution of the nations took place according to the divine principles and for reasons which are unknown to human beings, even to the ancestors of the Jewish nation. This kind of interpretation apparently suggests that 'the divine initiative' is the dominant element in election and other related issues. However, Philo also frequently refers to the merits of the Patriarchs, and of Abraham in particular, who left his homeland and its polytheistic customs in order to search for the Creator and put his trust in him (*Virt.* 211–12; *Quis Her.* 92ff.). In another passage Philo interprets Genesis 12:7, 'God was seen by Abraham', by saying that it was only after he left Chaldea to change his thinking, and freed himself from his false opinion, and knew that the world was dependent on and governed by its Maker and First Cause, that God appeared to him (*Abr.* 77–8, 212–16). Philo continues:

> He in His love for mankind, when the soul came into His presence, did not turn away His face, but came forward to meet him and revealed His nature, so far as the beholder's power of sight allowed. That is why we are told not that the Sage saw God, but that God was seen by him. For it were impossible that anyone should by himself apprehend the truly Existent, did not He reveal and manifest Himself.
>
> (*Abr.* 79–80)

Thus Philo asserts that it is Abraham who, by proving himself worthy in God's eyes, brought about the vision of sight, the instrument that made the Jews into a great nation, namely 'Israel' in its real sense. Jacob, in a similar way to Abraham, gained the ability to see God as depicted in Genesis 32:30 where, after wrestling or struggling with (the angel of) God and receiving his blessing, Jacob said, 'I have seen God face to face'. Philo here gives a kind of spiritual interpretation of Jacob's wrestling with God, namely that Jacob actually wrestled with thoughts preventing him from reaching the wisdom of God, in order to make his belief firm and stable (*Mut.* 81). So, Israel, for Philo, is the people, whether ethnic or religious or both, who strive for the good and for the knowledge of God (*Cong.* 51). Abraham gained God's promise and friendship only when he came to the point of having true faith in God (*Abr.* 273). Abraham made the first step by changing his habitation and seeking the Creator; then God responded to Abraham's efforts to find the truth by revealing himself (*Abr.* 77–8). In a similar way, Philo points to the joy of God when human beings turn from their sins and wrongdoings and follow his commandments by their own 'free-will choice' (*Som.* ii, 174–5). In his interpretation of Deuteronomy 30:15, 'Behold I have set before your face life and death, good and evil; choose life', Philo writes,

> He puts before us both truths: first, that men have been made with a knowledge of good and of its opposite, evil; second, that it is their duty to choose the better rather than the worse, because they have … within them an incorruptible judge in the reasoning faculty, which will accept all that right reason suggests and reject the promptings of its opposite.
>
> (*Immut.* 50)

Nevertheless, as indicated above, Philo, like his contemporary Jews, does not think of human free will as independent of God's guiding act or divine grace.[15] So, Philo understands human free will as a faculty that allows one to take the initial, but not the ultimate, step (*Immut.* 47, 48). In this context, Wolfson quotes what Philo wrote in his lost fourth book of *Legum Allegoriarum*:

> It is a happy thing for the soul to be able to choose the better of the choices put forward by the Creator, but it is happier for it not to choose, but for the Creator to bring it over to himself and improve it. For, strictly speaking, the human mind does not choose the good through itself, but in accordance with the thoughtfulness of God, since He bestows the fairest things upon the worthy.[16]

Wolfson maintains that, according to Philo, human free will, even in its absolute sense, is a gift from God as one portion of his own power of freedom. Indeed, Philo declares in several passages that human effort is not sufficient itself to acquire a virtue, but it requires God's help (*Leg. All.* iii, 136). Accordingly, for Philo, God's guidance always exists in direct or indirect ways, especially for those who deserve and seek it, as he wrote: 'Some even before their birth God endows with a goodly form and equipment, and has determined that they shall have a most excellent portion' (*Leg. All.* iii, 85). On the other hand, Philo highlights a kind of human effort or human initiative as a prerequisite for God's taking an active role to reveal himself, as it happened in the cases of Abraham and Jacob. So, as maintained by E.R. Goodenough, Philo's standpoint is not one that accepts either the divine or the human initiatives as the dominant element, but one in which the human and divine free wills are juxtaposed.[17]

Either way, the virtues of the Patriarchs are what make Israel, for Philo, a nation of a 'royal priesthood' on behalf of humankind (*Mos.* i, 149; *Spec. Leg.* i, 303). Philo refers to the 'priesthood' and 'prophecy' as gifts given to the nation of Israel by God. However, they were given first to the Patriarchs, from Abraham to Moses, due to their goodness and nobility (*Abr.* 53, 56–8; *Mos.* i, 148–9).[18] Philo, in parallel to the biblical notion of chosenness, interprets the purpose of Israel's consecration above other nations in terms of setting an example of a model nation, the nation of 'priesthood', which will act in a wise and righteous way to bring others to 'good' (*Mos.* i, 149; *Abr.* 98). He also points out that the Jewish law has already had a wide appeal among the nations, especially among those who have more virtue in honouring it (*Mos.* ii, 17–20, 41–4).

At this point, it should be noted that although Philo is known as a Jewish philosopher who mostly addressed non-Jews in his writings, this is strongly questioned by some scholars. According to Emil Schürer, for example, Philo's 'concerns were focused largely on the important Alexandrian Jewish community of which he was a member'.[19] Schürer also maintains that, despite discerning some universal elements in Philo, he hardly influenced Alexandrian proselytes if it is thought that proselytism was his aim.[20] On the other hand, Martin Goodman refers to the absence of a Jewish theology, at least a systematic one, in Philo's environment at the time.[21] However, he points to Philo's perception and praise of the good and wise men among non-Jews, those who enjoyed moral excellence, not as observers of the Noahide Laws but rather, as 'the closest observers of nature' (*Spec. Leg.* ii, 45). In fact, there are some passages in which Philo shows his admiration of those non-Jews, as they strove to reach the knowledge of God through reasoning and through their virtue in respecting the Jewish law (*Mos.* ii, 17; *Praem.* 43). At this point, Wolfson points to Philo's perception of the nature of the Jewish community as consisting of the native-born Israelites and proselytes, by writing:

> The admission of proselytes on equal terms with native-born Jews into the Jewish polity indicates, according to Philo, that the basis of that polity is not common descent but rather the common heritage of the Law which was revealed by God to the people of Israel. Even the native-born Jew is a member of that polity, in the full sense of the term membership, not only because he is a descendant of the stock that founded that polity but also, and primarily so, because he remained loyal to the Law which is the heritage of that stock.[22]

It is probably not wrong to say that Philo's concern with non-Jews was mainly on the grounds of their attachment to the Jewish law, an attachment which ranges from a full observance to a mere honouring. Despite a discernible universal element in his presentation of Judaism, Philo's interest was focused mainly on his Jewish environment.

In the light of these remarks, it is possible to think that Philo's definition of Israel is based primarily on ethnic grounds, given his great emphasis on the virtues of the founders of the people of Israel.[23] On the other hand, Philo also recognizes the perception of Israel in a broader sense, integrating those who are the lovers of wisdom and knowledge, Jew or non-Jew. According to the law, as admitted by Philo, the children will be judged in accordance with their good or wicked behaviours without taking into account the goodness or the wickedness of their parents (*Virt.* 227). But surely the children of Israel did, and would, benefit from the fruits of the good deeds of their ancestors, the Patriarchs, as long as the former remained obedient (*Som.* ii, 176).

Paul's letters

As for Paul, three arguments constitute his theology of chosenness; these are the replacement of the old Mosaic covenant with the new Messianic covenant, righteousness/salvation by faith instead of law, and the notion of 'true Israel' as against physical Israel. In this way, Paul seems to try and establish a new religious community, which includes both Jews and non-Jews on equal grounds, without any privilege being giving to the former. W.D. Davies argues that since the Torah represents a kind of national religion, which requires not only an initiation into a religion, but also an incorporation into a nation, Paul sought a neutral criterion, such as faith, to bring both Jews and non-Jews into the covenant on a completely universal basis.[24] Indeed, Paul clearly rejects any kind of Jewish superiority over the gentiles in terms of salvation, by writing: 'For Christ is the end of the law so that there may be righteousness for everyone who believes' (Rom. 10:4) and 'For there is no distinction between Jew and Greek; the same Lord is Lord of all and is generous to all who call on him. For, "Everyone who calls on the name of the Lord shall be saved"' (Rom. 10:12–13; cf. Gal. 3:28). Such a universal religious community, according to Paul, is the realization of what Isaiah prophesied beforehand. In Romans 14:11 Paul quotes Isaiah 45:23, by writing: 'For it is written, "As I live, says the Lord, every knee shall bow to me, and every tongue shall give praise to God"'.

Some scholars maintain that Paul opposed the idea of righteousness through law because it was impossible to completely fulfil the latter. Such an argument, in fact, derives from a widely held belief that at the time of Paul there was little place for God's mercy and grace in Judaism's understanding of covenant and salvation, which were, instead, based on minute observance of the law. However, such depiction of early rabbinic Judaism is not without its critics. Sanders, for example, maintains that the system of early Judaism was based on what he calls 'covenantal nomism', in which Israel's obedience to the law is regarded not as a condition of election, but rather as a response to it, as election is based on God's grace. Therefore, as long as the Israelites agreed to obey the Torah, their sins would result in punishment, but not annulment of the covenant.[25] It seems that, despite an apparent emphasis on obedience to law in early Judaism, the religion of Israel, as depicted both in the apocryphal and rabbinic writings, was not unaware of the notions of God's mercy and his redeeming grace. On the contrary, as seen above, obedience and mercy were regarded as complementary elements in salvation, and this was also the case in rabbinic literature in general. So what was problematic with the Jewish notion of salvation was not the lack of mercy in the idea of salvation but, instead, the lack of salvation for non-Jews. This is why, Paul insisted on salvation by faith; it was so not because of the difficulty in observing the law, but because only faith would lead to salvation for both Jews and non-Jews.[26] Apparently Paul, who, on every occasion, declares himself as an observant Jew (Acts 22:3; 24:14; 26:5), does not question the fact that Jews do and should observe the law (Acts 24:14; I Cor. 7:17–18). He rather questions the idea of righteousness through law, as he writes: 'neither circumcision nor uncircumcision is everything; but a new creation is everything' (Gal. 6:15). He also maintains that Abraham was reckoned righteous on the grounds of faith and received an oath from God that every nation in the world would be blessed in his name (Gal. 3:8; Rom. 4: 11, 17). Only in reference to gentiles do Paul and the Apostles regard the law as unnecessary and difficult to observe (Acts 15: 7–11, 19–20). So, the real obstacle in Paul's mind as regards the law was its association with particularity and Jewishness, which apparently did not suit Paul's mission in terms of establishing a universal religious community.

On the other hand, it should be noted that Paul had a firm belief that he was living in the messianic age and that 'the Messiah came to be a hope for both Jews and Gentiles'.[27] In Romans 9:30–2, Paul gives the essence of his argument by declaring that the law has no place in the messianic age as an instrument for salvation; faith, instead, will count for righteousness and salvation. He also implies that since the Jews could not see this fact and sought righteousness through works, salvation came to gentiles. Again, in Galatians, Paul declares that those who seek salvation through faith are the heirs of the Abrahamic message and therefore Abraham's true descendants: 'Just as Abraham believed God, and it was reckoned to him as righteousness, so ... those who believe are descendants of Abraham' (Gal. 3:6–7, 16–17). It follows that Paul's definition of the true Israel, in accordance with his understanding of righteousness, excludes any physical or historical relationship, as he writes, 'it is not the children of the flesh who are the children of God, but the children of the promise who are counted as descendants' (Rom. 9:6–8). In fact, Paul underlines the notion of God as the one of love and mercy by insisting on a new covenant based on faith. In other words, to have faith in Christ, for Paul, means to have faith in God's mercy for both Jews and non-Jews. This is why, according to Paul, law is equated with sin and wrath (Rom. 3:20; 4:13–15; 7:7–8; Acts 13:38f.), whereas faith is considered to represent freedom and mercy. What Paul offers both Jews and gentiles in this way is a world where an individual does not have to struggle against sin with actions because he is already under God's mercy (Rom. 6:14).

However, what is also essential to Pauline theology is the special and irrevocable place of the physical Israel, as the people of God, in salvation. Although Paul clearly states that 'not all Israelites truly belong to Israel', yet he still does not give up calling them Israel (Rom. 11:11, 26). He also points out that the Messiah, Christ, who symbolizes the spiritual kingdom, comes according to the flesh (Rom. 9:5). So, Paul, in a similar way to Philo's insistence on blood relationship as the primary factor in the covenant, places an emphasis on the physical Israel. This is why many scholars argue that Paul's mission was aimed first at Jews, that 'Paul might have been primarily apostle to the gentiles (Rom. 1:5; 11:13; Gal. 1:15, 17; 2:7–8) but he was an apostle to gentiles for the sake of Israel'.[28] Indeed, according to Acts 18:5–6, Paul turned to gentiles only after Jews rejected his message (see also 13:46; 26:19–20, 23; 28:26–8. Cf. Gal. 2:7).[29] Besides, despite the fact that the transformation or incorporation of gentiles into the people of God is a significant part of Paul's mission, the ultimate goal seems to be the mysterious salvation of all Israel, as it is written: 'a hardening has come upon part of Israel, until the full number of the Gentiles come in. And so all Israel will be saved' (Rom. 11:25–6).[30]

Thus Paul indicates that as the Jews have been chosen once by God, even if they fail to fulfil the requirements of the new covenant, which is the acceptance of Christ, they will still be saved by God's grace (Rom. 11:1–6). For they were chosen by the same grace and, therefore, God will not reject them or let them lack redemption. In Romans Paul mentions a 'remnant, chosen by grace' for the sake of which all Israel seems to gain salvation in the end (Rom. 11:5). What makes one chosen or rejected, to quote Karl Barth as regards his commentary on Romans, is 'not the good or bad will of the one but the word of God.'[31] Indeed, Paul believes that chosenness is not based on actions but rather on God's call, 'not as something due but as a gift' (Rom. 4:4–5; 9:13–14; cf. Ex. 33:19). It is, in fact, such mercy that in the end will enable the Jews to repent even if they do not accept Christ at the time (Rom. 2:4f.).

Apparently, both Philo and Paul, as two Jewish figures of antiquity, sought to define the concepts of the Jewish covenant and chosenness in more universalistic terms than most of their contemporary fellow Jews. But they did so in their own separate ways. Philo carried the biblical notion of the law into his own philosophical system as the embodiment of the good and the standard for a great and wise nation, namely the nation of priesthood. He also incorporated all lovers of wisdom and knowledge, both Jew and non-Jew, within the category of the great nation. However, a sort of superiority attached to the Israelites as the chosen nation still remained. As for Paul, to be able to incorporate both Jews and non-Jews equally into the covenant, he proposed even more universal means, such as faith in God's redeeming grace, symbolized in the figure of Christ. However, Paul, just like Philo, achieved this without giving up the physical Israel. This was, in effect, the acceptance of the 'eternity' of Israel, albeit in a rather controversial way.

3 Rabbinic literature

As in the case of ancient Jewish literature, the central message stemming from rabbinic literature as a whole is the belief that 'Israel's holiness endures'; to put it in other words, the covenantal relationship between God and Israel is eternal. But before dealing with the rabbinic discussion of chosenness, it is important to highlight a distinction between the early (tannaitic) and late (amoraic) rabbinic writings. For these two sets of writings present the same belief in the holiness of the people of Israel, yet they do it in two different ways. While the amoraic writings of the fourth and fifth centuries are involved in an intense discussion and justification of the biblical notion of chosenness, the tannaitic writings of the second and third centuries display only an implicit recognition of it. As regards this, Jacob Neusner points to the fact that the Tannaim and Amoraim had differing experiences and, therefore, responded to different circumstances, which, consequently, influenced the nature of their receptions of the biblical notion of chosenness. Accordingly, as far as the mishnaic formulation is concerned, the recognition and retention of Israel's holiness was presented in response to the catastrophic defeats of 70 and 135 CE, which led to the destruction of the Temple and also the collapse of the last Jewish hope for a national–religious restoration. In the Talmud and related writings, on the other hand, it was placed against the challenging presence of Christianity and the Christian version of chosenness, i.e. the rhetoric of 'true Israel'.[1] So, it is interesting, but not totally surprising that the strategy adopted in the tannaitic writings was a renewed acceptance of the holiness of Israel as an obvious fact. Indeed, in the Mishnah, in particular, the apologetic tone prevailing in the amoraic writings of the fourth and fifth centuries is completely absent. There is, instead, an incontestable commitment to the 'sanctification' of Israel; a sanctification which is expressed, not through the Temple and sacrifices in particular, but within the everyday life of the Jewish people, including the Temple cult. In other words, what the Tannaim did in the Mishnah is the transformation of Israel from a 'political religious entity', centred around the sanctity of the Temple, into an unquestionably and inherently 'sacred community' in its everyday life.[2] So, the mishnaic system does not engage with the problematic questions embedded in the biblical presentation of election. Nor does the existence of Christianity have any bearing on the mishnaic world as framed by the Tannaim. They do not deal with the question as to '*why* is Israel chosen by God?' but, instead, affirm the fact that 'Israel *is* chosen by God'. In this way, they suggest a harmonious picture of Israel (the mishnaic emphasis on order) and an unproblematic presentation of chosenness and holiness. This is presented mostly within a ritual (*halakhah*), instead of a theological (*aggadah*), framework and is based on the assumptions that 'God stands for paradox' and that 'Strength comes through weakness', namely that Israel endures as the holy people of God, despite destruction and defeat.[3]

According to this picture, the challenge of Christianity as a competing system was first seriously felt in the Palestinian Talmud (Yerushalmi, 400–450) and in the Midrash Rabba (400–600), alongside some other exegetical writings of the same period, such as *Sifré Deuteronomy*,[4] and was carried on through to the Babylonian Talmud (Bavli, 500–600); a process which resulted in an increasing emphasis on the doctrine of Israel's election in a polemical mode. It is important to note that the emergence of an apologetic rabbinic discussion of the doctrine of Israel's election is the result of Christianity's turning from a subordinate sect into an institutionalized and predominating system; a shift which took place due, to a great extent, to Christianity's becoming a religion officially recognized by the Roman Empire in 312 CE.[5] This triumph of Christianity to political power meant the rule and control of the Christian Roman Empire over the Jews and the area which was sacred to them. Such a political change also had theological implications for both Christians and Jews. From the Christian point of view, it looked like a victory for the new Israel, represented by the Church, over the old Israel, i.e. the Jewish people. As a result of this, the ancient rabbis had to stick even more vigorously to the mishnaic conviction that 'Israel's holiness and chosenness endure'. Moreover, they had to show that Christianity did not supersede Judaism, nor did the Church replace the chosen people of God. By so doing, the rabbis made use of a sort of asymmetry between two types of power: the spiritual and the physical, the former applying to Israel and the latter to other nations. This was in a way the repetition of the mishnaic conviction that 'Strength comes through weakness', namely that spiritual power is superior over physical power.

Accordingly, the early rabbinic writings, which emerged as an answer to a political change in the life of Israel, that is the destruction of the Second Temple, placed emphasis on the sanctity of the community of Israel in its everyday life. As for the later rabbinic writings, which were produced in response to the theological question of the emergence of Christianity as an opposing religious system, they had to further the idea of the sanctity of Israel as a worldly situation (the theme of sanctification here and now) to that of the sanctity of Israel as an eternal reality (the theme of salvation at the end of time). Although the emphasis is thus laid on the 'social' (*halakhic*) dimension in the early rabbinic writings, and on the 'supernatural' (*aggadic*) dimension in the later rabbinic writings, Israel is presented, in both cases, as an everlasting entity. So, the 'purpose of Israel's election', as C.G. Montefiore and H. Loewe point out, 'is that it shall sanctify God's name, and be a holy people dedicated to God's service'.[6] Indeed, in a midrashic comment on Leviticus 19:2, 'For I the Lord am holy, who made you holy', God says, 'I am holy, do I need sanctification? But I will hallow Israel, so that they may sanctify Me' (*Ex. R.* 15:24; also *Lev. R.* 2:5). The reason why God needs to hallow Israel is also presented in universalistic terms, as written in another rabbinic statement: 'So is Israel indispensable for the existence of the world; as it is said: "And in thy seed shall all the nations of the earth be blessed" (Gen. 22:18)' (*Num. R.* 2:13).

On the other hand, in the Mishnah, as a result of the notion of holiness, there is an apparent 'recognition' of the separation of Israel from other nations on religious as well as social grounds. In the later rabbinic writings, however, a theological 'justification' is brought forward for the differentiation between Jews and non-Jews in the world to come, as well as in this world. God's choosing Israel because of their acceptance of the Torah is frequently placed alongside his rejecting the gentiles due to their refusal of the Torah. In other words, a sort of taken-for-granted mishnaic separation between Israel and the gentiles is reformulated by the Amoraim, within the notion of the salvation of Israel and the dismissal of the others based on their relation to the Torah. This late rabbinic emphasis on the theme of election and rejection through the Torah can be seen as an answer to Christianity's substitution of 'the old Israel' (Jewish) with 'the new Israel' (Christian) and of 'law' with 'faith'. This emphasis on the Torah is occasionally presented in inclusive terms, as in the statement 'even an idolater who studies the Torah is equal to a High Priest' (A.Z. 2b–3a).

In fact, the way that the rabbis discuss the relationship between God and Israel is not free of ambiguity. In rabbinic literature a wide diversity of opinions exists on the question of God's relation to Israel, and most of the time different statements that seem to prove opposite parts of the question are given at once. This might be related partly to the ambiguous attitude of Scripture itself towards the question of the chosenness of Israel, and partly to the nature of the exegetical method employed by the ancient rabbis, which allows a diverse range of statements and comments on a particular topic. Above all these, the belief in an eternal Israel is sought to be justified in rabbinic literature against a conflicting background, as mentioned earlier. This is why the rabbinic formulation of chosenness incorporates a sort of rationality and purposefulness, on the one hand, and an element of mystery and arbitrariness, on the other.

As regards the reason for Israel's chosenness, namely God's election of the people of Israel from among all others as a holy people, different explanations are given in both later tannaitic and amoraic writings, which can be classified under the three headings:

1   God's love for Israel.
2   Israel's merit.
3   The merits of the Patriarchs.

These three rabbinic explanations regarding the chosenness of Israel also yield some further questions and categories, such as: whether chosenness is a historical event which took place under certain conditions at a particular time or a cosmic act which had been planned by God, even preceding the creation of the world; whether Israel actively (choosing) or passively (chosen) participated in this event; whether one should understand chosenness as a conditional or an unconditional matter. What lies behind all these questions, on the other hand, is the broader question of whether the ancient rabbis interpreted Israel's chosenness and holiness as a quality or duty.

God's love for Israel

There is a prevailing notion of an 'unmerited' favour and love of God towards Israel and a concomitant emphasis on an eternal–cosmic election, which altogether lead to a substantialist understanding of chosenness. In one midrashic passage God declares his love for Israel by saying, 'Of all the nations whom I have created I love only Israel' (*Dt. R.* 5:7; also *Num. R.* 1:9f.; *Cant. R.* 18:1; *Sifré Dt.* 344). The theme of God's love for Israel is usually presented by the ancient rabbis in terms of the association of God's name with the people of Israel. Such an association, in fact, suggests a notion of God that is less than a 'universal' one, as it is written:

> R. Simeon b. Yohai taught: I am God to all the inhabitants of the world, but I have associated My name only with my people Israel. I am not called the God of the nations, only the God of Israel.
>   (*Ruth R.* 1:1; also *Sifré Dt.* 31; *Cant. R.* 33:1; *Ex. R.* 32:2; *Num. R.* 20:21)

In parallel to this, Israel is also presented as a people that are more than 'chosen'. In the following rabbinic comment the people of Israel are depicted as a special people who are so created by God for the sole reason of sanctifying his name.

> Israel were created for the purpose of declaring the praise of the Holy One; as you read: 'The people which I formed for Myself, that they might tell of My praise' (Isa. 43:21). For the reason, then, that His name might be glorified through them he made them [Israel] His seal of goodness: 'Set me as a seal upon your heart, as a seal upon thine arm' (Song 8:6). 'That I cut thee not off' (Isa. 48:9).
>
>   (*Num. R.* 4:1)

Again, in a similar statement Israel are declared to be 'created only for carrying out religious duties and doing good deeds' (*Lev. R.* 23:6). Moreover, alongside the association of God's name with Israel the rabbis speak of an interdependence between what is called *Shekhinah*, that is the divine presence of God in the world, and Israel (*Num. R.* 7:8; *Pesik.* 5:6; *Mek.d.r.Ish.*, Beshallah, 4:80), by attributing to the latter a supernatural function. However, as emphasized by many, this rabbinic belief in a special connection between God and Israel as well as the subsequent differentiation and separation of Israel from other nations (*Sifré Dt.* 314; *Pesik.* 5:5), which establish the kernel of rabbinic theology, is understood and displayed in purely religious and social terms, with no implication of any genetic difference.[7]

In the wake of a powerful rabbinic notion of God's love for Israel, one should also speak of the 'emotional' element involved in the separation of Israel from other nations. While this special position that Israel enjoys imposes upon them a great number of responsibilities, i.e., detailed commandments, (*Ex. R.* 30:5–6) and sufferings, i.e. chastisements (*Ex. R.* 1:1; Ber. 5a), it also guarantees them a reward in the world to come, namely an eternal life (A.Z. 4a; also *Koh. R.* 1:7, 8; Men. 53b). In other words, chosenness incorporates privilege and responsibility at one and the same time. In reference to God's punishment of sins in this world and the gaining of salvation at the end of time, the rabbis point to an apparent distinction between Israel and other nations, who are mostly associated with the idolaters. God shows an 'unlimited capacity to forgive Israel',[8] as is manifest in one midrashic comment on Deuteronomy 32:9, in which it is maintained that even when the people of Israel 'deserved to be cursed they were not cursed' (*Num. R.* 20:19). Again, in another midrashic passage God says: 'I will not banish Israel, even if I destroy my world' (*Ex. R.* 31:10). In parallel to this, there are some other rabbinic statements that explain the eternity of Israel in relation to the eternity of God's name. One rabbinic comment on Isaiah 48:9, which reads, 'For my name's sake I defer my anger, for the sake of my praise I restrain it for you, so that I may not cut you off', states: '["My name's sake"] refers to Israel, with whom the Holy One, blessed be He, particularly connected His name by declaring, "I am the Lord thy God"' (Ex. 20:2), and with whose name "Israel" He combined His own' (*Num. R.* 5:6).

Moreover, in relation to the world to come it is written: 'In the hereafter they [Israel] will enter Gehinnom and the nations of the world will also enter. The latter having entered will perish, but Israel will come out therefrom unscathed' (*Num. R.* 2:13; also *Sifré Dt.* 311). At this point, it is important to indicate a well-known mishnaic statement which reads, 'All Israelites have a share in the world to come' (Sanh. 10:1). Neusner argues that to be 'Israel', based on this statement, comes to mean 'to be those destined to rise from the dead and enjoy the world to come'. With the same token, the non-Israelites, namely the gentiles, are those who are judged to eternal damnation and who will perish. As for the righteous gentiles, they will not be subjected to eternal damnation, but will not be rewarded with eternal life either. Accordingly, 'all Israelites have a share in the world to come', can be read in reverse, namely that 'all who have a share in the world to come are Israelites'.[9] However, in the later rabbinic writings, and the talmudic discussion in particular, there is an attempt to find a place in the world to come for the righteous ones of the other nations.[10] The formulation of the Noahide Laws, as a measurement for righteousness and therefore salvation for non-Jews, is mentioned again in these later rabbinic writings (Sanh. 56–60; A.Z. 64b). The presence of such a formulation in the Talmud and other rabbinic writings of that period, again, can be understood in reference to an apparent rabbinic need to respond to the Christian notion of salvation for all the nations of the world, but without giving up the biblical doctrine of chosenness.

In parallel to the notion of God's special love for Israel, there is also a rabbinic conviction that 'the heaven and the earth were created for the sake of Israel' (Ber. 32b). In a statement ascribed to Rabbi Berekiah, the word *reshith* in the opening sentence of the book of Genesis, 'because of *reshith* (in the beginning) God created the heaven and the earth', cannot but signify Israel, as it is written in Jeremiah 2:3, 'Israel is the Lord's hallowed portion, his *reshith* (first fruits) of the increase' (*Lev. R.* 36:4). In another midrashic passage it is also declared, in reference to Psalm 74:2, 'Remember your congregation which you acquired long ago', that the intention of God to create Israel preceded everything else (*Gen. R.* 1:4). Accordingly, for some rabbis Israel was actually created before the creation of the world, while for some others the creation of Israel, unlike the nations, was already contemplated, which in any case indicates that Israel's election was predestined before the creation of the world. The idea of a cosmic election, which takes Israel's creation, and therefore its holiness and distinctiveness, to a time prior to the creation of the world, suggests in this way an eternal and therefore unconditional form of chosenness.

The unconditional doctrine of chosenness was supported especially by Rabbi Akiba, a pre-eminent rabbi of the first century, who believed that Israel were chosen to be given the Torah through which the world was created, and that they are the children of God, independent of any circumstances. Rabbi Akiba, in reference to Deuteronomy 32:5, 'yet his degenerate children have dealt falsely with him', argued that even though the children of Israel are full of blemishes they are still the children of God for they are called 'His children', despite their corruption: 'Is corruption His? No, His children's is the blemish'.[11] In another rabbinic comment on Deuteronomy 32:6, 'Is not he your father, who created you, who made you and established you?', it is stated, however, that 'as long as Israel performs the will of God, He is merciful towards them like a father towards His children, but if they do not perform His will, He chastises them as one does His slave' (*Ex. R.* 24:1). Rabbi Meir, like his master Rabbi Akiba, holds to the view that it makes no difference whether the people of Israel observe the commandments or not, they are his children in either case. Again, Rabbi Abba bar Zavda is also stated to have a similar view to that of Rabbi Akiba and Rabbi Meir, namely that although the children of Israel sin they are still 'Israel' because they are always called Israel. In opposition to this majority view of unconditional chosenness, there is also the minority view, attributed to Rabbi Judah, which argues that the people of Israel are the children of God as long as they are obedient (*Sifré Dt.* 96).

God's love for Israel is also presented in relation to the Torah. Yet, again, two different emphases are given in this rabbinic connection between Israel and the Torah: one refers to the unconditional love of God for Israel as evidenced in the giving of the Torah, and the other to the active involvement of Israel in the acceptance of it. So, according to one rabbinic interpretation, God says to Israel: 'See how beloved you are unto Me, for no being in My palace is acquainted with the Torah, yet to you have I entrusted it' (*Dt. R.* 8:7). In other words, God gave his most precious gift, i.e. the Torah, to his most beloved one, i.e., Israel (*Ex. R.*

1:1; 30:9; *Sifré Dt.* 311; Ab. 14). The important point here is not any merit on the part of Israel but rather God's unconditional love for it. In other words, God has chosen the people of Israel out of his own free will and for his particular love for them, and has, therefore, given them the Torah. In order to emphasize God's free will in the election of Israel, it is also written:

> 'Is not He thy father that has got you?' (Dt. 32:6): Moses said to Israel, 'You are precious to Him. You are His own possession and *not* His inheritance.' ... a person who had inherited ten palaces from his father purchased one palace of his own, which he loved more than all the palaces that he had inherited from his father. So also did Moses say to Israel, 'You are precious to Him. You are His own acquisition and not His inheritance.'
>
> *(Sifré Dt. 309)*

In parallel to the notion of God's free will, a particular emphasis is placed on the biblical notion of the weakness of the people of Israel – in terms of both size and physical power (*Num. R.* 11:1; *Ex. R.* 31:13; see Dt. 7:7–8). Indeed, the conditions of poverty and humility are frequently attributed to the people of Israel. The ancient rabbis, by pointing to the physical weakness of Israel, aim to underline two crucial points. First, God's choice of Israel as his people was not because Israel was any better than other nations; on the contrary it was the poorest and the smallest of all. It was because God loved the people Israel out of his free will that he chose them for himself. Second, Israel is still a great nation, not physically but spiritually, because it possesses the Torah. In other words, Israel's power, unlike that of other nations, is not dependent on any physical and, therefore, temporary characteristic. Instead, it comes directly from God and the Torah and is therefore eternal (*Mek.d.r.Ish.*, Shirata 3:10–25). Such a comparison between physical and spiritual powers might have also served to explain the reason behind the subordinate situation of the Jews at the time. This is, in other words, the confirmation of the rabbinic belief that 'Strength comes through weakness'.

Israel's merit

There is also the notion of the merits of Israel, which indicates much of the historical aspect of chosenness. That Israel alone accepted the Torah among all other nations is frequently used as evidence of Israel's merit. In one midrashic passage it is written:

> When God was about to give the Torah, no other nation but Israel would accept it. Similarly, when God revealed Himself on Sinai, there was not a nation at whose doors He did not knock, but they would not undertake to keep it; as soon as He came to Israel, they exclaimed: 'All that the Lord has spoken will we do, and obey' (Ex. 24:7).
>
> *(Ex. R. 27:9; also Sifré Dt. 343; A.Z. 2b)*

In the following rabbinic comment, there is also an explicit affirmation of the historical dimension of chosenness, as well as Israel's active participation in it: 'Why did the Holy One, blessed be He, choose them? Because all the nations rejected the Torah and refused to accept it, but Israel gladly chose the Holy One, blessed be He, and His Torah' (*Num. R.* 14:109).

Again, in a rabbinic attempt to combine the cosmic and historical definitions of chosenness, it is declared that although God knew Israel long before (Hos. 11:1), it was only when the people 'stood before Mount Sinai and received the Torah' that 'they had become completely God's people' (*Cant. R.* 42:1; also *Pesik.* 12:23). In a similar rabbinic interpretation of Deuteronomy 7:8, 'because the Lord loves you', it is also written that only when Israel 'stood at Sinai and received the Torah' that God wrote 'I love you' (*Ex. R.* 32:2). On the other hand, the cosmic election of Israel is directly associated with the Torah and the notion of the merits of Israel, by asserting that: 'The intention to create Israel preceded everything else ... had not the Holy One, blessed be He, foreseen that after twenty-six generations Israel would receive the Torah, He would not have written therein, "Command the children of Israel!" (Num. 28:2)' (*Gen. R.* 1:4).

In fact, such interpretations can be seen as an affirmation of another rabbinic conviction that the creation was actually carried out for the sake of the Torah (*Lev. R.* 36:4). Accordingly, God knew that Israel alone would accept the Torah, and therefore he chose the people of Israel as his people and bound his name to them before actually creating them along with everything else. This is why it is also written that if Israel had not accepted the Torah, God would have caused them to disappear from the nations (*Ruth R.* 1:1). A similar understanding is that the world was created for the sake of the Torah and was saved for the sake of Israel only because they accepted the Torah (*Lev. R.* 33:3; *Cant. R.* 19:1). According to this, the world was created for the sake of the Torah, but Israel, by accepting it, firmly established the creation.[12] In other words, Israel are God's people, whether cosmic or historical, for the sake of Torah.

However, does this mean to say that the chosenness of Israel as God's people is conditional on Israel's complete obedience to Torah? Given the overall emphasis in rabbinic literature, the answer to this question should be in the negative. For, despite an apparent rabbinic emphasis on the recognition of the Torah as the main cause of the difference between Israel and the heathen nations,[13] it seems quite clear that, according to the ancient rabbis, since God once bound his name with Israel due to their acceptance of the Torah at Sinai (covenant agreement), as long as they stay within the covenant by showing an ongoing 'willingness' to obey the Torah, He will not forsake them. At this point, it is written:

> When Israel stood at Sinai and received the Torah, the Holy One, blessed be He, said to the Angel of Death: 'Thou hast power over all the heathen but not over this people, for they are My portion, and just as I live for ever, so will My children be eternal...
>
> (*Ex. R.* 32:7)

Indeed, there are quite a few rabbinic passages in which 'covenant' and 'mercy' are mentioned together (*Dt. R.* 3:4f.; *Num. R.* 16:22). In another passage God says, 'I will not banish Israel even if I destroy the world ... nevertheless I have made a condition with them that if they sin, the Temple will be seized in pledge' (*Ex. R.* 31:10). Again, the rabbis state that evil deeds can be forgotten by God but not the covenant (Ber. 32b). So, the main emphasis in rabbinic writings is, that even if God punishes Israel for their sins and hides his face due to their disobedience, Israel are holy to God and will be redeemed in the end (*Num. R.* 16:22; Men. 53b). The rabbis restate that it is in spite of their sins that the people of Israel are called the children of God (*Sifré Dt.* 308) and that *Shekhinah* dwells among them. 'Even if they have become rebellious', God says, 'I do not abandon them; but with them I dwell' (*Ex. R.* 33:2). Moreover, there is a rabbinic confidence in Israel's overall righteousness, as it is written:

> There is no nation in the world to compare with them. One moment they are asleep, far from the Torah and the precepts. The next moment they rise from their sleep like lions, quickly proceed to read the *shema* and, proclaiming the sovereignty of the Holy One, blessed be He...
>
> (*Num. R.* 20:20)

At this point it is important to refer to the concept of 'covenantal nomism' as coined by Sanders to describe the characteristic of Rabbinic Judaism, according to which the 'acceptance of God's kingship', that is the covenant, 'always precedes the enjoining of the commandments', namely the minute observance of the law. Therefore, 'the result of not being obedient is punishment', through exile and/or destruction, but 'not the loss of election'.[14] Accordingly, while the initiative in election belongs to God, Israel's obedience to the law is demanded as a response to God's grace, and not as a condition of election. Apparently, while the Temple, the land, and the kingship are gifts which are conditionally given to Israel, their holiness endures, in any condition, as long as they agree to obey the Torah. Sanders maintains that one should understand the famous mishnaic passage which guarantees salvation for all Israelites (except the three groups) within the same context of the covenant consciousness. Accordingly, 'all Israelites have a share in the world to come unless they renounce it by renouncing God and his covenant', not for as long as they stay completely righteous.[15]

On the other hand, there is a broader criterion drawn by later rabbis regarding the redemption of Israel. The redemption is to take place for the sake of Israel itself when Israel deserves it, or for God's own sake when Israel does not deserve it,[16] or for the oath that God promised (*Lev. R.* 23:2; *Dt. R.* 3:2), or for the sake of the Torah through which the world was created (*Lev. R.* 33:3; *Est. R.* 7:13). As a matter of fact, all these principles are presented in connection to one another. The ultimate conviction is that Israel is precious to God and indispensable to the world, and therefore will be eternal. This is why the rabbis seek to justify the eternity of the election of Israel rather than the election itself.

Sometimes they refer to God's love for Israel (the notion of God's grace), and sometimes to Israel's love for God (the notion of Israel's merit). In one rabbinic comment on Deuteronomy 26:17–18, it is written:

> 'You have avouched the Lord this day ... and the Lord has avouched you this day' [26:17–18]. The Holy One, blessed be He, said to Israel: You have made me a unique object of your love [Dt. 6:4] in the world, and I shall make you a unique object of My love [1 Chr. 17:21] in the world.
>
> (Hag. 3a–b)

Moreover, in order to emphasize Israel's active involvement in chosenness, the rabbis also write: 'God said to Israel: "because you exalt Me through justice I too will act righteously and will cause My holiness to dwell amongst you"' (*Dt. R.* 5:7; also 7:12; Ber. 6a–b). God also says to Moses: 'The idol-worshippers are worthless grain ... Israel, however, are righteous; they are all wheat fit for storage' (*Num. R.* 5:1; also Hul. 89a). There is also a universal–cosmic dimension attached to the rabbinic conviction of the merit and eternity of Israel. Not only the creation, but also the continuity of the world, depend on the people of Israel in respect to their relation to the Torah, and therefore to God, as it is suggested in several midrashic interpretations. In one of them it is written, 'the world would long have gone into dissolution had not Israel stood before Mount Sinai' (*Ruth R.* 1:1; also *Ex. R.* 15:6; *Num. R.* 2:13). Again, in another passage, there is a clear universalistic and other-worldly emphasis, as it is written:

> ...were it not for Israel no rain would fall nor would the sun shine. For it is due to their merit that the Holy One, blessed be He, brings relief to this world of His. In the World to Come when the idolaters behold how the Holy One, blessed be He, is with Israel they will come to join them...
>
> (*Num. R.* 1:3)

The merits of the Patriarchs

In some other rabbinic interpretations, however, the notion of merit is formulated more in relation to the Patriarchs, than in relation to Israel. According to such a formulation, the creation of the world, as well as the election of Israel, is believed to actually take place for the sake of the Patriarchs, in particular Jacob. What is interesting with this rabbinic notion of the merit of the Patriarchs is that it is of an opposing nature. The rabbinic emphasis on the merit of Abraham, due to the fact that his biblical mission is a blessing for all the nations of the world, conveys a universal and an inclusive message (*Num. R.* 14:11; *Cant. R.* 3:4). The same emphasis made on Jacob's merit, on the contrary, gives the issue of chosenness an exclusivist tone. It is emphasized that in contrast to Abraham and Isaac, who generated Esau and Ishmael, respectively, two wicked generations, Jacob did not generate any unfit descendants (*Lev. R.* 36:5; *Sifré Dt.* 312), and therefore will suffer no humiliation in the world to come (*Num. R.* 2:13). This overemphasis on Jacob and his all-righteous descendants, though not entirely unknown to the Hebrew Bible, can, again, be seen as a response to the Christian rhetoric of 'the new Israel', according to which not all descendants of Abraham belong to the chosen people (Rom. 9:6–8). The ancient rabbis thus assert that the true descendants of Abraham and Isaac were carried on through Jacob, whose descendants are regarded as 'perfect' before God (*Lev. R.* 36:5), and therefore eternal.

In fact, faith in the eternity of Israel as demonstrated in rabbinic literature is also preserved and even further developed, with all its ramifications, in medieval Jewish literature. Among the medieval Jewish scholars, Judah Halevi pioneers the idea of an unconditional, even a genetic, chosenness of Israel based on what he calls 'divine will/influence' (*'amr ilahi*) that uniquely and eternally rests in Israel as a people and also as individuals. This is why a convert, for Halevi, as much as he shares the good fortune of Israel, i.e. the reward in the world to come, still cannot be equal to a Jew by birth.[17] Gersonides, too, formulates Israel's chosenness in reference to an 'inherited providence', which, in a similar way to Halevi's divine will, indicates an unconditional, if not genetic, principle underlying it.[18] However, Halevi's genetic chosenness finds its foremost recognition in kabbalistic literature, the book of Zohar in particular, where a clear division is made between Jewish and non-Jewish souls in terms of their sources, one deriving from the 'holy side' (*sitra di-qedusha*) and the other from the 'other side' (*sitra ahra*).[19] Therefore, according to the author of Zohar, the rabbis talk about the converts coming under the 'wings' of the *Shekhinah*, and not unto her 'body' as it is the place allocated only to the Jews by birth.[20] This division of souls into Jewish and non-Jewish is later developed by some kabbalistic and Hasidic figures, so that while the souls of Jews are seen as identical with the 'divine soul' or *neshamah*, the souls of non-Jews are regarded as equivalent to the 'natural/animal soul' or *nefesh*. On the other hand, although Saadiah Gaon and Maimonides, two important medieval Jewish scholars, write little on Israel's chosenness in a direct way and understand it mainly in terms of 'virtue of the law', not as any genetic trait on the part of Israelites/Jews, they do still accept the 'eternity of Israel' as a fundamental principle. Accordingly, while being part of Israel is, for Maimonides as well as for Saadiah, dependent on obedience or allegiance to the law, which works equally for a Jew by birth and a convert, unless one deliberately and intentionally abandons the law, a Jew, despite his sins, remains a part of Israel and, therefore, has a place in the world to come.[21]

In the light of these explanations, it becomes clear that in the formation of the Oral Torah the conviction of Israel's 'eternal holiness' serves as the overruling principle on which a new Jewish identity is built in the absence of a national–political independence. The challenge of Christianity, on the other hand, which recognizes the divine covenant made with Israel, but at the same time introduces the theme of the rejection of the physical Israel or the Jews (Rom. 9–11) as reinforced later within the Church tradition, amplifies the unsteady nature of the biblical doctrine of chosenness. The Jewish people, in parallel to their contradictory experience with the Christian world – as well as with Islam to

a certain extent – during the medieval period, began to see themselves as a people not only 'elected' by God, but also 'rejected' by the nations, which only proves and also strengthens their faith in chosenness as it serves as a remedy for the inferior position of the Jewish people in the medieval period. The history of the Jewish people in the modern period, on the other hand, witnesses a shifting emphasis on either part of the formulation of chosenness, namely on being an elected and/or a rejected one. This is what will be discussed in the next two parts.

Part II
Chosenness as 'mission'

4 Universalist Jewish philosophies
Spinoza and Mendelssohn

The early modern period witnesses a transition of the Jewish people from a closed and homogenous (traditional) outlook to an open and divergent (modern) one. This transition is of particular importance for the purpose of the book, as it indicates the beginning of a shift in the Jewish understanding of chosenness from holiness to mission, from particularity to universality. Put briefly, in the pre-modern period a fairly straightforward understanding of the idea of chosenness, as a taken-for-granted fact, was retained by the majority of Jews. Jewish isolation from the outside world was a direct consequence of an internal demand, which can be attributed to Jewish belief in being the holy people of God. Such a belief, in turn, provided the Jews with an explanation for their current socially inferior status and a reason to endure it. So, despite a feeling of inferiority, which was the product of both social and theological factors, the Jews had confidence that they were superior in a religious sense, and that their full reward was preserved in the world to come. What is meant by social and theological factors is the structure of society (the status society), which was based on religious affiliation and required a strict hierarchy between Christians and Jews, and the Christian rhetoric of the true Israel and rejection of the Jews. This rhetoric, coupled with the social inferiority of the Jews, gave an impetus to an increasing Jewish hold on the idea of chosenness. Thus, the idea of chosenness rendered the Jewish people with a more other-worldly outlook and a sense of religious superiority at one and the same time. Besides, when the structure of society was based on the authority of the religious system, the Jewish communities could naturally enjoy, under a single religious authority, a homogeneous and, to a certain extent, an autonomous existence. As a result, Jews, at least those who were from the same region, could understand and practise their religion in the same way. This was the case notwithstanding some geographical (Ashkenazi and Sephardic) and theological (Rabbinic and Karaite) divisions.

In the modern period, however, when the Enlightenment turned religion into a private and ordinary matter, stripping it of its supernatural and normative nature and rationalizing and secularizing society, Jewish communities lost their religious authority and their coherency. The result was the compartmentalization of life and the fragmentation of religion. What lay at the centre of Judaism in rabbinic and medieval times was the Jewish community, shaped in accordance with the Torah, as an absolute authority. In modern times, however, in the absence of any religious authority, the question of Jewish identity and Jewish self-definition as based on a premise other than Torah came to the fore. The new source of authority became the 'individual' or 'the Jewish people'. Parallel to this, the idea of chosenness, once understood in the context of religious status, was received by modern Jews as part of their quest for identity, which was of an obvious philosophical–existentialist nature. And most importantly, 'choosing' rather than 'being chosen' became the key term. On the other hand, the Jewish Emancipation generated an attempt by the Reform Jews, in particular, to minimize the burden of chosenness and normalize the people of Israel by transforming them from a holy people, who were mysteriously chosen by God and therefore ultimately different, into a religious community with a worldly mission. This was, in fact, an attempt to end the exile of the Jewish people by making them part of the surrounding cultures, though to different extents. It is possible to trace this tendency back to Moses Mendelssohn, who pronounced his famous catchphrase 'be a Jew at home, outside be like everybody else.' Although Emancipation was thus understood by the enlightened Jews as liberation from the ghetto life, for Orthodox Jews it meant an escape from the yoke of election and thus was seen as a major threat to Judaism.

Accordingly, what follows will be a discussion of the impact of modernity on Jewish self-understanding and the traditional notion of chosenness, as exemplified in the writings of Baruch Spinoza and Moses Mendelssohn. Spinoza and Mendelssohn, two important Jewish figures in the pre-Emancipation period, are probably the examples that best highlight the transition in the history of the Jewish people and Jewish religion from the medieval, or pre-modern, to the modern period. While the notion of 'one universal truth', which was later adopted by progressive Jews in Germany, lay at the centre of their philosophical endeavours to universalize the Jewish religion (Spinoza) and to integrate the Jewish people with other peoples (Mendelssohn), they adopted different positions on many issues, including the doctrine of chosenness, and apparently had different impacts on the coming generations. The ideas of neither Spinoza nor Mendelssohn were well received by the majority of the Jews of their time. On the contrary, Spinoza was even excommunicated by the Jewish community of Amsterdam due to his radical views concerning the Jewish or biblical God as well as Jewish religion. Nevertheless, the models they set would later witness the growth of modern Judaism and, in particular, progressive Judaism, based on universal and rational principles. Thus this chapter aims to establish the background for the Jewish Emancipation and the development of modern Jewish movements from between the late eighteenth and the nineteenth centuries in the light of the universalistic theologies of Spinoza and Mendelssohn. Despite the fact that neither of them, especially Spinoza, interpreted chosenness in terms of a mission on the part of Israel, they opened up the way for universalistic developments among German Jewry, albeit with a negative outcome like the problem of assimilation.

Baruch Spinoza

Baruch or, to give his Latin name, Benedict Spinoza is one of the most controversial figures in Jewish history. Yet it would probably not be wrong to regard him as a 'Jewish' thinker, due to his visible contribution to the understanding of the Jewish religion and Jewish identity in the modern period. He is regarded by many as the founder of Jewish secularism, i.e. the first secular Jew and even the first Zionist.[1] Besides, the Jews of his time referred to him as 'our Jew from Voorburg' and so he remained in the eyes of both Jews and non-Jews.[2] One should also remember the attempts made by the contemporary Jews to lift the ban on him and to grant him back the title of 'Jew'.[3] Although Spinoza was bitterly critical of the main principles of the Jewish religion, for some Jewish writers like Jacob Agus, his ideas cannot be seen outside the parameters of the Jewish thought and Jewish experience.[4] Indeed, Spinoza's rejection of the biblical and rabbinic views of the Jewish religion and Jewish people can be understood as an endeavour to establish a 'universal religion'; a notion which was first generated in prophetic universalism. So, as asserted by many, what Spinoza sought to achieve was to make Jewish history 'the model and lever of world history'[5] by depriving the former of its national and particularistic precepts. Of course, Spinoza's philosophy, in its own right, is a huge subject and lies beyond the scope of this book. Therefore, the focus of interest here will be limited to Spinoza's view of Jewish religion in general, and his interpretation of the biblical idea of chosenness in particular. This focus will highlight some similarities to and differences with Paul, another controversial Jewish figure. In fact, what makes a comparison between Spinoza and Paul an interesting one is the fact that they both were at least originally Jewish figures and established their own theologies within a kind of interaction with the figure of Christ. Besides, universalist concerns played a tremendous role in the theologies of both.

Indeed Spinoza's philosophical thought seems to be based on his perception of one 'universal truth', in relation to which the concepts of God, nature, and religion take shape. He certainly does not believe in a personal God, like that of Abraham, Isaac, or Jacob, one that interferes in history, that is a lawgiver or forgiving, or merciful; all of these, for Spinoza, are human attributes, not divine.[6] By rejecting the biblical God, however, Spinoza does not suggest a transcendent God but rather presupposes a world that is truly divine, in which 'nothing can be, nor can be conceived, without God, but that all things are in God'. And this God, for Spinoza, is the 'substance consisting of infinite attributes each one of which expresses eternal and infinite essence'.[7] So, in the understanding of Spinoza, what is natural is not other than what is divine, and vice versa. And apparently, such an identification of God with Nature has implications of atheism.[8] In fact, the rejection of a personal God by identifying him with the universe implies, as Yovel points out, a more profound rejection of Judaism and Christianity than ordinary atheism.[9]

Nevertheless, the identification between 'God's eternal decrees' and 'the universal laws of Nature' is so crucial to Spinoza's thought that nationalist and particularist notions evident in the Hebrew Bible are dismissed by him as the product of the Jewish mind and understanding, rather than as parts of the universal truth. According to Spinoza, the more knowledge we have of the nature of the world the better we understand the nature of God.[10] And as the Hebrew prophets, including Moses, had limited knowledge of the world, their understanding of God and the world turned out to be nationalistic, namely immature and imperfect. Moses, just like other Israelites did not know that 'the universal laws of Nature, according to which all things happen and are determined, are nothing but God's eternal decrees, which always involve eternal truth and necessity'.[11] And, as a result, he 'perceived all these things not as eternal truths, but as instructions and precepts, and he ordained them as laws of God'.[12] Spinoza also goes further to argue that 'we must believe the prophets only with regard to the purpose and substance of the revelation; in all else one is free to believe as one will'.[13]

In order to show a categorical difference between the universal/eternal and particular/temporary decrees of God, or the necessities of nature which are based on those decrees, Spinoza refers to what he calls the external and internal help of God. In fact, this is the point on which Spinoza's explanation of the idea of chosenness is based. Accordingly, God 'chose' the people of Israel, not because of or for the purpose of their wisdom and virtue, but because of their social organization and material prosperity.[14] At this point, Novak and Yovel claim that Spinoza's use of the term 'God's election' should be understood in a purely metaphorical way, because there is no place in his philosophy for recognition of any kind of election on the part of God.[15] So it is Israel who actually chose God for its national security and social welfare. Mason, on the other hand, argues for Spinoza's recognition of a kind of vocation from which Israel benefited, but apparently not as it was understood in Jewish tradition. Indeed, in a section devoted to the question of 'the peculiar vocation of the Hebrews' in his *Tractatus Theologico–Politicus*, Spinoza writes:

> we do not mean to deny that God ordained those laws in the Pentateuch for them alone, nor that he spoke only to them, nor that the Hebrews witnessed marvels such as have never befallen any other nation. Our point is merely this, that Moses wished to admonish the Hebrews in a particular way, using such reasoning as would bind them more firmly to the worship of God, having regard to the immaturity of their understanding ... the Hebrews surpassed other nations not in knowledge nor in piety, but in quite a different respect; or that the Hebrews were chosen by God above all others not for the true life nor for any higher understanding but for a quite different purpose.[16]

In fact, nowhere in *Tractatus*, does Spinoza deny the existence of a sort of election on the part of Israel. He rather rejects the traditional Jewish understanding of election, which is unacceptable to Spinoza for several reasons. First of all, the biblical notion of covenant requires a mutual relationship between God and the people of Israel and also takes place out of possibility, conditions which are completely incompatible with Spinoza's definition of God.[17] Indeed, this formulation of covenant ascribes to God certain attributes, such as the making of contracts and the choosing or loving of one group among others as a matter of chance, of which Spinoza's God is completely free. Thus Spinoza uses the terms 'vocation' and 'election' in a purely metaphorical way. What he means by these terms is God's external, namely particular and temporary, decrees. Second, Spinoza rejects the notion that the people of Israel were chosen in respect of their knowledge and piety. In terms of knowledge the Israelites, for Spinoza, held quite customary ideas of God and nature, and in respect of true life they again were on the same level with other nations. Besides, 'knowledge and virtue', Spinoza maintains, 'are not peculiar to any nation but have always been common to all mankind'.[18] Therefore, deuteronomic statements such as, 'God has chosen you out of all the peoples' (7:6; 10:15), 'he is nigh unto them as he is not unto others' (4:7), 'for them alone he has ordained just laws' (4:8), and 'he had made himself known only to them before all others' (4:32), were only meant to speak 'according to the understanding of those who knew no true blessedness'.[19] For God, according to Spinoza, is equally gracious to all humankind in respect of virtue and understanding. In fact, Spinoza classifies the main objectives that every human being naturally seeks to attain under three categories:

1   To know things through their primary causes.
2   To acquire the habit of virtue.
3   To live in security and good health.[20]

Of these categories, the attainment of the first and the second objectives, namely knowledge/understanding and virtue/piety, falls within the bounds of human nature and, therefore, is not special to any particular group or people. For they are the objectives resulting from God's decrees as eternal and universal gifts; that is to say, their attainment is the result of God's inner help. As for the third objective, that is well-being/security, it is a matter of God's external help, namely something that is given to a particular group, at a particular time, and under particular circumstances.

As a matter of fact, what Spinoza means by God's external help towards Israel's collective security and prosperity is nothing other than Israel's perception of God through national laws and rituals, instead of a universal truth. So, what is called the election of Israel is a means to ensure their survival as a people, and not a sign of Israel's superiority over other nations in respect of its understanding or virtue, the attributes that are common to all humankind. In other words, in order to establish Israel as a secure social organization, the prophets of Israel presented God in terms of particular degrees and laws of religion. So this is what Spinoza calls the external help of God, which also works in accordance with perfect necessity.[21] For the desire for self-preservation, which lies at the heart of religion in general and Judaism in particular, is the 'basic motivating force in human behaviour', and therefore natural.[22]

Moreover, according to Spinoza, this kind of vocation of God, which is involved only in the material prosperity of human beings, is not special to the people of Israel, but had been performed in previous times for other peoples as well. Before the Israelites the land of Israel was allocated to the Canaanites in the same way; that is they were meant to settle down and establish a social organization there, as Spinoza writes:

> I show from Scripture itself that God did not choose the Hebrews unto eternity, but only on the same terms as he had earlier chosen the Canaanites. These also had priests who devoutly worshipped God, and yet God rejected them because of their dissolute living, their folly, and their corrupt worship.[23]

Spinoza, in this way, proclaims that God's decrees are realized in the world either as eternal/universal or temporary/particular divine acts, the latter of which are called God's external help and are concerned only with matters of social well-being, as was the case with Israel. Since the Israelites did not recognize God's decrees as a universal truth, Moses presented this external help or vocation of God as the precepts of the law of God, namely as the practice of religion.[24] This law thus relates to the Israelites only as long as they live under a social organization, namely as long as they remain as a state in the land of Israel.[25] At this point, Spinoza again refers to the Scripture to show the particularistic and temporary character of the election, by saying:

> [T]heir election and vocation consisted only in the material success and prosperity of their state; nor do we see that God promised anything other than this to the Patriarchs and their successors. Indeed, in return for their obedience the Law promises them nothing other than the continuing prosperity of their state and material advantages, whereas disobedience and the breaking of the Covenant would bring about the downfall of their state and the severest hardships.[26]

Spinoza also maintains that while the Jewish law meant to establish the Israelites as a 'special kind of society and state', the universal law taking place in the Scripture can be summarized in one single rule, which is the representative of the divine law: 'to love God as the supreme good'.[27] Accordingly, only the universal law involved in 'the knowledge and love of God' leads to true blessedness and happiness, whereas the Jewish law, which is based on the temporary election of Israel, is intended solely for material and social prosperity.[28] So, in terms of universal divine law there is no difference, for Spinoza, between Jews and non-Jews.[29] Besides, the prophets, according to Spinoza, prophesied one universal truth, namely the love of God ('You shall love the Lord, your God' – Dt. 6:4; Ps. 40:6, 8; Hab. 2:14; Zeph. 3:9–10; Zech. 2:11) and charity ('you shall love your neighbour as yourself' – Lev. 19:18; Isa. 1:16f.). Spinoza firmly states that since the election of the Israelites is related only to their political prosperity, it cannot be eternal in any respect. 'For Moses', Spinoza maintains, warns the Israelites not to defile themselves with abominations like the Canaanites, lest the land spew them out as it had spewed out those peoples that used to dwell there [Lev. 18:27, 28]. And in Deuteronomy 8:19, 20 he threatens them with utter destruction in the plainest possible terms, speaking as follows, "I testify to you this day that you shall surely perish; as the nations which the Lord destroyed before your face, so shall you perish."

So if the prophets foretold for them a new, eternal covenant involving the knowledge, love, and grace of God, it can be easily proved that this promise was made for the godly one only. For it is explicitly stated that God will cut off the rebellious and the transgressor from them (Ezk. ch 20; also Zeph. 3:11–12).[30] There is only one eternal law and it is promised to the godly alone, among both Jews and non-Jews. Again, if there are some statements in the Scripture promising the Israelites God's eternal mercy, these should be understood in relation to the godly ones among Israel, those who possess the eternal/universal law, namely 'the love of God'. The expansion of the universal law,[31] having already begun in the late biblical period, is the foundation for Spinoza's concept of a 'universal religion'.

As a matter of fact, the correlation between Spinoza and Paul lies mainly in their attempts to universalize the Jewish religion by using the same token, namely the figure of Christ, albeit in somewhat different ways. Spinoza recognizes and admires Christ as a 'man' of righteousness and wisdom and sees him as a model of the moral man. Paul, on the other hand, regards him as the 'son' of God and a redeemer. As emphasized by many, Spinoza could not possibly accept the main Christian doctrines, such as original sin, and the divinity and physical resurrection of Christ.[32] First of all, there is no place in Spinoza's theology for an understanding of a divine and resurrected Christ, as Spinoza is against any kind of myth, whether the election of the Jewish people for eternity or the divinity of Jesus, which is considered by Spinoza as irrational and anti-natural. Besides, showing no willingness to join any Christian groups after having been excommunicated, Spinoza openly displays that he approves of Christianity no more than Judaism. However, he puts a great deal of importance upon the figure of Christ and this is so mainly for two reasons: first, that Christ is the embodiment of knowledge and virtue, and second, that he, unlike the prophets and the Apostles, perceived God's decrees as eternal truths rather than as instructions and laws.[33] Spinoza ascribes Christ's unique personality to his ability to communicate with God 'mind to mind', as he writes:

To him God's ordinances leading men to salvation were revealed not by words or by visions, but directly [2 Cor. 3:3], so that God manifested himself to the Apostles through the mind of Christ as he once did to Moses through an audible voice. The Voice of Christ can thus be called the Voice of God in the same way as that which Moses heard. In that sense it can also be said that the Wisdom of God – that is, wisdom that is more than human – took on human nature in Christ, and that Christ was the way of salvation.[34]

In fact, to be the voice or mind of God means, for Spinoza, to know God's decrees as eternal truths and to pass them on to all human beings as the universal law, just as Christ did. So, Spinoza believes that since the universal law and the Jewish law are intended to serve completely different purposes, the former being a blessing for all humanity and the latter being designed for the particular needs of the Jewish people, Christ did not mean to abrogate the law of Moses.[35] Indeed, in Spinoza's thought, the Jewish law was annulled not with the coming of Christ but with the destruction of the Temple because the Jewish people, from that point, ceased to be a nation in a particular territory. Accordingly, Christ's unique status in Spinoza's thought of universal religion has much to do, as rightly emphasized by Misrahi, with 'his preaching a Jewish virtue (charity) on a universal plane after, and as a consequence of, the destruction of the Hebrew State'.[36] Apparently, when saying that there is only one law for salvation and that is the law of Christ (Rom. 10:12), Paul, for Spinoza, was drawing attention to the fact that the Jewish law was meant to serve for the commonwealth of the Israelites, and even in that sense is no longer valid after its destruction. However, by presenting the reason for the abrogation of the Jewish law as the coming of Christ,[37] even Paul did not understand properly that the law and the message of Christ had separate functions and that the former was not superseded by the latter. Perhaps Paul, as implied by Spinoza, meant to reject the Pharisaic claim that blessedness comes from the observance of the law of Moses.[38]

Accordingly, Spinoza praises Christ as one who is the embodiment of the eternal truth and also gives credit to Paul as the Apostle who best understood Christ's message. What Paul understands, for Spinoza, is the fact that Christ's message bears a unique and universal character that leads humanity to happiness, whereas Moses's message is the law of commonwealth delivered only for the Jews.[39] Spinoza also asserts that if Paul talked about attributes of God, such as mercy and anger, and that if he sometimes did not speak openly, it was because of the need to adapt his language to the understanding of the ordinary people.[40] Therefore, when talking about 'God's mercy' (Rom. 9:18) Paul meant the will of God working out of necessity; and in the same way the term 'faith' referred to the full consent of the mind.[41]

Misrahi argues that although Spinoza uses the figure of Christ as a model for his ideal man of knowledge and virtue, his true source of inspiration is Solomon the sage,[42] to whom Spinoza often makes references as in the following:

> I refer to Solomon, who is commended in the Scriptures not so much for prophecy and piety as for prudence and wisdom. In his Proverbs he calls man's intellect the fount of true life.... Thus, he says in chapter 16 verse 22, 'Understanding (is) a wellspring of life to him that has it...'.
>
> Thus Solomon ... takes the view that the happiness and peace of the man who cultivates his natural understanding depends not on the way of fortune (that is, on God's external help) but on his own internal virtue (or God's internal help), because he owes his self-preservation mainly to his own vigilance, conduct and wise counsel.[43]

But in any case, Spinoza, like Paul, accepted one path to happiness and blessedness for both Jews and non-Jews and rejected the Jewish law as something national and temporary;[44] though he did so by isolating himself from the mainstream understandings of both Judaism and Christianity as he was opposed to any kind of election as a means to universal truth. In this way, he presupposed the universalization of the Jewish, as well as non-Jewish, man on the model of Christ.

Moses Mendelssohn

Mendelssohn, on the other hand, is one of the forerunners of the German Enlightenment and the forefather of the Jewish Emancipation and progressive Judaism. Just like Spinoza, but this time as an attempt to make the Jewish population a part of German society and equal citizens of the state, he voiced somewhat novel and challenging views about the nature of Jewish religion and Jewish people. He also called for the eradication of the external, as well as internal, walls that stood in the way of Jewish Emancipation.

What lies at the heart of Mendelssohn's philosophy is, reminiscent of Spinoza's distinction between the eternal/universal and temporary/particular degrees of God, a differentiation between what Mendelssohn calls eternal and historical truths. What he means by eternal truths are those universal principles which can be reached by reason and observation and therefore apply equally to all human beings. The external truths, on the other hand, refer to particular rules and beliefs as drawn from specific historical events in the history of different peoples, and are therefore the subject of a personal or local experience and testimony. Parallel to this, Mendelssohn maintains that while eternal truths stem from the creation in eternity, historical truths depend on revelation(s) that occur in a particular place and at a particular time, as in the case of the Sinai revelation. Accordingly, the Torah, ordained by God for a particular people, namely the Jews, and for a particular purpose, namely their earthly felicity, includes no universal dogmas or eternal truths that are not open to other peoples, but rather historical commandments and laws. 'The voice which let itself be heard on Sinai', Mendelssohn writes,

> did not proclaim, 'I am the Eternal, your God, the necessary, independent being, omnipotent and omniscient, that recompenses men in a future life according to their deeds.' This is the universal *religion of mankind*, not Judaism; and the universal *religion of mankind*, without which men are neither virtuous nor capable of felicity, was not to be revealed there.[45]

So, for Mendelssohn, Judaism is best defined as a 'revealed legislation', and not a 'revealed religion', which is represented instead by Christianity. In other words, it is not a way of thought or belief but a practice confined to one's personal life; and, for this reason, Jews can participate in their host societies in all particulars and still remain Jewish. At this point, Mendelssohn regards the Torah as consisting mainly of national and individual laws. As far as national laws are concerned, he, just like Spinoza, argues that as the Jews ceased to be a nation after the destruction of the Temple, they were now free to do away with those laws and to accept the dominion of the state for their socio-political life.[46] But, unlike Spinoza and more similar to Paul, Mendelssohn believes in the ongoing validity of the individual laws for the Jews.[47] Perhaps the main difference between the attitudes of Spinoza and Mendelssohn towards the Jewish law lies in their quite diverse understandings of God and of his relation to the world. According to Spinoza, as we saw, God is nothing more than the ultimate principle ruling in nature. As for the Torah, it is a product of the limited prophetic understanding of God's will, and because of this, does not contain any universal/eternal decrees, but only particular/temporary ones. And the latter serves but one purpose, which is the survival of the Israelites as a people with socio-political prosperity. So Spinoza believes that what the Jews as individuals need is a system based on universal and rational laws. In other words, according to Spinoza, there is one type of law for all individuals, and it is the universal/eternal one.[48] As far as the Torah and its particular/historical laws are concerned, Jews should certainly do away with them, alongside their claim to chosenness, as they are no longer a nation. For Mendelssohn, however, there is no way to get away from the Torah, which contains not only the temporary/historical laws that Israel as a nation needed, but also individual laws that are ever-binding on individual Jews. In addition to this, Mendelssohn regards God as the one who enters a personal relationship with men. He is a personal God and the Torah is the divine book which contains both historical/national and eternal/individual truths. So the validity of the Torah should be everlasting for every individual Jew.

Accordingly, by making a distinction between eternal/universal and historical/particular laws, Mendelssohn unifies the Jews, both with the world, on the basis of universal principles, and with other Jews, through Jewish law and the Jewish way of life.[49] In other words, in Mendelssohn's thought, the eternal laws are those which every human being can attain directly through reason and observation; they are universal laws embedded in creation, not written with letters and script, and not given to one people alone. In this way Mendelssohn seems to make a clear-cut distinction between the universal/eternal laws of the Creation and the particular/historical laws of the Torah. However, he recognizes in the teaching of the Torah some eternal truths as well.[50] Apparently when saying this, Mendelssohn does not mean to say that those beliefs and values are the exclusive providence of Judaism. On the contrary, they are attainable by reason and therefore taught by other religions as well.[51] It is also important to note that Mendelssohn not only denies the Jewish religion any special doctrine, but also any particular moral instruction, by identifying it with mere legislation.[52] So, one might argue that if the eternal truths, whether intellectual or moral, do not exclusively belong to either the Torah or the Jewish religion, and the function of the latter mainly lies in its historical, and therefore temporary, importance, there is no point in retaining the Jewish way of life. At this point, Mendelssohn refers to the 'mysterious' character of the relationship between God and the Jews and the ongoing function of the Torah for the world as an example of the Jewish way of life. Jacob Agus paraphrases Mendelssohn, by writing:

> The precepts of the Torah were designed by God to express His truths through the patterns of observances of a living people.... These truths are indeed available to all men, but while mankind is liable to forget and distort these truths from time to time, the people of Israel will never forget and never pervert these teachings of reason. At all times, Mendelssohn concluded, the great truths of religion will be treasured and illustrated by the 'very existence' of the 'Jewish people'.[53]

While Mendelssohn, in this way, attributes to the Jewish people, through the Torah, the role of an eternal guide or custodian, he also makes it clear that salvation is open to both Jews and non-Jews through the attainment of universal truths. He maintains: 'Judaism boasts of no *exclusive* revelation of eternal truths that are indispensable to salvation, of no revealed religion.... This is the universal *religion of mankind*, not Judaism...'[54]

Again, on the questions of chosenness and salvation Agus quotes Mendelssohn, by writing: 'Whatever the purpose of God may have been in singling out the Jews as the objects of special legislation, He cannot have intended to make the observance of the Torah a prerequisite for salvation.'[55] Agus also states that, according to Mendelssohn, 'the "seven principles of Noah" which all men discover by searching their hearts' are those which are 'alone necessary and sufficient for the bliss of the soul here and in the hereafter'.[56] However, it should be noted that Mendelssohn also attributes to the Jewish people an important role in the continuity of truth and salvation. He sees them as a people 'chosen by Providence to be a *priestly* nation', a nation which 'through its establishment and constitution, through its laws, actions, vicissitudes, and changes' will be a testimony among the nations to the 'sound and unadulterated ideas of God and his attributes'.[57] Mendelssohn's insistence on the eternal validity of the law for the Jews and the continuity of Judaism and Jewishness seems to be based upon some political grounds as well. Indeed, Mendelssohn sought to end Jewish distinctiveness to a certain extent, but at the same time, like Paul, endorsed a definition of salvation as accessible to all humankind. This was the only way to demolish the barrier between Jews and non-Jews and make the former part of the wider non-Jewish society, without giving up the Jewish way of life. So Mendelssohn sought, on the one hand, to unify Jews internally through the law and, on the other hand, to bond them to other peoples through reason. Jews should be united with the world, but in order to remain a separate group they had to retain their special role as the priests of God. According to many, Mendelssohn might have been successful in unifying the Jews both with one another and with the outside world in the short run, but he left them defenceless against the challenge of modernity in the long run, by depriving the Jewish religion of any doctrinal, spiritual, or exclusively eternal dimension.[58] The early modern Jewish thinkers and theologians in Europe and in America, however, would do more justice to the Jewish religion and Jewish distinctiveness by associating the universal and rational principles of the Enlightenment with the monotheistic and messianic ideals of the prophetic Jewish message. Thus, the main emphasis would be laid on the superiority of the Jewish religion in terms of its monotheistic and universalistic principles and on the mission of the Jewish people to sustain and convey those principles to all humanity.

5   Jewish Emancipation and modern Jewish movements in Germany

The European Enlightenment and the following Jewish Emancipation are two crucial events that had a great impact on the Jewish people and Jewish religion during the nineteenth and early twentieth centuries. German Jewry in particular, in the wake of Jewish Emancipation, witnessed the emergence of three modern Jewish movements, which would later turn into three well-established Jewish congregations, namely what we know today as Reform, Conservative and Orthodox Judaisms. In fact, each movement developed as a response to the question of Jewish Emancipation and the concomitant need to reshape Judaism in accordance with the requirements of the new conditions. In other words, all these modern Jewish movements, from the most radical to the most traditionalist, emerged as alternatives to the danger of assimilation.

Nevertheless, while the Jewish Reform movement, pioneered by Abraham Geiger and Samuel Holdheim, was busy redefining the Jewish religion in a rationalist–universalist line and introducing radical new changes into Jewish theology and the Jewish prayer book, the majority of the traditional Orthodox Jews continued to be dominated by the talmudic outlook, with no contact with modernity whatsoever. According to this latter group, the leading spokesman of which was Moses Sofer, the culture of the outside world was completely hostile to and incompatible with Judaism. Between these two extreme groups there were also the Positive–Historical School and Neo-Orthodoxy, led by Zacharias Frankel and Samson Raphael Hirsch, respectively. These two movements would later turn into the Conservative congregation and modern Orthodoxy. Frankel's Positive–Historical School, in a similar way to the Reform movement, displayed openness to the need for change. However, for such purposes the sentiments of the Jewish people, instead of the rationalist spirit of the time, were regarded as the yardstick. According to Frankel, Judaism was 'the historical achievement of the Jewish genius' and in this way was 'lodged primarily in the Jewish people, rather than in the principles of ethical monotheism that underpin Jewish faith'.[1] What Frankel emphasized, therefore, was not the Jewish faith, but the national–ethnic nature of the Jewish religion. As for Hirsch's Neo-Orthodoxy, it represented a system called by him *Torah im derekh eretz* (Torah with the way of the land), a system that advocated the traditional Jewish view with an open attitude to secular culture in certain aspects. There was also what can be called

Jewish existentialism, which was basically represented by Franz Rosenzweig and Martin Buber. So, these modern Jewish movements, namely Reform, Positive–Historical School, Orthodoxy (both traditional and modern), and Jewish existentialism, suggested different definitions of the Jewish religion and Jewish existence in the wake of modernity. Nevertheless, it was Reform thought, based on the principles of rationalism and universalism, more than any other tendency, that had become the predominant representation of Judaism in that period, particularly in America. Reform thinkers in both Germany and the USA not only universalized the Jewish religion by their emphasis on the notion of mission and a messianic unity of humanity. They also proposed the normalization of the Jewish people by seeking to turn the Jews from the 'ultimate other'[2] living among the Christians into the 'messengers' of the universal truth and messianic unity.

In what follows, the doctrine of chosenness as understood by the leading universalist and existentialist Jewish thinkers, plus by relatively progressive figures in Orthodoxy, will be discussed under the subtitles of 'the Reform movement', 'Neo-Orthodoxy' and 'Jewish existentialism': in this way certain differences among them will also be highlighted. As for Conservative Judaism and traditional Orthodoxy, the former will be discussed under the title 'The American Experience' in Chapter 9. As far as mainstream Orthodoxy is concerned, however, it should suffice to note that it carried on the traditional talmudic understanding of chosenness by presupposing a fundamental separation between Jews and non-Jews on the basis of the covenantal responsibilities of the former. Yet, there are two exceptional Orthodox figures that deserve a particular mention, and their ideas, alongside those of Samson Raphael Hirsch, will also be discussed under the title of Neo-Orthodoxy.

The Reform movement

Enough has been written regarding the emergence of the German Reform movement and the new regulations created by the leading rabbis of the movement.[3] Among those early Reform figures Abraham Geiger is of particular interest, due to his influence on the changes promoted by the movement in many facets of German Jewish life. Later on, Hermann Cohen set a good example as an enlightened German Jew and indicated the direction that the German Reform movement was taking, a direction which would have an obvious impact on the shape of the American Jewish community in general. Geiger and Cohen both placed an emphasis on reason and universality in their theologies and interpreted Jewish particularity in terms of a universal 'mission' to be undertaken by the Jews until the establishment of the messianic age. In this context, one can speak of two points of difference between the universalist–messianic stress embedded within the German Reform notion of mission and the traditional idea of the redemption of all humanity in the end, which has usually been emphasized by Orthodox Jews as the ultimate goal of Jewish chosenness. First, the German Reform idea of mission, unlike the traditional notion of chosenness, is based solely on the universal–ethical dimension of the Torah. This is, in fact, an attitude totally unacceptable to a traditional Jew. Second, and consequently, the German Reform notions of mission and messianism do not presuppose a fundamental difference and separation between Jews and non-Jews. On the contrary, such difference is understood as purely functional and is to be completely overcome through messianic achievement. In the traditional Jewish view, however, the separation between Jews and non-Jews, as well as the authority of the Torah with its legal rules, is considered to be valid even after the establishment of the messianic kingdom of God. In addition to its emphasis on mission and messianic unity, central to the nineteenth-century German Reform movement was a determined opposition to Jewish nationalism, and particularly Zionism.

As far as Geiger's understanding of Judaism is concerned, Michael Meyer points to two stages, by writing:

> [A]lthough Geiger throughout his life remained a strict religious universal-
> ist, his early belief that for Jews a universal faith could be achieved only by
> overcoming Judaism gradually gave way to a conviction that universalism
> was inherent within Judaism itself, and there alone.[4]

In fact, this is the case with Cohen and Rosenzweig, too, as they both went through a process of transition leading them back to the Jewish religion and Jewish people, albeit in different ways and to different extents. As far as Geiger is concerned, this kind of transformation seems quite natural. For, unlike Samuel Holdheim, the leading figure in the radical wing of the German Reform movement, Geiger saw the present only as 'a stage between past and future', rather than an end in itself.[5] Besides, Geiger, like most liberal Jews of his time, believed in historicism in terms of an ongoing historical process as based on reason. Therefore Geiger recognized a continuous progress in everything through which essence (faith) remains the same whereas the form (ritual) can continually change. So for Geiger, Judaism was all about an 'ongoing spiritual process', with a fixed essence underneath, a formula which has been the motto of the Reform movement from its early days. In parallel to this, in his earlier writings, Geiger displayed a clear humanistic and universalistic orientation, as he wrote in 1833: 'I have never considered it my purpose to lead toward Judaism … but rather toward humanity in general … and to have Judaism permeated at all times by humanity's concepts.'[6] Geiger's goal was, thus, to accommodate Judaism to the universal scientific truth. The question that most concerned him, like other liberal Jewish scholars of his time, was of a theological and intellectual nature, not a socio-political or national one; the latter rather being the case for the late-twentieth-century Jewish scholars. At this early stage there seems to be no distinction in Geiger's mind between Judaism and any other (monotheistic) religion, as he believed back then that reason is the key term for any religion that leads to salvation.[7] Until the 1850s, in fact, Geiger did not make any explicit reference to the concept of chosenness in his writings. He just referred to a 'Jewish task' that was based on the principles of a monotheistic faith and universal justice and that was aimed at the welfare of humankind, rather than at one particular group.[8] At that stage Geiger seems to have been interested mainly in the Jewish spirit emanating from the prophetic universalist message, making a distinction between the message of the prophets, which he understood as purely universalist, and that of the Pentateuch, which was particularist. Again, at that time Geiger was solely concerned with the intellectual progress of German Jewry, so he was not interested in either the physical survival of the Oriental Jews or worldwide Jewish unity, as he confessed in 1840:

> We can term as 'of universal Jewish concern' only whatever goes on among those Jews who comprise the upper stratum of Jewry; i.e., once again, those Jews who reside among the civilized nations, particularly in Germany, and who later will be emulated and followed by those who now are still among the uneducated.... And as for the Jews who were murdered, no one will be able to bring *them* back to life. Of course it is a fine humanitarian deed to take up the cause of individuals who are victims of oppression; but it is not a specifically Jewish problem, and if we make it so, we distort the outlook and confuse the gradually developing good sense of the Jews.[9]

In a work from 1858, Geiger focuses on the issue of chosenness by stating that Jews are 'not chosen from among the nations', but 'have a vocation', which, for Geiger, relates to the 'religious genius' of the Jewish people.[10] This genius makes Jews, as Geiger states later in 1865, 'discern more clearly the close relationship between the spirit of man and the Universal Spirit'.[11] The ancient Israelites, especially the Patriarchs, being a people of revelation had a divine vision, which placed them above other nations. Although here, and in his later writings, there is an emphasis on peoplehood and nationhood, Geiger still understands the unifying factor for Jewish peoplehood as a spiritual bond. So, the main concern here is faith rather than ethnicity.

It seems that, whereas in his early writings, Geiger advocated a purely universalistic message in the name of religion and tried to make Judaism conform to this, he later came up with a notion of a transformation taking place in the Jewish religion. According to this, an early nationalist emphasis had gradually given way to a universalist orientation, which was implicit in Judaism right from the beginning. So, the origin of the Jewish religion, as Geiger came to understand, was revelation given to the Jews as a whole, providing them with a genius and a vision that enabled them to achieve a close relationship with God. Yet Geiger also maintained that 'Israel never lost the awareness that it embraced all of mankind and that its labors were on behalf of humanity as a whole'.[12] As he sought to prove in his *Judaism and Its History* (1864), this duty of the Jews was what made their religion valid in every age. Judaism, with its emphasis on monotheism and social ethics, had a mission to fulfil on earth, not only in antiquity as against the pagan world, but even today, as it is still the only true holder of the monotheistic and universalist message in the wake of Christianity, which was based on Trinity, and Islam, whose message, for Geiger, was mostly taken from Judaism.[13] In fact, it is not till the 1860s that Geiger began to talk about the superiority of the Jewish faith, as based on the national life of a particular people, over the Christian faith, which is grounded on individual commitment. Although Geiger points to the existence of a higher mission implicit in national chosenness and the capacity of Judaism to go beyond national bonds, he also seems to advocate a sort of Jewish nationhood. His earlier concern with the idea of leading Judaism toward humanity is thus replaced by his later thought that displays an apparent recognition and even appreciation of Judaism in its entirety as a universal religion based on national grounds. 'Let us', Geiger writes in 1870s, 'look back with joy on our former life as a nation, as being an essential transitional era in our history'.[14]

So, it is possible to summarize the transformation that Geiger went through as follows: he first believed in one universal religion based on faith and reason, and later saw Judaism as the first and most suitable religion for that definition and for a strong universal purpose. So the essence of Judaism, for Geiger, has always been universalist, as he wrote, 'Judaism is permeated with spirituality; it does not deny the earthly world, but transfigures it instead. It is rooted in one particular people with a language and history of its own, and yet it embraces all of mankind.'[15]

Despite this transformation, however, Geiger seems not to have changed his attitude toward the idea of chosenness. It is still understood as a special religious task through which Jews have to work for the improvement of humankind. However, this time the Jewish religion and the Jewish people have an apparent superiority over other religions and peoples, due to the revelation and prophetic vision that prevails among them, even today, in terms of a progressive spirit. Although Geiger retained his insistence on the spiritual character of Jewish existence and the universal task that the Jews as a religious community have to undertake, he, as stated by Meyer, came to adopt a more ethnocentric theology. This change can be observed in Geiger's reaction to the suffering of Romanian Jewry. He displayed quite an active and caring attitude towards the persecution of the Romanian Jews in the 1860s, in a clear contrast to his obvious indifference to the Damascus Affair two decades earlier.[16]

On the other hand, when one compares the two Jewish prayer books prepared by Geiger, one dating 1854 and the other 1870, no big difference is found between the two in terms of the formulation of the idea of chosenness. And at this point the *Aleinu* prayer is of particular importance.[17] While any reference to a distinction between Jews and non-Jews, to returning to Jerusalem or the restoration of the Jews is absent in both editions, in the 1854 edition the main emphasis is placed on the (covenant) relationship between God and Israel, as it is revealed in the English translation of the Hebrew text:

> He hath revealed Himself to our fathers and hath made known His will unto them. He hath made the eternal covenant with them [this sentence is omitted in the German text]; and unto us He hath given the holy teaching as an inheritance.

The 1870 edition, on the other hand, emphasizes the Jewish obligation to proclaim the unity of God, as the English translation reads:

> We, who acknowledge His Unity and are called to dedicate ourselves to His Name and to His service, we, in particular, are obligated to praise the Lord of the Universe, and to proclaim the greatness of the world's Creator...[18]

Apparently, Geiger, by writing 'we, in particular', gives some credit to other peoples too in praising God's unity. As a matter of fact, in most editions of the European Reform prayer book, from the 1880s and early 1900s, the emphasis in the *Aleinu* prayer is placed on a distinction between a monotheistic Israel and heathen nations or idolaters, with an implicit and sometimes explicit recognition of other monotheistic peoples.[19] In other words, the tone that is prevalent in these Reform prayer books, at least in reference to the *Aleinu* prayer, is a positive and mission-oriented paraphrase of Jewish particularism, in contrast to the traditional version of the prayer, which gives importance not to duty and responsibility, but to Jewish particularism in terms of an organic separation of Jews from other peoples,[20] as it is written:

> It is our duty to praise the Lord of all things, to ascribe greatness to him who formed the world in the beginning, since he has not made us like the nations of other lands, and has not placed us like other families of the earth, since he has not assigned unto us a portion as unto them, nor a lot as unto all their multitude...[21]

In this way, Geiger's understanding of Jewish religion and Jewish chosenness seems to display a general tendency among the European Reform leaders at the time. As far as Cohen's understanding of Judaism is concerned, there is, as stated earlier, a similar transformation leading him from an endorsement of 'a universal faith ultimately transcending Judaism to a reaffirmation of his ancestors' particular religion'.[22] Marvin Fox points out that during an early period Cohen was attached to Judaism with 'emotional ties' only, without seeing any point in 'maintaining the distinctiveness of Judaism'.[23] Yet, even then, those emotional ties must have been so strong that, as stated by Samuel Bergman, in one of his early articles, a testimony written to defend Judaism against Christian attacks, Cohen points to 'the essence and uniqueness of Jewish monotheism'.[24] Again in another article ('Brotherly Love in the Talmud') he interprets the Jewish concept of chosenness in terms of a 'mission' which has been 'directed at the unity of mankind'.[25] It is important to note that even before Cohen developed a mature and more positive attitude towards religion in general and Judaism in particular, he began to see Judaism as a religion based on reason and universalism and wanted Jews 'to take their religion seriously'. According to Bergman, this is what distinguished him from the easy assimilationist Jews of his time.[26] What lies at the heart of Cohen's thought is, thus, the idea of 'universal humanity', which was central to the philosophies of Geiger and Spinoza as well. In the *Religion of Reason* (1919), which is the product of his later thought, Cohen emphasizes the principles of pure monotheism and social ethics as the prerequisite of a religion of reason; the principles which, for him, are best represented by the concept of 'prophetic messianism'. In fact, the ideal of a messianic age, as based upon the basic principles of 'just relations among men and a universal recognition of the one true God', takes the most significant place in Cohen's understanding of religion of reason.[27] Apparently, in this projection of an ideal this-worldly future, in which in order to establish an extended community the recognizing of the stranger in one's midst is undertaken, Cohen greatly depends on the experience of his fellow Jews living as strangers in the midst of the German people. The Jewish people are provided, in this way, with a particular role and character, namely that of being the 'suffering servant' of God for the achievement of a messianic future. Cohen's intent was, thus, to unite Jews and Christians in Germany into a democratic society grounded upon the principles of pure monotheism and social ethics, the principles which originated, for Cohen, in the sources of Judaism. Although Cohen believed that the prophetic spirit and pure monotheism first emerged, in a mysterious way, within the people of Israel, namely the chosen people, this did not have, for him, anything more than a symbolic meaning. So, for Cohen, messianism was the goal that the election of Israel was meant to serve, as he wrote:

> The continuity of the spiritual power of one people was necessary in this case.... But this people is less for the sake of its own nation than as a symbol of mankind. A unique symbol for the unique idea: the individual peoples have to strive to the unique unity of mankind.... Thus, Israel, as a nation, is nothing other than the mere symbol for the desired unity of mankind.[28]

This is why Cohen clearly states that not every member of the chosen people is really chosen, while the pious ones among other peoples could be considered part of the mission, either in terms of spreading the knowledge of one God or in participating in the suffering for humanity.[29] In fact, as far as the distinctiveness of Judaism is concerned, there are two important concepts that Cohen refers to: messianism and vicarious suffering. Corresponding to these, the Jews also undertake two roles: the role of being the 'chosen people', i.e. being a symbol for the unity of humankind through monotheism and social ethics, and the role of being the 'suffering servant of God', suffering vicariously for the sins of humankind. However, as much as the mission is essential to Jewish identity in the sense of a 'religious confession', it is not confined to the Jews alone as individuals.

In fact, Cohen uses the term 'chosen people' in a symbolic way. For, considering his understanding of God, which refers not to a personal God, but rather to a 'moral idea',[30] it becomes quite obvious that it is, in effect, Israel who actually chose God. In Cohen's thought the idea of the chosen people refers to a fact and, is therefore true. So what is problematic and needs to be eliminated in Judaism, for him, is not the idea of the chosen people, but the notion of the particularity attached to it. For, according to Cohen, the idea of a unique God, which is the prerequisite of pure monotheism, presupposes the unity of humankind, for the uniqueness of God refers not only to being 'one' in terms of his relation to other gods, but also, and more importantly, to being 'only' in accordance with his relation to the world. Due to his uniqueness, God 'does not decree particular commands to a particular people, but gives commandments that are valid as laws for all men'.[31] Thus Cohen, in contrast to Mendelssohn and in parallel to Spinoza, understands the Torah to consist of moral universal laws alone, which, aimed at the moral perfection of man, are meant for the chosen people, then through them for messianic mankind.[32] In this way, Cohen's theology regards the messianic goal (essence), which is concerned with the unity of all humanity in monotheism, as prior to the chosen people (existence), which is a mere instrument to bring about that messianic end. This is the point on which David Novak puts forward a critique of Cohen's understanding of chosenness. According to Novak, Cohen betrays the traditional doctrine of election in two main points. First of all, by presuming that 'the human subject as rational moral agent can only will and choose, he or she can never be chosen by anyone who addresses him or her from above', he has been reducing the election of Israel to the revelation of the Torah. Second, by recognizing the Torah merely in terms of its moral laws, he has been assuming that 'only those who morally merit being of Israel – the symbol of ideal humanity – are in fact the elect of God', namely those who 'have truly elected God themselves'.[33]

Actually, Cohen, in this way, seeks to unify the Jews with humanity by presupposing a transformation for both Jews and non-Jews into a messianic humanity. Yet he ends up separating the Jews internally, with his emphasis on pure universalism and ethics, rather than on ritual-based particularity. At this point, W.Z. Harvey argues that Cohen, through his reduction of Judaism to reason, internally divided the Jews, and moreover, with his notion of Judaism as the 'primary origin of the religion of reason', separated them from the rest of the humanity, while Mendelssohn sought to unify the Jews with the Jewish world, on the one hand, and the outside world, on the other, with his separation of what is particular (law) and universal (reason).[34] Indeed, Mendelssohn might have presupposed a more successful way of unifying the Jews with both other Jews and humanity by declaring a single path to the eternal and universal truths for both, without reducing Judaism to reason and universalism or giving up the laws and the related Jewish particularity. However, in the absence of any superiority or originality attributed to Judaism, Mendelssohn's interpretation of chosenness, as a mere particularity planned for a good, yet mysterious, reason, did not render Jewishness, at least in the eyes of his followers, indispensable enough.

Notwithstanding certain differences, Geiger and Cohen both attributed to the Jewish people a special, yet somewhat different, role in reference to one universal religion. Cohen also, like Mendelssohn, regarded other monotheistic religions as performing a similar, yet inferior, role to Judaism. In other words, according to both Mendelssohn and Cohen, the Jewish people alone could undertake the role of the witness of God, yet there might be pious individuals among other religions, such as Christianity and Islam, who would help to spread the monotheistic message. So Mendelssohn sought to defend the Jewish distinctiveness (a priestly nation) by referring to its 'symbolic' function as a testimony to pure monotheism. Cohen, on the other hand, interpreted Jewish existence in reference to its 'instrumental', yet indispensable, role or mission for the establishment of a universal humanity. The liberal Jewish tendency in general suggested a system that is universalist yet 'hierarchical' in nature, as based on the superiority of the Jewish religion over other monotheistic religions.

Neo-Orthodoxy

In contrast to a universalist tendency represented by the progressive Jews, traditional Orthodoxy in Europe, in a similar way to today's Haredi Orthodoxy, urged a fundamental separation of the Jewish people from other peoples in every facet of life, based on their assumption of a qualitative difference between Jews and non-Jews. This was, in fact, a strict 'dualistic' vision of the world, as Marc Gopin points out, which presupposed a system of a 'dark contrast of righteousness and unrighteousness, good and evil'.[35] At this point, Gopin refers to two exceptional Italian Orthodox thinkers of the modern period, namely Samuel David Luzzatto and Elijah Benamozegh, who suggested a perfect tolerance, even to non-monotheistic religious systems, by advocating a 'universal spiritual unity' among all faiths. To put it briefly, both Luzzatto and Benamozegh proposed the idea of a universal religion on the basis of ethics (Luzzatto's 'moral-sense theory') and a framework of theology and ethics (Benamozegh's 'Noachism'), as a common denominator for all religions.[36] What is interesting here, for our purposes, is the fact that these two early modern Orthodox figures attributed to the Jews the role of a global 'mission', namely a role of a 'pedagogy teaching a compassionate ethic and simple monotheism' (Luzzatto), and of 'a synthetic unity' of theology and ethics, including 'the best expression of all spiritual human insights' (Benamozegh). Moreover, Luzzatto and Benamozegh both rejected the existence of an oppositional duality between Jews and non-Jews, considering the truths of Judaism to be given not only to Jews, but rather to all humanity. On the other hand, they, like Cohen and other universalist thinkers and in strong contrast to the traditional Jewish position, understood the biblical commandment to 'love one's neighbour' as applying to all human beings. In this way Luzzatto and Benamozegh promoted an exceptionally tolerant and inclusivist approach toward not only other peoples, but also other faiths, on the basis of a universal humanity.

Samson Raphael Hirsch, the leader of what is called Neo-Orthodoxy, on the other hand, despite his open attitude towards western civilization and his interpretation of Jewish chosenness in terms of a mission, disagreed with what was achieved by Mendelssohn and other progressive Jews, namely the rationalization and universalization of the Jewish religion. According to Hirsch, there were 'no rational moral laws' which could be attained 'by reason without any dependence on divine commandments'.[37] So there was no way to reach morality or truth other than through the Torah. Hirsch, in his *The Nineteen Letters on Judaism*, makes a clear distinction between Israel, as the sole agent of religion and spirituality, and other nations, as characterized merely by secular power and materialism, by writing:

> [A] nation, poor in everything upon which the rest of mankind reared the edifice of its greatness and power; externally subordinate to the nations armed with proud self-sufficiency, but fortified inwardly by direct reliance upon God, so that, by the suppression of every enemy force, God might reveal Himself directly as the sole Creator, Judge and Master of nature and history.[38]

However, the reason for the difference between Israel and other nations, as emphasized by Hirsch in his *Horeb*, is ascribed solely to the fact that Israel upholds the Torah, namely the truth, and their concomitant 'mission' to 'be man and Israelite; called upon to serve the eternal God'.[39] Accordingly, in respect of their attendance to the requirements of the Torah, the Jewish people are seen as having an instrumental, not a fundamental, value in God's project for the world. 'Israel, according to Hirsch', David Rudavsky asserts, 'was created for the Jewish religion and not the Jewish religion for Israel'.[40] Thus, the mission of the people of Israel, which was their *raison d'être* as a people, required them to declare the existence and unity of God and fulfil his will 'through its history and life'.[41] This mission, Hirsch maintains, necessitates some other duties as well, such as 'spiritual' separation, suffering and exile. It is important to note that, unlike Cohen and some other Jewish thinkers who understood Jewish suffering in terms of its being undeserved or vicarious, namely for the sake of the sins of other nations, Hirsch saw suffering mainly as a means of discipline for the Jewish people, through which they came to realize that 'their real strength lies mainly in upholding the laws of the Torah', not in power and force.[42]

Hirsch also proposes quite an altruistic interpretation of the separation of Jews from other peoples, as he writes:

> It must remain alone and do its work and live its life as a separate entity until, refined and purified by Israel's teachings and Israel's example, humanity as a whole might turn to God and acknowledge Him as the sole Creator and Ruler. Once that is attained, Israel's mission will have been accomplished.[43]

Again, as regards Israel's separation, Hirsch gives an inclusive meaning to Deuteronomy 33:3, which is usually translated as 'O favourite among peoples, all his holy ones were in your charge', with no mention of God's love for other nations. Hirsch, however, reads the passage as 'Though He loved all the nations, His holy ones were implements in Your hand'.[44] In this way Hirsch de-emphasizes, if not rejects, the traditional notion of God's special love for Israel. For Hirsch, it is rather on a basis of mission and duty than love that the Jews were chosen by God. Moreover, as regards the relation between Israel and the land, Hirsch maintains that the land and statehood are given to the people of Israel as a gift, which is not 'an end unto itself', but 'a means for carrying out the Torah'.[45] He emphasizes the fact that Israel became a nation by receiving the Torah long before it conquered the land. Accordingly, it is the Torah, not the land that is to be Israel's soil, Israel having a spiritual rather than a political character.

It is important to note that the Torah is understood by Hirsch in terms of all the commandments, which go beyond monotheism and morality. In other words, in Hirsch's understanding of the Torah the law stands at the centre.[46] So, there is a fundamental difference between a universalist Jew such as Cohen and the Neo-Orthodox Hirsch, in terms of their understanding of mission. Hirsch, unlike Cohen and Mendelssohn, regards the Torah, instead of reason, as the only way to truth. Besides, no matter how altruistic and universalist is the idea of mission imposed on Israel, the Jewish people, in terms of the role they undertake, are seen as being significantly different from other nations, and the former alone is understood to have a claim to truth.

Jewish existentialism

As discussed so far, for universalist Jewish thinkers such as Geiger and Cohen, the Jews had a divine mission to bring humankind to a way of unity on the basis of monotheism and social ethics. What those thinkers emphasized through the idea of mission was a religious system based on reason and universalism, which, they believed, was best represented by Judaism. On the other hand, modern Orthodoxy, led by Hirsch, advocated the traditional view of Judaism as based on obedience and law, and of the idea of chosenness with its particularist, as well as universalist, implications. Accordingly, in defining Judaism and Jewishness, either 'true faith alone' (Reform) or 'true faith and conduct at once' (Orthodoxy) happened to be the key terms in those movements. However, as far as the theologies of Franz Rosenzweig and Martin Buber are concerned, which together constitute another line in twentieth century German Judaism, the question at stake was mainly centred on the question of 'religious experience'. This is, in effect, a period in which for the first time the Jews, in the wake of Emancipation and of growing modern anti-Semitism, had to encounter a question 'Why should I remain a Jew?'[47] And they came up with different answers and formulations, among which are Zionism, Diaspora nationalism, socialism, and, even, assimilation. For both Rosenzweig and Buber, on the other hand, 'experience', either in terms of con-sciousness/awareness (Rosenzweig) or dialogue/relationship (Buber), was the essence of Judaism. So they placed a particular emphasis on individuality and the need for making one's life meaningful through religious experience. Individuality, in particular, is very important to their theologies as it is the term on the basis of which both Rosenzweig and Buber reject the prevailing tendencies due to their reduction of the individual either to an abstract universalism or to history, by failing to make the 'whole' relevant to 'individual' lives.

Rosenzweig, as the first existentialist Jew, came to this conclusion through his personal experience. Born to an assimilated Jewish family, he at one time came to the point of converting to Christianity yet, after having an extraordinary experience on a Day of Atonement (*Yom Kippur*) he decided to remain a Jew. His theology, therefore, is based on the need to have Judaism 'brought into living contact with the "worldly" life of man'.[48] Since Rosenzweig understands Jewishness in terms of an awareness or consciousness of being a Jew, Judaism, for him, reveals itself in 'being' rather than 'doing' something. So unlike traditional particularist or modern universalist understandings, Judaism, for Rosenzweig, is designed to render a meaning rather than a task or mission. As paraphrased by Bergman, 'by its very existence Israel bears witness to God in the world'.[49] Rosenzweig's Jewishness is, therefore, not about 'belief' or 'conduct' but about 'existence'. Although that awareness of 'being' has ultimate universal implications, the task of a Jew, for Rosenzweig, is not to bring about that universal end, either in a passive or active way, but solely to remain a Jew, which also includes the achievement of such an end. Rosenzweig frequently uses the expression 'born a Jew'[50] by which he refers to the notion of 'being chosen' in the sense of being with God. In his theology, Israel is the people chosen by God eternally. Despite being chosen as a people, however, every individual Jew, for Rosenzweig, should also make a personal decision at some point to remain a Jew and live a Jewish life; this is what he means by the expression of 'narrowing down to Jewish man'.[51] In fact, this emphasis on 'being' is the point that differentiates Rosenzweig's existentialism from that of Buber, for whom 'becoming' instead of 'being' is the correct word. This is also what makes Eugene Rosenstock, a contemporary Jewish convert to Christianity, highly critical of Rosenzweig. According to Rosenstock, Jewish insistence on being (chosen) per se, as exemplified in Rosenzweig's theology, is not different from the claim of a particular Judah or Lucifer, as both see their chosenness as a 'divine right' with no obligation, or 'a divine title for privileges' rather than 'a divine mandate for duties'.[52] There is also a fundamental difference between Rosenzweig, the existentialist, and the universalist Jewish thinkers such as Geiger and Cohen on the one hand, and an Orthodox rabbi such as Hirsch on the other. Chosenness for the universalists is something to be 'externalized' through the messianic mission, whereas for Rosenzweig it is something to be 'internalized', namely what is necessary is solely 'being' a Jew or 'feeling' Jewish. As for the Orthodox view of chosenness, despite its apparent particularistic orientation, Orthodoxy imposes on the Jews certain responsibilities, i.e. law, as the prerequisite of being chosen. For Rosenzweig, however, Judaism means mainly 'to be a Jew', whether one follows the law or not. In fact the Torah symbolizes, for Rosenzweig, a divine commandment to live a Jewish life rather than a law to be strictly observed.[53] Although at one point Rosenzweig refers to law as a precondition of chosenness or Jewishness,[54] the question here is for an individual Jew to turn the law into a 'commandment', by 'taking upon himself the yoke of the Kingdom of God'.[55] So the law becomes a part of 'being' in Rosenzweig's thought, rather than a measure to define who is a true Jew. It is also important to note that, for the universalist thinkers, chosenness was not a criterion according to which one could determine the true religion; it was instead a mere instrument. As for the criterion, it was none other than 'reason' leading to 'messianic unity', which reached its climax in Cohen's 'religion of reason'. As a result, Cohen regarded all monotheistic religions, i.e. Christianity and Islam, as having a role in spreading the true knowledge of God. As far as Rosenzweig is concerned, however, chosenness was the main, if not the only, criterion, and this is why he, in contrast to Cohen, included Christianity alone in his 'religion of chosenness'.[56] According to Rosenzweig, Judaism and Christianity are complementary traditions in fulfilling God's plan for the world. The Jew, being 'himself the belief', should remain Jewish, whereas the Christian, representing 'belief in something', is to convert all non-Jews to Christianity.[57] In this way, Rosenzweig narrows down not only Jewishness, but also the Jewish notion of redemption, substituting Christian baptism for the Noahide Laws as the only way for the salvation of the gentiles. Moreover, although in this way, for Rosenzweig, Judaism and Christianity together make 'authentic manifestations of the one religious truth', there still remains an important difference between the Jews and Christians. As paraphrased by Bergman, 'Israel "bears witness" to God by "bearing children", by the very fact of her biological existence and continuity. Christianity bears witness by its mission and numerical growth'.[58] In other words, a Jew, as Rosenzweig maintains, is someone who 'has already reached the goal towards which the "nations" are still moving'.[59] In fact, the notion of Israel as a trans-historical entity is quite a common one in both rabbinic and modern Jewish traditions. Nevertheless, it seems to be that this super-historical quality of Israel, as understood by Rosenzweig, does not refer so much to a circumstantial meaning as to an existential one. For whereas the universalist Jewish thinkers consider chosenness solely in relation to the messianic end, as far as Rosenzweig is concerned, there is an indirect relation between chosenness and redemption. He regards chosenness and redemption as two separate and equally important tasks. This is why the role of Christianity in redemption is indispensable to his theology, as the Jews represent chosenness rather than redemption, the latter being the task of the Christians. Rosenzweig believes that the Jewish people are already with the Father and therefore they do not need to be redeemed as the non-Jews do; the former cannot be brought to God through Christianity, as they are already there.[60]

> No one can *come* to the Father! This excludes him who no longer has to come to the Father because he already is with Him. This is the case with the people of Israel (though perhaps not with individual Jews).... The synagogue knows and admits that what the works of law and ritual do for Israel, the works of love do for the world outside of Israel.[61]

In other words, since both Jews and Christians are already with the Father, the former by birth, and the latter by baptism, redemption is something that is meant for the world. However, Rosenzweig does not consider redemption as something already fulfilled. The aim of redemption is to make all humanity like the chosen people. In this way, Rosenzweig points to a form of aspiration towards the unity of humankind through redemption as represented in Sabbath service. Accordingly, during the morning prayer, Rosenzweig states, the emphasis is made on election, while in the afternoon it is on creation and revelation, which both lead eventually to the redemption of humankind.[62]

According to Novak, although Rosenzweig with his strict belief in 'the direct election of Israel by God' confirms the biblical doctrine of election, his understanding of redemption differs from the traditional view. What Rosenzweig suggests by redemption, Novak argues, is a transformation of both Judaism and Christianity into a 'new humanity' rather than 'judaization' of humankind.[63] So Rosenzweig's theology goes against tradition on two main points: first, Rosenzweig sees the election of the Jews in the sense of the election of humanity and, second, he deprives Jewish redemption of its trans-historical nature by associating the former with Christian proselytising. So, for Novak, Rosenzweig does not hold to a complete universalist approach and totally abandon the traditional Jewish notion of election for the sake of a pure universalist interpretation, as Cohen did, by placing the Jewish mission at the centre of chosenness. Nor does he prove to be true to Judaism as he endorses a finished redemption in the name of Christianity instead of attributing the realization of redemption to God's mysterious plan; for this is, for Novak, no less contrary to traditional Jewish understanding than the universalist one. In fact, Rosenzweig's inclusion of Christianity in the messianic plan is one of the issues on which Buber also disagreed. However, Novak still finds Rosenzweig's theology to have universalist implications as it is obvious in his attitude to the question of the relationship between Jews and non-Jews. Novak explicitly states that the term 'neighbour' in a well-known biblical command, 'you shall love your neighbour as yourself' (Lev. 19:18), refers to the 'fellow Jew' in Jewish tradition, because what is involved here is the covenantal love and this, by nature, includes Jews alone. The Jews are supposed to 'love' their fellow Jewish neighbours to whom they are related through the covenant, while doing 'justice' to the rest of humankind to which they are linked through creation.[64] According to Novak, not only a universalist Jewish philosopher like Cohen, but also Rosenzweig, regards the term 'neighbour', in contrast to the traditional understanding, as referring to 'man' in general.[65] This is why Rosenzweig, Novak states, does no less injustice to the particularist emphasis of the traditional doctrine of election than Cohen. Accordingly, despite a kind of particularism emphasized in his theology, Rosenzweig incorporates, through love (of God and neighbour), all individuals, Jewish and non-Jewish, in his existentialist system.

As for Buber, his starting point also seems to be the problem of 'spiritual crisis' that the modern man in general and the Jewish man in particular were going through in those days. In a similar way to Rosenzweig's concern about *the* Judaism which, for him, had been completely deprived of its relevance to Jewish lives, Buber insisted on the need to restore the trust of the modern man in the Jewish faith.[66] So, for Buber, as much as for Rosenzweig, the renewal of the Jewish faith was meant primarily for the individual. Nevertheless, Buber insisted on the significance of the 'collective memory' and has understood the uniqueness of the Jews in reference to their being a people of a collective memory. For what is really significant in Buber's thought is the relationship itself, emanating from the experience, rather than the components, whether individuals or the community.

As an existentialist thinker, Buber's main concern in his writings seems to centres on different types of relationships, namely those between people and nature, human beings with each other, and human and spiritual beings.[67] In his well-known 'I–Thou' formula Buber points to the relationship between man and God as the purest of all. According to Buber, man can be an I in its real sense only through the achievement of the I–Thou relationship. Because, for Buber, 'all real living is meeting' and that meeting appears in its purest form only between man and the Eternal Thou (God); this is so, due to the nature of him who 'is the Being that is directly, most nearly, and lastingly, over against us, that may properly only be addressed'.[68] Moreover, in Buber's philosophy, the connection between I and Thou is fully realized in the unique relationship between Israel and God, as there is a special bond connecting them. He wrote:

> The great deed of Israel is not that it taught the one real God, who is the origin and goal of all being, but that it pointed out that this God can be addressed by man in reality, that man can say Thou to Him, that he can stand face to face with Him, that he can have intercourse with Him.[69]

According to Buber, even the relationship between man and God is exhausted through addressing and responding. However, as far as the relationship between God and Israel is concerned, those acts of 'address' and 'response' realize themselves in a covenantal relationship, making Israel the chosen people. So, in respect of the relationship between God and Israel, the acts of addressing and responding turn into those of 'being chosen' and 'choosing', respectively, in the complete sense of the terms; and this subsequently brings about some mutual obligations.[70] For Buber, what makes Israel unique is its ability to respond to God and enter a covenantal relationship with him, but the meaning of its election lies in the fact that 'any offence against the *berith* [covenant] is "visited upon" it'.[71]

Buber, following the mainstream rabbinic interpretations, maintains that Israel's election by God over other peoples has only one meaning and therefore serves one purpose, namely 'to set an example of harmony in obedience to God for the others'.[72] This is the ultimate plan of God for humankind. In other words, the purpose of God's choosing one people among the others is to make a model people having a dialogue and partnership with God. This emphasis on 'relationship' as the essence of Judaism is, in fact, what most differentiates Buber's theology from that of Rosenzweig, for whom 'existence' alone is the consummation of Jewishness. So, according to Rosenzweig, one does not become, but rather is born a Jew, as he states: 'one is Jewish'.[73] According to Buber, however, being Jewish is ultimately about undertaking the role of a model community whose essence lies in a 'dialogical', and not an 'existential', relationship between the community members themselves, on the one hand, and between the community and God, on the other. In other words, the task of man in general, and of Israel, in particular, is not 'being' but 'becoming'. As an ideal community, the Jewish people also incorporate in themselves the whole of humanity. For Buber it is not mere existence, but rather a dialogue which matters; an aspiration towards an ideal relationship with the Eternal Thou and humanity, as he writes: 'In genuine Judaism ethics and faith are no separate spheres; its ideal, holiness, is true community with God and true community with human beings, both in one.'[74]

In another passage Buber makes it clear that the 'spirit' (or the ideal) that Israel is believed to possess should refer 'not to ourselves but to the living truth, which is not our possession, but by which we can be possessed, which is not dependent upon us, but we upon it'.[75] For Buber, unlike Rosenzweig, to be chosen, or one's realization of being chosen, is not sufficient in itself. What is more important than this is to 'respond' to the choosing act of God; this is the achievement that Buber means by the term 'dialogue'. As pointed out earlier, Buber's insistence on 'becoming' frees Judaism, at least as he understands it, from the danger of believing that the Jewish people, as a concrete entity, form an ideal community in itself. Rosenzweig's definition of Jewishness in relation to 'being', namely as something finished and waiting to be discovered, however, is not immune to the above-mentioned risk of confusing the ideal with the real. Again, as far as the issue of suffering is concerned, there remains a considerable difference between the two thinkers. Buber imposes a two-fold meaning on suffering: one refers to the deuteronomic notion of punishment for sins in relation to Israel's failure in its responsibilities, and the other to the idea of the suffering servant of God, as introduced in the book of Isaiah. So, whereas for Rosenzweig suffering seems to be the pay-off for being one with the Father,[76] a condition which is already fulfilled, for Buber it is a result of Israel's voluntary participation in the covenant.[77] It is not an unexpected result of a fulfilled position but, on the contrary, as unfortunate as it may seem, is the guarantee of the continuity of the task.

Despite all these differences, however, one thing remains certain, namely that all these modern Jewish thinkers emphasized 'a positive symbiosis between Judaism and elements of modern German culture' and also advocated a programme towards universal unity as the goal of Jewish chosenness, albeit in different ways and to different degrees. This was done through reason and mission (Geiger and Cohen), or love (Rosenzweig) or dialogue (Buber). In fact, American Judaism would be successful in carrying out and making useful the European Jewish emphasis on reason and mission, on the one hand, and on the existentialist concepts of identity and experience, on the other, for its own agenda.

6 Modern Jewish congregations in America

The Reform congregation

One of the advantages the Jewish people found in the New World was the Puritan tradition underlying American self-understanding. Caroline Gleason gives an account of the experiences of the first Puritan colonists in America, which sheds a light on the American use of the idea of the 'chosen people'. Gleason states that those colonists had interpreted their encounter with the Native Americans in reference to the traditional concepts of divine providence and covenant. They believed that their relationship with the Natives was orchestrated by God and that they had 'a duty to fulfill their covenant with God by serving as an example of an ideal Christian community to the world'.[1] So, under the impact of Puritanism, the Americans came to regard themselves as the 'chosen people' and their country as the 'chosen land'. By quoting Reinhold Niebuhr, Eisen also points out that it was thanks to this Puritan legacy that America 'came into existence with the sense of being a "separated" nation, which God was using to make a new beginning for mankind'. Accordingly, 'the destiny of "Christ's people in New England" was the destiny of all mankind'.[2] As far as American Jews are concerned, the obvious peculiarity that was attached to their insistence on (cultural, ethnic or religious) particularity when trying to be part of the American nation was thus overcome by a similar American insistence on being the chosen people.

Besides, Jews, finding a tolerant environment in America, the land of immigrants, did not have to fight for emancipation, as their European brethren did – sometimes at the expense of their faith and identity. This is why an apparent optimistic attitude and a hope for the future of Judaism prevailed throughout the first generation of American Reform leaders, in contrast to the confusion and ambiguity the following generations would go through as regards the main Jewish theological issues. But fear of Jewish assimilation has been there right from the beginning, which explains the rapid success of Reform and Conservative movements among American Jewry. Alongside an emphasis on spiritual progress and morality, what is also common to both German and American Reform movements is their use of the prevailing tendencies in accommodating Judaism to the relevant societies. Accordingly, among the German Reform leaders 'reason' and 'universalism', the concepts on which European Enlightenment grounded itself, were the ideas that mainly shaped the movement's self-understanding, as well as its world-view. The American Reform leaders, on the other hand, during the first generation in particular, frequently made use of terms such as democracy and unity, alongside universalism, which were dominant notions then in American society. The idea of the Jewish mission also continued to be the leverage of the movement, not only for the sake of pure universalism, but also to justify the Jewish right to remain a separate entity. However, the Reform Jews, even during the first generation, had to confront some challenges, such as modern science, in particular Darwinism, with its anti-religious rhetoric, and higher biblical criticism. They were quite successful in combining those scientific rules with their notion of mission. As put by Michael Meyer, to 'complete the evolution of man', for instance, 'was simply another way of stating the mission of Israel'.[3] Besides, the majority of the first generation of Reform Jewish leaders continued to stick to the traditional belief that 'God chose Israel', albeit interpreting it on rather universalist and moralist grounds.

In the theology of Isaac Mayer Wise, in particular, the traditional belief in the Sinai revelation and in a personal God is strongly displayed alongside an emphasis on rationalism and morality. Whereas Wise and David Einhorn, two leading figures among the first generation of Reform rabbis, were both rationalist and universalist, they differed mainly on the issues of the authority of the Scripture and the methods to embrace in order to pursue a safe future for Reform Judaism in America. Einhorn, as a radical reformer, sought to reshape Jewish theology in a more rationalist and universalist direction, whereas Wise, being moderate, placed more emphasis on the ancestral faith of ancient Israel as defined in the Torah. However, what he considered to be the legacy of the Torah was 'the complete and rational system of religion for all generations and countries'[4] and ancient Israel, as understood by Wise, was 'the prototype of American democracy'.[5] Yet, he was not so much interested in consistency and rationalism as in the continuity and unity of the American Jews. This is why he had an ambiguous attitude towards rituals and the authority of the sources.

Although Wise and Einhorn adopted different methods and set different priorities in their theologies, there was, however, one important similarity. Einhorn strongly argued that monotheism and morality, as qualities inherent in the human spirit, existed long before the people of Israel appeared in history. Therefore, Israel's role in this world was not to teach any previously unknown theological or moral laws but, as a priest people, 'to impress the ancient divine teaching more deeply upon itself and then to bring it to universal dominion'.[6] So, in contrast to the traditional Jewish view, which associated the sole truth with the Torah, Einhorn took into account the example of the people, rather than the truth of the Torah. In other words, Einhorn, just like Mendelssohn, argued for the universality of the monotheistic message while regarding the Jewish people as the bearer, rather than the originator, of it; i.e. a reminder of the universal message through their unique way of life. In fact, the idea of a 'mission of the priest people to the nations' was stressed by Einhorn more than any one else among contemporary Reform Jews, and this was directly related to his notion of universal religion. 'It was not a religion', Einhorn states, 'but a religious people, that was *newly* created at Sinai',[7] indicating that Judaism as a religion does not possess any unique or exclusive message but the Jews as a people have a special task to carry universal monotheism to humanity until the messianic end. So the idea of chosenness, for Einhorn, was not about the uniqueness of the Jewish religion/ faith but, instead, the uniqueness of the Jewish people in terms of having greater responsibility for the future of humanity.

Wise, on the other hand, in a similar way to Einhorn, held that 'the very ground-work of the system of ethics and religion taught in the Bible', as well as the rejection of paganism were already established with the first covenant God made with the first human couple, Adam and Eve.[8] Although with the two later covenants, one made with the Patriarchs and the other with Israel, the idea of monotheism and the moral laws gained more clarity, the foundation was already set in the beginning. So Wise believed that Israel was 'the chosen people, to possess forever, and to promulgate among all nations and tongues, the true know-ledge of the one'. And they were dispersed for the same reason as they were given the land, namely to 'be the custodian and expounder of the true knowledge of God and his will, until the human family enter the three-fold covenant between God and man'. There is a difference this time, that they could now fulfil the goal 'in all lands and generations'.[9] It should be noted that, while insisting on the uni-versality of the truth and special responsibility of the Jewish people, Einhorn and Wise have been referring not to the ideal Israel, but to the human Jews who were seeking to justify their separate identity in the New World.

Nevertheless, one thing that leads to severe disagreements between Wise and Einhorn is the fact that Wise, as much as being a universalist, was keen on uni-fying the American Jews, sometimes making certain compromises, such as giving full authority to the Talmud as decided in the Cleveland Platform (1855), which was against the essence of the Reform movement.[10] He wanted to estab-lish a 'strong and united Judaism' in America, with the help of the notion of the Jewish mission. Einhorn, on the other hand, as a strict rationalist, stuck to the principle of 'first truth, then peace'.[11] It seems that, while both leaders advocated Jewish separateness due to their special responsibility towards humanity, for Wise this was more for the sake of the Jewish people than for the mission they were to fulfil. This is why, Wise unconditionally believed in America as a haven for Jewish existence and prosperity, as well as a platform for Jewish mission. Einhorn, on the other hand, despite the rise of anti-Semitism in Germany, was more drawn to 'the greater value Germans placed on serious intellectual endeav-our in religion as opposed to practical activity'.[12] Besides, Wise's early support of Zionism also indicates that a particular concern for the Jewish people was dominant in his agenda, in contrast to Einhorn's purely universalist thought.

The other two figures worth mentioning among the first generation of American Reform Jews are Kaufmann Kohler and Emil Hirsch, who both hap-pened to be Einhorn's son in-laws. Interestingly enough, Kohler and Hirsch, like Wise and Einhorn, and also Geiger and Holdheim, before them, represented mod-erate and radical attitudes, respectively, and employed the same concepts in their theologies, such as prophetic heritage, the mission of Israel, and the universal messianic goal. Kohler, in particular, devoted a huge section in his *Jewish Theology* to the questions of the election and mission of Israel. These two concepts are understood by Kohler as two dimensions of the question of God's plan for the world. Although in his thought the election of Israel serves a universal goal, not so novel an idea, Kohler, reminiscent of the traditional Jewish justification of Israel's election, emphasizes that it is Israel alone which deserves, due to its qualities, to be chosen by God for the purpose of being a messenger. In other words, he sees election in terms of a kind of 'superiority' of Israel 'over other peoples in being especially qualified to be the messenger and champion of religious truth'.[13] So Kohler's discussion of chosenness seems to display an apparent emphasis on the universal dimension, as much as serving as a justification for the election of Israel on the basis of the notion of 'merit'.

As for Hirsch, despite having a more radical attitude towards Jewish sources and rituals, the idea of the mission of Israel, with its social and universal implications, gained more credit in his thought.[14] At this point, the similarities between Hirsch and certain European socialist Jews are striking. Indeed, the latter, in a similar way to Hirsch's concern with oppressed groups in America, carried the traditional notion of mending the world (*tikkun*) and put Jewish messianism on their agenda in dealing with social problems. Furthermore, despite their rejection of the traditional idea of the chosen people as exclusivist and chauvinist, the socialist Jews advocated instead, a chosenness by history to preach 'a salvation open to all mankind',[15] which was based on the prophetic message, particularly that of Isaiah, and was very much socialist in nature. Again, Hirsch placed the concepts of public action and social service at the centre of his notion of mission. In fact, the eighth principle of the Pittsburgh Platform (1885), which is 'to regulate the relations between rich and poor' and 'to solve the problems presented by the contrasts and evils of the present organization of society', was included through his efforts.

Nevertheless, it is important to note that the direct impact of the prophetic notion of social justice on certain modern Jewish ideologies, such as socialism in Europe and Jewish liberalism in America, is not easily discernible. At this point, Nathan Glazer argues that despite the fact that those socialist Jews 'were attracted to socialism in part because of certain elements in the Jewish religious tradition', the Jewish passion for social justice was essentially motivated by the fact that the Jews were 'an underprivileged element' in Europe and America and had to achieve their own political and social liberation.[16] In other words, the modern Jewish idea of social justice was instrumentalist rather than essentialist. Besides, as far as the American Jews were concerned, they had to be pioneers of liberalism with an emphasis on social justice and civil rights in order to enjoy the same rights as the Protestants. In parallel to this, for the American Jews liberalism always coexisted with ethnic loyalty.[17]

It should also be noted that in the 1920s, when Zionism began to gain growing sympathy and support from the Reform movement in the wake of the Balfour Declaration (1917), even Kohler became a proponent of the idea of establishing a Jewish home, if not state, in Palestine. By so doing, Kohler placed his argument on the fact that 'religion and peoplehood in Judaism constitute an indissoluble entity',[18] a notion which went against mainstream Reform thought. Some Reform Jews, on the other hand, including Hirsch, being attracted to cultural Zionism, understood the Jewish home to be established in Palestine 'as a beacon for the Jewish mission of bringing light to the nations'.[19] It is interesting to note that in the 1920s the American Reform movement had already taken a completely different direction than that of the 1880s, when the Pittsburgh Platform, led by Kohler, was held. The guiding principles of Judaism, as decided in the conference, mainly centred around strict universalism, in which there was no place for Jewish restoration in Palestine nor for a notion of Jewish nationhood. Judaism was defined as a progressive and God-centred religion, whereas the Jewish law was understood as consisting of moral laws alone. In the 1920s, however, only a few Reform Jews approved of the Jewish restoration to Palestine with reference to the idea of mission while even Kohler saw it as 'a center of Jewish culture and a safe refuge for the homeless'.[20] Such transformation, in fact, would set the seal on American Reform Judaism during the second generation.

Accordingly, what had shaped American Reform understanding of Judaism and Jewishness during the first generation was an indisputable commitment to universalism and to the idea of Jewish mission. In fact, this was the legacy of the German Reform movement, which the American followers sought to adapt to their newly adopted land of freedom and democracy. When coming to the 1930s, however, the relation between Judaism with its ethical–universal goals, as long advocated by Reform Judaism, and the Jewish people as a concrete entity became more problematic than it had been three decades before. Thus, the old question of whether the Jews were a religion or a nation, which had already been rekindled towards the 1920s, occupied the agenda of the second generation of American Jews more than anything else. This was also the period when the radical–universalist and moderate–particularist tendencies within the movement transformed into separate groups. Growing anti-Semitism, especially in Eastern Europe and Germany, the emerging nationalist tendencies and Jewish nationalism, Zionism in particular, began to be taken seriously even by rabbis from the American Reform movement.

The new guiding principles of the movement as formulated in the Columbus Platform (1937) were completely antagonist, in certain aspects, to those of the Pittsburgh Platform, which was the voice of classical Reform Judaism. In the Columbus Platform, Judaism was defined not as a religion, but as 'the historical religious experience of the Jewish people', indicating an inseparable relation between Judaism and the Jewish people, that is religion and nationhood. The overall emphasis shifted from ethics and individuality to rituals and peoplehood/community, albeit with an ongoing universalist tone. To denote Israel's world task, the term 'vocation' was used instead of 'mission', the former having an apparent social connotation. In fact, one of the paragraphs is devoted to the issue of social justice and social improvement of the world, in an open contrast to some kind of abstract and spiritual perfection, which had once put the seal on Reform Judaism. Looking at this from the perspective of body–spirit relations, the

American Reform movement of the 1930s seems to embrace a body-orientated outlook while the earlier classical Reform leaders, such as Geiger and Cohen in Germany, and Einhorn in America, held a spiritual–philosophical orientation. The influence of Kaplan's Reconstructionism with its emphasis on Jewish peoplehood, is also detectable in the former case. It was 'charity, social justice, and group life' which constituted American Judaism in general.[21]

In parallel to these, the new Reform understanding of chosenness also came to the fore with a slightly different meaning attributed to it. In fact, as far as the question of chosenness is concerned, it is possible to talk about two groups of Reform rabbis. One group, led by Julian Morgenstern, Samuel Goldenson, Samuel Schulman, and Bernard Bamberger, continued to use the language of classical Reform Judaism by putting an emphasis on Jewishness as a religious identity and on an unshaken universalist notion of chosenness as understood in terms of the Jewish mission. The other group, on the other hand, among which were Solomon Cohon, Abba Hillel Silver, and Stephen Wise, adopted a more peoplehood-centred position, albeit with an ongoing acceptance of universalism and mission. It was this group that controlled the movement to a great extent, with the draft prepared by Cohon accepted in the Columbus Platform over that of Schulman.

It is important to note that, despite their unquestionable loyalty to the religion of reason and spiritual progress, classical Reform thinkers strongly advocated the idea of chosenness and a unique mission for which the Jews as a people had been appointed. Although there is no clear statement in the Pittsburgh Platform that they literally believed in being chosen by God, a paragraph like 'We recognize in the Bible the record of the consecration of the Jewish people to its mission as the priest of the one God' indicates that they at least believed in the concept of chosenness as a holy mission which had been imposed upon the ancient Israelites by their prophets and sages. Besides, even a radical Reform Jew like Emil Hirsch had once written that 'the Jews were chosen by God, just as nature chooses',[22] by pointing to a similarity between the evolution theory based on natural selection and the Jewish idea of chosenness which depends on divine election.

As for the language of the Columbus Platform, here the Jewish mission is understood in terms of being 'witness to the Divine in the face of every form of paganism and materialism', attributing to the Jews a rather passive role. Again, in reference to 'the establishment of the kingdom of God', which was seen as being central to the Jewish mission by the first generation of American Reform Jews, in terms of a messianic unity of humankind, it seemed to suffice for the second generation to 'cooperate with other nations' instead of taking the lead. Besides, in the eyes of the latter, Jewish religious obligation does not consist of struggling for universal brotherhood and establishing social justice alone. The Jews are also required to build a Jewish homeland in Palestine and to make a 'faithful participation in the life of the Jewish community' in every way; the kind of concerns long forgotten by classical Reform Jews.

In fact, the second generation of Reform rabbis was no less universalist than the first generation but the former represented, at the same time, a nationalist orientation. So they sought to demonstrate in their writings that religion and nationhood were not incompatible. 'Though brought forth, preserved and cultivated by the Jewish people', Cohon states, 'Judaism is universal in its aims and ideals'.[23] Silver, on the other hand, in his attack on the Pittsburgh Platform declares that

> [i]t is the *total* program of Jewish life and destiny which the religious leaders of our people should stress today – the religious and moral values, the universal concepts, the mandate of mission, as well as the *Jewish people itself*, and all its national aspirations.[24]

On the other side, however, there were those Reform Jews who, in conformity with the mainstream classical Reform thought, attributed to Jewishness only a religious–spiritual meaning, completely rejecting any ethnic element in it as anti-universalist.[25] Morgenstern would continue to resist Zionism even in the wake of the extermination of European Jewry when he wrote on Jewish chosenness in 1947:

> We of the Reform wing conceive of Israel as a people, a chosen people, endowed from very birth a genius for seeing God in every aspect of existence and of interpreting all of life, nature and history from the standpoint of the one, eternal God ... chosen by God, therefore, to be His servant, the bearers of the highest knowledge of Him and of His way of life for mankind, unto all nations and peoples and throughout all time.[26]

Again, Samuel Goldenson would make a similar statement by playing down Jewish particularism and nationalism for the sake of a universal mission:

> If we insist, as I believe we should, upon the moral basis and universal validity of democracy, we should at the same time emphasize less and less the particularism in our Jewish heritage, those particularisms that separate us from others, and stress the universal concepts and outlooks more and more.[27]

However, the question to answer in the wake of the Nazi threat to Jewish existence was, for the majority, whether the Jews should carry on seeing themselves in purely religious-altruistic terms, as a people chosen for the sake of the world, as the suffering servant of God. So in contrast to the universalists, such as Morgenstern and Goldenson, on the one extreme, and the militant Zionists like Stephen Wise, on the other, the majority of Reform rabbis chose to find a middle way between pure religious and pure nationalist interpretations of Jewishness and chosenness. They would voice an argument which was based on the premise that 'universalism could not exist without particularism', and 'Jews, like all men, were members of a group, not of society in the abstract.'[28] So Judaism, for them, was a universal religion based on the historical religious experience of the Jewish people. As for the Jews, alongside their contribution to the amelioration of the world, they held responsibilities for their own people, as elaborated in the Columbus Platform. Although Reform figures such as Cohon and Silver insisted on the ongoing Jewish mission and the universal ethical message of the Jewish religion, by so doing they placed more emphasis on the people than on God. Judaism is defined by Silver as a religion 'created' by the Jewish people.[29] Again for Cohon, Judaism was 'the spiritual creation of the Jewish people'.[30] As shown by Arnold Eisen, during the second generation the term 'chosen people' gave way to the term 'choosing people'.[31] Cohon in particular, in the face of the rationalist interpretation of Judaism by classical Reform thinkers, defended 'the personal religious experience of the sacred' as the starting point for Jewishness,[32] just as Rosenzweig and Buber had done earlier in Germany. The need to make Judaism a religion of the physical also required American Jews to support the idea of the restoration of a Jewish homeland in Palestine. It is not surprising that Silver and Wise were both sincere Reform figures and ardent Zionists at one and the same time.

On the other side of the ocean, however, European liberal Jews were also going through a similar change when Leo Baeck declared that '[i]n the nineteenth century Judaism had been too concerned with conformity, with how it appeared to others rather than with what it really was. Now the time had come to throw away the mirror and to look inside'.[33] Although European liberal Jews were more cautious about Zionism then, they were apparently advocating a Judaism which was more concerned with the requirements of the Jewish community than of the times, albeit without entirely losing a religious and mission-oriented perspective. However, when coming to the 1930s, the rhetoric of the Jewish mission began to prove old-fashioned for at least the majority of American Reform Jews.

The Conservative congregation

The Reform theology, as reshaped by the second generation of American rabbis, was in many ways quite similar to the theology of American Conservatism, founded by Solomon Schechter. The centre of authority in Judaism, for Schechter, was not the revelation itself or any particular group within the people, but what he calls 'the religious conscience of the bulk of the nation or "Catholic Israel"'.[34] Schechter's Conservatism was an attempt to follow a middle path between Reform and Orthodox interpretations of Judaism, both of which, for him, failed to understand what Zacharias Frankel called the 'Positive-Historical' Judaism. In this, as explained by Louis Jacobs, an investigation of 'the origins of Jewish beliefs and institutions' is strongly advocated, whereas 'the need for strict observance of the precepts' is left to the 'mystical consensus of the Jewish people'.[35] So the need for continuity, on the one hand, and the importance of the community as the decision-making mechanism on the other, became dominant principles in the movement. These two principles in effect indicate the enthusiasm of the Conservative movement for the idea of a Jewish peoplehood. There have been various opinions within the movement regarding the idea of

God – from a biblical–personal to a very abstract–impersonal definition – and the revelation (Torah), yet the traditional belief in an intimate relation between God and Israel, as well as the idea of the Jewish peoplehood have always been given certain credit. Schechter's concept of a 'Catholic Israel' served to legitimize change only on the basis of the general approval, the people as a whole taking precedence, in this way, over the Torah. Arthur Cohen states that Conservativism 'marks the Jew as an historical God'. According to Cohen, 'Jewish catholicity too often degenerates into the vulgar response of mere collectivity – kinship feeling and camaraderie'.[36]

The idea of chosenness has a central place in Schechter's theology. In fact, election, in Schechter's interpretation, is just one dimension of the special relationship between God and Israel, a relationship which is based on God's love for Israel, as it is written, 'I will love them freely' (Hos. 14:5). Schechter states that 'the great majority of the rabbis are silent about merits, and attribute the election to a mere act of grace (or love) on the part of God'.[37] He also elaborates on different forms of the love relationship between God and Israel, as described in the Scripture and later interpreted in rabbinic literature, using such metaphors as paternal and bridal loves.[38] It seems that what stands at the centre of the Jewish religion, for Schechter, is the belief in a special intimate relationship between God and the people of Israel, the latter being the chosen people. Moreover, Schechter regards this relationship as an unconditional covenantal relationship, pointing to a well-known rabbinic statement, 'the Israelites are God's children even if they are full of blemishes'. So unlike classical, and to some extent nationalist, Reform theologies and even the Conservative theology of the second generation, which understand chosenness in terms of a 'mission/responsibility', Schechter sees chosenness primarily as a 'status'. Thus what is essential to Judaism, in Schechter's view, more than anything else, including the purpose for which the people of Israel have been chosen, is being the people of God, being chosen, which as an 'unformulated dogma',[39] Schechter asserts, has been passed down through the generations. This is why the Jewish peoplehood is placed at the centre of the movement. For Schechter, there is not only 'one God through Israel', but also 'one Israel through God'.[40] Indeed, David Novak, a contemporary American Conservative rabbi and scholar, clarified the same point in his *The Election of Israel* by pointing to the rabbinic understanding that 'Israel is for Torah as much as Torah for Israel',[41] Accordingly, in Schechter's theology, chosenness, in a similar way to the existentialist Jewish interpretation presented by Rosenzweig, refers to an existential reality on the part of the Jewish people. It is first a status and then a duty.

Nevertheless, it is important to note that although Schechter regarded chosenness mainly as a status, he was careful to present it on the basis of religious factors instead of national/cultural ones.[42] Accordingly, the Jews collectively and eternally were the people of God. However, as far as individual Jews are concerned, they are required to have faith in order to remain a member of the chosen people and to have a share in the world to come. At this point, Schechter makes a distinction between two types of Jewishness: one in the sense of nationality and the other in the sense of religion. So, in Schechter's theology atheist Jews were Jews only in the former sense.[43] Schechter furthermore maintains that the people of Israel, due to the fact that God's name is specially attached to them, are 'devoted to the proclamation of God's unity' and the 'mission of preaching the kingdom of God'.[44] This idea of a special task, in fact, is what renders Schechter's view of the election of Israel with an apparent universal dimension. However, Schechter also binds the realization of Jewish mission to the spiritual and physical redemption of the Jews. By spiritual redemption, Schechter means the redemption of the Jewish soul from the *galut* (exilic condition), while by physical redemption he means that the Jewish people will be living their own life again, apparently as a nation in their own land.

> History may, and to my belief, will repeat itself, and Israel will be the chosen instrument of God for the new and final mission; but then Israel must first effect its own redemption and live again its own life, and be Israel again, to accomplish its universal mission.[45]

When saying that 'Israel will be the chosen instrument of God for the new and final mission' and 'Israel must be Israel again', Schechter seems to make a separation between two types of Israel: one as a concrete people, such as the Jews, and the other as an abstract condition. This is in fact quite a crucial point in highlighting the marginal rabbinic view that the Jews become 'Israel'[46] only when they embody certain conditions within themselves. In the light of Schechter's earlier thoughts, it is possible to regard his view of chosenness and mission as two different entities. Accordingly, the Jews, in respect of being the chosen people, enjoy an unconditional status. As for the mission stemming from the status of chosenness, it requires Jews to meet certain conditions by becoming a proper religious people in their land again.

Coming to the 1930s, however, new interpretations emerged within the movement, placing more emphasis on the purpose of chosenness as a purely universal one. It seems that Conservative rabbis, especially in the second generation, took on the question of chosenness in as serious and painful a manner as the contemporary Reform rabbis did, if not more so. This was the period in which a need emerged within the Conservative movement to universalize its rhetoric more, but without underestimating the importance of the Jewish peoplehood. In this way, Conservative Judaism took quite an opposite direction to Reform Judaism, which had ended up by nationalizing its theology to a greater extent. Even those opinions that were quite similar to Kaplan's Reconstructionist understanding of chosenness in terms of a multiple vocation found voice within Conservative Judaism. The interpretation put forward by Ben Zion Bokser, in particular, is worth mentioning. He believed that 'all groups are equally God's chosen – they are unique vehicles of his revelation and the instruments of his purposes in history'.[47] On the other hand, the majority of the Conservative rabbis, such as Simon Greenberg, Louis Finkelstein and Robert Gordis, argued for the unique contribution of the Jews to civilization by attributing the election of the

Jews to their holding of the Torah,[48] rather than to God's love. Chosenness thus came to be understood not as a status, but as an obligation/responsibility, similar to the ongoing Reform accent on mission. The Jews, being chosen for the sake of the Torah, were 'the instrument of revelation to humanity'.

On the other hand, there were some other rabbis, such as Ira Eisenstein and Jacob Agus, who announced chosenness as a dangerous concept and opted for the renunciation of it, albeit for different reasons. Eisenstein believed that there was no way to determine whether one people's claim to chosenness was really legitimate. As far as Agus was concerned, however, the question was more than a technical one. It was very much related to the problem of the Jews being set apart from humanity in the name of chosenness; it was this to which he was strongly opposed. In response, Max Kaddushin argued that 'election', as understood in tradition, was the combination of 'God's love, Torah, and Israel', and thus no 'biological superiority or any special talent' was intended, but rather only 'gratitude for God's love in giving the Torah'.[49] Finkelstein too affirmed the uniqueness of the Torah and the election of Israel for the sake of the Torah, albeit in a rather vague and ambiguous way.[50] Milton Steinberg, on the other hand, appreciated the value of Judaism in respect of its being 'a rich culture' and 'a contribution to the civilization of the world'[51] but, as far as chosenness was concerned, he argued, in a similar way to Gordis, for a multiple vocation. It seems that Steinberg, like the majority of Conservative rabbis, saw chosenness in terms of the Jews choosing God.

Nevertheless, one issue was of more significance for Conservative rabbis than the question of choosing or being chosen; belief in election, either in terms of a choosing or a chosen people, should be allowed to Jews as much as to any other people, as long as it served for the good. In fact, Conservative rabbis in the second generation were well aware of the negative implications of the concept of chosenness and this is why they sought to present it in a language in which any terms that might lead to chauvinistic meanings were eliminated. According to Morris Silverman, the editor of the Conservative prayer book in 1946, chosenness meant that the Jews were to be 'judged by higher standards', and on them was to be imposed a 'great moral responsibility', and that they would make a 'contribution to mankind' through Torah. So, instead of eliminating the problematic passages related to chosenness, Silverman explained and rephrased them. The passage recited in the *Aleinu* prayer, for instance, read as 'who hast chosen us from among the nations to give us Thy Torah', not 'and given us Thy Torah'.[52]

So, when emphasizing the universal purpose of the idea of chosenness, the rabbis placed a stress on the idea of the covenant and the Torah. It was a unique responsibility emerging from the covenant relationship between God and Israel, an idea which, reminiscent of Kaplan's view, did not reject the possibility of the uniqueness of other nations in certain aspects. In fact, the Conservative attitude towards the idea of chosenness was grounded on the premise that the Jews were attributed with a unique and greater responsibility, without rejecting the responsibilities of other nations. In other words, the Conservative movement in the second generation opened up the way towards the idea of a multiple chosenness, by encouraging particularities, based on the idea of serving universal purposes. It is not surprising that Mordecai Kaplan, with his theology of a multiple vocation, would have emerged from the lines of the Conservative school, though he ended up with a new movement.

The Reconstructionist congregation

Mordecai Kaplan, founder of American Reconstructionism, having first studied at the Conservative Jewish Theological Seminary in New York, later went on to adopt a philosophy which went against Conservative theology in many ways. According to this new philosophy, Judaism was not a religion, but an evolving religious civilization created by the Jewish people and based on a humanist–rationalist understanding of God. Kaplan's Jewish civilization is also well-known for its renunciation of the idea of the chosen people and its particular emphasis on the Jewish peoplehood. Kaplan, in a clear contrast to mainstream Reform and Conservative theologians, asserted that the Jews make up an ethnic group rather than a religious community (Reform) or a religious nation (Conservative), and Judaism is not a religion but a religious civilization that preserves the Jewish group identity. In fact, Kaplan's renunciation of chosenness is not independent of his definition of religion. For Kaplan understands religion in terms of Emil Durkheim's 'conscience collective', namely that is 'the shared beliefs and practices of a community'. In other words, Kaplan, following the Durkheimian interpretation, justifies religion as something reduced to its function, which is about 'integrating the lives and consciousness of communities'.[53] In parallel to such a definition of religion, the purpose of Jewish civilization is understood as 'to ensure the continuation of the group'.[54]

It is interesting to note that one of the best means to keep Jewish group solidarity throughout Jewish history has been the concept of chosenness, an historic fact which is accepted even by Kaplan himself. However, according to him, while the idea of chosenness worked well in the previous stages of Jewish history when national, ecclesiastical, and rabbinic elements, respectively, had shaped the Jewish religion, chosenness is no longer the appropriate vehicle in a 'democratic civilization', taking into account the changing worldviews and the changing situation of the Jews within society.[55] Kaplan thus places his charge against the traditional doctrine of chosenness on certain theological, socio-ethical, and psychological grounds. First of all, according to him, chosenness was the result of an other-worldly theological system of previous periods, when the Jews, in the face of national disasters, believed that their God would reward them in the world to come. In the light of modern scientific developments, however, it is no longer possible to maintain such a belief in either a transcendent personal God or in the notion of the hereafter. For God is nothing but the power, manifesting itself in the universe as well as in individuals, that makes salvation possible. Salvation is thus not an other-worldly deed but, instead, it is within the capacity of human beings to bring about a world order based on justice and peace. Jews are not a people chosen by a transcendent God, but rather a people who are in search of a God, namely the power that is the epitome of all goodness. In this way, Kaplan shifts the emphasis from God to people. 'In its personal aspect', salvation means 'the faith in the possibility of achieving an integrated personality'. As far as the social aspect is concerned, however, it amounts to 'the ultimate achievement of a social order in which all men shall collaborate in the pursuit of common ends' with their full capacity of 'creative self-expression'.[56]

The other reason for Kaplan's opposition to chosenness is socio-ethical, based on the fact that one of the inevitable implications of the idea of chosenness is racial superiority. Such claim to Jewish superiority over other peoples is compatible, for Kaplan, with neither the modern Jewish demand to be a part of American society nor the 'highest ethical ideals' to be pursued by the modern Jews.[57] Kaplan also asserts that the doctrine of 'election', by associating the Jewish people with a sort of supernatural order, had worked as 'a psychological defense to counteract the humiliation to which the Jewish people was subjected', and in this way the idea of chosenness had a certain value. 'But nowadays', Kaplan continues to write,

> when only present achievement tends to satisfy the human spirit, the doctrine of Israel's election, in its traditional sense, cannot be expected to make the slightest difference in the behavior or outlook of the Jew. From an ethical standpoint it is deemed inadvisable ... to keep alive ideas of race or national superiority, inasmuch as they are known to exercise a divisive influence, generating suspicion and hatred.[58]

In addition to these theological and socio-ethical impediments or inconveniences, the idea of chosenness, as a means of preserving the Jewish identity and Jewish survival, proves dysfunctional on psychological grounds as well. For chosenness, in Kaplan's view, first emerged as 'a poetic idealization of the Jewish people', and later developed into a substitute for the Jewish inferiority complex and within this form it has been breeding even more inconvenience for Jews, causing more suspicion and hatred. So what modern Jewry really needs, in order to lead a meaningful life and to preserve the unity of the community, is a humanist system that recognizes national 'uniqueness' as based on the idea of 'vocation', instead of national 'superiority' promoted by the doctrine of 'chosenness'.

The term vocation, as used by Kaplan, denotes a particular call for the establishment of justice, truth, goodness, and peace on earth, a goal for which Jews, as well as other nations, are to strive. Kaplan's substitution of the concept of vocation for the doctrine of election serves several goals. First of all, Kaplan, in this way, eliminates the idea of a transcendent God, albeit without denying his existence as a complex of forces manifest in the universe. Moreover, he also transfers the Jewish religion from a God-centred, other-worldly, and exclusivist religious system to a people-centred, this-worldly, and humanistic civilization. At this point, Louis Jacobs asserts that 'the precepts of Judaism', are understood by Kaplan as commanded 'not by the God of tradition but by the God within the Jewish soul'.[59] Finally, Kaplan frees the Jewish people from any kind of feelings of inferiority or superiority, for the concept of vocation, unlike chosenness, does not include any exclusivist meaning. On the contrary, the former can be applied to more than one group. According to Kaplan, the notion of multiple chosenness, as suggested by some Conservative rabbis, is 'doomed to failure by the meaning of the word "chosen" itself', which is applicable only to a few instead of many.[60] As a matter of fact, even in the most universalist Jewish theologies, the disadvantage attached to the term chosenness, namely that it implies some kind of exclusivist meaning, is not completely eliminated. By the term vocation, however, Kaplan seems to achieve two things: preserving the Jewish particularity on the one hand, and making the Jews part of civilized society through and/or despite their particularity on the other. Vocation, in this way, works as a magic word, as it does not convey any meaning of superiority or exclusivity but rather gives a sense of particularity, which the Jewish people needed most in order to survive. Jews, by their vocation, make up a nation like other nations, who have their own vocations, and again Jews with their own civilization make up a separate ethnic group like other ethnic groups, no more or no less. Thus, the 'value of Judaism', for Kaplan, 'is in no wise dependent on its ability to demonstrate its superiority to other ways of life. So long as it serves as a way of salvation for the Jew, that is its own justification'.[61] Accordingly, 'in the task of preserving and developing the spiritual heritage of the human race', Kaplan argues, every group has to 'assume responsibility, each one for the maintenance of its own identity as a contributor to the sum of human knowledge and experience'.[62] As far as the Jewish people is concerned, 'the sense of the nation's responsibility for contributing creatively to human welfare and progress in the light of its own best experience becomes the modern equivalent of the covenant idea.'[63]

Yet, the problem endemic to the traditional concept of chosenness is also taken into Kaplan's quite advantageous concept of vocation. For, as Arnold Eisen points out, the Jews' 'unique "god-consciousness"', according to Kaplan, enables them 'to experience "the reality and meaning of Divinity" more than any other people'. 'All vocations', Eisen continues, 'were not equal; one was far "more equal than others"'; so '[c]hosenness, ushered unceremoniously out the front door, was in more modest dress smuggled in through the back'.[64] Indeed, the rewording of certain passages in the Reconstructionist prayer book does not seem to entirely eliminate the theme of election, though this is what is intended. For instance, in the *Aleinu* prayer, instead of 'who has chosen us', the passage reads 'who has called us to God's worship', ignoring the close association between the verbs to choose and to call.

It seems to be that what is common to all American Jewish theologians discussed above is that, instead of coherently expounding, or creating a systematic theology of, chosenness, they use it as a symbol – either in the sense of mission (Reform), or multiple chosenness (Conservative) or multiple vocation (Reconstructionist) – to be part of America on the one hand and to stay apart from it on the other. In the end the Reform, Conservative and Reconstructionist

Jewish movements had emerged as alternatives to the threat of assimilation and a stagnant Orthodoxy. 'Contemporary Jewish life', as suggested by Arthur Hertzberg, 'must be made so attractive that Jews will find rich, positive meaning in their Jewishness'.[65] They sought to win Jews back to Judaism by reinterpreting the traditional concept of chosenness in a way that would also prove compatible with American democracy. However, the American Jewish evaluation of the idea of chosenness failed to see chosenness beyond this function. And that characteristic of American Judaism seems to have been carried into contemporary times.

7   Zionist understanding

Zionism, as a Jewish national movement aiming to re-establish the Jewish people in their ancestral homeland, Palestine, developed mainly as a response to the new socio-political circumstances caused by modernity and Jewish Emancipation.[1] For, after the Emancipation, the Jews encountered an unprecedented identity crisis, on the one hand, and the problem of anti-Semitism, on the other. Yehezkel Kaufmann maintains that 'Emancipation is the due of the individual Jew, whereas the problem of the Exile is the problem of the Jewish group, one which Emancipation cannot solve'.[2] However, Zionism, as well as providing Jews with a haven, generated serious divisions among the Jewish communities, as much as modernity did in the beginning of the nineteenth century. Indeed, despite the fact that Zionism would become a civil religion for the Jewish settlements in Palestine as early as the 1920s and that it would be accepted by many Jews as a legitimate movement after the creation of the state of Israel in 1948, its transformation into a dominant ideology for world Jewry would only be achieved in the late 1960s.

Zionism, when it first emerged, was rejected by both traditional and liberal Jews due to its secular and nationalist nature. According to the nineteenth-century Reform leaders, who, by defining the Jews as a religious community, had long ago done away with the notion of 'the return to the land', Jewish nationalism only meant the betrayal of universalism and of the idea of Jewish mission.[3] The dispersion of the Jews among other nations, which was seen as an abnormality by the Zionists, did not yield a negative meaning within Reform thought; on the contrary, it was understood as a result of unique Jewish mission. 'Whatever purpose it may have served initially', Hermann Cohen wrote, 'the very notion of the rebirth of a Jewish state had become antithetical to Judaism's universal aims'.[4]

The Orthodox leaders, on the other hand, were mainly concerned about the secular nature of the movement, according to which human effort, rather than the coming of the Messiah, would bring about Jewish redemption in the Holy Land.[5] Exile was mainly understood by the traditional Jews as a divine punishment for the sins of the Jewish people and, therefore, the realization of the ingathering of the exiles was seen as a matter of divine will. Even in the eyes of those religious Jews that supported Jewish settlements in Palestine as a preparation for the divine redemption, Zionism was an anti-religious movement pioneered by secular and assimilated Jews. Moreover, the Zionist reduction of the Jews from a religious people built around the Torah to a mere nation established in a land was no less problematic for the Orthodox than it was for the Reform. Accordingly, Zionism, as a national movement, encountered strong opposition from world Jewry on the basis of its anti-universalist and anti-religious orientation at one and the same time.

Nevertheless, Zionism, which first emerged in a period when secular nationalism was the dominant movement in the world, bore characteristics which did not easily fit in with the nationalisms of other nations. First of all, as Arthur Hertzberg points out in his *The Zionist Idea*, 'all of the other nineteenth-century nationalisms based their struggle for political sovereignty on an already existing national land or language'.[6] As far as Zionism is concerned, however, the struggle was not carried out in the name of the liberation of the Jews as an existing nation in their homeland. On the contrary, the Zionist claim that the Jews were a nation generated great opposition among Jewry, on religious as well as historical grounds. So the Zionists would have to turn the Jewish people, dispersed all over the world, into a nation before turning Palestine, which was to a great extent inhabited by the Palestinian Arabs, into a Jewish homeland. Ironically enough, Zionism, as a Jewish national movement, functioned as a reversing process in which the strategy of occupation and colonization was employed. In fact, some scholars and historians regard Zionism as part of the general colonialist trend in history,[7] and this was exactly what other national movements were fighting against. Moreover, the dilemma would not end here, but the Zionist efforts to colonize Palestine would, in turn, bring about the Palestinian national liberation movement to counter Zionism.

Second, Zionism possessed both modern secular and traditional religious elements, with its use of modern nationalism on the one hand and Jewish messianism on the other. There was a consensus among all Zionist groups on the issue of the 'return to Eretz Israel', whereas on the question of whether 'the Jewish people should be defined by religion or nationality', religious and secular Zionists had differing views.[8] Although Palestine did not at the time belong to the Jewish people, it had always been the focal point of their religion through their belief in redemption, which would take place in the Holy Land. For secular Zionists, the Jews had a right to the land on the basis of historical and ancestral ties. As far as religious Zionists are concerned, however, both ancestral ties (the past) and redemption (the future) at the same time legitimated their right to the land. In other words, Zionism was grounded on two traditional Jewish premises:

1　The Jews are a people/nation, not (only) a religious community.
2　They are to be restored to the Holy Land.

This is why, although Zionism encountered opposition from different Jewish circles, it also aroused messianic expectations among some Orthodox and Hasidic Jews and won supporters from the American Reform congregation as early as the 1920s.

So it is not surprising that Zionism had also quite an ambiguous relation with Jewish tradition. It greatly employed the traditional idea of a 'return to the land', which had been at the heart of Judaism since the destruction of the Second Temple in 70 CE but, at the same time completely negated another well-known Jewish notion, namely that redemption will be established in a miraculous way through divine intervention. Zionism instead placed emphasis on personal responsibility for the destiny of the Jewish people. In other words, it suggested a secularized version of Jewish messianism, which aimed at the establishment of the Jews back in their homeland as a proper nation, not particularly religious, and by means of human efforts instead of divine acts. By so doing, Zionism also shifted the language of redemption from a religious-eschatological tone to a secular–historical one. The latter becomes especially obvious in the Zionist negation of the Diaspora and in its desire to create a new Jewish identity, in contrast to that of the exilic periods. Indeed, as stated by Silberstein, Zionism based its discourse on a group of confrontations: exile–homeland, Hebrew–Jew, culture–religion.[9]

On the other hand, classical Zionism, as a movement seeking to normalize the condition of the Jewish people by rendering them with their own homeland, brought about an understanding of exile which stood in sheer contrast to traditional messianic understanding. 'Religious messianism', as Hertzberg states, 'had always imagined the Redemption as a confrontation between the Jew and God', namely in terms of 'resolving the tension between the Jew and his Maker', which had resulted in the 'exile' as punishment and atonement for Israel's sin. In classical Zionism, however, the confrontation was seen between Jews and nations and for mainly socio-political, not religious, reasons.[10] The goal for the Zionists was thus to end the struggle between Jewry and the outside world by turning the Jews into a normal people.

Thus Zionism appeared as a secular political movement, displaying a sort of continuity with Jewish tradition, in particular with Jewish messianism, on the one hand, and a repudiation of the Jewish past, on the other. In terms of continuity, Zionists, at almost every stage, had a utilitarian and selective attitude towards traditional Jewish concepts and symbols. Yet in diagnosing the Jewish problem, which generated modern anti-Semitism, and in shaping the new Zionist Jewish identity as a solution to it, they adopted different attitudes towards religion and tradition. Some rejected the pre-modern Jewish tradition as passive and religious-oriented (e.g. Micha Berdichevski, Joseph Brenner, etc.). For others, however, it was the Emancipation that actually created the Jewish suffering (e.g. Max Nordau, Nahman Syrkin, etc.). According to this second group of Zionists, the Jewish Emancipation, as something that happened not for the sake of the Jews, but 'for the sake of logic', ended up depriving them of their collective identity.[11]

The question of how Zionists understood the idea of chosenness was also part of their evaluation of the past, present, and future of the Jewish people, and was not free of ambiguity. Zionism, as a secular national movement, ended up including a variety of positions, ranging from secular political to religious messianic ones. Yet, in general, secular Zionists sought to turn the Jews from an 'abnormal people' into a 'normal people like other nations'.[12] Accordingly, the theme underlying this early Zionist definition of Jewishness was a sense of 'normalcy', based on Jewish nationalism. However, this programme of normalization did not mean depriving of the Jews of their 'privileged' or 'unique' position as the chosen people, but rather abandoning their 'abnormal' condition as a people without a home. In other words, while Zionists, for the most part, did away with the element of 'difference' embedded in chosenness, they retained, to a great extent, the notions of 'uniqueness' and 'superiority'. Although it was difficult to combine an aspiration for normality with an ongoing sense of chosenness, either in terms of divine election or the unique national genius of the Jewish people,[13] classical Zionism softened the apparent contradiction, turning the notion of chosenness into a useful factor for Jewish national liberation and a necessary element for the improvement of world civilization.

Accordingly, the notion of chosenness provided the Zionist movement with a missionary role. In this way, the universalist and redemptive implications of the traditional doctrine of chosenness, particularly in terms of 'leading the world', were employed to a great extent by the Zionists to justify their goal of establishing a Jewish state in Palestine. The new Jewish nationhood established in their ancestral homeland would aspire to the role of a 'mentor of the Middle East' (Moses Hess), or represent a 'moral priesthood whose authority is accepted by all mankind' (Ahad Ha-Am), or become 'the shining star of humankind' (Martin Buber). The traditional notion of chosenness, which originally referred to the Jewish people as a physical collective entity, was transformed in this way into the Jewish nationhood as a political–ethical entity. The theme of 'leading the world' was also used by the socialist Jews of the Diaspora. They would attribute a 'vanguard' role to the Jews, as 'a chosen people not of God but of history', a people 'preaching a salvation open to all mankind'.[14] However, unlike the Zionists, they would place an emphasis on the Jewish socialist nationality in the Diaspora instead of a Jewish state in the land.

On the other hand, the sense of uniqueness attached to Jewish chosenness rendered Zionism a unique form of nationalism, which might be seen in connection with the above-mentioned missionary role. In this notion of uniqueness, once doubled with the idea of mission, a sense of greatness came to be included; this would work out very well in the process of freeing the Jews from their abnormal and inferior sense of being and elevating them in the eyes of other peoples, as well as their own, to a distinct and indispensable position. Thus, the Zionist formula built around the secular notion of chosenness would be that the Jews, as a great and model nation deserved to have a homeland as much as, or even more than, any other people, for their own sake as well for the sake of the world. In other words, the secularized notion of the chosen people, in terms of the greatness of the Jews, would be used as a justification for the Jewish colonization in Palestine. At this point, it is important to note the Zionist insistence on Palestine over any other alternative territory. Any available territory formulation, particularly Uganda – in fact Kenya – as proposed by Israel Zangwill, an

Anglo-Jewish Zionist and the founder of the Jewish Territorial Organization (1905) in opposition to Herzl's World Zionist Organization (WZO), did not find much support among the Jews. Apparently, what lay behind this Zionist insistence on Palestine must have been mainly pragmatic concerns, as Herzl himself, at one point, was very close to the Uganda formulation before realizing that any territory other than Zion and any terminology other than the biblical would not get much Jewish attention and support.

However, the choice of Zion also indicates the emotional, as well as ideological, connection that Zionism had with biblical terminology. By choosing Zion as the place for the Jewish homeland, the Zionists were able to maintain the aforementioned traditional Jewish concept of chosenness and redemption, albeit in an apparently secular and nationalist tone. Return to Zion, in this way, meant a return to the condition of being 'a great nation' again, in fulfilment of what is said about Israel in the Hebrew Bible: 'surely this great nation is a wise and discerning people' (Dt. 5:7). Moreover, Zion was the appropriate place, not only to re-establish the Jews as a great or chosen nation in their homeland in the minds of Jews, but also to link this greatness to the notion of the redemption of the world in the eyes of Christians. This latter point is manifest in the Zionists' calling Harry Truman, the American President, a 'Messiah' serving 'Eternal Divine Israel' when he declared the creation of a Jewish state in 1948.[15] Here an association between Truman and Cyrus, the ancient Persian King, is apparent as the latter was also called the 'Messiah of the Lord' (Isa. 45:1) due to his order to rebuild the Temple in the sixth century BCE.

In the light of these remarks, in what follows the Zionists' interpretations of Jewishness and their use of the language of chosenness will be examined in four well-known categories, namely political, cultural, socialist, revisionist and religious Zionism, which prevailed primarily in Europe and later in Israel and America.

Political Zionism

The problem of modern anti-Semitism, the pogroms of 1881 and the Dreyfus affair, apparently had an important impact on the development of Jewish nationalism. This appears to be the most dominant force in the ideologies of the early Zionists in particular, such as Theodor Herzl, Max Nordau, and Leo Pinsker. However, the solution proposed by these early Zionists, especially Herzl, was based on a positive understanding of the Jewish problem. For both Herzl and Nordau, the Jewish problem was the result of certain socio-political conditions such as the homelessness of the Jews, and not some irrational and mysterious form of anti-Semitism. Therefore they suggested political solutions that would end the Jewish problem through normalizing the condition of the Jews.

As far as Herzl was concerned, the only goal of Zionism was to bring the age-old problem of anti-Semitism to an end by rendering the Jews with their own state, originally anywhere in the world, but preferably in Palestine. In parallel to his secular, western background, Herzl pioneered a programme of colonization in Palestine. The Jewish state in this way would be 'a part of a wall of defense for Europe in Asia, an outpost of civilisation against barbarism'.[16] According to Herzl, the Jewish state would represent 'the most blessedly modern small state',[17] apparently as a secular version of the to-be-established messianic state of Israel, as he declared 'we do not mean to found a theocracy, but a tolerant modern civil state. We shall, however, rebuild the Temple in glorious remembrance of the faith of our fathers'.[18] He was thus careful to highlight the implications of Jewish religious tradition as well. Despite his secular orientation, Herzl stated that 'Our community of race is peculiar and unique, for we are bound together only by the faith of our fathers'.[19] In fact, Herzl grounded his endeavours to establish a Jewish state in Palestine on the fact that the Jewish people had never ceased to see themselves as the chosen people or to cherish the idea of the restoration of the Jewish state.[20] But the state as envisaged by Herzl suggested a secular process in which the Jewish people would become a normal, yet a great, nation.[21] 'The world', he wrote, 'will be freed by our liberty, enriched by our wealth, magnified by our greatness. And whatever we attempt there to accomplish for our own welfare, will react powerfully and beneficially for the good of humanity.'[22]

Nordau, too, adopted a colonialist attitude in his Zionist programme. He wrote in a positive way about traditional Judaism by frequently referring to the traditional language of 'separation' and 'uniqueness', which, he believed, had been successfully pursued by the Jews in order to preserve their community until the time of the Emancipation.[23] As an atheist thinker, what interested Nordau about separation and uniqueness, however, was their use of a distinctive national identity. He hoped that the Jewish people would become a strong nation again; the people would keep their unique qualities, but the nation would be based on a new Jewish identity which demanded 'not simply a broadening and secularization of the Jewish spirit' but rather 'a new physical Jew'.[24] The term 'muscle-Jews' was coined by him to represent this new Jewish identity.[25] Nordau, like many Zionists, had quite an ambiguous attitude towards the Jewish past, praising the traditional Jewish notion of collectivity on the one hand, and opposing the image of the traditional Jew, as physically weak and passive, on the other. According to him, the Jewish striving for 'superiority' was the result of the fact that they had been denied equality.[26] However, what he suggested on behalf of the Jews was a colonial instead of a religious, superiority; he wrote, in the same fashion as Herzl, that the European Jews, as 'a people more industrious and more able even than the average European', would bring civilization to the 'savage' world.[27]

As for Pinsker, he, unlike Herzl, regarded anti-Semitism as a problem which was inseparable from the existence of the Jews. Therefore, the Jewish state could not end anti-Semitism, which, for Pinsker, was a natural condition of Jewish existence. The Jewish state, instead, could be an instrument to emancipate the Jews as a nation. 'The Jews are aliens who can have no representatives', Pinsker wrote, 'because they have no fatherland'.[28] However, in his thought the solution of the Jewish problem did not lie on a political level only, that is the Jewish people becoming a normal people again through establishing their own state. It also required 'a psychological transformation', which is called 'auto-emancipation' by Pinsker,[29] that is the process of gaining 'self-respect' and 'consciousness of human dignity'. What is interesting in Pinsker's thought is that, despite his concerns for the normalization of the Jews by turning them into a people with 'self-respect', he recognized a 'unique' character within the Jews, as did Herzl and Nordau, a character which went beyond being a distinctive nationality. What was at stake in Pinsker's thought, too, was a 'uniqueness' based on a historically verified superiority. Apparently the Jews were meant, for Pinsker, to be more than an ordinary people. After all they were the people who once, like an 'eagle', Pinsker wrote, 'soared to heaven and recognized the Divinity' yet now the nations reproach the Jew 'because he cannot rise high in the air after his wings have been clipped'.[30] Pinsker's metaphoric use of 'eagle' to designate the people of Israel bears an apparent implication of the biblical 'eagle metaphor' that occurs in Exodus 19:4, 'You have seen what I did to the Egyptians, and how I bore you on eagles' wings and brought you to myself', and in Isaiah 40:31, 'but those who wait for the Lord shall renew their strength, they shall mount up with wings like eagles, they shall run and not be weary, they shall walk and not faint'. However, what Pinsker indicates in this way is hardly the biblical notion of election but, instead, a religious–spiritual genius possessed by the Jewish nation. He employs the term 'chosen people' in a rather cynical way, as he writes: 'He must be blind indeed who will assert that the Jews are not *the chosen people*, the people chosen for universal hatred'.[31] In fact, a similar notion of 'negative' chosenness was also implied by Herzl when he stated that 'We are one people – our enemies have made us one in our despite, as repeatedly happens in history'.[32] However, it seems to be that in Pinsker's thought there is also a positive/internal dimension of Jewishness, as manifest in the aforementioned eagle metaphor where Pinsker referred to the 'spiritual genius' of the Jewish people. The idea of a spiritual genius was also emphasized by the Reform leaders, such as Abraham Geiger and Kaufmann Kohler, as well as some socialist and cultural Zionists. As regards the Jewish claim to chosenness and mission, they all placed emphasis on the Jewish genius, instead of on God's act of choosing. What Pinsker sought was, in a similar way, to make the Jews retrieve their innate creativity by being a proper and leading nation.

On the other hand, there were those secular Zionists who rejected the idea of chosenness, such as Jacob Klatzkin, a late political Zionist and the most radical opponent of the idea of Jewish mission and of a future Jewish life in the Diaspora. Klatzkin followed a Zionist line similar to Herzl's. While strongly opposing the religious and spiritual definitions of Judaism, including the notion of 'a priest people, a nation of prophets', Klatzkin asserted that the Jews, as a nation, required nothing but their own land and language. 'We are', he wrote, 'neither a denomination nor a school of thought, but members of one family, bearers of a common history'.[33] Although the share of a common Jewish history makes one Jewish, Klatzkin argues that a Jew 'who no longer wishes to belong to the Jewish people, who betrays the covenant and deserts his fellows in their collective battle for redemption, has thereby abandoned his share in the heritage of the past and seceded from his people'.[34] Klatzkin suggests a Jewish covenant and redemption in secular–nationalist terms instead. The Jewish state, as he envisaged, does not have any mission whatsoever: messianic or colonialist. Instead, 'a third-rate, normal, national state and culture', should suffice, as far as Klatzkin's territorial Zionism is concerned.[35] What is even more important is the fact that he has shown clear contempt for the altruistic and ethical purposes represented by cultural–spiritual Zionists. What mattered for him was the survival of the Jewish nation. The Jews, as a secular nation, were not meant to serve any purpose other than their own continuity, and the Jewish state would serve that goal alone. Nevertheless, Klatzkin also held that 'Zionism pins its hopes, in one sense, on the general advance of civilisation and its national faith is also a faith in man in general – faith in the power of the good and the beautiful'.[36]

It seems to be that, alongside an effort to ameliorate the condition of the Jewish people by turning them into a people of home and self-confidence, the rhetoric of being a great nation and of bringing civilization to the savage world, which looks like a secular version of the idea of chosenness, dominated the political Zionist agenda to a great extent. What is even more interesting is that one can observe in the writings of many socialist Zionists an apparent implication of the ideas of chosenness and mission, as adapted to a socialist–secular terminology, which will be discussed later.

Cultural Zionism

Ahad Ha-Am (Asher Ginzberg), the chief proponent of cultural Zionism, was one of the severest critics of political and practical Zionism. According to him, the real Jewish problem was less about the physical survival of the Jews than spiritual survival. Moreover, the goal of mass Jewish immigration to Palestine, as suggested by political Zionists, was thought by him to be unrealistic. Thus, he was critical of political Zionism both in its goal and strategy. This is the main difference between Herzl's western Zionism, which was involved with 'the problem of the Jews', and Ahad Ha-Am's Hibbat Zion (Love of Zion), which was interested in 'the problem of Judaism'.[37] Commenting on the First Zionist Congress, Ahad Ha-Am wrote:

> After thousands of years of unfathomable calamity and misfortune, it would be impossible for the Jewish people to be happy with their lot if in the end they would reach [merely] the level of a small and humble people.... It would be impossible for an ancient people, one that was a light unto the nations, to be satisfied with such an insignificant recompense for all their hardships.[38]

However, Ahad Ha-Am seems to have quite an ambiguous attitude towards the idea of mission, as his starting point is Judaism as a national entity, not as a religion.[39] In a similar way to Rosenzweig's definition of Jewishness as 'being' a Jew, Ahad Ha-Am understood the Jewish feeling as 'a natural sentiment' that needed no further justification than its own reality. 'Why are we Jews?' he wrote,

'How strange the very question!.... It is within us; it is one of our laws of nature'.[40] This was also the way that Mordecai Kaplan defined Jewishness when he wrote, 'If Jewish life is a unique way of experience, it needs no further justification'.[41] So, it was no surprise that Ahad Ha-Am, understanding Jewishness in terms of a secular–existential identity instead of a religious–ethical one, was critical of the doctrine that 'the Jewish right to survive was dependent on a mission to teach ethical monotheism in the diaspora'.[42] In fact, Ahad Ha-Am's understanding of the Zionist goal as well as his critique of Reform thought, was quite similar to that of Hess. Both thinkers opted for a nationalist definition of Judaism and also gave certain credit to Orthodoxy, as long as it sustained the collective identity among the Jewish people.[43]

Yet Ahad Ha-Am, despite the fact that he had quite an existentialist approach to Jewishness, needed to find an explanation for the existence of the Jewish people. According to him, it was no coincidence that the people of Israel became 'a kingdom of priests and a holy nation' – as depicted in the Torah. Judaism, being a product of the Jewish national spirit, was an answer to the human search for 'spiritual perfection' as based on 'a body to serve as its instrument'.[44] In this way, the Jewish nation was 'destined from the very beginning to be an example to the whole of mankind through its Torah'.[45] In other words, the Jewish people were the living example of the unity between spirit and body. Accordingly, for Ahad Ha-Am, Judaism represented not only a natural, but also some sort of redemptive fact, through which the Jewish people became the bearer of 'the task of creating a society that would be an example to all peoples'.[46] He advocated the establishment of a Jewish spiritual centre in order that a revival of Jewish culture could be realized, something that was necessary for the continuity of the Jews before all else.

It is also important to note that there are striking similarities between Ahad Ha-Am's cultural Zionism and Mordecai Kaplan's Jewish civilization. In fact the former had inspired Kaplan's theory of 'two sorts of Jewish civilization', according to which, 'in the land of Israel Jews could fashion a complete national civilization, receiving salvation from their revitalized Jewish religion, while in the Diaspora they would participate in (and be enriched by) two civilizations, the Jewish and American'.[47] For both thinkers, Judaism, being a product of the Jewish national spirit, was meant primarily to respond to the changing needs of the Jewish people, enabling them 'to live a life developing in a natural way' (Ahad Ha-Am)[48] and providing them with 'self-respect' (Kaplan).[49] However, in the thoughts of both Ahad Ha-Am and Kaplan, the aspirations to a Jewish unity and Jewish renascence, in the Diaspora as well as in Palestine, were eventually aimed at contributing to the improvement of world civilization. Yet, in parallel to this idea of improving the world, Ahad Ha-Am's cultural ethics as well as Kaplan's notion of vocation, appeared not so immune to a hidden claim of Jewish superiority.[50] For the idea of mission, in terms of either being a model of collectivity for other peoples (Ahad Ha-Am) or having a particular call for the establishment of justice, truth, goodness, and peace on earth (Kaplan), was regarded by both thinkers as a result, not of divine initiative, but rather of the Jewish national spirit. It goes without saying that, for them, it was only because the Jews had an innately higher spirituality than other nations that they were able to come up with the idea of a mission or unique vocation; and this is a notion that implies an apparent superiority on the part of the Jewish people. In fact, the main difference between the Zionist and Reform recognitions of the idea of a Jewish mission was that the former saw it, not at the expense of, but due to, Jewish nationality.

On the other hand, Horace Kallen, another American Zionist Jew, in a similar way to Kaplan, saw the Jews, like other groups in America, as centred on a cultural–ethnic, instead of a religious, identity. He, in this way, argued for a 'cultural pluralism' working like an orchestra made up of different ethnic or cultural groups in which each group plays its instrument to get a 'harmony', not a 'unison',[51] namely making its contribution to the wider society not to the detriment but on account of its own difference and particularity. Therefore, Zionism, as a movement, was important to Kallen in terms of both affirming the Jewish cultural loyalty in America and enabling the establishment of a secular Jewish society in Palestine.[52] Zionism, in this way, would function as a new religion, entitling American Jews to be different and making them preserve their own separate identity.[53] Accordingly, for Kallen, the Jewish particularity was not about any mission, but about a right on its own. He wrote a lot about the Zionist response to the 'arrogant' doctrine of the 'chosen people' and the idea of the 'Jewish mission', by regarding the Jews as 'a historic people among other peoples, neither better nor worse'.[54] He, in a similar way to Kaplan, interpreted the appeal of the idea of chosenness to the Jews in reference to 'the state of inferiority' in which they had found themselves in the Christian world.[55] As pointed out by Eisen, to be able to answer the question of why one should remain Jewish if there is no special role on its behalf, Kallen reverted to a position similar to that of Kaplan's, trying to find 'a core of inherited Jewishness'.[56] Kallen's inherited Jewishness, in terms of certain 'cultural habits' (i.e. kitchen, calendar and celebration) to be cultivated through Jewish education, was more immune to the accusation of being arrogant but less to the threat of a loss of Jewish distinctiveness than Ahad Ha-Am's cultural superiority. Being aware of it, Kallen stressed the 'Jewish national life' to be established in Palestine as an element indispensable to the survival of the Jewish people as well as Judaism. He even found some historical truth in the biblical notion of the chosen people, understood as a 'contract' agreement based on Israel's devotion to the worship of God and God's leading them to the 'Promised Land' to live there in prosperity. This 'hope for the Promised Land' and the 'consciousness of a goal to be attained collectively in turn for the assumption of a collective obligation to a supernatural being' was, for Kallen, what made 'a congeries of tribes' turn into 'a nation'.[57] Kallen also referred to 'prophetic universalism', in terms of an 'ideal of international peace under a general law for all nations', which was aimed not at abolishing but harmonizing the nations. Therefore, Kallen stressed, it also retained its nationalist outlook in 'giving to Israel a dominant note in the international harmony, and Zion the foremost place'[58] (the metaphor of orchestra). So Kallen, despite his denunciation of the idea of Jewish mission and superiority, with his emphasis on the notion of prophetic universalism as well as Christian eschatological anticipation – i.e. the return of the chosen people to the Promised Land[59] – ended up advocating, albeit for pragmatic reasons, a sort of pseudo-messianic role for the Jewish people.

Socialist Zionism

Although the ideologies of the socialist Zionists were based on different premises, such as 'ethical socialism' for Moses Hess and Nahman Syrkin, and 'dialectical materialism' for Ber Borochov, one thing that was common to all socialist Zionists was the emphasis on physical labour and social justice. Moses Hess was the precursor of Zionism though his views did not find much support until the establishment of the WZO in 1897. He, after having made his turn to nationalism with his *Rome and Jerusalem* (1860), placed his earlier ethical socialism in a new Zionist context and came to see the former as something to be achieved in a Jewish state. He declared that such a state 'would serve as a model for other peoples' with its 'just and equitable social order'.[60] It is important to note that despite his use of the theme of 'leading the world', which is reminiscent of the notion of mission, Hess was extremely critical of the classical Reform claim that 'Judaism had some special mission to teach gentiles the elements of humanitarianism'.[61] According to Hess, the Reform idea of mission was wrong on two grounds. First of all, the presence of the Jewish state would not deprive the world of any of the benefits promised by the Reform mission, such as 'pure' theism, the principles of humanitarianism, morality, industrial and commercial endeavours, which were indispensable to the future development of the world. In other words, 'the national character of Judaism', Hess maintained, 'does not exclude universalism and modern civilization; on the contrary, these values are the logical effect of our national character'. Second, according to Hess, it was not true that the world needed Judaism for all those spiritual and material consequences, at least not any more. As far as the concepts of 'tolerance' and 'humanity' were concerned, for instance, the enlightened Christians were not less entitled to these than the enlightened Jews; and it was the case for other benefits derived from the Jewish mission.[62] However, it seems to be that, in Hess's thought, Judaism, within the form of a Jewish state, still had something to offer the rest of the world, mainly on social and economic grounds. And this is what Hess indicates by quoting Ernst Laharanne, a French patriot: 'A great calling is reserved for the Jews: to be a living channel of communication between three continents. You shall be the bearers of civilization to peoples who are still inexperienced and their teachers in the European sciences...'[63] In fact, the Jewish mission so understood by Hess, which was based on the idea of establishing a 'socialist commonwealth', 'social and economic justice' through a Jewish state, proved quite similar to the notion of mission as advocated by second-generation Reform leaders in America, such as Abba Hiller Silver, who emphasized the Jewish nationality, as well as the idea of universal social justice.

Nahman Syrkin, in a similar way, endorsed an 'ethical and utopian' national-ism, which was rooted in 'the ideals of biblical prophecy'. For Syrkin, as much as for Hess, socialist values were nothing but 'a rediscovery in the modern context of the biblical concern for social justice found in the prophetic visions of the messianic age and in the Mosaic legislation protecting the widow, orphan, and slave'.[64] In fact, a similar view would also be voiced by Louis Brandeis, an American socialist Zionist. What is interesting about Syrkin's thought, however, is a clear acceptance, not only of the idea of a messianic age, but also of the traditional Jewish concepts of mission and chosenness. Indeed the critical dis-tinction that Hess made between a messianic hope represented by traditional Jewish values and an abstract idea of mission as volunteered by Reform Judaism is not so obvious in Syrkin's ideology. He directly referred to a 'unique historic mission', taken on by the Jewish people, albeit in a rather concrete form, which first required the liberation of the Jews as a nation.[65] However, the Jewish people themselves, with their mission, took a more significant place in Syrkin's Zionism than the Jewish state. In other words, the Jewish state functioned as an instrument to prepare the people for its 'high mission'. Syrkin highlighted this notion of mission by declaring that the Jewish man 'will redeem the world which crucified him'.[66] In this way, he also attributed to the Jews the role of 'the suffering servant', which was also emphasized by the German Reform thinker Hermann Cohen. Moreover, when Syrkin wrote that '[f]rom the humblest and most oppressed of all peoples it will be transformed to the proudest and great-est',[67] it echoed like a certain deuteronomic passage, where it is written that when God chose the people of Israel they were 'the fewest of all peoples' and then became a 'great nation' through law.[68] Syrkin proclaimed that Israel would 'once again become the chosen of the peoples', but this time apparently on the grounds of socialist principles such as freedom and justice.

Louis Brandeis, on the other hand, suggested a parallel between American democracy and Jewish law, both being based on 'the brotherhood of man' and 'social justice'.[69] When he talked about the Jewish duty to survive and contribute to 'the advance of civilisation',[70] he was implying the prophetic notion of being a light unto the nations, albeit in rather socialist terms. Accordingly, what is appar-ent in most socialist Zionists is that they clearly carried into the universal mes-sianic hope in their socialist–nationalist agenda by believing that the 'new society they intended to create in the land of Israel would be a more powerful "light unto the gentiles" than the Diaspora Jewish communities'.[71]

Nevertheless, in contrast to the Zionisms of Hess, Syrkin, and Brandeis, which successfully applied the traditional language of messianism and the idea of mission to their socialist–nationalist agenda, there were other socialist Zionists such as Micah Berdichevski and Aaron Gordon, who rejected any connection with the Jewish past. In the writings of both Berdichevski and Gordon, in parallel to the notion of physical labour, a strong metaphysical bond is suggested between the Jewish people and the land. Berdichevski, being one of the severest critics of Ahad Ha-Am's cultural Zionism, endorsed a revolution which required the replacement of an abstract Judaism with the living body of the Jewish people, declaring that 'Israel precedes the Torah'.[72] He also pointed to the contrast between the 'lofty ethical culture destined to be a light unto the gentiles', of which the traditional Jews boasted, and the current situation of the Jews as 'a beaten, tortured, and persecuted people'.[73] The name 'Hebrew', denoting a people of labour in a concrete and active sense, was preferred by Berdichevski over the traditional name 'Jew', which had an abstract religious connotation.[74] In this context, Berdichevski also used the biblical term the 'holy people' in reference to the Jewish people having physical power, instead of a religious–spiritual virtue. Moreover, the fact that God revealed himself to the people of Israel at Mount Horeb (Sinai) was taken by Berdichevski as a sign of nature's supremacy, the emphasis being shifted from God to Sinai.[75] Gordon, too, wrote about establishing 'a new relationship with nature',[76] reminiscent of the biblical theme of renewing the covenant with God.[77] The main emphasis in this Gordonian type of Zionism was on the idea of 'redemption of the land'. The traditional Jewish emphasis on worshipping God was replaced by the idea of labouring the land, an emphatic contrast being held between the 'secular activity' of 'settling the land and tilling its soil' and the '"holy" activity of pious Jews who spent their days in the study of sacred text.'[78] Moreover, Gordon placed an emphasis on 'human brotherhood',[79] though he did not see this as a legacy of Judaism, as some other socialist Zionists did, but rather as a prerequisite for the creation of a new people by Zionist efforts, 'a human people', in contrast to the traditional Jewish people. Thus, both thinkers aspired to the transformation of the Jews from a supernatural people that were covenanted to God with law and faith into a normal people related to nature with labour and physical power.

In a similar fashion, Joseph Brenner, another secular socialist Zionist, advocated a new Jewish identity which had no dependence on the Jewish religion or Jewish religious history. Brenner's interpretation of Jewish nature is particularly worth mentioning. According to him, the Jews struggled throughout their history not for the sanctification of God, as claimed by the traditionalist Jews, but for assimilation. '[S]uch is our history', Brenner deplored, '[t]he expulsions and ghettos – these assured our survival.' And the Jewish belief in being the chosen people was the result of, or rather was compensation for, the Jewish failure to be like other nations, prosperous and rich.[80] Therefore, Brenner, in a similar way to Berdichevski and Gordon, bound the new Jewish identity to normalcy, by writing, 'It would be a sign of steadfastness and power, of productive strength, if the Jews would go away from those who hate them and create a life for themselves. That I would call heroic sacrifice.'[81]

The traditional Jewish idea of a 'renewed covenant' made with God was formulated by Brenner in a completely secular way, to be recited in a kibbutz *haggadah*:

> Now we have arisen to throw off the yoke of exile and to make for ourselves a new land and a new sky with a strong hand and faithful arm ... and to renew our covenant with this land and with the plants that grow.[82]

So this second group of socialist Zionists sought not only the survival of the Jews as a separate nation in their Jewish state, but also, and more importantly, to transform them into a normal and self-confident people, one whose survival did not depend on chosenness, either by God or history, creating an abnormal and humiliating life for the Jews. In other words they sought to make the Jews into a nation that would be intimately related to their land with labour, power, and loyalty, in sheer contrast to the traditional Jewish view that requires the people of Israel to connect with their God through worship, faith, and covenant.

However, as formulated in a Zionist–socialist statement of faith, which reads, 'The land and only the land will be the holy of holies for the Hebrew soul',[83] even within that secular process there was an attempt to sanctify the Zionist–socialist values. What is also sanctified is the Jewish nation, albeit with no relation to God, covenant, and chosenness. The *Shema* prayer, the most sacred passage of the Jewish liturgy, which reads 'Hear O Israel, the Lord is our God, the Lord is One' was transformed into 'Hear O Israel, Israel is our destiny, Israel is one.'

Revisionist Zionism

As a nationalist–militarist movement founded by Viladimir Jabotinsky, Revisionist Zionism mainly followed the Herzlian political Zionist tradition. Unlike the labour Zionists who had established their ideology on the basis of the land and physical labour, revisionist Zionists gave priority to the establishment of the Jewish state through military and diplomatic means. They advocated militarist fascism by trying to form a Jewish majority in the land through mass immigration and colonization. The Jewish state, as envisaged by the revisionists, became not 'simply an instrument to solve the problem of Jewish suffering and oppression in the Diaspora', but also a state of 'an intrinsically sacred value'.[84] For socialist Zionists, it was socialism which eventually aimed at overcoming nationalism by reaching a classless society.[85] For the revisionists, however, nationalism was the foremost and only goal. So they needed to underscore what is national and unique, namely what is Jewish.[86] Jabotinsky emphasized in his writings the need to engender a state of Jewish national character,[87] which meant an association with Jewish tradition, particularly with the Bible. In this way, nationhood, alongside the idea of Jewish statehood, was attributed some kind of holiness. Indeed, Jabotinsky described the Zionist activity undertaken by the revisionists as 'the work of one of the builders of a new temple to a single God whose name is – the people of Israel'. This new religion, which was called 'Zionist monism' by Jabotinsky, 'meant the subordination of all values and interests to the Zionist idea and to the national interest'.[88] This is in fact quite a different formulation from the messianic Zionist vision. However, it seems possible to associate Jabotinsky's consecration of the Jewish people with some other reasons than his Russian nationalist background, though apparently this played a significant role in his militarist ideology. In a letter submitted to the Palestine Royal Commission (1937) as evidence for the Jewish right to a state in Palestine, he made an allusion to the apparent role of the Jewish people in world civilization, by writing,

> Yes, we do want a State; every nation on earth, every normal nation, begin-
> ning with the smallest and the humblest who do not claim any merit, any
> role in humanity's development, they all have States of their own. That is
> the normal condition for a people.[89]

Thus Jabotinsky, like most Zionists, combined two separate features in the new
Jewish identity: normalcy and greatness. The Jews are to have their own state for
two reasons: first, this is the requirement of every normal nation, and second, they
deserve it more than any other nation through their merit of being a great nation.
Here Jabotinsky shows a clear openness to the traditional Jewish belief that the
Jews have a special role to play in the world. So, as far as Jabotinsky and other
revisionists are concerned, this is a sanctification of the people and the state on
both secular–national and traditional–Jewish grounds. However, there were other
revisionist groups, the most important one of which was Lehi (Lohamei Herut
Yisrael – Fighters for the Freedom of Israel), which saw the right of the Jewish
people to the entire land as sacred and absolute. Leaders of Lehi also spoke of
conquering the land 'by force from the hand of aliens'.[90] Jabotinsky, however,
acting more diplomatically, wrote that although 'in that process the Arabs of
Palestine will necessarily become a minority', yet 'Palestine on both sides of the
Jordan should hold the Arabs, their progeny, *and* many millions of Jews'.[91] As
observed by Peter Beyer, even in Jabotinsky's formulation exclusivism based on
separation between Jew and non-Jew served as a leverage to create national
unity.[92] On this point, Charles Liebman and Eliezer Don-Yehiya point to the
growing revisionist disposition towards religion for the sake of preserving 'the
unity and uniqueness of the people', which would become the sole purpose of the
Zionist civil religions of Israel, particularly after the Six Day War.[93]

Religious Zionism

While the discourse of other Zionisms, as seen so far, involved the Jewish nationality and the relationship between a nation and a land, that of religious Zionism
was based on Judaism as a religious nationality and the relationship between the
'chosen' people and the 'Holy' Land. Thus, secular Zionists adopted, as we have
seen, either a colonialist–socialist/militarist or spiritual–cultural vision in general
whereas the religious Zionists mostly embraced a religious–messianic thrust.

Rabbi Yehudah Alkalai and Rabbi Zvi Hirsch Kalischer, first religious Zionists
or activist–messianists, alongside other Orthodox Zionist figures, known as the
'Harbingers of Zionism', espoused the idea of 'redemption coming by a natural
process', namely through Jewish efforts. As broadly explained by Aviezer
Ravitzky in his *Messianism, Zionism, and Jewish Religious Radicalism*, although
there were inner tensions and disagreements in Jewish tradition as regards the
nature of the messianic era, 'for many generations the passivist tendency had
enjoyed the upper hand'.[94] According to this tendency, the messianic redemption
would come as a result of miraculous acts of God. The Jews were warned against
forcing the end, not even through excessive prayers, let alone by other human

efforts. Ravitzky emphasizes that although there were some traditional figures (e.g. Maimonides, Nahmanides, Gaon of Vilna), who encouraged Jewish settlements in Palestine as a preparation for the redemption, or predicted the coming of the redemption as a result of a natural process, these were restricted to elite circles of eschatologists.[95] Besides, it is noted that Maimonides, in parallel to his vision of the messianic era as a natural and historical, albeit ideal or utopian, one, did not consider the advent of the messianic era, which mainly referred, for him, to national–political redemption, as an indispensable stage for earning a part in 'the world to come', the latter rather symbolizing the individual–spiritual redemption. On the contrary, for Maimonides and some others, it was quite possible to achieve a personal spiritual redemption in the most exalted sense, even in exile, an idea which served to neutralize the messianic idea by minimizing the urgency of messianic expectations.[96] It seems to be that, although there have been different theories regarding the nature of messianic redemption, passivist interpretations usually had more appeal to the majority and gained ascendancy in periods when the Jews felt betrayed by false messianic movements.[97] What shall be discussed here, however, is the activist interpretation of the messianic age, as employed by the leading religious Zionists.

According to both Alkalai and Kalischer, redemption was to begin gradually by building up the land through Jewish efforts. It is no surprise that in their activist interpretations Alkalai and Kalischer both frequently referred to the activist views of earlier rabbis and traditionalist Jewish figures. The rabbinic notion of two Messiahs, in particular, i.e. 'the true miraculous Redeemer' and his 'forerunner', was often used.[98] The first Messiah (son of Joseph), who, as a forerunner to the second Messiah (son of David) would conquer the land of Israel, taking it from the infidels, but would fall in battle, was understood by Alkalai to refer to a process inaugurated by the Zionist pioneers.[99] Again, the old spiritual notion that 'the awakening from below will bring about an awakening from above'[100] was also among those traditional views used by Alkalai and Kalischer.

However, it is interesting, but not altogether surprising, that the religious Zionism of Alkalai and Kalischer had an apparent modern–nationalist orientation as well; it was actually a mixture of the traditional and the modern. Alkalai strongly supported a colonization programme in Palestine, while Kalischer widely used the current socialist–nationalist arguments, referring to examples of other nations that were struggling for national independence:

> Are we inferior to all other peoples, who have no regard for life and fortune as compared with love of their land and nation? ... while we, the children of Israel, who have the most glorious and holiest of lands as our inheritance, are spiritless and silent.[101]

What underpinned all these early religious Zionist endeavours was, certainly, the belief in chosenness as an accepted fact. But, as clearly seen in the above passage, the language and the means used were mainly nationalistic. Kalischer also encouraged a programme of organized agriculture in Palestine, in a similar way to socialist Zionist endeavours. It is important to note that the plight of East European Jewry played a significant role in these two early religious Zionists' involvement in Zionism. What they were searching for was less an eschatological redemption than a this-worldly national liberation with a religious thrust. Perhaps this is not surprising, considering that redemption was usually understood in Jewish tradition in terms of the restoration of the Jews to the land in this world.[102] There were surely implications of the idea of glorifying God in the writings of Kalischer and Alkalai, and they saw the Zionist efforts mainly as a preparation for the final redemption. Yet, the main motivation behind their Zionism remained the amelioration of the situation of the Jews. This is why their idea of redemption did not go beyond the radical notion of 'self-redemption', despite all the references they made to traditional Jewish sources regarding the messianic faith. They failed to mention even the prophetic notions of social justice and being a light unto the nations – the universal dimension – which were employed to a great extent by some secular Zionists, as we have seen. However, it was these two rabbis who showed, long before the emergence of secular Zionism, that the Zionist movement could have religious potential. During the 1960s and 1970s, Zionism, as a dominant discourse of Israeli society, would follow a similar direction, creating more ethnocentric policies and placing a growing emphasis on the religious–messianic dimension.

On the other hand, there were Hasidic rabbis who, despite their antagonistic attitude towards Zionist ideology, due to its secular orientation, saw the Jewish settlement of Palestine as a divine duty (*mitzvah*) and regarded the building up of the land as the beginning of divine redemption. Rabbi Shneur Zalman, the founder of Habad Hasidism, believed that 'the rebuilding of the land will commence before the coming of the Messiah, and the rebuilding of Jerusalem will take place before the ingathering of the exiles'.[103] The leaders of Ger and Vishnitz Hasidim were as fervent supporters of Jewish settlements in Palestine as Zalman. Rabbi Yehudah Leib once wrote, 'Just as the Jews need the Holy Land so the Holy Land needs the Jews to bring out its intrinsic holiness'.[104] Again Rabbi Hayyim, to encourage his followers to make *aliyah* to Palestine, quoted a certain talmudic passage which reads, 'If a man dwells in the Diaspora, it is as if he has no God'.[105] The only exception to this was the Satmar Hasidim, who strongly opposed those who settled in Palestine and those who believed that the Jewish conquest of the land of Israel was 'the beginning of the Redemption'. However, even the Satmar Hasidim ended up establishing two Jewish settlements in Palestine.

Among other religious Zionists are Rabbi Meir Bar-Ilan and Michael Pines. Bar-Ilan insisted that the Jews as a people and Judaism as a religion are essentially different from other peoples and religions.[106] Pines, on the other hand, stated his opposition not only to Zionism, but also to secular Jewish nationality.[107] For both of them, the Jews were a religious people too unique to reduce to a secular national entity. They more or less shared the views of Agudat Israel. Despite their original anti-Zionist attitude, however, the Agudat leaders promoted a religious-Zionist objective, according to which '[t]he colonisation of the Holy Land in the spirit of the Torah shall be directed towards creating a source of spirituality for the Jewish people'.[108] On the other hand, the religious Zionist group called the Mizrachi (1902) held the notion of re-awakening the hope of a return to Zion. They voiced the traditional view that 'only out of Zion will the Lord bring redemption to the people of Israel'.[109] In a similar messianic fashion, albeit within a relatively universalist manner, Hayyim Bialik called the Balfour Declaration (1917) 'the gospel of redemption to the whole humanity'.[110]

However, it was Abraham Isaac Kook (Rav Kook), the first chief rabbi of the Ashkenazi Jews in Palestine, who most ardently advocated the Zionist goal. Rav Kook's interpretation of Jewish chosenness is a combination of particularist and universalist elements. He understood the Jews, both in terms of individuals and collectivity, as 'different' and 'higher' than other peoples, as he wrote: 'We are not only different from other nations, differentiated and set apart by a distinctive historic existence that is unlike that of all other nations, but we indeed surpass the other nations.'[111] According to Rav Kook, the Jewish people are of a 'real and organic holiness' because the 'divine spirit exists in the community of Israel in the most sacred concealment'. He warned the Jews that, this being the fact, the holy spirit could exist among them 'only within the context of an attachment to God'.[112] However, Rav Kook's later thoughts on the existence of the divine spirit in the Jewish people in relation to secular Zionists clearly show that the Jews, both as individuals and as a people, whether attached to God or not, were regarded as vessels in which the divine spirit dwelt. Rav Kook believed that 'Jewish secular nationalism is a form of self-delusion: the spirit of Israel is so closely linked to the spirit of God that a Jewish nationalist, no matter how secularist his intention may be, must, despite himself, affirm the divine'.[113] In fact, the same idea was also shared by Rabbi Avraham Mordechai Alter, the third Rebbe of the Ger dynasty, who asserted his belief in Zionism, saying:

> I have no doubt that the Zionists are motivated by *mitzvot*, even if they consider themselves to be irreligious … By choosing the Land of Israel, they depart from secular ideology and cling to an irrational demand of their soul, the longing for the God-given land. And since they fulfill the obligation to the Land of Israel under harsh circumstances, this one obligation is counted as equal to the rest of the 613 commandments.[114]

Rav Kook, as shown by Ravitzky, even in his earlier anti-Zionist stage, when he was strongly opposed to secular nationalism, remained a pro-activist and a fervent supporter of the idea of a national rebirth. After he left for Jerusalem in 1904, however, a dramatic change occurred in his thoughts. He modified his secular Zionist views on the basis of a new definition of 'Israel'. He developed his mystical doctrine of the inner power of the 'uniqueness of Israel'.[115] His earlier definition of the *Knesset* of Israel as constituting exclusively those who observe the Torah, was replaced by a new definition, based not on the Torah but, instead, on the 'uniqueness of Israel', that is the '*segullah* quality of Jewish identity'.[116] In other words, his view of chosenness was shifted from a conditional position to an everlasting/inherent status. Accordingly, as argued by Charles Liebman, Rav Kook held that 'the Jewish nation (people) possessed absolute sanctity unconditioned by their behavior – a result of their natural and unchanging qualities'.[117] Indeed, this is what is indicated by him when he writes that '[t]here is an eternal covenant which assures the whole House of Israel that it will not ever become completely unclean. Yes, it may be partially corroded, but it can never be totally cut off from the source of divine life'.[118]

It is also interesting to note that the idea of the divine spirit, on the basis of which Rav Kook came to incorporate secular Jews into the chosen people, was also the criterion that he applied to all humankind. This is the meaning of what Rav Kook called the 'all-encompassing unity', according to which, as paraphrased by Liebman and Don-Yehiya, 'everything that is good and positive ... stems from Judaism and the Torah even when no association is apparent'.[119] Besides, 'the world of the gentiles', Rav Kook maintained, 'will be redeemed, once and for all, with the redemption of the Holy People', and this could only take place in the Holy Land.[120] In this way, all the civilizations of the world would be renewed by the renaissance of the Jewish spirit; as the realization of the 'active power of Abraham's blessing to all the peoples of the world' and the basis for renewed Jewish creativity in Eretz Israel.[121] According to Shlomo Avineri, Rabbi Kook viewed the election and redemption of Israel not in terms of 'national–religious domination', but rather as 'part of a universal salvation'.[122] Avineri also asserts that Rav Kook was aware of the fact that the creation of a Jewish state in an unredeemed world would result in its involvement in power struggles. So, for him, the only way to redemption was 'the complete salvation of all mankind', and not holy wars.[123] It seems that Rav Kook, in effect, made a distinction between an organic demand of living in the land, as a necessary element for the personal Jewish realization of complete holiness, and the establishment of a Jewish state in the land, which, as the epitome of universal redemption, was to follow 'a global transformation of the world of politics'. Accordingly, Rav Kook, following the traditional Jewish view, found an organic relationship between not only the people and God (chosenness), but also between the people and the land (redemption). Nevertheless, his mystical philosophy of chosenness and redemption, which encompassed an eventual universalist outlook, was short of the theoretical equipment necessary to handle the risk of a premature establishment of a Jewish state. So it is interesting, but not surprising, that his ideas would take on, transformed by his son, Zvi Yehudah Kook, a completely particularist and radical perspective. The insistence of Rav Kook on activating 'the elements of sanctity within the nation' as a whole, including the secular Zionists, would be reduced by Zvi Kook and his disciples to sanctifying the Jewish state along with all its political policies and the adoption of a hostile attitude toward non-Jews (more on this later).

At this point, it is important to note that few religious-Zionist Jewish leaders openly referred to a universal redemption that would begin with religious-

Zionist efforts; and few, if any, concerned themselves with the ethical and humanitarian dimension of the question of Zionism. As indicated above, Rav Kook, as one of those who had an ultimately universalistic notion of redemption, failed to see the gap between the reality as lived now and here (i.e. occupation and colonization) and the ideal yet to come in some future period of time (i.e. universal redemption). The only exception to this religious-Zionist dilemma came from somewhere else. The approaches of Judah Magnes and Martin Buber to the questions of Jewish nationalism, Jewish mission and the land seem quite different from that of Rav Kook and other religious Zionists. In fact, Magnes and Buber both had a critical relationship with Zionism and rejected Zionist colonialism as something against the spirit of the Jewish mission. Both thinkers made a distinction between the centrality of the Holy Land to the Jewish mission – not to the physical survival of the Jewish people – and the Zionist desire to build a Jewish state in Palestine. Magnes, in particular, made this point very clear by writing: 'Palestine can help this people perform its great ethical mission as a national–international entity. But this eternal and far-flung people does not need a Jewish state for the purpose of maintaining its very existence.'[124]

As far as anti-Semitism is concerned, which was the main force behind the ideologies of most Zionists, including some religious ones, such as Kalischer and Alkalai, Magnes again put a different light on the subject by arguing that:

> Palestine cannot solve the Jewish problem of the Jewish people. Wherever there are Jews there is the Jewish problem. It is part of the Jewish destiny to face this problem and make it mean something of good for mankind.[125]

In Magnes's thought, the Jewish people and the Torah came before the land. In the same way, the people were meant to be 'poor and small' but 'faithful to Judaism'. So, the Jewish life to be established in the land, as envisaged and supported by Magnes, was not meant to turn the Jews from a poor and powerless people into a 'large and powerful' one 'like all the nations'. Although, in Magnes's thought, the people took priority even over the Torah, the role attributed to them in his theology, namely the achievement of an ethical mission, made them a purely function-oriented people in contrast to being a self-centred one. In other words, the people came before the Torah and the land, but not before the mission. In this way, Magnes managed to go beyond the physical and literal meanings of the traditional Jewish concepts of people, Torah, and land. After pointing to the danger lying in Zionist colonialist thought that 'we, being the ruled everywhere, must here rule; being the minority everywhere, we must here be in the majority', Magnes referred to the meaning of the *Aleinu* prayer by interpreting its stress on the Jewish difference in a positive way:

> In the face of such danger one thinks of the dignity and originality of that passage in the liturgy which praises the Lord of all things that our portion is not like theirs and our lot not like that of all the multitude.[126]

Again, in respect of the present inhabitants of Palestine, Magnes showed an exceptional concern by writing:

> The fact is that they are here in their overwhelming numbers in this part of the world, and whereas it may have been in accord with Israelitic needs in the time of Joshua to conquer the land and maintain their position in it with the sword, that is not in accord with the desire of plain Jews or with the long ethical tradition of Judaism that has not ceased developing to this day.[127]

In a similar way, Buber was one of the most steadfast critics of political Zionism from within, on the basis of what he called 'Hebrew humanism'. 'I am setting up Hebrew humanism in opposition to that Jewish nationalism which regards Israel as nation like unto other nations and recognizes no task for Israel save that of preserving and asserting itself.'[128] Nevertheless, Buber made his critiques, like Magnes, without denying the Jewish people's claim to the land of Israel. Buber has always supported the Zionist cause in respect of the 'realization of Judaism' and defended it not only against political Zionists but also against anti-Zionist liberal Jews such as Hermann Cohen.[129] Buber disagreed with both Cohen and Rosenzweig in his emphasis on the nationality of the Jews and the importance of the Holy Land to their realization of their messianic mission. Yet he defended the Jewish claim to the land within the limits of his Hebrew humanism. As a separate section is already devoted to Buber's existentialist definition of chosenness, here we shall look at his thoughts on Zionism, after briefly mentioning his views of Jewish uniqueness. Buber's starting point was the idea of the uniqueness of Israel, which he understood as 'something counter to history and counter to nature'.[130] Apart from assuming the 'burden of its uniqueness' and 'the yoke of the kingdom of God' there was 'no security' for Israel.[131] 'Israel is chosen', for Buber, 'to enable it to ascend from the biological law of power, which the nations glorify in their wishful thinking, to the sphere of truth and righteousness'.[132] Zionist efforts to normalize the Jewish people, by having them incorporated in power politics,[133] meant, to Buber, negating this uniqueness. As pointed out by Ehud Luz, Buber made a crucial distinction between 'Zionist ideology' and 'Zionist practice'. According to him, 'Zionist ideology' as a way of normalizing the Jewish people, 'severs itself from the organic memory of Judaism and aspires to create a new chain of continuity', whereas 'Zionist practice' as an attempt to 'return to the Land of the Fathers', stems 'from a desire to *return* to the *ancient* roots and *revive* the *tradition*'.[134] It seems to be that returning to the land, in Buber's theology, was a spiritual obligation – not a *halakhic* one, as some religious Zionists understood it. It was more about being involved in the development of the unity of the Jews and of humanity than being involved in a land/state in a physical/political sense. In other words, even the sacredness of the land – either in terms of a homeland (secular emphasis) or a Holy Land (religious emphasis) – was understood by Buber in a way which was more spiritual than physical. This is why the inner relations of the Jews with the nations, and with their neighbours in particular, had great importance in Buber's thought. And this is why Buber was opposed to secular colonialist Zionism, as he wrote:

> Our settlers do not come here as do the colonists from the Occident to have natives do their work for them.... We have no desire to dispossess them: we want to live with them. We do not want to dominate them: we want to serve with them...[135]

It is important to note that, in their opposition to the Zionist normalization of the Jewish people, Magnes and Buber were pointing to an ethical/theological dilemma in which religious Zionists were caught more than any other Zionist group. By endorsing both Jewish chosenness/uniqueness and nationalist/political means at the same time, the religious Zionists had not been very successful in reconciling these two opposing claims regarding the Jewish people; namely being outside (power) history, on the one hand, and taking part in it as other nations, on the other. Within this dilemma the uniqueness of the Jewish people proves even more problematic. They are a people who are different from other peoples, but at the same time are just like them, in a rather peculiar way. They are both a spiritual and political people. The religious Jews believed that the existence of the Jewish people and Jewish religion was ultimately for the sake of all humanity but the question of what would happen if the survival of the Jewish people was to be juxtaposed with that of another people was left unanswered by many, while the needs of the Jews were given open priority in the unfolding events. Indeed, it is already an uneasy task to reconcile the universalist and particularist dimensions of the traditional Jewish doctrine of chosenness even when the Jewish people are regarded as being outside history. This is why, as put by Louis Jacobs, 'the problem of how to reconcile Jewish nationalistic aspirations with universalism, the secular with the sacred, belief in divine providence with human endeavour, justice for the Jews with the rights of the Arabs, love for the Holy Land with the loyalty Jews outside Israel owe to the lands in which they reside'[136] has been at the heart of Zionism right from the beginning. And this tension would give rise to quite problematic ideologies in the course of Zionist history in the state period, as will be discussed.

Consequently, in parallel to the spirit of the time, most nineteenth-century Zionists felt an urge to justify their claims to the land and to a Jewish state on the basis of their own definitions of 'mission'. As pointed out in the beginning, the Jewish society/state to be established in the land entailed either a 'moral priesthood' (Hess's socialist Zionism) and a 'model society' (Ahad Ha-Am's cultural Zionism), or 'an outpost of civilization against barbarism' (the colonialist Zionism of Herzl and Nordau). On the other hand, religious Zionists interpreted Zionist efforts in reference to the notion of the 'beginning of redemption'. Again, an apparent universalistic attitude was adopted by socialist Zionists in the pre-state period, which would continue to some extent during the first years of the state, under the civil religion of Statism. On the other hand, there was revisionist Zionism with its exclusivist and militarist rhetoric, which began to loom in the 1920s. When coming to the 1960s, however, especially after the 1967 (Six Day) and 1973 (Yom Kippur) wars, the increase in Jewish control of the land would arouse a totally self-justified and self-redemptive and a more unanimous Zionist discourse, in which the idea of 'mission' would be totally replaced by that of 'survival'.

Part III
Chosenness as 'survival'

8 The discourse of 'Holocaust and Redemption'

In the previous part, mostly European Jewish understandings of Jewishness and chosenness, produced under the conditions following the aftermath of the Jewish Emancipation, were explored. One unexpected result of those conditions happened to be the transfer of the Jewish centre from Europe to America and Israel. Therefore, the aim of this final part will be to discuss mainly American Jewish and Israeli interpretations of Jewishness and chosenness in the aftermath of two very important events for the contemporary Jews, namely the extermination of European Jewry and the creation of the state of Israel. In this way, the dynamics of the Holocaust discourse and its effects on the formation of a new interpretation of chosenness will be examined here. As a matter of fact, this new version of Jewishness and chosenness as consummated in a unique sense of 'victimhood' and 'survival' did not become the dominant view in American Jewish theology but, certainly it was the most effective one on a public scale, from the late 1960s on, particularly throughout the 1970s and 1980s. The emphasis on the relation between the Holocaust and the state of Israel came to be emblematic of sacred suffering and redemption for American Jewry and created, what Jacob Neusner calls, 'American Judaism of Holocaust and Redemption'.[1]

Nathan Glazer, in his well-known *American Judaism*, describes American Jewish life in the 1940s and 1950s under the rubric of 'institutionalism', which points to the flourishing Jewish ethnicity in the guise of religiosity. In fact, the victory of Jewish ethnicity was partly the heritage of the 1920s and 1930s and, in the wake of American Jewish awareness of the Holocaust, would be carried to the late 1960s and 1970s in terms of 'survivalism'. However, the immediate post-war period would, in contrast, display an apparent 'integrationist' attitude among American Jewry, which was then primarily occupied with securing a better status within American society. A new development in American Jewish life, namely more and more Jews moving from old Jewish neighbourhoods in the city centres to Christian neighbourhoods in suburban areas, which is an obvious sign of Jewish willingness to integrate into wider society, also required a new Jewish willingness to redefine and preserve Jewish identity within a gentile community. The increasing attendance at synagogues and affiliations with Jewish institutions, and the growing number of Jewish parents sending their children to Jewish schools, all appeared on the surface to be a Jewish religious revival, yet were actually the result of the need to create a 'socially' Jewish environment. So, it was not Jewish religiosity that was flourishing, but rather the number of Jewish institutions and Jewish participation in those institutions that were increasing – for quite instrumentalist reasons.[2] Perhaps it would be even more appropriate to interpret this trend of institutionalism as part of a growing secularization among American Jewry. For, 'the more secular society becomes', as Dow Marmur rightly asserts, 'the greater is the need for religious institutions'[3] to fill the spiritual gap through materialized means.

This being the case on the social level, Arnold Eisen in his *The Chosen People in America* observes an increasing Jewish interest in theology in that period. He points to the 'new Jewish theology' that emerged among the third-generation American Jews during the late 1940s and 1950s and would later draw emotional strength from the notion of chosenness.[4] In parallel to the universalist approach of the 1940s, in articles written on chosenness, this basic concept of Judaism would be interpreted in reference to the notion of a spiritual mission and be placed against the Teutonic idea of the master-race.[5] However, as regards the situation in the 1950s Yosef Gorny asserts that 'as the problem of existence eased' – through American Jewry's achievement of a speedy integration into American society and the creation of the Jewish state – 'the question of identity gained urgency and won increasing attention'.[6] Accordingly, the welcoming American attitude towards the Jews as well as the following Jewish need for a new way to present Jewish identity, from within, and the more religious orientation America was taking on, from without, led Jewish intellectuals to focus on the 'cultural, religious and existential' aspects of the question of Jewish identity.[7]

As brilliantly examined by Peter Novick in his *The Holocaust and Collective Memory*, during the immediate post-war period American Jews were careful not to bring up their ethnic particularity. In fact, this was the period in which an emphasis on unity and integration had prevailed in American society in general. In respect of American Jews, in particular, this was also the period that witnessed 'the rapid collapse of anti-Semitic barriers to Jewish ascent in every area of American life'.[8] As emphasized by various Jewish writers, American Jewry, especially the Reform wing, – during the process of integration in a wider society – were mainly occupied with issues related to social consciousness, such as 'supporting humanitarian causes', 'aiding the underprivileged', and 'helping blacks achieve equality'. These, they believed, were 'more important to being a good Jew than supporting Israel or observing the basic tenets of Judaism'.[9] Glazer asserts that although 'Judaism in America had been for a long time not much more than ethnic loyalty on the one hand and "liberalism" on the other', it was not before the late 1960s that the amalgam between ethnicity and religion, which had been current in American Jewish life up until this time, began to come apart, forming a more ethnic-oriented self-definition.[10] By the mid-1960s the Jews had already managed to successfully penetrate American society and had preserved their Jewish identity through institutionalism. Yet, they had also begun to face a continuity problem even more vividly than before. So the main reason for a growing sense of alienation among American Jewry, which would mount during the 1960s, was not fear of anti-Semitism, but rather that of the assimilation that they encountered after full integration into American society.

As pointed out by Glazer and others, before the late 1960s there was little concern about anti-Semitism among American Jews, and no major specific impact of the Holocaust or the creation of the state of Israel on Jewish self-definition before Israel's war of June 1967 (Six Day War).[11] It is interesting to note that in a survey conducted by *Commentary* magazine in 1966 the Holocaust did not figure among the questions, but the issue of chosenness was treated as a separate question. And, with the exception of the Reconstructionist rabbis, Mordecai Kaplan and Ira Eisenstein, two Conservative rabbis, Jacob Agus and Harold Schulweis, as well as Richard Rubenstein, the rest of a total of 38 respondents (Reform, Conservative, and Orthodox) confirmed the Jewish doctrine of the chosen people in one way or another. Moreover, the motive behind the doctrine of chosenness was mostly understood in traditional lines with reference to commitment to God and Torah in a covenantal relationship as well as a 'unique' responsibility/service and suffering/sacrifice.[12] Even if the idea of mission in terms of a 'spiritual vocation' was attached to their interpretation of chosenness, it was put in terms of a 'mysterious', yet astonishing, role that the Jews did and should play in the world. There was also an emphasis on the 'perennial *survival* of Israel' seen as a testimony to its chosenness.[13] This was, in effect, an apparent disassociation from the mission-centred American Jewish theology of the earlier periods. In other words, coming to the 1960s the disenchantment with the ideas of mission, universalism, and integrationism, which had once shaped first-generation American Judaism, had already begun to take place and would lead, in the 1970s, to the development of a new Jewish identity based on 'survival'.

At this point, the 1967 war is of great importance in terms of its influence, not only on the emergence of the American Jewish awareness of ethnicity and of the destruction of European Jewry, but also on the development of 'Holocaust chosenness'. This growing ethnic awareness and a concomitant interest in Israel, is seen by many as the direct result of some domestic and foreign socio-political developments such as the Eichmann trial of 1961, the fear of assimilation that was growing among the American Jews as well as the upheaval in American politics and the renewal of ethnicity in American life.[14] As indicated by Murray Polner and Adam Simms, the passage of the Civil Rights Act in 1964 and the publication of *Nostra aetate* by the Second Vatican Council in 1965 may have also helped to shift the central agenda of Jewish organizations from domestic-liberal causes, i.e. 'securing civil rights and ending anti-Semitism', to particularly Jewish ones.[15]

However, as stated above, the Jewish intellectuals had already begun to return to the traditional idea of chosenness by that time. So this emerging sensitivity on the question of chosenness in the 1950s and 1960s would intermingle in the 1970s, under the shadow of the rhetoric of the 'uniqueness' of the Holocaust, with a 'mysterious' sense of distinctiveness and a concomitant Jewish alienation from wider American society. European Jewry's survival of the Nazi camps, as much as it amazed American Jewry, would arouse the question of whether they were able to survive Americanization and assimilation this time.[16] On the other hand, the 1967 war, despite the fact that Israel 'was hardly in serious peril'[17] during the war and won an immediate victory in the end, would bring to Jewish minds the example of the Holocaust, due to the image in American and Israeli Jewish minds of Israel as an isolated and vulnerable country.[18]

As regards the question of why American Jews did not have a strong reaction to the extermination of European Jewry during or right after the Second World War (or even to the 1948 war), Novick points to two different explanations. One is based on the 'social unconscious' theory, which explains memory in relation to 'trauma' and 'repression'. According to this theory, the Holocaust had been 'a traumatic event' for American Jews and therefore they repressed their response to it during the immediate post-war years; but exploded in recent years through 'the return of the repressed'.[19] This explanation is widely accepted by Jewish scholars, despite the fact that during the post-war years the Holocaust survivors' deliberate choice to keep silent about their experience was because of the lack of interest of fellow Jews on the subject.[20] Besides, as emphasized by Novick, Neusner and others, even before the 1967 war, there was a certain emphasis on Nazi crimes in American and Jewish public thought, but it was more in relation to a universal danger attached to Nazi totalitarianism, and the 'problem of evil' as understood in general terms. Thus the general tendency was to see the Jews as constituting only one group among the various victims of the Nazis and to consider Nazism as a threat to all humanity.[21] 'Before June 1967', Norman Finkelstein, American Jewish historian, points out, 'the universalist message of concentration-camp survivor Bruno Bettelheim resonated among American Jews. After the June war, Bettelheim was shunted aside in favor of Wiesel', the result being a particular emphasis on the 'uniqueness of Jewish suffering' and the 'uniqueness of the Jews'.[22] As it is also apparent in the formulation of the question on the doctrine of the chosen people in *Commentary* magazine's survey and in the nature of the responses given to it, American Jews in 1966 were not aware of the idea of the uniqueness of the Nazi extermination. They were mainly concerned to show that the modern theories of national or racial superiority, finding their most hideous and deadly example in the racism of the Nazis, bore no real analogy to the Jewish doctrine of chosenness. So, what happened after the 1967 war was a primarily political shift from a universalist reception of Nazi totalitarianism to a uniquely Jewish interpretation of what is called the Holocaust, a shift which is based not on the past experience of the survivors, but rather on the perceptions of Americans, both Jew and non-Jew, of the current events.

And this takes us to the other explanation that Novick gives, which is based on the theory of 'collective memory' developed by Maurice Halbwachs, a French sociologist. According to this theory, memory is not something 'imposed' or given, but something 'chosen'. In other words, it works not through an imposed cycle of trauma, repression, and the return of the repressed, but by choices 'shaped and constrained by circumstances'.[23] 'Our conceptions of the past', Lewis Coser paraphrases Halbwachs, 'are affected by the mental images we employ to solve present problems, so that collective memory is essentially a reconstruction of the past in the light of the present'.[24] At this point, it is important to note what Judith

Plaskow, the American Jewish feminist scholar, states about the dynamic nature of memory, and particularly that of Jewish memory. 'As members of living communities', Plaskow writes, 'Jews continually re-member; we retell and recast the Jewish past in light of changing communal experience and changing communal values'.[25] For Novick, in the same way, what happens within the Jewish consciousness of the Holocaust can be best explained by the concept of collective memory, as a dynamic and re-shaping faculty that belongs to social groups.[26] For the emergence of the American Jewish awareness of the Holocaust after the 1967 war, that is the transformation of a marginalized event into a central symbol, of a history into a myth,[27] was not disconnected from the changing needs of American Jewry, or from changing American policies over some socio-cultural and political issues. As regards the changing needs of American Jews, Novick states that those were mainly the result of

> the decline in America of an integrationist ethos (which focused on what Americans have in common and what unites us) and its replacement by a particularist ethos (which stresses what differentiates and divides us).... The Holocaust, as virtually the only common denominator of American Jewish identity in the late twentieth century, has filled a need for a consensual symbol. And it was a symbol well designed to confront increasing communal anxiety about 'Jewish continuity' in the face of declining religiosity, together with increasing assimilation and a sharp rise in intermarriage...[28]

Again, as far as the changing circumstances in American cultural and political life are concerned, apart from the transformation from an integrationist into a particularistic ethos, Novick points to the changing American policy towards Israel, which demonstrated its strength in the 1967 war as 'a force to be deployed against the USSR and its clients in the Middle East'.[29] So, it was about a semi-conscious and semi-circumstantial decision made by American Jews as well as non-Jews to turn what had been understood as Nazi totalitarianism into the Jewish Holocaust. The similarity drawn between the position of European Jewry in the Second World War and that of the Israelis during the 1967 war could, and did, have a bearing for American Jewry only in the wake of certain circumstances.

Accordingly, as far as American Jews were concerned, the Holocaust did not pose a direct threat nor did it become a matter of concern in America during the 1950s, due to the prevalent circumstances, which offered the Jews an opportunity to integrate into American society, as well as the socio-political and cultural ethos that was at the time embraced by American society, namely universalism, integrationism, and optimism. Any talk of Jewish victimhood was not in the best interests of the Jews, not only in America but also in Europe and Israel. As Marc Ellis states, 'Western Jews were busy with life in Europe and America, and Jews in Israel were distancing themselves from suffering as a long, shameful chapter in Jewish history that they were determined to end'.[30] As regards the Israeli leaders' attitude to the Holocaust, Tom Segev, Israeli journalist and historian, asserts that for Ben-Gurion, like many other Zionists, the extermination of European Jewry was a catastrophe for Zionism as it jeopardized the chances of establishing a Jewish state. For if there were not enough Jews to build a country with, there would be no reason for the continuing existence of Zionism.[31] By the same token, the 1967 war would not pose a danger to American Jews if the circumstances in America had not been different then from those of the 1950s. In other words, the American Jewish awareness of the Holocaust in the wake of the 1967 war was primarily a reaction to a domestic, but serious, problem of spiritual and physical continuity. To meet the challenge of assimilation, American Jews resorted to the example of the Holocaust and proclaimed the traditional view even more strongly than ever before: Judaism is a national religion. The implication of this confirmation was, however, working from the Jewish people to Judaism, rather than from Judaism to the Jewish people: instead of 'if there are no Jews, then there is no Judaism', it read 'if there is no Judaism, then there are no Jews', a formula indicating the necessity to survive as a Jewish person. This is the situation that Michael Meyer points out by writing, 'Concern for the future of the Jews seems to run deeper than concern for the future of the *Jewish religion*'.[32] So, to answer the question of 'what differentiates us from other Americans' the Jews would turn to the example of the extermination of European Jewry. Because, first, as Novick argues, the emphasis on Jewish victimhood would mirror the changing American attitudes towards victimhood as a concept that was beginning to attain a positive implication; second, no concept or value other than Jewish victimhood would secure a place of unity and identity for American Jewry, who had mostly severed their ties with any distinctively religious principles or cultural traits.[33] In a similar way, Meyer points out that 'American Jewish identity was for most Jews either a religiously based morality or a loose bond of ethnic solidarity', but 'the rise in awareness of the Holocaust produced in many individuals a much more determined Jewishness'.[34] Again, Zionism, Novick argues, would function as 'a thin and abstract variety', considering the American Jewish lack of knowledge about Israel and the inner tensions going on within Israeli society at the time between the secular and the religious, between the hawks and the doves. As observed by Susser and Liebman, the example of the Holocaust would prove not only 'the "most vivid and ethnically alive" aspect of American Jewishness' but also the 'easiest and most accessible of Jewish themes to employ'.[35] The only common grounds for American Jews would thus be attributed to their East European background and the destiny attached to it. So, the need for a transformation among American Jews from integrationism into particularism, which was also the result of a similar transformation taking place within American society, would be reflected in mobilizing a Jewish awareness of the extermination of European Jewry. In other words, Jewish victimhood, which had been marginalized for various reasons[36] during the immediate post-war years, would be brought to the fore towards the late 1960s under the title of the Holocaust.[37]

It should be noted that American Jewish awareness of the Holocaust would also beget a concomitant attachment to the state of Israel, as the other component of American Judaism of Holocaust and Redemption. Moreover, the influence of the 1967 and, later, 1973 wars, especially the latter, would work in a similar way within Israeli society, namely as a means for unity and consolidation. Indeed, the result would be the emergence of an emotional tie to unify the Israelis, not only among themselves, but also with Diaspora Jewry.[38] This unification would be achieved on the basis of a common goal, namely 'survival'. This point is of particular importance in showing the intersection of the needs of two separate Jewish communities with one another. Both had a simultaneous need for unification and survival, and also adopted similar means to meet that need, by building up a new Jewish identity on the grounds of Jewish victimhood and redemption. In short, the emergence of the Holocaust consciousness among the American Jews, as well as the Israelis, and a more ethnocentric definition of Jewishness and Jewish religion were the result of a conscious Jewish choice made in the wake of some socio-political circumstances. What happened, in this way, was, as put by Neusner, the transformation of an 'historical memory' into an 'evocative symbol', which bore 'its own, unexamined, self-evident meanings', and imposed 'its own unanalyzed significance'.[39]

For the purpose of this book, the implications of the mythicization of the Holocaust in Jewish theology are of special importance in respect to the emergence of a new definition of Jewishness and chosenness. These implications would result, as mentioned earlier, in the creation of what is called Holocaust theology and a new version of chosenness, i.e. the Holocaust chosenness. In fact, the American Jewish insistence on the uniqueness of the Holocaust seems a tacit confirmation of the traditional Jewish belief that 'the Jews are a unique people'. However, the notion of Israel's uniqueness as embedded in the Holocaust chosenness differs from the traditional Jewish premise in certain aspects, which mainly concern the nature of uniqueness as defined by the Holocaust theologies.

It is a belief shared by all advocates of the uniqueness argument that the Jewish suffering in the Holocaust is of an unquestionably 'singular' nature. Yet the idea of uniqueness reveals different definitions in relation to the meaning attributed to the term. It is possible to mention some three grounds on the basis of which the understanding of uniqueness has been shaped in the Holocaust writings. These are what can be called 'transcendental (metaphysical)', 'qualitative (form-related)', and 'quantitative (scale-related)' understandings of uniqueness. The metaphysical uniqueness of the Holocaust is best represented by Emil Fackenheim, who argues that since the Jews have had a unique relation to the God of history and their collective survival alone was bound up with God, it is Jewish belief as well as Jewish life that is 'most traumatically', or uniquely, affected.[40] Again, Abraham Foxman, national director of the Anti-Defamation League, holds to a similar view by claiming that the Holocaust is a 'singular event' on the basis of its being an 'attempt on the life of God's chosen children and, thus, on God himself'.[41] Elie Wiesel, too, who is the champion of the rhetoric of the uniqueness of the Holocaust, believes that the Nazis targeted the Jewish God more than they targeted the Jewish people, or, to put it this way, they targeted the Jewish people on the basis of their God. Wiesel maintains that 'What the Germans wanted to do to the Jewish people was to substitute themselves for the Jewish God', as one SS soldier once said, 'We are your masters, even in the other world.'[42] In a similar vein, Irving Greenberg, Orthodox Jewish rabbi and theologian, asserts that 'to "destroy God", Hitler had to destroy God's witnesses, the Jewish people'.[43] The notion of the transcendental uniqueness of the Holocaust was, in fact, a by-product of a common view among the religious Jews that 'the Jew represents one thing in this world and it is religion'. Thus it follows that the rhetoric of uniqueness is directly related to the notion of Jewish chosenness.

For many Jews, however, the Holocaust was unique not on any metaphysical grounds but merely due to the rate of extermination or the means of destruction or even the ideology and irrationality underlying it. If we put aside the question of whether the Holocaust was really unique *in a unique way*,[44] the whole discussion of uniqueness, in which the Holocaust is rendered unprecedented and incomprehensible, and even undebatable, seems to serve for one thing: the mystification and mythicization of the Holocaust – as a 'sacred truth', as a 'new religion', for the Jews. Even for those who do not find any transcendental meaning attached to it, the Holocaust works as a 'mysterious' event. This is for no other reason than the 'unique status' applied to the Jews, be it in a secular or religious, direct or indirect way. The doctrine of the uniqueness of the Holocaust finds its thrust in the Jewish belief in being 'special'. 'Most American Jews', Charles Silberman asserts,

> no longer believe in a God active (or undemocratic) enough to choose one particular people, yet they continue to believe in their own specialness – in their own destiny as Jews. And this in turn serves to keep Jewishness alive even in those who have abandoned any semblance of a Jewish way of life.[45]

So, it is not even the '*suffering* of Jews' that matters, but the fact that '*Jews* suffered'.[46] Indeed, according to the advocates of the uniqueness doctrine, the Jewish suffering in the Holocaust is singular because

1   The Jews were killed by the Nazis solely for the reason of being Jews.
2   The Jews alone were the primary and ultimate target of the Nazis, whereas other peoples' victimhood was merely accidental and therefore of less worth.[47]

According to this understanding, the Holocaust is unique due to the 'fact' that what the Nazis intended to achieve was 'a messianic, global, even cosmic racial imperative commanding "that all Jews must die, and that they must die here and now"'.[48] Such a view, which is particularly upheld by Steven Katz, functions as a confirmation of the traditional Jewish idea of chosenness, by presenting itself within the opposite corner of the same spectrum. The Jews, being regarded as the only deliberate target of the Nazis, are rendered 'chosen' in both cases: either for life (the Sinai chosenness) or for death (the Holocaust chosenness). Accordingly, in their eyes, even if the Jews are not of an inherently transcendental identity, that quasi-religious non-Jewish hatred renders them so. In other words, unlike the pre-modern and, to a great extent, early modern parameters of Jewish self-definition, the Holocaust

Jewishness presupposes a uniqueness that is not necessarily or directly based on an inherent religious premise but rather on an externally forced and internally accepted pseudo-religious one. This understanding is best exemplified in a statement such as this: the Jews 'are chosen people because they have no choice. We are chosen: the choice is outside us'.[49] The Jews, due to the Holocaust, have been proven to be an everlastingly unique phenomenon, not only in the eyes of religious Jews, but also in the eyes of secular Jews, even non-Jews. In this way, even secular Jews, who do not normally picture Jewishness as a unique phenomenon, end up accepting that in the eyes of Jew-haters, at least those of the Nazis, Jews are a unique people. As confirmed by the liberal Jewish theologian, Eugene Borowitz, this 'over-determined hatred of the Jewish people' is understood by some Jews as the 'sign of something cosmic' about themselves.[50] It is exactly on this point that David Novak, Conservative rabbi and scholar, criticizes post-Holocaust Jewish theologies. According to him, the Jewish attempt to make the Holocaust 'the central orienting event for Jews' is nothing but an approval of Jewish secular distinctiveness.[51]

The insistence on the uniqueness of the Holocaust on the basis of the magnitude of the brutality or the techniques used in it does not automatically lead to a metaphysical or pseudo-metaphysical uniqueness. Insistence on a pseudo-messianic or pseudo-religious notion of the Holocaust, however, inevitably opens up the way to a transcendental uniqueness, even chosenness, by creating an unbridgeable gap and a fundamental difference between Jews and non-Jews, as well as between their sufferings. In this way, the Jewish insistence on the uniqueness of Jewish suffering becomes tantamount to an acceptance of a fundamentally different Jewish condition and existence, as Elie Wiesel writes: 'Everything about us is different'; 'Jews are "ontologically" exceptional'.[52] Ironically enough, this is exactly what the Nazis thought of the Jewish people – albeit in a negative sense. This is also what Ismar Schorsch, the chancellor of the Jewish Theological Seminary, points out by putting sarcastically, 'We are still special – but only by virtue of Hitler's paranoia'.[53]

It is important to note that the whole question of uniqueness and difference, under the surface of a negative identity, implies an apparent Jewish 'superiority', on the one hand, and a strong sense of 'particularism' and 'exclusivism', on the other.[54] As stated by Charles Silberman, 'it is Jews' monopoly on suffering that sets them apart from and makes them morally superior to others'.[55] For the uniqueness of Jewish suffering renders Jews not only a 'unique' but also an eternally 'innocent' people, while the other victims of Nazi extermination are regarded as 'by-products' of the Holocaust, namely the 'incidentally dead'.[56] The relation between a unique Jewish victimhood and an exclusive Jewish innocence is also emphasized by Gulie Ne'eman Arad, who maintains that the 'culture of victim', as represented by the uniqueness argument, renders Jews 'morally superior, as victims'. Arad also refers to the link built between victimhood and holiness, by highlighting the changing attitudes towards survivors and the concomitant terminology used for them:

> At first they were called 'survivors', which is a very neutral term. You can be survivor of anything, survivor of an earthquake, survivor of a car

accident. There's nothing unique about the term. Then they were made into 'martyrs'. But not all [are] martyrs. Because it was first only those who fought with weapon in hand [who] were martyrs. But then they became 'holy', *qedushim*. This is literally translated as 'holy people'; in other words, superior to you and me.[57]

As a matter of fact, in the absence of any purpose linked to Jewish survival, which is consummated by merely the psychology of 'never again', Jews are left with the feeling of otherness/difference, on the one hand, and that of superiority/betterness, on the other, feelings bereft of any positive essence/substance. This psychology of otherness and betterness, in fact, finds an open confirmation in some Jews, like Philip Roth. According to Roth, what an American Jewish child inherits from his parents is 'no body of law, no body of learning and no language, and finally, no Lord ... but a kind of psychology', which is translated as 'Jews are better'. 'There was a sense of specialness', Roth maintains, 'and from then on it was up to you to invent your specialness; to invent, as it were, your betterness'.[58] In a similar way, Charles Silberman also attests, 'Jews would have been less than human had they eschewed any notion of superiority whatsoever'.[59]

As for the sense of particularism and exclusivism promoted through the Holocaust uniqueness, this was the basis of its allure for American Jewry, in particular. For through that 'uniqueness', which is exclusively attached to Jewish suffering, all descendants of European Jewry are inevitably included in a 'mysterious' feeling of victimhood, innocence, and betterness, which, as a common denominator, shapes their unique/distinctive identity, while automatically leaving out other victims and survivors of the Nazi extermination. In fact, the appointing of the role of a common denominator to the Holocaust functions as a barrier, not only in relation to other peoples, but also in relation to other Jews, who were not of European origin. Indeed, one of the reasons for the ongoing conflicts between Ashkenazi (European) and Mizrahi (Eastern) Jews in Israel is attributed to the failure of the idea of the Holocaust uniqueness as a common denominator in Israel.[60] This is why the great stress placed on the Holocaust by American Jews is interpreted by many scholars as a worship of an 'American civil religion' or 'civil Judaism'.[61] To show the degree of the significance, even holiness, assigned to the Holocaust by American Jewry, Michael Goldberg writes: 'For them, the first of the Ten Commandments has been revised: "The Holocaust is a jealous God; thou shalt draw no parallels to it"'.[62] In the eyes of the proponents of the doctrine of the uniqueness of the Holocaust, such as Wiesel, 'the big truth' about the Holocaust was not its universal lessons but 'its Jewish specificity'.[63] At this point, Neusner points to the main, and perhaps the only, function of the Holocaust – as a symbol in the 'mythic life' of American Jewry – which is 'to explain to themselves the meaning of their distinctive existence as a group and of their individual participation in that group'.[64]

Nevertheless, the question of whether the Holocaust reveals any religious meaning or bears any religious connection – and, if so, in what sense – as a purely theological question, has witnessed a heavy debate among Jewish theologians and scholars. As indicated by Neusner, as far as some secular Jews are concerned, the Holocaust validated atheism. 'God could not stop those events, so is not God; or God could stop them but did not do so, so is evil'.[65] On the other hand, there were religious Jews, who found some kind of a religious meaning or purpose stemming from the Holocaust. They believed that it was inflicted on Jews by God as a punishment for their sins – as this was the explanation given for the previous catastrophes in Jewish history. However, those sins were understood in different, and sometimes contradictory, ways: assimilation,[66] support of Zionism, or even rejection of Zionism.[67] However, for some others like the modern Orthodox theologian, Eliezer Berkovits, any sort of sin on behalf of the Jewish people was out of the question. According to Berkovits, the Holocaust was not about punishment for any sins, but about the suffering of the innocent. It was the result of the fact that God let evil happen on earth for the sake of providing human beings with free will, to enable them to choose between right and wrong for themselves and be fully human (the idea of a long-suffering God).[68]

At the heart of the question of the religious significance of the Holocaust is, as indicated earlier, the Jewish belief in a special relationship between God and the Jewish people. However, the debates on the religious significance of the Holocaust involve not only the age-old problems of theodicy and the suffering of the innocent but also the rather modern phenomenon of historicism.[69] To borrow the division made by Neusner, it is possible to divide post-Holocaust Jewish theologies into two categories in relation to the theory of historicism: one is the 'Holocaust theology' (historicist) and the other the 'theology that takes account of the Holocaust' (non-historicist).[70] Holocaust theologies in general have a tendency to interpret the Jewish religion and Jewish faith in the light of historical events, particularly the Holocaust, and with apparent secular implications. As for the theologies that take account of the Holocaust, they rather receive and understand the Holocaust as well as other historical events within the eternal framework of revelation.

In parallel to the Jewish belief in a special relationship between God and the Jewish people, the big question facing Jewish theologians in the aftermath of the Holocaust was whether the Jewish faith stands firm or proves vulnerable in front of a historical challenge or catastrophe like the Holocaust. For some, the answer was in the negative. 'The faith of Israel', as asserted by Jonathan Sacks, Britain's chief rabbi,

> cannot be summarised in a set of theological statements which might be true whatever happened in space and time. It is peculiarly tied to the physical existence of the people of Israel.... If there were no Jews, Judaism would have proven to be false.[71]

In fact this is the point which both historicist and, to a certain extent, non-historicist Jewish interpreters of the Holocaust take into account. For the non-historicists as long as the Jewish people survive, no matter how great the catastrophe, the Jewish faith should continue, whereas for the historicists, even if the Jewish faith continues it does not remain unaffected.

For some non-historicists, the Holocaust is understood as a confirmation of the covenant between God and Israel. At this point, Orthodox Rabbi Mordechai Gifter wrote, 'For if, Heaven forbid, *Hashem* would have forsaken us, this *Churban* could never have occurred. The *Churban* itself is evidence and testimony to the fact that "we have a Father in Heaven"'.[72]

For religious Jews in general, what was confirmed through the Holocaust were simply the chosenness and greatness of the Jewish people and their centrality to world history. 'When other nations sin', Rabbi Gifter maintains, 'their actions did not make the imprint on the universality of history that the deeds of *Klal Yisrael* do.' Because, he goes on saying,

> History is not impressed by insignificant individuals; only the great *Klal Yisrael* occupies a central position in history as the *Am Hanivchar* (Chosen Nation) whose chosenness is manifested through times of redemption and through times of destruction. *Churban* is testimony to the status of *Klal Yisrael* as the *Am Hanivchar*.[73]

Some non-historicists, such as Berkovits, on the other hand, explicitly maintain that as vast and brutal a catastrophe as it was, the Holocaust has no unique bearing in the history of the Jewish people, either morally or theologically. Morally, because there is no difference between the suffering of many and of a single soul as far as the justice of God is concerned.[74] Theologically, because, as far as the Jewish experience as a whole and the problem of theodicy are concerned, the Holocaust, as another *hurban* (catastrophe) in Jewish history, is neither the first nor the last and, thus, carries no unique meaning.[75]

For the modern Orthodox theologian, Michael Wyschogrod, too, the Holocaust has no religious significance whatsoever; it gives Jews neither an opportunity to strengthen their faith nor a reason to question or abandon it. 'If there is hope after the Holocaust', Wyschogrod argues, 'it is because to those who believe, the voice of the Prophets speaks more loudly than did Hitler, and because the divine promise sweeps over the crematoria and silences the voice of Auschwitz.'[76] According to Wyschogrod, who sees the continuity of the Jewish religion as independent of any historical event,[77] the reality of the times when God is silent does not annihilate the existence of the 'wonderful favors bestowed by him', such as his love for Israel. This unconditional and eternal love of God for Israel is understood by Wyschogrod as the pinnacle of chosenness and also the very reason why Israel should praise God in every situation, including the Holocaust. For God's free love for Israel, which is the reason for the election of Israel, makes it obligatory for Jews to-be-ever-grateful to God.[78]

The Conservative Jewish scholar, David Novak, also takes up a non-historicist stance regarding the relation between faith and history, or Sinai and Auschwitz, albeit on a different premise. Whereas for Wyschogrod, God's arbitrary, unconditional and eternal love for Israel builds the foundation for the doctrine of chosenness, in Novak's thought nothing but the Torah, as a timeless truth, makes Jewish chosenness possible and meaningful, and therefore, irreversible, even in the face of Auschwitz. Novak writes:

> there is a responsibility to understand the historical context of the various utterances of the Torah's truth.... Nevertheless, this does not lead to relativism or historicism ... for a vertical responsibility to the historical continuity of the Jewish people as the covenanted people of God means that we regard history as the *medium* for the transmission of the Torah *to us*, not as Torah itself.[79]

Accordingly, for those who see the Sinai experience as the yardstick for an authentic Jewish faith, either in the sense of a mark of a covenant made between God and Israel or of God's unconditional love for Israel, 'the eternal Israel meets God in the Torah and through Sinai', irrespective of historical changes.

As far as the historicist interpretations are concerned, however, Israel's encounter with God in a covenant relationship finds or loses its meaning in accordance with the Holocaust experience. Among the most well-known advocates of the historicist interpretations of the Holocaust are Emil Fackenheim and Irving Greenberg, who created the Holocaust theology by placing the Holocaust at the centre of Jewish history and Jewish faith. What they have proposed is in effect a new view of covenant and chosenness, which is not based on Sinai but on Auschwitz. This new understanding of covenant and chosenness is represented by the terms the '614th commandment' (Fackenheim) and a 'broken covenant' (Greenberg). In both formulations what is suggested is a reaffirmation of the covenant between God and Israel, albeit on a totally new basis. First of all, survival is the key term in both theologies. Second, of the two parties which are essential to the traditional covenant relationship, namely divine and human, the latter is given an upper hand in the Holocaust theologies. Thus the new covenant is considered to be bound mainly with the decision, will, and wish of the Jewish people to survive. In this emphasis on survival, as the only commanding voice coming out of Auschwitz, faith seems not so much an issue. What is asserted in this way is a formulation that 'Jews must rely on themselves'.

As far as Fackenheim is concerned, both secular and religious Jews have only one duty in this post-Holocaust age, and it is to survive as a Jew, with or without faith. For Fackenheim, the Jewish need to respond to God (or to his absence) in the Holocaust, which is a repeating theme in his theology, is rendered compulsory not so much on the basis of the previously made divine covenant of Sinai, but more for the sake of giving Hitler no posthumous victory. 'To dedicate oneself as a Jew to survival in the age of Auschwitz', according to Fackenheim, 'is in itself a monumental act of faith'. Fackenheim confesses that he

> used to be highly critical of Jewish philosophies which seemed to advocate no more than survival for survival's sake. I have changed my mind. I now believe that, in this present, unbelievable age, even a mere collective

commitment to Jewish group-survival for its own sake is a momentous response, with the greatest implications.[80]

Greenberg, on the other hand, goes even further to declare a 'voluntary covenant' by saying that 'the covenant was broken but the Jewish people, released from its obligations, chose voluntarily to take it on again and renew it'.[81] He also adds that in the post-Holocaust age '[t]he ultimate goal will be achieved through human participation.... Human models, not supernatural beings will instruct and inspire mankind as it works toward the final redemption'.[82] In this way Greenberg sees the Holocaust as a turning point for a new stage in Jewish tradition as well as for a new pattern of faith. To justify his formulation of a 'voluntary covenant' Greenberg also comes up with the idea of three major stages in Jewish covenantal history with 'the innovative role' of the rabbis 'in further interpreting the meaning of the covenant'. Accordingly, after the previous two catastrophes, namely the destruction of the First and Second Temples, the interpretations of the rabbis displayed a transformation in their understanding of God and covenant. After the destruction of the First Temple, the dominant theme of rabbinic response centred on the idea that 'for our sins we are punished'. This was a result of the rabbinic understanding of covenant, in which God was seen as the absolute active party. After the destruction of the Second Temple, the rabbis understood the motive behind that catastrophe as being that of a mainly self-refraining God, rather than that of an interfering and punishing one. This kind of interpretation, too, took place due to the changing rabbinic understanding of covenant, in which the divine and human parties were understood to participate more equally. As for the Holocaust, through this catastrophe the Jewish history of covenant has entered a new stage that requires a more radical response than those of the previous two stages. This new stage, for Greenberg, displays a 'broken covenant' on the side of God and a 'voluntary covenant' on the side of the Jewish people.[83]

Elie Wiesel, too, sees the Holocaust experience as central to Jewishness and to Jewish faith, due to the covenantal relationship between God and the Jewish people. This is, in fact, what Wiesel indicates by suggesting that 'the Holocaust may be compared with Sinai as revelatory significance'.[84] Wiesel finds God guilty of forsaking European Jewry, on the basis of a 'unique' relationship established at Sinai. Yet Wiesel, in a similar way to Fackenheim and Greenberg, proposes a middle way between godlessness and an unbroken faith, by attacking the notion of a caring and active God yet, at the same time, refusing to abandon Judaism.[85] On the other hand, Richard Rubenstein pushes further the idea of a voluntary covenant by rejecting the traditional God of covenant and election altogether.[86] As paraphrased by Oliver Leaman, Rubenstein claims that after Auschwitz '[w]hat is required is a form of Judaism without God, and consequently without the notion that the Jews have a special relationship with such a deity'.[87]

For almost all Jewish theologians, however, who write about the Holocaust, the covenant is still there, albeit with different premises. In fact, the Holocaust theologians, by seeing the Holocaust as an unquestionably unique episode in the history of humankind and a cardinal event of important theological implication in the history of Jewish people, have been confirming the idea of covenant in one way or the other. If one should denounce the Jewish idea of covenant and concomitant belief in Jewish uniqueness, there would be little reason for insisting on the uniqueness of the Holocaust, especially in a transcendental sense. However, the notion of covenant as proposed by the Holocaust theologians, in effect, is based on the need for eliminating God, at least as an active entity, from the lives of Jews and declaring a new covenant based on new conditions which demand first of all the survival of the Jewish people. Thus, in this new covenant, the priority shifts from the demands of God on Israel to the needs of the Jewish people, from an ultimately religious and universal mission to a primarily and ethnically Jewish redemption. And this is the point that takes us to the other component of American Judaism of Holocaust and Redemption, namely the role of the state of Israel in the Jewish faith and destiny.

As emphasized by Neusner, if the first lesson to be deduced from the Holocaust is that 'the gentiles wiped out the Jews of Europe, so are not to be trusted', the second should be 'if there had been the State of Israel there would have been no Holocaust; and so for the sake of your personal safety, you have to support Israel'. In this way, the state of Israel and its achievements are seen as what gives 'meaning and significance, even fulfillment, to "the Holocaust"', as 'the redemptive myth'.[88] On the other hand, as indicated by Ellis, secular Zionists in Israel take advantage of this myth to gain political and economic support from American Jewry and world-wide sympathy for the existence of a Jewish state and its expanded occupation in Palestine.[89]

Nevertheless, regarding the theological implications of the relation between the Holocaust and the state of Israel, one representing suffering and the other redemption, Jewish scholars held different opinions. For the traditional the connection was supernatural in nature; for the less traditional it was a 'causal nexus'.[90] In Israel, the view of the creation of the state of Israel (1948) and the settlement of the occupied territories (1967) as a stage in the coming divine redemption is fervently supported by the religious-Zionist segment of the society, and particularly by Gush Emunim, the fundamentalist organization founded after the 1967 war. Among those American Jews, who find a direct and positive relation between the Holocaust and the state of Israel, in a religious sense, Greenberg deserves a special mention. He wrote that 'if the experience of Auschwitz symbolizes that we are cut off from God and hope, and the covenant may be destroyed, then the experience of Jerusalem symbolizes that God's promises are faithful and His people live on'.[91] In Fackenheim's thought, however, although there might be found a causal connection between the Holocaust and the rise of the state of Israel, 'any attempt to justify Israel on the grounds that it is the answer to the Holocaust' is 'intolerable'. This is so for Fackenheim, because 'No purpose, religious or otherwise non-religious, will ever be found in Auschwitz. The very attempt to find one is blasphemous'.[92] For Rubenstein, on the other hand, no matter what position other theologies hold regarding the Holocaust, one particular bizarre but genuine explanation, that 'because the Jews are God's

Chosen people, God wanted Hitler to punish them',[93] was a direct result of the (traditional) doctrine of chosenness.[94] Thus, in the face of this dramatic reality what Rubenstein suggests as the only way out is to normalize or mediocritize the Jewish people by recognizing the Reconstructionist view, namely that what makes a religion unique is its civilization and not its being 'the centre of the divine drama of perdition, redemption, and salvation for mankind'.[95] So, the question for Rubenstein becomes not so much why did God let his people suffer in that way, but rather why one particular people should be either chosen or rejected by God. This is why neither the creation of the state of Israel nor the Six Day War is, for Rubenstein, a 'royal road back to the God of History'.[96] Nevertheless, Jewish insistence on the uniqueness of the Holocaust would serve for nothing but the restoration of the Jewish people back into the centre of a world drama, one that is written by Hitler, this time, instead of God.

Thus, the idea of a unique Jewish suffering has both theological and existentialist implications for Jews. Either the relationship between God and the Jewish people (religious point) or the existence of the Jewish people per se (secular point) should be regarded so unique, special, and indispensable that they would work, in both cases, towards the creation of a civil religion of the Holocaust and Redemption. The reason why many Jews see the Holocaust as unparalleled and unique, in relation to the history of both Jews and humankind, lies primarily within the notion of the chosenness/uniqueness of the Jews (transcendental/pseudo-religious uniqueness), and only secondarily within the claim that the Holocaust represents a greater/higher evil in terms of scale and brutality. As indicated earlier, even this second reason can be seen as a direct result of the first, that is to say, if the Jews are, or should be, unique, then their suffering must be unique too. The problem of theodicy,[97] which is mainly a 'universal' phenomenon and therefore minimizes the amount of Jewish particularity embedded in the Holocaust, takes a significant place in Holocaust discussions mainly in relation to the 'particular' nature of the Jewish encounter with God's presence/absence in history. So it goes without saying that it is the uniqueness of the Jewish people, as a traditional Jewish belief, that renders the Jewish encounter with God or with history a particular phenomenon, which in turn underlines the uniqueness of the Holocaust and of Jewish suffering.

Nevertheless, as far as the question of Jewish suffering in general is concerned, there happens to be one substantial difference between traditional and modern Jewish responses on the one side and the Holocaust response on the other. It is certain that, even in traditional and modern Jewish theologies, Jewish suffering was understood as a unique phenomenon due to its transcendental meaning. Yet, it was also pre-justified in relation to the idea of the chosen people. It has been a common view in Jewish tradition that the Jewish people, on the basis of their being the chosen people/witnesses of God, are meant to suffer more than any other people do. This notion, in fact, has a two-fold character related to biblical and rabbinic interpretations of two different types of sufferings: one as punishment and the other as vicarious suffering. Yet both were understood to function as a confirmation of the chosenness of the Jewish people.

In relation to Jewish suffering as punishment, Amos 3:2 can be seen as the best example, which reads, 'You only have I known of all the families of the earth; therefore I will punish you for all your iniquities'. Again, a similar theme of suffering as punishment runs through the books of Deuteronomy (11:26 and chs 28, 31) and Leviticus (ch. 26). The corresponding idea in rabbinic literature occurs in several passages, in one of which it is written: 'Israel will be redeemed through five things only, through distress, through prayer, through the merits of the fathers, through repentance, and through the End' (*Midr. Ps.* 229a).[98] As for the vicarious suffering, it is exemplified by the theme of the 'suffering servant of God' as appears in Isaiah 53:5, 'he was wounded for our transgressions, crushed for our iniquities', which is understood to refer to the people of Israel. Again, the notion of the vicarious suffering of the Jewish people for the sins of other nations is presented in quite a few rabbinic passages, such as this: 'As the dove atones for sins, so the Israelites atone for the nations' (*Cant. R.* 15:1).

Moreover, when we look carefully into the rabbinic literature we notice that the general tendency among the rabbis was to interpret even the most problematic passages in Scripture in a rather positive way.[99] As strongly advocated by Berkovits,

> the men of faith in Israel, each facing his own Auschwitz, in the midst of their radical abandonment by God, did not hesitate to reject the negative resolution of the problem ... even though the Jewish people were fully aware of the conflict between history and teaching, yet they staked their very existence ... on the view that all history was ultimately under divine control, that all depended on doing the will of God, on living in accordance with his Torah.[100]

There has certainly been some variation between different rabbinic works in terms of the extent and the way in which they discussed the question of suffering in general. However, while rabbinic discussions of suffering were mostly generated in relation to the suffering of the individual rather than the suffering of the people, the difference of opinion among ancient rabbis was usually the result of social and political conditions and varying scholarly approaches as well as, and even more than, different disasters.[101] On the other hand, although in most rabbinic passages different reasons are given for the destruction of the First and Second Temples, these are mostly products of the same period and the general approach underlying those reasons does not differ from one another. In both cases, the destruction of the Temple is attributed to Israel's failure to conduct themselves correctly in one way or another.[102]

In short, in traditional Jewish thought the suffering of the Jewish people was unique only in religious, not humanitarian, terms. Jewish suffering, unlike the suffering of non-Jews, was regarded as bearing a transcendental and a positive, affirmative meaning. Positive, because even in the case of suffering as punishment the outcome was a confirmation of God's continuing concern for the Jews. This was a relation between a transcendental (Jewish) and an ordinary (non-Jewish) suffering, rather than a greater and a lesser suffering. In Holocaust Jewish theologies, however, two new meanings are attributed to Jewish suffering as experienced in Auschwitz. In relation to God, the Holocaust is seen as his betrayal of the covenant with the Jewish people. In reference to the Jews, however, their suffering is bestowed with even more uniqueness. Thus the Holocaust is considered unique not only in relation to the mundane sufferings of other peoples, but also in relation to previous Jewish sufferings. It is unique because it is both transcendental and unprecedented. It is unique not only because Jews are 'transcendentally' unique, but also because they have to be 'unprecedentedly' unique. This is also the answer to the question asked by some, like Gulie Arad, as to 'why Jews keep the Holocaust alive', since 'when one goes to a terrible trauma the natural way is to forget it'.[103]

The Jewish insistence on the uniqueness of the Holocaust makes sense only when one takes into account the fact that the Holocaust is seen by the Jews as a sacred truth, rather than as an extremely dreadful (and in many ways unprecedented) earthly catastrophe, like many other peoples did, and do, experience at some point in the course of history. In the absence of religiously/culturally fed Jewishness (positive factor) and of a provoking anti-Semitism (negative factor), both of which had worked to preserve Jewish identity in the past, the Holocaust, as put by Ismar Schorsch, becomes 'the primary source of fuel to power Jewish life in America'.[104] In this way, the claim to uniqueness proves important for the majority of American Jews for quite instrumentalist purposes. This is, perhaps, what is implied in an anonymous saying that 'He who mourns more than necessary does not mourn for the deceased but for someone else', perhaps even for himself. So what happens here is a sanctification of an historical event for social and psychological reasons. The uniqueness of the Holocaust is crucial to Jewish self-definition because it is the sole guarantor of their 'uniqueness', and their uniqueness is, in turn, the sole guarantor of their 'survival'. At this point, Arthur Hertzberg refers to the fact that the Holocaust awareness among Jews began 'at the point when anti-Semitism in America had become negligible'. He maintains,

> Every major area of American life ... was open to Jews.... Middle-aged parents saw what freedom had wrought and became frightened at the evaporation of the Jewishness of their children. The parents evoked the one Jewish emotion that had tied their own generation together, the fear of anti-Semitism. The stark memory of Auschwitz needed to be evoked to make the point that Jews were different.... Those who come [to the Holocaust memorials in the USA] to remember are transformed in this shrine into participants in the great sacrifice. They are confirmed in their Jewishness, leaving with 'never again' on their lips.[105]

In this way, a new form of anti-Semitism, Holocaust anti-Semitism, was introduced into the Jewish consciousness as the main denominator of Jewish self-definition, and a new form of Jewish–gentile opposition. David Stannard maintains that at the heart of the uniqueness of Jewish suffering there is the dichotomy of being a 'chosen Jew' and an 'un-chosen non-Jew'.[106] Again, according to Schorsch, the Jewish 'obsession with uniqueness is a "distasteful secular version of chosenness" which introduces pointless enmity between Jews and other victims'.[107] Under the banner of the Holocaust, Jews, both in America and Israel, would come to see the relations between Jews and non-Jews from the perspective of separation and particularism. At this point Novick states that '[t]o the extent that one became convinced that only Jews could be depended upon to care about Jews, it made less and less sense for Jews to care about those who didn't care about them'.[108] Again, as stated by Meyer, after the 1967 war Judaism in the Israeli mind was also 'associated with an intense particularism that values the Jews above others'.[109]

In fact, the portrayal of Jewish–gentile relations in such antagonistic terms, reintroduced by the Holocaust experience, lies in an age-old view in Jewish tradition, which grasps humanity through the spectacles of 'us' and 'them', 'Jews' and 'gentiles', Jacob and Esau, elected and diselected or rejected.[110] It was mainly the example of the conflict between Jacob and Esau that shaped the Jewish perception of other nations. According to a well-known rabbinic teaching, 'Esau [the gentile] is not really capable of kissing Jacob [the Jew] ... even when he appears to do so; what seems to be a kiss is, in fact, a bite'. This perception, which was abandoned to a great extent with Jewish Emancipation, was given a new credence through the experience of the Holocaust.[111] Indeed, some antagonistic statements made by rabbis in the past, which were mainly the product of hard times when Jews were oppressed by non-Jews, would be frequently repeated in Holocaust writings and even turn into a norm for Jewish–gentile relationships. Lucy Dawidowicz, an American Jewish historian of the Holocaust, would see the Holocaust 'as the result of an active (but negative) interrelationship between the Jewish and gentile worlds, a clash between the Jewish uniqueness and the gentile unwillingness to accept it'.[112] Again, Cynthia Ozick, an American Jewish novelist, in her famous article, 'All the world wants the Jews dead', would write, 'The world wants to wipe out the Jews ... the world has always wanted to wipe out the Jews'.[113] On the other hand, in Israel, right after the victory of the 1967 war, the most popular song would be 'The Whole World Is against Us'.[114] To recall the theory of collective memory, the way in which the Jewish perception of themselves and others works refers to the fact that although 'collective memory is essentially a reconstruction of the past in the light of the present', it is 'made of continuity as well as change'.[115] In a similar way, Plaskow points to the interaction between past and present, writing that the 'remembered past provides the basis for a particular present, but the nature of the present also fosters or inhibits particular kinds of memory'.[116] Applying this principle to the case of the Holocaust, it becomes clear that, while on the surface Jewish collective memory based on the example of the Holocaust presents a new Jewish condition in parallel to the requirements of the present circumstances, it also repeats, underneath, the deep-down and age-old Jewish dilemma of seeing the world from the perspective of the Jacob–Esau conflict. The whole question of Jewishness becomes in this way tantamount to being a product of people's memories.

In the light of these remarks, what is of particular importance for our purposes is that the Holocaust chosenness, which is based on the notion of the uniqueness of Jewish suffering, differs from the traditional and modern versions of chosenness, namely holiness and mission, respectively, in two basic points. First, unlike previous concepts of chosenness, the Holocaust chosenness proposes a 'negative' identity, negative in the sense that it negates something instead of verifying something, which can be best demonstrated by Fackenheim's well-known formula: 'not to give Hitler any posthumous victory'. This formula, presented as the second *Shema Yisrael*[117] by Fackenheim, would control the American Jewish socio-political arena throughout the 1970s and 1980s in the form of 'never again': 'No second Auschwitz, no second Bergen-Belsen, no second Buchenwald – anywhere in the world, for anyone in the world!' It is possible to see this psychology of 'never again', in relation to what Hitler did to European Jewry in Auschwitz, as a post-Holocaust equivalent of a positive biblical command to 'remember', referring to how God rescued Israel from bondage in Egypt.[118] However, while the same themes of 'oppression, deliverance, and liberation' are available in cases or stories of both, i.e. Exodus and the Holocaust, the differences between them are considerable. According to Michael Goldberg, one of those differences is related to the question of confirming or repudiating God and the covenant, as he writes:

> The Exodus narrative would have us see Israel's outliving Egyptian persecution as evidence of a powerful God who makes and keeps generation-spanning covenants. But if we view Jewish existence through the perspectives of a Holocaust-shaped narrative, neither God nor covenant worked to save the Jewish people from Hitler…[119]

Moreover, Goldberg refers to two opposite messages, as attributed to the stories of Exodus and the Holocaust, by asserting that

> For the Israelites, deliverance meant more than merely getting out of Egypt; freed from Egyptian servitude, they were free to enlist in God's service as a "kingdom of priests and a holy nation" (Ex. 19:6). By contrast, for those rescued from Auschwitz and Bergen-Belsen, there was no goal beyond getting out alive. For such as these, survival itself became not a means to an end, but instead an end, a mission, in and of itself.[120]

This, in fact, refers to the second point differentiating post-Holocaust chosenness from its traditional and modern versions. Accordingly, the Holocaust chosenness grounds itself on a mainly 'existential' condition or status, which is to be fulfilled by mere 'survival'. Despite the fact that Jewish survival, as a commanding voice emerging from the Holocaust, was believed to refer to a meaning still-to-be-found in life and a hope for the redemption of humanity (the *tikkun* idea), survival (form) was regarded as preceding the purpose (content). Fackenheim, for example, believed that in the face of the most cruel and unprecedented idolatry of the Hitler regime, what a Jew is required to do is to reaffirm his mission of testifying against the idols, which once was trivialized through the Emancipation.[121] So, although this testimony, in the case of victims, was without their own choice, survivors could and must reaffirm it freely and consciously. In this way, Fackenheim seems to find a kind of connection between the modern Jewish situation and the past religious understandings, and presuppose a return to these as an inevitable prerequisite for Jewish survival. However, he also makes the Holocaust an overruling constituent in Jewish faith and Jewish self-definition by formulating the 614th commandment and placing it somewhere before the other 613 biblical commandments, which suggests a kind of survival primarily for the sake of survival. The contrast between the traditional notion of 'holiness', as well as that of 'mission', stemming from the Sinai experience, which requires Jews not only to 'be' but also, and more importantly, to 'become' something, and that of 'survival' for its own sake, which rises from the Holocaust experience, is striking. This emphasis on survival would in effect lead to a great anxiety among many Jewish scholars as early as the 1970s, as indicated above.[122]

As a matter of fact, in its two earlier, i.e. pre-modern and modern, uses, 'chosenness' also partly implied a kind of existential, inescapable, and mysterious reality, particularly in the case of holiness. As we have seen in previous parts, that reality was regarded, in the pre-modern period, as the reference point for God's unconditional love, on the one hand, and for an inevitable gentile hatred, on the other.[123] On the other hand, in the modern period, existentialist Jewish theologies, and particularly that of Rosenzweig, proposed the notion of 'being Jewish' in a minimalist and existentialist definition of the term. However, even in the existentialist theology of Rosenzweig the bottom line was not survival but a special/ existential awareness of being covenanted to God and the concomitant responsibilities, both particularist and universalist. So this was the case in the traditional existentialist interpretation of holiness too, notwithstanding certain exceptions. Alongside the notion of an eternal and mysterious, even genetic, divine chosenness as advocated by Judah Halevi in particular, there was also a more common acceptance that the Jews were holy/special/chosen only in relation to the Torah, as advocated by Saadiah Gaon.

As far as Holocaust chosenness is concerned, however, what is quite new and distinct, in terms of uniqueness (of the Holocaust and therefore of the Jews), is very much related to its two-fold nature. First, what is proposed with the example of the uniqueness of Jewish suffering is mere survival, representing almost a total withdrawal from the ideas of mission and responsibility of earlier periods, making the Jews hooked on their self-preservation alone. At this point, it is worth noting a stimulating comparison, made by Schorsch, between the medieval Jewish response to the catastrophic expulsion of Spanish Jewry in 1492 and the modern Jewish response to the Holocaust. In his comparison, Schorsch refers to the sixteenth-century Safed Kabbalists who, by using 'the symbol of the broken vessels', interpreted the 'trauma of exile' as 'built into every stage of the world's unfolding'.' According to this symbolism, the hole or the chaos, which emerged as a result of God's contraction into himself (in order to give man freedom of choice), would be fixed through the task of restoration (*tikkun*). This task provided 'each Jew with the two-fold task of restoring harmony to his own soul and of advancing the completion of creation'.[124] In other words, the atmosphere of despair and imbalance created by God's becoming passive was encountered not by turning the Jews into a self-centred and static entity (survivalism), as is the case in the Holocaust response, but by attributing to Jews even a more active role (restoration) in the perfection of creation as well as the condition of exile. Despite the fact that the same kabbalistic tradition also engendered a substantialist interpretation of chosenness, by assuming a fundamental difference between Jewish and non-Jewish souls,[125] Schorsch's emphasis on the active and positive nature of this kabbalistic response to Jewish expulsion is still crucially important.

As for the second point, Holocaust chosenness is employed by Jews to ameliorate a particular condition instead of that particular condition being understood as the verification for chosenness. To put it this way, in the previous use, because Jews were 'chosen' – either literally by God (pre-modern) or symbolically through their own spiritual genius (modern) – they were supposed to become something, namely holy, obedient, or on a mission, and endure a particular condition, namely suffering, exile, and so on. In the case of Holocaust chosenness, however, as Jews are something, namely they are in danger of assimilation or facing the problem of physical/spiritual continuity or simply in an insecure condition, they need to be unique. For uniqueness, as applied to the Holocaust experience, is the best means to mobilize unity among Jews and secure their survival in this way. This is, in effect, a re-introduction of the traditional idea of chosenness into American Jewish life for quite instrumentalist reasons. In this way, 'uniqueness' (content) follows 'survival' (form). This is also the point that indicates the impact of the post-modern condition on this new version of chosenness: the priority of 'form' over 'content'.[126] As asserted by Glazer, both in the case of the 'survivalism' of the 1970s and 'transformationism' of the 1980s, to remain Jewish (form) in one way or another would be given the highest priority, with not much significance being attributed to the way (content) in which Jewishness was being preserved.[127] Moreover, the Holocaust emphasis on particularism and the sense of uncertainty or even despair (of the late 1960s and 1970s) as set against universalism and optimism of the previous periods (the 1940s and 1950s) is also another sign of an apparent post-modern condition effective during that period. On the other hand, the Jewish identification of the Holocaust with irrationality and mystery seems to have played an important role in the creation of an inexplicable and mysterious sense of chosenness, as described in many Jewish writings of the 1960s and 1970s.[128]

There is also one further point that confirms the reversal nature of the Holocaust chosenness, as based on the idea of a unique victimhood and survival. This point, in fact, displays itself in comparison with the attitude of early Zionism to Jewish particularity. In fact, the Holocaust chosenness with its emphasis on uniqueness and anomaly has reversed what was an aim of Zionism, namely, the normalization of the Jewish people through the normalization of their condition. Early Zionism, too, proposed some kind of particularity, even superiority, mainly in ethnic or national terms. However, notwithstanding the

Jabotinsky type of militarist Zionism, the sense of particularity and superiority generated by Zionism was understood in relation to a colonialist (political Zionism) or messianic (social and cultural Zionism) role that it was to play, as much as in relation to the fact that there was a unique status to preserve on the part of the Jewish people. In the Zionist messianic emphasis of certain socialist and cultural Zionists the uniqueness of the Jews was understood, not only for their own sake, but also in relation to their putative messianic role in the world. In other words, the Zionists' claim to Jewish chosenness depended on some sort of unfulfilled redemption whose completion was regarded as their duty – at least it was what was promised.

As far as Holocaust chosenness is concerned, however, within the rhetoric of the Holocaust and Redemption, Jewish victimhood has a redemptive effect, in a similar way to that of the crucifixion of Jesus, as understood in Christianity.[129] The emblematic victimhood of the Jews, i.e. their chosenness by the Nazis as the main target, is read into their redemptive uniqueness (passive chosenness), which was fulfilled by the creation of the state of Israel, rather than into their ongoing universal–messianic role (active chosenness). The Jewish chosenness stemming from the uniqueness of the Holocaust, as Levi Olan rightly states, 'more adequately fits the Christian doctrine of the vicarious atonement than his role of witness to the living God who chose Israel to be a light unto the nations'.[130] In other words, the process of turning the Jewish suffering in Auschwitz into a unique phenomenon becomes at the same time a process of turning the Jewish anomaly, which ironically both the classical Reform Jews and the early Zionists tried to cure, into an eternal Jewish condition, and even a matter of identity, for all Jewry. Moreover, it is this culture of uniqueness and distinctiveness that shapes contemporary Zionism – in America as well as in Israel – by engendering a self-justified and self-redemptive discourse.

It is also important to note that what are called the lessons of the Holocaust referring to Jewish centrality to humanity, meaning in life and hope for redemption, prove almost void in the face of the uniqueness rhetoric. Indeed, according to Ismar Schorsch, the Jewish 'fixation on uniqueness has prevented us [Jews] from reaching out by universalizing the lessons of the Holocaust'.[131] Again, Michael Goldberg makes a similar point by asserting that 'in saying that there are no significant similarities [with other sufferings] that matter, we will be saying in effect that the Holocaust lacks any real significance beyond itself, then in the end, it was only an historical oddity'.[132] Accordingly, this is the way in which the unparalleled, unique, even sacred, Jewish victimhood functions as a payoff, as a confirmation of Jewish uniqueness and distinctiveness. In other words, this is a confirmation not of the Jews' unique role *for* the world (mission) but of their unique status *in* the world (survival).

After this long introductory section to the post-Holocaust Jewish understanding of chosenness, next will be a survey of specific interpretations and applications of it in both American and Israeli Jewish communities.

9   The American experience

Reform Judaism

Among all American Jewish congregations, Reform Judaism is certainly the one that most radically severed itself from its original discourse. Perhaps this is not so unusual, considering the progressive and somewhat radical nature adopted by the movement right from the beginning. American Reform Jewry has been quite successful in using the early German Reform emphasis on going with the spirit of time, but after the 1960s this turned out to mean a withdrawal from the principles of universalism and rationalism. In their answers to *Commentary* magazine's question on chosenness in 1966, Reform rabbis and scholars referred to notions such as 'unique experiences of Jewry', 'the miracle of Jewish survival', 'mystery', 'myth', 'historic fact', 'messianic hopes' as well as the 'uniqueness of the covenant' and 'special responsibility'. 'What Judaism can contribute to the world', Eugene Borowitz wrote:

> is not an idea or a concept. What Judaism can uniquely give to the world is Jews ... that live by their social, messianic hopes.... The story of the survival of this improbable people is its chief testimony. Just by being here, the Jewish people is an evidence of hope.[1]

This rhetoric of survival is also observed in the statement of principles adopted in the Centenary Perspective of 1976. It is important to note that it was held not in the immediate post-war period of the 1950s or 1960s – i.e. not as a response to the end of the Second World War or to the creation of the state of Israel – but in the years following the 1967 and 1973 wars, which had helped to create a discourse of a unique Jewish suffering and survival as embodied in the Holocaust. In the opening section of the statement ('One hundred years: what we have learned') 'the survival of the Jewish people' is declared as being 'of highest priority'. There is also a special praise of 'pluralism' and 'particularism', alongside an underlying unity, which was believed to have been established by the survival of the people, despite all the inner differences. The early Reform insistence on defining Judaism as a religion and the Jews as a religious community is clearly seen to have given way to a new definition of Jewishness, based on 'an uncommon union of faith and peoplehood'. The statement continues, 'Born as Hebrews in the ancient Near East, we are bound together like all ethnic groups by language, land, history, culture, and institutions'. In addition to this emphasis on the ethnic and cultural aspects of Jewishness, the process of withdrawal from the idea of mission, which had partly been introduced into the movement through the Columbus Platform (1937), becomes even clearer in the Centenary Perspective (1976). Here what the Jewish people are supposed to achieve is presented as a 'unique' existence instead of a universal mission. In parallel to this, it is also suggested that the Jews are 'to be less dependent on the values of' western society and 'to reassert what remains perennially valid in Judaism's teaching'. What this suggests is a shift from the principles of the Enlightenment and the spirit of Emancipation, as exemplified in Jewish integration with wider western society, to a more traditional and more particularist, in short, a more Jewish, way of life.

This American Reform emphasis on 'separation' and 'uniqueness' on the part of the Jewish people is also apparent in the new prayer book. The English version of the *Aleinu* prayer reads: 'We must praise the Lord of all, the Maker of heaven and earth, who has set us apart from the other families of earth, giving us a destiny unique among the nations'.[2] In the Hebrew text, on the other hand, which is the same as the traditional one used in both Orthodox and Conservative synagogues, a negative account of other nations with a repeated stress on the Jews being not like them has been preserved:

> We must praise the Lord of all, the Maker of heaven and earth, who has not made us like the nations of the earth, and has not placed us like the families of the earth, and has not assigned unto us a portion as unto them...[3]

The reason for retaining the Hebrew version of the prayer in the new prayer book is attributed, for the most part, to the fact that the rhythm of the Hebrew text better suits the melody during recitation in the service. What is even more important is that in both the Hebrew and English versions of the prayer, as they appear in the new prayer book, there is no mention of 'God's giving Israel the Torah', which is present in the British Reform version of the prayer: '...who has chosen us from all peoples by giving us His Torah'.[4] Nor is there any explicit reference to 'chosenness', with the omission of the word *bahar* (chose), which, as seen above, is also kept in the British version. At this point, it is worth noting that the exclusivist language, which is central to the traditional Jewish prayer book, seems to be greatly played down in the British Reform prayer book, despite a continuing emphasis on chosenness. The idea of being chosen for service is specifically highlighted in the *Aleinu* prayer, while any negative attribute given to other nations is omitted. As a matter of fact, the same applies to the general attitude of the British Reform congregation towards the idea of chosenness, which, unlike the American Reform, retains an apparent universalist and mission-centred language.[5] In the American version of the *Aleinu* prayer, however, the emphasis is placed on 'separation' by virtue of a unique Jewish destiny, instead of 'chosenness' for the sake of the Torah, covenant, and mission. Nevertheless, under the banner of 'Special themes', a later addition to the prayer book, the question of 'Israel's mission' is separately addressed, in which the doctrine of chosenness is presented in terms of serving God, being a witness to the world, and possessing the Torah. Again, during the Sabbath morning service the sages and teachers of all faiths are praised for having brought many to a deeper understanding of God and His will.[6] Apart from the fact that there is an apparent tension between these two emphases, namely separation and uniqueness on the one hand and responsibility and mission on the other, the stand taken by American Reform Judaism seems overall more pro-separation than pro-mission. Indeed, one immediate result of this recent Reform emphasis on separation and particularity is an emerging Jewish concern with the meaning of Judaism, first and foremost, for the Jews themselves rather than for the world. The American Reform movement, Nathan Glazer writes,

> once so concerned with formulating a creed, is now indifferent to that problem, but rather asks itself: What example of a Jewish life should we present, what rituals should we urge for the home, how much Hebrew should we require a Jew to know, what kind of ethical behavior should being a Jew impose on one?[7]

Indeed, in the 1976 statement of principles, under the rubric of 'Our religious obligations: religious practice', an apparent emphasis is made on practice and ritual, especially the type related to the Jewish home, rather than on morality and ethics. Accordingly, the new religious obligations of the Jews, as understood by Reform Judaism, go beyond ethical issues to include:

> creating a Jewish home centered on family devotion: lifelong study; private prayer and public worship; daily religious observance; keeping the Sabbath and the holy days; celebrating the major events of life; involvement with the synagogues and community; and other activities which promote the survival of the Jewish people and enhance its existence.

This Reform need to return to more traditional ways of defining and living Judaism was mostly the result of the developments of the late 1960s when 'a new ethnic consciousness' was emerging among the Jews and they began to lose interest in mainstream American Judaism which, with its mere emphasis on social action and institutionalism, fell short of offering a concrete Jewish identity and a fulfilling religious life.[8] This return to tradition would also mark the end of the notion of mission. Alongside Eugene Borowitz, the author of the 1976 statement of principles, most Reform rabbis and thinkers declared a common disenchantment with the idea of mission in the 1970s. This, in fact, meant taking a huge step back from the notion of being 'indispensable to the development of world civilisation', a notion which was once confidently expressed under the banner of mission by the European forerunners of the

Reform movement, as well as their early American successors. At the turn of the century, Isaac Wise had even gone so far as to envisage Judaism as the future civil religion of America. Again in 1928 Samuel Cohon had declared the Jewish people as 'a light unto the nations' and 'a covenant to the peoples', as put in the Union prayer book.[9] In contrast, Borowitz, on behalf of the third generation, would announce the transformation taking place in Reform Judaism, by writing,

> our experience in recent history having been so negative, the doctrine of the mission of Israel has as good as disappeared from Reform Jewish thinking.... [Who] among us can still confidently proclaim that our group has a special message for all peoples, a unique idea they have not truly heard of, or a teaching that would solve the basic spiritual problems of humankind...[10]

In this way, the American Jews were giving up an active role in bringing about universal redemption. However, this did not mean that they would give up the idea of Jewish centrality to world history. Jews, in effect, were offering the example of their 'survival' instead. In other words, the Jewish people were not the people of a 'messianic mission' working for the improvement of the world here and now any more, but rather they were a people of a 'messianic hope' that humanity will be redeemed one day. Previously emphasized qualities of the people of Israel, such as 'the priest of the one God' and the people with a 'mission', were also replaced by one quality, namely that of being a 'unique' people on the basis of their 'involvement with God'.

This is why Borowitz suggested a kind of return to the idea of covenant as well as more traditional, yet revised, understanding of chosenness, in other words to the particular Jewish roots, for American Jewry, after a period of heavy secularization. He wrote:

> The failure of secular humanism means that chosenness can no longer be reduced to the spirit of the nation, or a vocation the people of Israel chose for itself. At the same time, the continuing emphasis on autonomy prevents a return to the traditional relationship in which God was so dominant that people were reduced to a relatively passive role.[11]

Borowitz admitted that, due to the outer aspects of chosenness, which are separation and service, Jews, particularly Diaspora Jews, 'must set a high example of personal conduct before humanity'. Though the idea of service here, as much as it indicates the activist aspect of chosenness, is understood mainly and ultimately in terms of service to God, as Borowitz asserted: 'What a Jew does reflects on God'. In fact, this special involvement with God, as Borowitz argued, makes Jewish 'nationhood' and Jewish 'survival' a 'divine imperative'.[12] It also enables Jewish 'particularity' to have an implicit 'universality'. However, Borowitz also stressed that the inner aspects or responsibilities of chosenness in terms of the Torah, commandments, life of holiness and redemption should have more effect in the lives of Jews.[13]

Thus the most immediate Jewish concern in this new Reform orientation was the question of 'how Judaism could enhance Jewish lives'. It became almost a common view among Reform leaders that the value of Judaism should have been measured more by what it gave to the Jew than what it gave to the world.[14] As a matter of fact, this period witnessed not only a reflexive/passive, even natural, withdrawal into what was particularly Jewish but also, and more importantly, a conscious/active disassociation with what is non-Jewish. For the process of Jewish assimilation into America, as occurred in the 1950s and early 1960s, which was the reason for the emergence of the ideology of affliction and the concomitant particularist orientation among American Jewry, had resulted in not only the American acceptance of Jewry but also the Jewish acceptance of America. The fact that '[n]on-Jews ceased being "the other" and began being comrades and colleagues'[15] turned out to be the biggest threat to the Jewish feeling of difference and exclusivity, and therefore to the continuity of the Jewish people. The American Jews in this way lost 'the other' against which they could define their Jewishness. At this point, Novick refers to a 1988 survey, in which 'more than a third of Reform rabbis – traditionally the most "integrated" and "outreaching" of the major Jewish denominations – endorsed the proposition that "ideally, one ought not to have any contact with non-Jews"'.[16] Ironically enough, this was the stand taken by the traditional Jews in Germany in the nineteenth century when the Reform movement was pioneering the principles of universalism, progress, and integrationism.

Furthermore, as regards the issues of the state of Israel and Zionism, which had become a scene of heavy debate in the previous platform, the tension between the obligations to humanity and obligations to the Jewish people seems to have been more openly admitted in the Centenary Perspective and, in parallel to this, a more Zionist or pro-Israeli position was adopted. While it is emphasized that Judaism calls Jews 'simultaneously to universal and particular obligations', those obligations appear to have changed in terms of both content and importance. As Eisen points out, 'even the purpose of Israel's service has been altered', by being transformed from representing an ethical monotheism into witnessing that 'history is not meaningless'.[17] As far as individual Reform rabbis are concerned, however, the interpretation of chosenness and Jewishness in the wake of the awareness of the Holocaust witnesses an apparent variation. For some, the Holocaust is the end of the idea of mission, whereas for others it serves as a confirmation of Jewish chosenness. It seems clear that the Jews had to accept their chosenness once more, albeit in the form of Jewish separation and distinctiveness, instead of mission.

What is of special importance in this apparent Reform shift from an active, integrationist, and mission-centred position to a passive, particularist, and survival-centred one is closely related to its two-fold nature. With this transformation, Jews, especially Reform ones, seem to have chosen a passive or indirect involvement in the world's progress and in the redemption of humanity, while coming to take a more active role in their own destiny. What is proposed in this way is that Jews place their trust neither in God nor in other peoples, but solely in themselves by working for their own redemption. Moreover, in cases of both universalist and particularist Jewish obligations, 'survival' is employed as the key term. Through the example of their survival, Jews enable themselves to justify the changing balances in their obligations to the world and to the Jewish people. The mission of Israel, as argued by Gunther Plaut, is a 'dynamic' and 'changing' one, so that every generation in Jewish history has their own 'missions' and their own 'tasks'.[18] And apparently this change occurs in accordance with the changing needs of American Jewry. While Jewish survival, as a passive instrument, is regarded as indispensable to the redemption of the world in a rather 'mysterious' way, excessive Jewish concerns with the fate of the Jewish people come to look, at the end of the day, not so particularist. In this way, Reform Judaism retains the idea of chosenness in the form of a mysterious uniqueness of the Jewish people, while doing away with the idea of mission and its primarily universal message.

This is, in fact, hardly an attempt to return to the traditional notion of chosenness but, instead, a way to accommodate the traditional language of chosenness, namely covenant, exile, and redemption, into a post-Holocaust Jewish condition. What most American Jews, both Reform and others, did in this way was to employ the traditional idea of chosenness for the confirmation of Jewish distinctiveness/otherness. This return to tradition was, in other words, the result of a search for a distinctive Jewish identity as well as Jewish continuity. In the same way, acceptance, or employment of the language, of chosenness was done for the sake of the Jews' separation from the world, not that separation for the sake of chosenness or covenant, as had been the case in traditional understanding. Jews were different and unique: that was the one and only component of the Holocaust proposition of chosenness. As indicated by Eisen, in the thought of many Reform Jews, retaining the 'idea of chosenness' in some sense was taken as an obligation in order to justify 'Jewish peoplehood'.[19] This is why contemporary Reform Jewish theologies, particularly during the 1970s, unlike traditional ones, generated confirming, yet non-apologetic, faith-related, but mainly experience-based, interpretations of chosenness with the intent of making Jews proud of themselves, proud of their difference and their otherness. So, instead of explaining the doctrine of chosenness, they ended up reducing it to a mysterious phenomenon, which best explained the ongoing Jewish alienation from American society, despite their full integration into it. The question at stake, in other words, was to make Jewish distinctiveness inescapable, even desirable, for Jews, instead of making it acceptable or reasonable for non-Jews. The idea of mission was an issue only during the first generation, and maybe the second as well, when the Jews needed to integrate into American society. It would prove redundant, however, for the third generation who, having become fully integrated into America, encountered a great challenge in keeping the Jewish community alive. This was the time of withdrawal from a 'purpose-centred' notion of mission to a 'survival-oriented' idea of uniqueness.

It is important to note that, this being the overall picture, different Reform theologians placed emphasis on different dimensions of chosenness and Jewishness. Some were even highly critical of the American Jewish overemphasis on survival.

Arthur Cohen and Will Herberg both put forward the idea of a special obligation/ vocation in the name of chosenness, to which survival, unlike what Fackenheim and others propose, was mostly instrumental. Cohen, in particular, in his *The Natural and the Supernatural Jew* wrote in a highly critical tone of the current Jewish emphasis on mere survival at the expense of Jewish vocation. With his well-known distinction between the 'natural' and the 'supernatural' Jew, one as the creation of history and fate and the other as the creation of Jewish faith and Jewish destiny, Cohen referred to a fundamental difference between a Jewishness of mere existence and that of a transcendental vocation.[20] According to Cohen, if survival, instead of vocation, is to be taken by the Jews as the condition of Jewish existence, Judaism turns into 'what its opponents say it is: a narrow, exclusivist, closed community'.[21] Cohen admits that although the Jewish religion is essentially an existentialist one, what justifies and also requires Jewish distinctiveness is a unique vocation attached to Jewish existence, and not a self-satisfying theology of survival. He goes on:

> The issue of self-definition is no longer that of coming to terms with the con- dition of Jewish history and the unique role which that condition has defined. The pursuit of self-definition consists presently in the achievement of the happy compromise: individuality amid homogeneity, ethnic distinctiveness amid the denial of significant difference, nationalist self-expression masked by the duties of charity and philanthropy. Judaism has all but disappeared, while Jewishness ... is well indulged.[22]

By associating survival with Jewishness and vocation with Judaism, Cohen in fact points out that Jewish survival, unless it is linked to a supernatural vocation – such a vocation only, he believed, gave 'substance and magnitude' to it – cannot but serve the natural condition of a natural people. In order to demonstrate that Judaism in effect represents an inclusivist and open community, the Jewish theologians should accept that the Jewish people are not 'a fact of history', as presupposed by Fackenheim's 614th Commandment, but 'an article of faith'.[23] Furthermore, in Cohen's thought, the idea of chosenness was not only an existen- tial issue. On the contrary, it was mainly concerned with the future, rather than with the past. In other words, the meaning of chosenness, for Cohen, lay more in its purpose (messianic fulfilment) than in its reason (God's love for Israel). However, by arguing that 'the meaning of chosenness cannot now be compre- hended',[24] and by pushing it in this way to the level of the unknown, Cohen, too, seems to end up with a 'mysterious' sense of chosenness.

As for Herberg, it is interesting to note the shifting themes that occur in two articles written by him, one in 1952 ('Jewish existence and survival: a theological view') and the other in 1970 ('The "chosenness" of Israel and the Jew of today'). In the earlier article the focus is on notions of 'covenant', 'supernatural commun- ity', and 'vocation', with a powerful concluding sentence: 'there is one and only one way of survival as Jews: *authentic, responsible covenant–existence*'.[25] In the later article, however, the previous critique of survivalism seems to be toned down. Instead, the emphasis is on 'otherness', 'difference', and the feeling of being an 'outsider', even an 'eternal stranger'. When presenting Jewishness as a built-in quality that calls into question 'the self-idolizing, self-absolutizing tendencies in men and society',[26] Herberg seems to overlook the danger that the Jewish overemphasis on uniqueness and survivalism in the name of chosenness might turn into another version of self-idolization and self-absolution. By seeing the 'chosenness' of Israel as 'an inescapable fact for the Jew' and a 'destiny', as well as a burden/responsibility,[27] Herberg presents Jewishness, and therefore chosenness, mainly as an existentially and psychologically unique phenomenon, as many other contemporary Reform Jews have done. It is existential, because in this way every Jew, religious or secular, is regarded as having 'an implicit religious affirmation' embedded in their beings. Yet, it is also psychological, as the Jews have come to accept this sense of chosenness not through reason/will or faith, which represents modern and traditional modes of understanding, but rather as a result of a pure inner necessity.

Accordingly, although the idea of chosenness as a vocation and responsibility found some voice in the Reform theologies of the 1970s and 1980s, especially when placed against mainstream survivalist theologies, what was common to all these theologies was the emphasis on an unnatural, unclassifiable, inescapable sense of 'uniqueness', which carried the mark of the post-Holocaust Jewish self-definition in terms of obligatory chosenness. Coming to the 1990s, however, the understanding of Jewishness and Judaism among American Jewry, particularly the non-Orthodox, seems to have been placed on more positive grounds, despite an ongoing language of uniqueness and distinctiveness. This period witnesses the emergence of alternative definitions of Jewishness, which are mainly based on principles such as universalism, moralism, voluntarism, and personalism.[28] Although the necessity to survive is not denied or given up by most rabbis, and is still vigorously supported by some, the need to become or to remain a Jew is attributed to positive meanings one can obtain from one's Jewishness, instead of being related to anti-Semitism or some sort of Jewish fear of everything non-Jewish. 'We now truly enter the age of Judaism-by-consent', Leonard Fein wrote in the early 1990s, and 'the question, therefore, becomes: To what have we consented when we say "I do"?' He went on:

> The traditional answers of organized American Jewry are barely adequate today, and they are likely to diminish in their appeal tomorrow. Those answers focus on our activity on behalf of Israel and our concern with anti-Semitisim ... a Judaism of consent wants to be something more than a political action committee or a lobby.... "Never again" tells us what to avoid, but it says nothing about what to embrace.[29]

At this point, the interpretation of Jewishness and chosenness as proposed in the 1999 Pittsburgh Convention is crucial as a theoretical response to this Jewish need. In a brief three-section declaration of principles, an equal amount of emphasis is placed on God, the Torah and Israel, respectively, these being the components central to traditional Judaism. In the section on 'God' what is confirmed is not only a 'hope' but an ongoing 'partnership' between 'God and humanity'. The Torah is also seen as the manifestation of 'God's eternal love', not only for the Jewish people, but also for humanity. Thus, through the Jewish faith in God and Torah the universal dimension of Judaism is brought to the fore. On the other hand, the emphasis on the Jewish commitment to, and love for, the community of Israel (*k'lal yisrael*) indicates the particularist aspect of Jewishness. What is suggested is a middle way between the radical universalism of the classical Reform movement and the strict particularism of traditional Judaism. Israel has been declared as a people not holy, but 'aspiring to holiness', and 'singled out' through 'covenant' and a 'unique history' to be 'witnesses to God's presence'. Again, there is an equal emphasis on two components of Jewishness: faith (covenant) and destiny (history). However, it seems quite obvious that among ordinary Jews the feeling of belonging to a community (positive element) outweighs that of being compelled to accept a common destiny (negative element) in their decision to remain Jewish. The search of the younger generation of American Jews for meaning in their 'Jewish' lives paves the way to the creation of what is called a 'post-ideology of affliction phenomenon',[30] which refers to a Jewishness that is a mixture of positive and personally chosen, cultural, social and spiritual elements. The result becomes the renewal of interest in ethics as something which gives positive meaning to one's self-identification as well as the continuing importance of family, as a concrete element in the making of Jewish identity.

According to the results of the survey conducted by Steve Cohen in 1998, religiosity remains stable among younger American Jews, whereas there is a decline in ethnicity. This decline in the ethnic aspects of American Jewishness displays itself basically in the rise of intermarriage, a decline in in-group friendship, the geographic dispersal of the Jewish population, and a weakening enthusiasm for Israel.[31] The universalist and moralist orientation becomes pivotal, particularly in the new regulations for synagogue ceremonies. One liberal congregation is noted for adding the following recitation to the list of sins asked forgiveness in the High Holy Days:

> For the sins we have committed before you and before us by being so preoccupied with ourselves that we ignored the social world in which we live…. And for sins we have committed by participating in a racist society and not dedicating more energy to fight it.[32]

On the other hand, Tony Bayfield, the current leader of British Reform Jewry, wrote in a 1993 article in an almost outdated universalist fashion of the early Reform movement, that when the Jewish religion, as a result of the idea of the chosen people, 'concentrates exclusively on its own love affair with God', it becomes 'oblivious of its role as a blessing to others', a notion that was a prerequisite of the classical Reform idea of mission. According to Bayfield, whereas the 'covenantal obligation', even in the prophetic tradition of ethical monotheism, was primarily limited to the Jewish community, today Judaism has 'an urgent need to enlarge its sense of mission' to all humanity.[33]

So, as a result of the weakened significance of rituals and ethnicity and an increasing emphasis on ethics, unconverted partners began to be readily accepted, even supported in those new liberal congregations.[34] In parallel to this universalist and moralist attitude, a voluntarist and personalist orientation was also adopted. Even during the 1980s Borowitz, writing on Sinai, maintained that the relevant question to ask, 'was not what occurred at Sinai but what the occurrence means to us'; each generation in this way would create 'its own covenant with God'.[35] A similar notion is later voiced by another Reform Jew who, in reference to the revelation at Sinai, declares his personal faith with these words: 'I am freely choosing to associate myself with a myth I find uplifting, informative'.[36] What is proposed in this way is an understanding of covenant that is experience-oriented and functional, as opposed to the law-centred and fixed one of traditional Judaism. Accordingly, in this privatized version of Judaism, 'Jewish identity is understood to be chosen rather than given, accepted rather than received'.[37] As opposed to traditional particularist and modern survivalist understandings of Jewishness, which are centred either on 'gentile hostility' or the 'precariousness of Jewish existence', the privatized Jewishness speaks through the 'terms of individual meaning, journeys of discovery, and the search for fulfillment'.[38] In such a personalist and voluntarist definition of Jewishness, the language of chosenness also loses its meaning. For the question at stake becomes less about justifying one's existence or preserving one's continuity in a hostile world than about fulfilling oneself as an individual. 'As a purely postmodern Jew', Tzvee Zahavy writes, 'I *know* that it [the Jewish community] will survive. It is now our task to make our lives as Jews meaningful to our present needs'.[39] Hence the current emphasis in many non-Orthodox congregations is more on individuality, spirituality, and morality than on community, ethnicity, and ritual.

This individualism can also be seen in terms of a post-modern search for freedom, an attempt to run away from the burdens imposed by tradition and history; a shift from being 'chosen' by God, i.e. from destiny, to 'choosing' one's own faith and identity. So, in a time when identity and spiritual continuity, and not the problem of existence and physical survival, gain urgency, the function of Jewish chosenness also changes from guaranteeing Jewish survival to rendering Jewish lives meaningful and purposeful. This is in fact a Jewish self-definition made against a meaningless and profane world, and not against a hostile and anti-Jewish one. Therefore, the question for many becomes a matter of choice rather than chosenness either as a positive, sacred or a negative, pseudo-religious category.

As a matter of fact, such a privatization process is not without its critics. They believe that this process poses a serious danger to the survival of the American Jewish community, undermining Jewish particularism and so accelerating the tendency to assimilation.[40] Several rabbis and Jewish leaders have made a call for the 'setting of clear lines' between Jewish and non-Jewish religions and for the 'working toward a consensus on who is a Jew'.[41] However, it needs to be remembered that there is evidence for an ongoing American Jewish concern with anti-Semitism though it seems less prevalent than one or two decades previously.[42] As for the alarmingly high intermarriage rate, relatively this is not as serious, considering that those Jews who marry out come almost exclusively from non-Orthodox congregations, whereas Orthodoxy displays itself as the strongest congregation in America, at least commitment-wise.

Moreover, there is another path contemporary liberal American Jews take, which is based neither on the ideology of affliction, nor on the privatization of Judaism. For many, Jewish particularism, albeit understood in a personalist and voluntarist way, seems inescapable. The statements presented by prominent American rabbis and thinkers from different congregations in a survey conducted by *Commentary* magazine in 1996, are of great importance.[43] One of the questions addressed in the symposium asks the participants in what sense they believe that 'the Jews are the chosen people of God' and what they think is the 'distinctive role of the Jewish people in the world today'. Based on eight statements selected by the magazine, the answers given by the respondents in relation to the question of chosenness focus on two groups of ideas. One sees the notion of Jewishness/chosenness mainly in terms of a mystery and intimacy (between God and the Jews) and the other places emphasis on the notions of a special mission and responsibility as attached to the idea of the chosen people. What is most surprising is that the answers given by two out of three Orthodox respondents, as well as by one out of two Conservative respondents, fall into the second category, whereas the answers of three non-Orthodox (one being Reform) respondents fit in the first category. David Ellenson, a Reform Jew, sees his Jewishness mainly in terms of 'belonging to the people of Israel'. He also emphasizes that his beliefs are 'to a great extent the products of subjective choices' which make his faith embedded at once in religion and culture, mystery and infinity, spirituality and community. What is even more interesting is that Ellenson does not directly address the question of chosenness, except for one reference he makes to messianism as a principle that obligates a Jew 'to work for the repair of the human condition'. In parallel to this, yet on a different occasion, Rabbi Eric Yoffie, President of the Union of American Hebrew Congregations, defines Judaism and Jewishness in almost completely traditional ways, placing emphasis on God, the Torah, and Israel, on faith, covenant, and *mitzvot*, on Sinai (rather than the Holocaust), and on the Jews making a holy community (rather than a private club). As regards this new Reform orientation towards a positive and spiritual identity-building, Yoffie also states:

> A certain number of young Reform Jews ... want to connect with God and to feel joy in being Jews. They are sending us the message that no one will be drawn to Reform Judaism with slogans of continuity or seminars on survival; no one will want to embrace a tradition that is one long, endless whine. And Judaism is not a tradition of tragedy; it is a tradition of celebration.[44]

On the other hand, Eugene Borowitz in his *Renewing the Covenant* offers a post-modern chosenness and a post-modern Jewish self-definition, which attributes an absolute and transcendent meaning to Jewish continuity by substituting the idea of Jewish uniqueness (based on inflexible and inexplicable anti-Semitism) with the traditional notion of a covenant with God, helping the Jews relate to themselves, to other Jews, and to the world in a much more positive way. 'Covenant with God', Borowitz states, 'gives us our personal significance and makes all God's covenant-partners an essential element of our selfhood'.[45] However, this post-modern covenant as proposed by Borowitz, unlike the traditional one, refers to 'a loving effort to live in reciprocal respect' rather than to 'a contract spelled out from on high'.[46] He suggests a middle way between traditional particularism and modern universalism by attributing the source of authority for covenant neither to God's will nor to the human will, but to the covenantal I–Thou relationship itself. According to Novak, what Borowitz calls for is a substitution of 'theorelatedness', namely 'the individual Jew's experience of being related to God', for 'theocentricity'.[47] Indeed, Borowitz also states in his *Judaism after Modernity* that the contemporary Jewish theological agenda 'should no longer centre on God or Torah but on the doctrine of Israel'.[48] What is at stake in this post-modern Jewishness is what the Jewish people need rather than what God commands. In other words, it is not God who requires the Jew for his mysterious plan for the world but the Jew who needs God for positive and personal reasons.

Conservative Judaism

It is interesting to note that Conservative religious leaders and scholars, unlike Reform ones, have placed, right from the beginning, almost no theological emphasis on the Holocaust. Those who most severely criticize the theology of survival also happened to be, to a great extent, Conservative rabbis and scholars, such as Jacob Neusner, Ismar Schorsch, and David Novak, to name just a few. Moreover, what was central to most Conservative Jewish interpretations of chosenness was an apparent traditional standing which took into account the classical problems attached to the doctrine, such as the tension between particularity and universality, and the question of exclusivity and superiority. This is why the Conservative understanding of chosenness did not display any obvious difference from one generation to the other, even in the aftermath of the Holocaust. Indeed, back in the 1970s, when American Reform theologies were heavily under the influence of the Holocaust discourse, most Conservative rabbis continued to associate the idea of chosenness with a special responsibility and duty as well as an inescapable, mysterious sense of uniqueness. Moreover, the traditional emphasis on the special covenantal relationship between God and the Jewish people, despite the Holocaust, was faithfully preserved. Perhaps this is because Conservative Judaism, due to the principle of 'Catholic Israel', has allowed certain modifications on which there was consensus, yet opposed radical and sudden changes in the notions of God, the Torah, and Israel. As a result, Conservative Judaism has been successful in creating theologically moderate and ethnically strong congregations.

It would not be wrong to say that Conservative Jewish theologians on the whole were quite careful to play down, even reject, exclusivist implications of the doctrine of chosenness. Louis Finkelstein, in particular, placed an ongoing stress on the 'universal faith in God' which was understood by him as the meaning of the messianic age and also the purpose of Israel's election, as he wrote:

> The fact that the people of Israel received the Law and heard the prophets does not, according to Jewish teaching, endow them with any exclusive privileges. But it does place upon them special responsibilities.... These responsibilities – to observe the Law, to study it, to explain it, and to be its unwavering exponents – are expressed in the term 'The Chosen People'.[49]

Seymor Siegel, in a similar way, interpreted chosenness mainly in terms of a special vocation and responsibility imposed on the Jews by God through the Torah. While the 'children of Israel living under a special covenant have additional responsibilities', Siegel writes, 'both Jew and gentile have a share in redemption'. However, despite this identification with responsibility and vocation, election is also understood by Siegel as a predestined, unconditional, and eternal reality.[50] According to this, the Jews are not *a* people but *the* people 'called into being by God to serve his purposes in the world'.[51] This is obviously the reason why chosenness, according to Siegel, is not only a matter of vocation or faith but also a question of identity, a feeling of uniqueness, which, as confirmed by Herberg, 'permeates the consciousness of most Jews even when they vociferously repudiate any kind of theological doctrine of chosenness'.[52]

In Robert Gordis's thought, too, the chosenness of Israel is considered central to Jewish theology as well as to Jewish self-identification. This was so, for him, on the basis of some empirical and objective facts, such as the special Jewish history which has lasted for thirty-five centuries, the Bible as a creation of the Jewish people, and the fact that the Jewish religion has paved the way for other monotheistic religions and modern humanitarian ideals.[53] This emphasis on 'historical facts' in verifying Jewish chosenness also finds a place in Louis Jacobs, British Masorti rabbi and scholar, as he writes:

> The world owes Israel the idea of the One God of righteousness and holiness. This is how God became known to mankind and clearly God used Israel for this great purpose. When Judaism declares that the covenant is still in force it reaffirms that Israel still has a special role to play.[54]

But it is most importantly the survival of the Jews – despite their loss of independence in their homeland – that has made the Jews, for Gordis, a unique people, or the only 'people' ('religio–cultural ethnic group') in the real sense of the term. This uniqueness, on the other hand, is seen by him as both the cause and the consequence of the Jews' unique history. In other words, while the above-mentioned historical facts confirm the chosenness of the Jewish people, the idea of being chosen in turn leads the Jews to feel special and act special, and in this way the feeling of uniqueness serves as a psychological stipulation for the survival of the Jewish people as well as for the continuity of the Jewish religion, as Gordis wrote:

If our generation is to accept Jewish fellowship and loyalty to Judaism willingly and joyously, accepting the disabilities of Jewish life and rejecting the temptation to desert, it requires a sense of consecration – a conviction that the Jewish people has played and yet will play a noble and significant role in the world.... Jewish loyalty is nothing petty and insular, but ... on the contrary, it ministers to the progress of humanity. The doctrine of the Chosen People is therefore a psychological necessity as well as a historical truth, an indispensable factor for Jewish survival today.[55]

And this is the reason why the idea of the chosen people, for Gordis, is retained in the Conservative prayer book. In it, he asserts, 'the election of Israel' is associated 'not with any inherent personal or group superiority, but with the higher responsibilities which come to the Jew as the custodian of the Torah and the devotee of the Jewish way of life'.' According to him, most liturgical sentences written in the classical Hebrew, which looks quite particularist to the modern mind due to its 'more primitive' and 'less complex' nature, are understood and interpreted by modern Jews in a more duty-oriented and universalist tone, as it is written in English: 'who has chosen us from among the peoples by giving us [instead of *and given us*] His Torah'.[56] Indeed in *Siddur Sim Shalom*, the traditional Conservative Prayer book of 1985, the original (Orthodox) Hebrew version of the *Aleinu* prayer is preserved, with an obvious separationist tone. However, various Conservative rabbis interpret the particularist emphasis of the prayer in a more universalistic way.[57]

Again, Arthur Hertzberg, to show the centrality and inevitability of the doctrine of chosenness for traditional Judaism, wrote, in response to *Commentary* magazine's questionnaire in 1966, that '[t]he essence of Judaism is the affirmation of the chosen people; all else is commentary'.[58] He proposed a traditional interpretation of Jewishness and chosenness by pointing to the complex nature of chosenness which involves 'merit and distinction' on the one hand, and 'duty and suffering' on the other. What is unique about the Jewish people, for Hertzberg, is the fact that their chosenness indicates a reality, not an assumption, because it stems from the idea of a choosing God of history. 'Such a God', Hertzberg writes,

can be imagined as choosing a particular people for the task of strictest obedience to His will, as an instrument in His hand for the redemption of mankind and as a teacher whom God Himself keeps from pride by applying to His chosen people the severest of judgments.[59]

Thus, chosenness requires a tangible distinction and separation between Jews and non-Jews, as Hertzberg goes on,

This people was chosen to be a corporate priesthood, to live within the world and yet apart from it. Its way of life is the appointed sign of its difference. At the end of time, in a completely redeemed world, this unique way will perhaps disappear...[60]

Although Hertzberg emphatically asserted that the doctrine of Jewish chosenness knows no 'special privilege' and no 'inherent biological superiority',[61] David Singer points out that in Hertzberg's view, Jewishness refers to a sort of innate character based on the triads of chosenness, otherness, and a 'sense of moral mission' as embedded in the nature of Jews, religious or non-religious. Singer also maintains that the term chosenness thus implies a 'conception of Jews as "aristocrats of the spirit" who have ever operated in the belief that what they do is of "transcendent significance to the whole of the human enterprise" '.[62] This is why the doctrine of chosenness, in Hertzberg's thought, remains a 'mystery' and a 'scandal' for the world, incorporating both particularist and universalist elements, yet ultimately belonging to the 'unknowable will of God'.[63]

As for Abraham Heschel, who had a Hasidic upbringing and was later affiliated with the Conservative tradition, in his thought the qualitative elements seem to intermingle with non-qualitative ones. He believed, on the one hand, that the idea of the chosen people signifies a 'relationship between the people and God', and not a 'quality inherent in the people',[64] and that Jewish existence, therefore, refers to 'the history of a responsibility'.[65] On the other hand, he suggested that belonging to Israel was in itself a spiritual act, as Israel is the creation of God's search, of God's discovery.[66] Therefore, the 'very survival of our people', Heschel wrote, 'is a *kiddush hashem*'; '[o]ur very existence is a refusal to surrender to normalcy'.[67] In this way, covenant (reciprocity) was understood by Heschel as being for the sake of chosenness (God's will), which belonged to an area of mystery.

Louis Jacobs, on the other hand, defends the idea of chosenness against both those who abandon it on the premise of universalism and those who turn it into an absolute condition for themselves (either within survivalist or qualitative renderings), as two ends of the same spectrum.[68] As implied by Jacobs himself, in both cases the Jewish people, as the chosen people, are given priority over the covenant. In other words, the quality or feeling of being chosen/unique/different surpasses the reciprocity of the covenantal relationship, and the accompanying responsibilities and duties. In this way covenant (condition) begins to serve chosenness (quality). Accordingly, in the qualitative understanding of chosenness, the Jewish people, as a concrete entity, are seen not in a state of aspiration to the spiritual Israel, but in a state of identification with it. In a similar fashion, in survivalist theologies the Jewish people are consecrated in a pseudo-religious way in which the survival of the Jews ceases to be an instrument for a higher purpose; it rather becomes an end in itself. Notwithstanding the common emphasis on the absoluteness of Jewishness, one main difference between qualitative and survivalist theologies lies perhaps in that, in the former Jewishness relates to something greater than itself, namely God, whereas this relation is absent in the latter.

It is important to note that, being aware of the danger of attaching too much significance to ethnicity, most Conservative Jewish thinkers hastened to warn against the exploitation of the doctrine of chosenness for chauvinistic purposes, and sought to rule out such exclusivist interpretations of the doctrine by attributing the latter to a divine covenant and concomitant human responsibilities, instead of to an inherent Jewish quality. This Conservative sensitivity towards the particularist implications of the concept of chosenness makes better sense if one considers that peoplehood and ethnicity have always been essential to Conservative Judaism. Besides, as admitted by the Conservative rabbis, the danger of chauvinism attached to the idea of chosenness was not that easy to eliminate. So some Conservative theologians advocated a reinterpretation of the traditional doctrine of the chosen people in terms of multiple covenants/vocations or even its total dismissal. Jacob Agus, in his response to *Commentary* magazine's survey in 1966, while rejecting the 'metaphysical uniqueness of the Jew', i.e. the core of the doctrine of chosenness, as a dangerous superstition, placed an emphasis, instead, on the 'historical uniqueness' of the Jewish people and Jewish religion as much as of any other people and religion.[69] 'As a component of faith', he wrote, 'the feeling of being "covenanted" should be generalized: every person should find a vocation and dedicate himself to it. So, too, the pride of belonging to a historic people should be universalized'.[70] Harold Schulweis, on the other hand, following the interpretation of Mordecai Kaplan, declared that in the light of modern Jewish experience and ethics the doctrine of divine chosenness became redundant. Yet he affirmed the uniqueness of every people in their 'life style', including the Jewish people.[71]

Most Conservative Jewish theologians, being sensitive in interpreting the doctrine of chosenness in non-exclusivist terms, saw it as a reason and a precious asset for Jewish being as well as the Jewish religion. As a matter of fact, in contrast to survivalist theologies that made up a pseudo-religious Jewish uniqueness to enable ongoing Jewish survival, most Conservative Jewish theologians interpreted survival as an indication of Jewish chosenness. This is so even though such an attitude looks quite contradictory in the face of the way in which Conservative congregations in America have established themselves. Marshall Sklare, the late American sociologist, states that Judaism, in general, and Conservativism, in particular, constitute what is called an 'ethnic church', in which maintaining group continuity, alongside providing group members with spirituality, are regarded as important tasks. The special contribution of Conservatism to this system, Sklare maintains, 'has been its relatively uninhibited "exploitation" of the new type of synagogue – the kind which is a house of assembly as much and more than it is a house of prayer – for the purposes of group survival'.[72]

Perhaps it is more reasonable to understand this Conservative emphasis on ethnicity in terms of continuity rather than survival. The Conservative discourse of the 1970s as well as 1960s, which promoted faith-centred and universalist interpretations of Jewishness and chosenness in general – with an emphasis on covenant responsibilities and the idea of plurality of covenants – seems to be preserved in the 1980s and 1990s alongside an increasing emphasis on the idea of multiple vocations. The latter had also been advocated by the second-generation Conservative Jewish leaders, under the influence of Kaplan's Reconstructionist philosophy. In *Emet ve Emunah*, the declaration made by the New York Jewish Theological Seminary in 1988 representing the more traditional wing of

Conservative Judaism, the possibility of multiple covenants is voiced in reference to Maimonides's recognition of other monotheistic faiths.[73] In the declaration there is also a particular reference to the recognition that other nations, too, might have their own covenants with God, as it reads:

> [A]lthough we have but one God, God has more than one nation. Our tradition explicitly recognizes that God entered into a covenant with Adam and Eve, and later with Noah and his family as well as His special covenant with Abraham and the great revelation to Israel at Sinai. It is part of our mission to understand, respect, and live with the other nations of the world, to discern those truths in their cultures from which we can learn, and to share with them the truths that we have come to know.

Alongside this acceptance of multiple covenants, the notion that the Jewish people undertake a distinct and sacred mission was retained by Conservative Judaism in general during the 1990s. At this point, the answers given by the Conservative rabbis to *Commentary* magazine's survey in 1996 are of special significance. David Dalin and Elliot Dorff both agreed that the Holocaust did not make an enormous theological impact on the Jewish religion, nor did it pose a philosophical problem for Jews any more than other examples of human depravity could. Dalin declared his affirmation of the idea of chosenness as a central tenet of the Jewish faith. He also made it clear that while the Jewish survival of the Holocaust served as a confirmation of the Jewish people's chosenness, it was the symbolism of Jerusalem, instead of Auschwitz, which provided him personally with a spiritual meaning and thrust in his Jewishness. Dorff, on the other hand, placed an emphasis on the ethical, rather than spiritual dimension of Jewishness and chosenness by repeating the well-known Conservative standing on the issue,

> Jews must strive to improve the world; that is our mission. Non-Jews may share in that mission, and ultimately the messianic era will be one in which Jews and non-Jews cooperate in making this world ideal. Modern communications and transportation have made it abundantly clear that any messianic view which speaks of Jews alone is, to that extent, unrealistic and inadequate; we are all indeed part of a global village. For that reason I prefer Micah's vision of pluralism (4:1–5) over Isaiah's monotheism (2:1–4).[74]

There was also a growing emphasis on universalism and ethics in many Conservative congregations, particularly under the influence of privatized Jewishness. Some Conservative synagogues declared their goal as 'from one group to one humanity.'[75] However, the general tendency of the Conservative leadership continued to focus on both particularist and universalist elements. The notion that the creation of the state of Israel, as opposed to Auschwitz, is central in Jewish consciousness was declared by Ismar Schorsch as one of the tenets of the American Conservative Congregation. According to Schorsch, whereas the national dimension of the Jewish religion – as exemplified in the Jewish peoplehood and the attachment to a particular land – is undeniable, what turns this religious nationalism into a universal monotheism is the Jewish belief in God. 'Remove God', Schorsch writes, 'the object of Israel's millennial quest, and the rest will soon unravel'.[76] He also retained the Conservative Jewish emphasis on the doctrine of the 'Catholic Israel', asserting that 'yearning for God' stems not from 'reason or revelation', but from the 'historical experience of the Jewish people'.[77]

Within contemporary Conservative Jewish theology, David Novak deserves particular mention. He is the author of *The Election of Israel*, which is an attempt to reclaim the doctrine of election as understood traditionally. Although Novak, like many other Conservative theologians, is highly critical of the Holocaust theologies and the radical interpretations of chosenness as promoted by them, he, in this work, is particularly concerned with philosophical interpretations of the doctrine as presented by Baruch Spinoza, Hermann Cohen and Franz Rosenzweig. It seems to be that Novak, like many other American Jewish scholars and theologians, is extremely concerned about the rise of privatized Jewishness and the growing universalist and moralist tendencies among non-Orthodox American Jews, Conservative as well as Reform. So, for Novak the 'permanent' danger to the tradition comes from adopting a rationalist–universalist direction, and not from a historicist one, notwithstanding the problems attached to the latter.

Novak clearly states that no reason is given in the Torah for either the election of Abraham or that of his descendants, the people of Israel. As for God's love for the patriarchs and the promise that he made to them, these, Novak asserts, do not refer to a proper reason, but to a fact. At this point, he portrays God in the same way as Michael Wyschogrod does; namely as one who is completely free and sovereign in his dealings with the world, which is nothing but his own creation. This is why God has the absolute freedom to make a covenant with any people He wishes. Nevertheless, Novak maintains that even if there is no obvious reason for the election of Israel there is certainly a definite purpose in it. What matters here then is not the question as to why God chose Israel instead of any other people, but rather what does God want to do with this particular people.[78] In other words, according to Novak, the people of Israel have no a priori bearing in election, except being the descendants of the Patriarchs, but rather they assume a special role after having been elected. Such an understanding of election and covenant is based, for Novak, on what he calls 'relational distinctiveness' against 'substantial distinctiveness'.[79] Israel thus obtains its uniqueness only through and after election. Therefore, the purpose of election, for Novak, seems to be very much related to the Torah. The true obedience to God's commandments is what God asks the descendants of Abraham to achieve in order that they become a blessing for all humankind.

In this depiction, Novak especially emphasizes three characteristics of election:

1   No reason is given for it.
2   It starts with God's initiative.
3   It is primarily generic or communal.[80]

Novak explicitly attributes to Israel a sort of passive role as the chosen party. He sees election not as a contract between two equally autonomous parties or with mutual free consent, but rather as a special relationship initiated by God and imposed on the people as an obligation. Novak also points out that Israel did not have any real choice but had to accept God's covenant. The only possible active role for Israel could be to respond to the covenant by receiving the law, using the term 'active' metaphorically. However, in one particular respect Israel is supposed to be an active party in the proper sense of the term. It was, in fact, the view of the ancient rabbis and some medieval Jewish theologians, such as Rashi and Nahmanides, that Israel chooses God as much as God chooses Israel.[81] Thus Novak points to other covenants or renewals of covenant as having taken place between God and Israel where Israel seems to have had more freedom in respect of confirming or rejecting the covenant – such as the covenant with Joshua. But what is more significant in Novak's view is the position of the Israelites when they returned from the Babylonian exile. The Israelites had a real choice in returning from Babylon and reconstructing their religion on the basis of the Torah. Again during the exile, after being rescued from Haman's conspiracy, when it is said about the Jews that they 'upheld and accepted', it is their re-acceptance of the Torah that is being referred to.[82] It seems to be that, according to Novak, whereas the first covenant made between God and the Israelites at Sinai is completely based on divine initiative, the continuity of the covenant in the course of history requires the initiative of the Jewish people as well. The next generations were totally free to retain or give up the covenant their ancestors had to accept at Sinai. So, although on God's side the covenant is eternal, not because God cannot cancel it, but because God does not cancel it, on the Jewish side the covenant depends on the will of the people to live with it.

Accordingly, like many traditional Jewish theologians, Novak sees the Torah as the point on which human initiative comes into the election. This is also the place where the third characteristic of election as understood by him, namely the communal dimension of it, comes into play. Accordingly, election is primarily about community and only secondarily about individuals, a notion which is widely accepted in Jewish tradition. Novak asserts that even the election of Abraham involved the whole community of descendants because Abraham was chosen not for his own sake but to be 'the progenitor of a people'.[83] In the same way, Abraham's response to God's election was in fact an archetypal response given in the name of all who come after him. In other words, election was about a common experience passing on through generations as depicted in Deuteronomy 29:10–15. Nevertheless, Novak is very keen not to confuse the generic dimension of election with the dangerous notion that sees election in terms of the national interests of the people. Novak writes:

> The practical implication of assuming that the Torah is solely for the sake of affirming the election of Israel is to see no transcendent standard governing Israel's relationships with the nations of the world. The only relationship

possible, then, is one where gentiles accept Jewish sovereignty and domi-nance, be it political or only 'religious'.[84]

According to Novak, what prevents election from turning into such a notion of *Herrenvolk* (the master nation) is the Torah. At this point, it is important to note the relation between election and revelation as understood by Novak. This relation also refers to a further connection between Israel and the nations. For Novak believes that the role of the Torah in election is two-fold: one as a 'higher standard by which nationalistic self-interest can be judged', and the other as a 'transcendental standard governing Israel's relationships with the nations of the world'. In terms of its first role the Torah becomes the 'normative content' of the relationship between God and Israel, whereas in terms of its second role, it functions as a means through which God's 'continuing concern' for the nations is expressed.[85] According to Novak, what is implied with the covenant between God and Israel is the 'subsequent participation' of the gentiles in it, to the extent that they accept the Jewish people as the one with whom alone God has a full relationship and that they live in accordance with some of the commandments of the Torah. In this way, Novak sees a sort of link between Israel and the nations through election and revelation, a link which is something other than God's love. In the same way, the redemption of all nations through the redemption of Israel is seen as part of God's plan for the world.

However, what differentiates Novak's view of redemption, which has an appar-ent universalist dimension, from that of Jewish philosophers, such as Spinoza, Cohen, and Rosenzweig, is that in the former the redemption of the world means the Judaization of the nations, and not the universalization of Israel.[86] In Novak's view, election has both particular and universal aspects, which are definitely inter-related, yet should not be mixed or reduced to one another.[87] As far as the univer-sal and particular dimensions are concerned, Novak points to three separate kinds of commandments, drawn from Deuteronomy 6:20, which deal with different aspects of the Jewish religion. These are *mishpatim* (universal laws), *edot* (histor-ical laws), and *huqqim* (laws depending on God's authority). Although election as a historical and singular event is governed and practised primarily within the realm of *edot*, it is also indirectly related to *mishpatim* and *huqqim*: namely, to universal laws because Israel was, and still is, part of the universal whole, as well as having a singular nature; and to mysterious laws because, especially as far as redemption is concerned, it also relates to a realm which is ruled by God's mysterious will. According to Novak, these two realms, those of *mishpatim* and *huqqim*, are the limits of the election of Israel, which is directly related to the practice of *edot*.[88]

It seems to be that in Novak's interpretation of chosenness, several aspects of the doctrine are simultaneously incorporated, such as factors of initial divine will and succeeding human choice, and universal and particular dimensions represented by revelation and election. It is obvious, however, that the fulfilment of the purpose of election, that is redemption, ultimately belongs to the realm of *edot*, the chosen people having no active role in it. It would not be wrong to say that Novak defines election as:

1   Dominated by divine will.
2   Based on legal principles, in the sense of what is lawful against what is good.
3   Particularist, in terms of being Jewish-centred rather than humanity-centred.

However, it is also true that Novak regards election as embracing universal, ethical, and human-related aspects in terms of its practice and purpose. According to him, the difference between the people of Israel and other nations is one of degree, not one of kind. This is why, for him, the covenant between God and Israel includes the covenants between Jews themselves and between Jews and non-Jews. God's relation to other nations is more than one of a creator to crea-tures. Through the universal commandments in the Torah, which equally apply to Jews and non-Jews, the latter too become covenanted to God in some way. On the other hand, Novak denies reducing Judaism to a part of a larger universal whole. Judaism, for him, is not part of a universal whole into which it will melt in the end but rather the ultimate truth, including the universal whole. According to him, if one regards Judaism as 'a partial source of truth' rather than 'the source of truth', one should also give up Jewish particularism, lest it turn into ethnocentric-ity or chauvinism.[89] To sum up, like many contemporary Conservative theo-logians, Novak understands election as a doctrine which, despite its universal purpose, ultimately belongs to the realm of law and mystery.

Orthodox Judaism

As for Orthodox Judaism, the second half of the twentieth century witnessed an Orthodox resurgence in America, both in its modern and traditional versions. However, for some Jewish scholars, the resurgence of Orthodoxy in America owed little to the 'ideology of affliction', and was mainly the result of a cultural flowering brought forward by East European Jewish immigrants plus a positive attitude towards religion and particularism emerging later in American society.[90] During the immediate post-war period the ultra-Orthodox group had managed to re-establish itself around what is called 'Yeshiva Orthodoxy'. However, the majority of the American Jewish community, being 'immersed in the quest for the material rewards of American life', was 'struggling with its own sense of identity',[91] and the modern Orthodox group was not exempt from this. It was only in the 1970s that modern Orthodoxy in America emerged as an alternative movement to Reform and Conservative Judaisms. Apparently the general Amer-ican return to religion as well as the sense of abandonment and alienation that prevailed among American Jewry (as a result of the Holocaust consciousness) also played a significant role in this Orthodox revival.

In this period the writings of Rabbi Joseph Soloveitchik, a central figure for second- and third-generation Orthodox Jews in America, were reprinted. In these he called for a 'renewed search for God: out of the depths of exile and idola-try' as a remedy for the current situation of American Jewry.[92] And he did so by employing the traditional language of 'exile and return', instead of the rhetoric of survival. However, the kind of Orthodoxy represented by Rabbi Soloveitchik, who had talmudic learning coupled with secular knowledge, differed from the traditional or ultra-Orthodoxy in some important points. Moreover, this difference, which was mainly related to the attitudes of different Orthodox groups or traditions to modernity, revealed two different Orthodox communities in America, with two subsequent understandings of Jewishness and chosenness. For the ultra-Orthodox Jews, who often lived within their exclusively ultra-Orthodox communities having little contact with the outside world, chosenness was an uncontested truth, a *raison d'être* of their existence. This was true, to a certain extent, of modern Orthodox Jews as well. However, for the ultra-Orthodox, who were almost entirely exempt from modernity and the values and beliefs attached to it, such as universalism, liberalism, and individualism, Jewishness found its meaning in a rather fixed and sectarian fashion, whereas for the modern Orthodox, who enjoyed living in an open society, the definition, or realization, of one's Jewishness became more flexible, sometimes even problematic, in parallel to one's changing needs and priorities.

Nevertheless, all the Orthodox rabbis who joined *Commentary* magazine's survey in 1966 confirmed the truth of the traditional doctrine of the chosen people by indicating that it was affirmed by the Torah and justified by a unique Jewish history. Yet they explained it in reference to mainly its universalist implications. Jews were chosen for 'special responsibilities', i.e. obedience to God and a commitment to his Torah, and bringing the message of God's existence to mankind, rather than for 'special merits'. It was about a 'spiritual vocation' and not a 'natural superiority'.[93] Even those who emphasized the 'human merit', i.e. Israel's acceptance of the Torah, 'special privileges' such as 'a closer relation to God' and a 'perennial survival' of the people, and a kind of 'superiority' as embedded within the doctrine, still understood the essence of chosenness to be consummated in 'covenantal obligations'.[94] And these obligations also entailed the 'separation' of the Jewish people from other peoples for their unique task as 'models for mankind' and concomitant 'suffering'.[95] It is possible to say that, with the exception of Irving Greenberg's radical theology, the Holocaust discourse did not change this mainstream Orthodox theology. The need and determination to preserve one's Jewishness was understood in spite of the Holocaust, not because of it. In other words, for most Orthodox Jews the Holocaust was not a challenge to the doctrine of chosenness but rather a confirmation of it – either in terms of the concept of the 'suffering servant of God' or the gentile hatred of the Jews or as a punishment for the sins of European Jewry. The simple truth was that, as put by Mordechai Gifter, one of the primary religious leaders of Orthodox Jewry, the '*Churban* [catastrophe] itself is evidence and testimony to the fact that "we have a Father in Heaven"'.[96] For the majority of Orthodox Jews the Holocaust was not a novel event in the history of the Jewish people. On the contrary, it fitted in as another example of Jewish suffering and evidence of Jewish chosenness. The imagery often applied to the Holocaust in this way was the conflict between Esau and Jacob,[97] an imagery which holds obvious particularist and separationist implications. Having said that, Orthodoxy, despite its discomfort with the survivalist theologies of the 1970s and 1980s, greatly benefited from an atmosphere of a return to tradition and particularism, an atmosphere which owed its existence mainly to the Holocaust discourse.

The idea that Israel is a people chosen by God as a model nation (kingdom of priests), the bearer of a true religion, was essential to all Orthodox groups. However, in relation to the extent that Orthodox Jewry integrated into surrounding societies, their understandings of the nature of chosenness displayed a variation ranging from an extreme particularism to a mild universalism. It is true that all Orthodox groups held the same view on basic Jewish tenets and, in the wake of what is called the Holocaust consciousness, modern and ultra-Orthodox Jewry concurred with each other through an increasing modern Orthodox Jewish emphasis on faith and separation. However, when coming to the 1990s, the difference between these two Orthodox groups, particularly in their attitude to Jewish identity, becomes more visible.

At this point it is important to note a 1990 survey conducted by Lynn Davidman on two Orthodox Jewish communities in America, one of which was a modern Orthodox and the other a Lubavitch hasidic group.[98] According to the survey results, there appear to be different, even opposite, motivations and principles underlying each community. In the modern Orthodox group (Metropolitan Synagogue) this-worldly, individualist, and choice-orientated criteria play an important role whereas in the ultra-Orthodox Lubavitch group (Pardes Sara) other-worldly, community-based and given motivations rule the community. So, in the modern Orthodox group Jewish (or Orthodox) identity is regarded as something to be chosen by a member of the group on the basis of rational, ethical, or social reasons. As far as the Lubavitcher attitude is concerned, however, Jewishness is believed to be something given: one is either Jewish or not; it is not a question of choice but that of an inner nature. The structural difference between these two Orthodox groups, for Davidman, is directly related to the fact that modern Orthodoxy employs accommodation as its survival strategy, by advocating 'a combination of traditional religious observance with active participation in the secular world'; the Lubavitch Hasidim, in contrast, represent a sectarian approach, resistance being the group's strategy for survival. As a matter of fact, these two opposite Orthodox approaches to modernity and Jewish identity are very much related to the way in which these groups understand the nature of Jewish separation and distinctiveness. In fact, the question of separation and distinctiveness, which lies at the heart of the doctrine of chosenness, is central to shaping the Orthodox worldview both in America and elsewhere.

Nevertheless, for some Orthodox groups the separation between Jews and non-Jews indicates, to use Novak's terminology, a 'relational distinctiveness', whereas for others it connotes a 'substantial distinctiveness'. So, in the case of relational distinctiveness, although the separation of Jews from non-Jews is strongly advocated (on the basis of the chosenness of the Jewish people) and its firm establishment sought after, other peoples are also given some credit, on the condition that they conform to the Noahide Laws. In fact, this has often been the view of the modern Orthodox rabbis and theologians in spite of the ongoing traditional Jewish reduction of all nations to Esau, the evil progenitor of paganism. In the theology of Rabbi Soloveitchik, for example, as paraphrased by Eisen, each community could cooperate with others in the 'cultural enterprise of humanity', as long as they held fast to their 'otherness as a metaphysical covenantal community'.[99] So, in Soloveitchik's theology, the Jewish people are seen 'unique' and 'different' in religious terms, namely by virtue of the Torah and covenant, and Jewish seclusion from secular America (reminiscent of Esau) is strongly required. However, no difference is observed between Jews and non-Jews in terms of humanity. Furthermore, Soloveitchik also adheres to the 'choice factor' in the covenantal relationship between God and the Jewish people, suggesting two types of covenants and/or Jewish existence: that of 'fate' and that of 'destiny'.[100] According to this distinction, Jewishness is primarily a matter of fate or coercion, as everyone born to a Jewish mother automatically becomes Jewish and therefore part of the covenanted people. Yet it also involves faith or choice, because after God chose Abraham and, together with him, all of his descendants, he asked Israel to voluntarily accept the covenant decrees at Sinai to become a 'priestly kingdom'. 'Man's task, according to Judaism', Solovetichik maintains, 'is to transform fate into destiny ... an existence of compulsion, perplexity and muteness into an existence replete with a powerful will, with resourcefulness'.[101] So, in Soloveitchik's understanding, the 'free and unrestricted search for the transcendent', Michael Berger asserts, 'is met by the commanding voice of Sinai, forcing Man into submission. But in the end ... Man's will unites with the divine will so that obedience is actually free'.[102] In other words, the notions of human free will and individual experience, though understood more in traditional terms than modern, are not totally absent in Soloveitchik's theology. Today, however, there is an increasing impact of modern values and modern thought not only on non-Orthodox Jewish groups and theologians, but also on some Orthodox ones. At this point, David Singer refers to a marked contrast between Soloveitchik's Orthodox theology and what he calls the 'new Orthodoxy theology', as represented by David Hartman and Irving Greenberg, in particular. As asserted by many, Soloveitchik has successfully combined in his theology what is traditional and modern, and adhered to an unconditional obedience to *halakhah*. Therefore his standing has been embraced by the majority of Orthodox Jews in America, albeit to the dissatisfaction of the ultra-Orthodox community. As far as the new Orthodox theology is concerned, however, Soloveitchik's stress on obedience is replaced by 'human autonomy', as reminiscent of Borowitz's post-modern covenant theology. Hartman declares, at the beginning of his *A Living Covenant*, that it was an attempt 'to characterize Judaism in terms of a covenantal anthropology that encourages human initiative and freedom and that is predicated on belief in human adequacy'.[103] According to Hartman, Singer states, 'experience' no less than 'tradition' can be a valid source of theological inspiration.[104] Indeed, although Hartman ascribes the social and historical existence of the Jewish people to the God of history 'through whose intervention it was born', he also declares that the commandments of God are such demands that are 'made by a personal will and presuppose a personal relationship to God'.[105] Thus, for Hartman, personal 'experience', as an ongoing process that began at Sinai, rather than unconditional 'obedience', which happened once and for all, lies at the heart of Judaism, as he writes:

> so long as the centrality of *mitzvot* and the eternity of the covenant are not undermined, there is enormous room for building multiple images of God and of his relationship to the community, nature, and history, a multiplicity that enables the covenant to remain a live option.[106]

A similar understanding can also be observed in Greenberg's post-Holocaust theology. In a 1968 essay, Greenberg openly suggested that Orthodoxy should 'go through the modern experience', to be able to transform from a 'normative, ascetic, ethnocentric, [and] judgmental' ethos into a 'more universalist, relativist, self- and pleasure-oriented' one,[107] which would include some post-modern values, such as relativism and individualism. Although in later years, under the influence of the Holocaust consciousness, Greenberg proposed that modern values should be approached in a 'discriminating fashion' and that one should be aware of their perils,[108] the impact of modernity on his theology still visible. The idea of 'human autonomy' in relation to covenant and chosenness occupies an important place in Greenberg's theology as well. According to what he calls the 'voluntary covenant', the participation of the Jewish people in the covenant is considered as that of a senior partner and the result of a voluntary act. Moreover, Greenberg defines 'chosenness' mainly as a 'unique experience' on the part of the Jewish people, writing in an existentialist fashion:

> The chosen-people concept expresses the Jews' experience of being singled out by God's love.... If one has truly tasted the experience, one would be reluctant to lose that feeling by dissolving back into the mass.... We lose neither connection – to God or to other humans – in the process of living the experience. Nor is the process reserved for us to the exclusion of everyone else. God's love – God's redemptive love – which is the basis of chosenness, is never the monopoly of any one people.... The chosenness flows from the fact that this particular redemption happened to us. Others ... may undergo their own experience of redemption. That cannot take away my unique experience or my feeling of uniqueness.[109]

In this way, Greenberg also advocates the idea of a multiple chosenness by affirming the uniqueness of each people's experience. He, however, does not play down the importance of the notions of being 'a light unto the nations' and *tikkun olam* (mending the world) for the Jewish concept of chosenness. According to him, while Jews are not intrinsically superior to other nations, the individual can by all means respond to election in a way that makes him 'more worthy and a truly constructive model and teacher' for the world.[110] In fact, what Novak says about Hartman, that he is 'a traditionalist thinker attempting to move in a more liberal direction',[111] seems to apply to Greenberg as well. Nevertheless, as emphasized by David Singer, these radical theologies do not represent the majority of the Orthodox Jews' viewpoint in America, who prefer to understand chosenness in more traditional terms, such as law and separation as well as mending the world. However, the emphasis that Hartman and Greenberg both place on human autonomy and on existentialist, personalist and voluntarist definitions of Jewishness and chosenness is certainly in accord with the orientation many contemporary American Jews take.

As for Michael Wyschogrod, although it is not easy to place him in any of the Orthodox categories, Singer introduces Wyschogrod under the banner of the 'New Orthodox Theology'. This is so, for Singer, despite the fact that Wyschogrod, with his rejection of 'human autonomy' and his emphasis on the 'sovereignty of the will of God', displays a contradictory approach to that of Hartman and Greenberg. According to Singer, what makes Wyschogrod's theology extremely modern (or post-modern), and therefore parallel to other new Orthodox theologies, is its being a 'direct response to the modern experience'.[112] Indeed, although Wyschogrod strictly opposes modernity, he ends up building his theology not on any given belief or fact but on 'a conscious philosophical-theological choice', which is a rather modern phenomenon. And this is why Wyschogrod in the end comes to the point of defending the 'individual decision based on the individual's understanding of the will of God', namely individual experience and concomitant choice, as against rabbinic authority as a taught (or given) truth. Again Wyschogrod seeks to establish Jewish uniqueness or chosenness from an internal (existential) point of view, just like Hartman, Greenberg, and Borowitz did, and not in relation to other faiths, namely not in relation to superiority or truth. This is why, in Wyschogrod's understanding, Jewish chosenness is grounded on no reason other than God's arbitrary love for Israel and has no purpose other than his embracing 'a people in the fullness of its humanity [namely in both its spirituality and carnality]',[113] while the role of bringing humanity to the knowledge of God is left to Christianity.

In a similar way, David Berger, one of the Orthodox respondents to the survey by *Commentary* magazine in 1996, speaks of the mysterious nature of chosenness by pointing to a blend of particularist and universalist elements included in the doctrine of chosenness. On the other hand, Saul Berman and Marshall Breger understand chosenness mainly in terms of a 'special mission' and 'duty and responsibility'. Breger, in particular, poses a critique of the current American Jewish emphasis on 'feeling' as against 'faith' and 'practice':

The intellectual thought of the 20th century is focused on the celebration (indeed the glorification) of the individual.... In rabbinic Judaism there is rarely any reference to rights; the operative terms are duty and responsibility. Nor is there much focus on feelings – one's duty is to practice the commandments. This focus on both duty and responsibility puts Judaism inextricably at odds with almost all species of modernism and political liberalism.[114]

As a matter of fact, the 1996 survey by *Commentary* is considered to witness the victory of traditionalism over liberalism, as represented by Orthodox and

Reform movements respectively, whereas the 1966 survey by the same magazine had the opposite result. Of this, Singer makes the following observation:

> [Thirty years ago] the Orthodox participants were comfortable in their modernity, but at pains to justify their Orthodoxy. In 1996, for me at least, the situation is exactly the reverse: my Orthodoxy is rock solid, but I am hard-pressed to justify any accommodation with modernity.[115]

However, despite an apparent consistency, even victory, of the traditionalist line, which advocates a Jewish uniqueness and a Jewish distinction for positive purposes and permanent reasons, the American Orthodox congregation does not seem to be successful, in the eyes of some Jewish scholars, in guaranteeing a place for itself that is safe from survivalist concerns. But, perhaps, it is possible to interpret these concerns in terms of a Jewish obsession with survival. In this context, it is important to recall a chapter entitled 'American Jewry: the ever-dying people' in Marshall Sklare's *Observing America's Jews*, in which he quotes the historian Simon Rawidowicz saying: 'He who studies Jewish history will readily discover that there was hardly a generation in the Diaspora period which he did not consider itself the final link in Israel's chain'.[116] Nevertheless, it is worth noting Rapaport's analysis on the future of modern Orthodoxy. According to him, 'despite the statistics, the future of Modern Orthodoxy is in jeopardy' and this is directly related to the fact that modern Orthodox Jews embrace modernity no less than non-Orthodox Jews. 'While adherence to the tenets of *Halakhah*', Rapaport maintains, 'classifies the individuals as Orthodox, their values and allegiances belong first and foremost to Western culture'.[117] According to Rapaport, by holding to wealth and success as a means of survival, Orthodox Jews transmit a weakened and transformed form of Orthodoxy to their children. Judaism becomes secondary to full membership in modern society.[118]

As far as the mainstream ultra-Orthodox theology is concerned, however, which holds to the idea of a substantial distinctiveness, the relation between Jews and non-Jews is seen as one of kind, not one of degree. In *Ha Tanya*, the basic book of Habad Hasidism, written by Rabbi Shneur Zalman, the idea of two different kinds of souls, one as the divine soul of the Jew and the other as the animal soul of the non-Jew, can be found.[119] This is in fact an idea that originated in kabbalistic literature. In the book of *Zohar*, the classical work of the Kabbalah, Jews are depicted as the possessor of 'the higher soul' (*neshamah*) in an exclusive way, while non-Jews, together with other living beings, are associated with 'the lowest part of the soul' (*nefesh*), namely what is also called 'the animal soul'.[120] As put by R.L. Kremnizer, this fundamental difference between Jewish and non-Jewish souls is manifested in two ways. The first way allows the Jew to interact with God directly, with no instrument being required, and this level of faith and knowledge of God is called the 'level of Sight' (*Reiya*).[121] On the other hand, the highest level of faith a gentile can reach is with the help of intellect, which is called the 'level of Hearing' (*Shemiah*). The second way in which the difference is manifested is indicated by the Jewish attribute of 'self-sacrifice for Godliness'. This attribute, which can be shared by non-Jews as well, works in a different way in the case of a Jew. Whereas a non-Jew displays self-sacrifice 'for the purpose of the completion of his being', as far as a Jew is concerned, self-sacrifice does not lead to any self-fulfilment; on the contrary, it becomes a natural and organic manifestation of his being. This is why, Kremnizer asserts, Jews 'have refused to change their religion and their allegiance to God' in the Nazi Holocaust as well as in the slaughter of the Crusades.[122]

In Habad theology, too, based on the above-mentioned fundamental distinction between Jew and non-Jew, the term 'chosen' is attributed to the Jewish people only in relation to the Jewish body, not to the Jewish soul, as the latter is considered not chosen but rather created as holy and divine. So, the Jews are not a people chosen by God, but rather a people whose soul (or substance) was created differently from the souls of all other beings. What is asserted here is an idea of chosenness that has an eternal unconditional nature. In other words, the 'chosen people' is used in a metaphorical sense, because the Jews were not chosen by God at some point in history but instead were created as the 'chosen people' right from the beginning. Moreover, in this substantialist definition of Jewishness, the Jews' inner nature, which has been so created by God and therefore is unchangeable, induces their actions and feelings, as put by one contemporary Lubavitcher rabbi:

> Why does a Jew do a *mitzva* [commandment]? For no reason. Because it's natural. They don't need a reason.... A Jew by definition wants to do *mitzvas*.... When God tells us what to do He's not telling us what to do but what we are.... A human being breathes, a Jewish soul *mitzvas*. That's a verb. God is *mitzvas*, we are part of God, therefore we are *mitzvas*. That's why a Jew who spent 40 years living a non-Jewish life and then studies *Yiddishkeit* [the traditional Jewish way of life] can be perfectly comfortable as a Jew in one week. If it was a new life-style it would be a struggle. But he's just being himself.[123]

At this point, the particularist and exclusivist emphasis on the concept of chosenness in relation to the Holocaust becomes obvious: 'History is not impressed by insignificant individuals; only the great *Klal Yisrael* occupies a central position in history as the *Am Hanivchar* (Chosen Nation) whose chosenness is manifested through times of redemption and through times of destruction.'[124]

Such a view of the chosen people as superior to and fundamentally different from other peoples has been promoted, before and after the Holocaust, by the Lubavitchers, who come from the tradition of the Habad Hasidic movement. Rabbi Menachem Mendel Schneerson, the last Lubavitcher rabbi, argued that:

> A Jew was not created as a means for some [other] purpose; he himself is the purpose, since the substance of all [divine] emanations was created only to serve the Jews. 'In the beginning God created the heavens and the earth' [Gen. 1:1] means that [the heavens and the earth] were created for the sake of the Jews, who are called the 'beginning'. This means everything, all

developments, all discoveries, the creation ... are vanity compared to the Jews. The important things are the Jews, because they do not exist for any [other] aim; they themselves are [the divine] aim.[125]

On the other hand, according to Rabbi Manis Friedman, a contemporary Lubavitcher rabbi, Jews, as much as being fundamentally different from other creatures, function for a divine purpose. 'A Jew', Friedman writes, 'is a Divine being sent to do something for the world, to accomplish something, to bring some Godliness to the worldly condition.... A Jew is a different kind of creature with a different soul...'[126] The impact of such interpretations on certain policies of the state of Israel and particularly on the activities of the religious–Zionist groups in Israel is obvious, as will be discussed in the following chapter.

Consequently, one can say that the influence of the Holocaust on different Jewish congregations and the relevant theologies during the 1970s and 1980s varied considerably. However, while the survivalist ideology was adopted by the Reform segment more than any other Jewish group, this period also witnessed the emergence of a 'mysterious' form of chosenness, which put a seal on every Jewish congregation in America to a certain extent. What is most interesting is that the Holocaust consciousness brought the Reform and Orthodox groups closer to each other by emphasizing the importance of Jewish distinctiveness and Jewish unity, albeit in reference to different premises. It was primarily the Holocaust that dictated to the Reform Jews the terms of the return to Jewish roots. And it was mainly God that mattered for most Orthodox Jews, whose voice could still be heard from Sinai, yet for some it was heard through Auschwitz. Coming to the 1990s, on the other hand, even a mere survivalism of the Reform congregation conceded its place to a new form of covenant relationship, which can be best defined as post-modern, due to its individualist and experience-oriented nature. As for the influence of the Holocaust on Israeli politics and society, it is possible to trace some similarities with the experience of American Jewry. However, the inner dynamics as well as the values and premises that rule these two societies have fundamental differences, which can be well observed in reference to the language of the doctrine of chosenness as employed by both societies.

10   The Israeli experience

The transformation that the Jews of the land of Israel (*Yishuv*) underwent in the second half of the twentieth century, measured by two great milestones, i.e. the creation of the state of Israel and the Six Day War, displays a parallel with the experience of American Jewry in many aspects. The first decades of the state of Israel (the period of Statism) witnessed a relatively universalist and anti-isolationist orientation in Israeli society and Israeli politics under the rule of Mapai, the left-wing Zionist party. The 1970s, on the other hand, witnessed a social crisis which promoted an atmosphere of particularism and isolation as well as a return to religion, with the emergence of the Holocaust discourse (the period of the New Civil Religion). As indicated by Laurence Silberstein, the way in which the Zionist ideology, either in secular or religious form, developed in Israel justifies post-modern theoreticians like Jacques Derrida, who argues that Zionism, like other social categories, is not a monolithic entity but 'a socially constructed discourse, formulated and disseminated by specific groups engaged in a struggle to establish their hegemony within the Jewish world'.[1] It is also true that Zionism, with its integration of basic Jewish myths and symbols into its own ideology, has become the most important and most powerful factor in Jewish self-understanding and self-expression in both Israel and America.

What is called Statism, civil religion created by the founders of the state of Israel, functioned as a 'substitute for traditional religion' and became a 'quasi-religion' for Israeli society, in which the traditional concepts of faith and covenant were redefined in relation to the State, instead of to God – thus the name Statism. The 'joy and enthusiasm evoked by the creation of the state of Israel', Charles Liebman and Eliezer Don-Yehiya assert, 'had the character of Messianic sentiments', and in this way many Israelis believed 'the state to be the fulfillment of the traditional Jewish vision of redemption'.[2] In fact, as mentioned earlier, the creation of the state of Israel had a biblical connotation, not only for Jews but also for Christians. The crucial role that President Harry Truman, called 'the American Cyrus', reminiscent of the biblical figure of Cyrus, played in the creation of the state of Israel, notwithstanding the political–electoral concerns, is attributed by some to his 'conversance with the history of the Middle East and his knowledge of the Bible'.[3] Again, President Jimmy Carter is quoted as saying in 1976: 'I am pro-Israeli, not because of political expediency, but because I believe Israel is the fulfilment of Biblical prophecy'.[4] Christian world's approval of a Jewish state in Palestine in reference to the Bible indicates its recognition of the Jews as the 'chosen people' and of their mysterious function in God's plan for the world, as indicated by Paul in the Letter to the Romans.[5]

However, the notion of the chosen people was transformed in the Statist rhetoric into the idea of 'mission'. The Jewish redemption, as expressed in nationalist, as opposed to religious, terms by David Ben-Gurion, Israel's first prime minister, included the 'redemption of all humanity' as well, providing the Jewish state with an indispensable mission for the world. It was, in effect, the realization of classical Zionism, which sought to establish its nationalist ideology in terms of a national salvation based on universal principles. Zionism, by so doing, 'secularized the religious myth [of chosenness and redemption] and thereby provided a synthesis of modern and traditional salvational ideas'.[6] If the first and foremost traditional Jewish concept employed by Zionism is thus 'redemption', the second such concept has been 'mission'. Indeed the notions of being 'a light unto the nations' and creating an 'ideal society' as an example for the entire world seem to have played an important role in the rhetoric of Statism as they did in the earlier political Zionist discourse – though in the latter what was meant by Israel was primarily the people, not the state.

Nevertheless, according to Yeshayahu Leibowitz, the late Israeli scientist and intellectual, while the idea of being a light unto the nations in its biblical context referred to the prophet Isaiah's mission 'to bring Jacob back' to God (Isa. 49:5) and to the position of the prophet Jeremiah as 'a prophet to the nations' (Jer. 1:5), it did not assume the people of Israel to be 'endowed with a capacity for instructing and guiding all of humanity'. Leibowitz maintains that such an idea was 'fabricated by the heretics – from the Apostle Paul to Ben-Gurion – who meant to cast off the yoke of Torah by substituting for it a faith in an abstract "vocation"'.[7] Indeed, such an idea of mission or vocation as understood in an active sense and deprived of the law, which is quite foreign to traditional Judaism, did not emerge in Jewish thought until the end of the nineteenth century and was the result of the Jewish Emancipation and the following Jewish encounter with western ideas and values. Therefore, in the Statist as well as in the earlier secular Zionist rhetoric, the idea of mission seems to be based on secular and elitist grounds. Statism's conception of the state of Israel as 'a light unto the nations', is taken to imply 'an elitism that found expression not only in Israel's responsibilities to other nations but also in its self-image of moral and intellectual superiority'.[8]

Apparently, the sense of superiority, parallel to the idea of mission, prevailing in Zionism in general and in Statism in particular, partly derives from the traditional Jewish doctrine of chosenness. For the idea of the holiness of Israel has something to do with Jewish 'merit' and Jewish 'superiority', as understood in spiritual terms, namely in terms of their acceptance and hold of the Torah. This is a notion that was later adopted by some modern Jewish scholars as well, such as Abraham Geiger who interpreted it in reference to 'Jewish genius'. The use of the Jewish concept of being 'a light unto the nations' by secular Zionists like Ben-Gurion, indicates the elitist nature of Zionism, as a secular counterpart to the traditional notion of Jewish chosenness and Jewish superiority. Leibowitz criticizes secular Zionists, 'who empty the notion of the people of Israel of its religious content, and still append the phrase "chosen people" to it', for transforming the expression into 'a reflection of racial chauvinism'.[9] This chauvinism becomes especially obvious in Israel's treatment of the non-Ashkenazi and non-Jewish Israelis, namely Oriental Jews and Arabs, respectively. As a matter of fact, Israeli society displays a hierarchical structure, the Ashkenazi (European) Jews being at the top, Sephardic and Mizrahi (non-European) Jews in the middle and non-Jewish Israelis (Druzes and Arabs, respectively) at the bottom. For the American Jewish feminist scholar, Judith Plaskow, this is mainly related to the nature of the Jewish religion, which, due to the notion of the chosen people, has created a hierarchical society based on an internal hierarchical differentiation and an external strong distinction between Jew and non-Jew. According to Plaskow, the Jewish concept of chosenness, in practice if not by definition, presupposes a hierarchical structure as being built on a multiple differentiation on various levels. For Jewish superiority or difference is 'not one among many'; it is, instead, 'a matter of God's decision, God's mysterious and singular choice bestowing upon the Jews an unparalleled spiritual destiny'. Plaskow maintains,

> to be a holy people was both to be different from one's neighbors and to distinguish between ... pure and impure, Sabbath and week, kosher and non-kosher, Cohen, Levi, and Israel (...), and male and female.... Differences in wealth, learning, and observance; differences in cultural background and customs (between ... Jews from Eastern Europe, Spain, or the Orient); differences in religious affiliation and understanding (...between Hasidim and Mitnagdim...) have all provided occasions for certain groups of Jews to define themselves as superior to different and nonnormative Others.[10]

Thus, according to Plaskow, the concept of being chosen by God is the biggest obstacle towards Jewish understanding of differences on a pluralist, rather than a hierarchical, ground and towards Jewish recognition of the other.

Indeed, despite the presence of quite a few passages in the Torah that emphasize the existence of one basic law or standard for all Israelites, including the resident aliens (*ger toshav*),[11] as well as the prophetic vision of equality and unity, the complicated nature of the law, which in many issues (such as marriage, purity, and diet) has different applications in different groups within Jewish society,[12] seems to have strengthened this differentiation by helping to create a hierarchical society. Accordingly, as asserted by Plaskow, the hierarchical structure of Jewish society, in turn, helped to create, or caused the social basis of today's Israeli civic system. As for the distinction between Jews and non-Jews, which originated in biblical times, this seems to have gained more of an anti-gentile orientation later in Jewish tradition. In rabbinic literature, alongside some positive statements, there are also some negative ones regarding the gentiles, in which they are depicted as 'idolaters', 'wicked', 'enemies of Israel', and even 'enemies of God'. Besides, their final destiny is understood, unlike that of Israel, in terms of complete ruin.[13] Apparently, one of the reasons for the rabbinic contempt of other nations was related to actual life experience between Jews and non-Jews. However, the need to justify the doctrine of chosenness by placing the righteous Israel against totally wicked nations must also have played an important role in this perception. Kabbalistic literature, on the other hand, introduced the notion of a fundamental difference between Jews and non-Jews, which had an important influence on the shaping of the religious–Zionist ideology in Israel. As a matter of fact, today every non-Jewish criticism of and opposition to the Jewish state would be seen, among the extreme religious–Zionist Jews, from this perspective of God's people versus their enemies, and Israel's revenge on the latter would be justified as a 'lofty matter of *Kiddush Hashem*'.[14]

Nevertheless, it seems to be that the Zionist, particularly Ashkenazi, sense of distinction and superiority is also strongly related to the supremacist character of western colonialist thought, which might be considered as constituting the political background of Zionism.[15] The question of the relation between colonialism and Zionism is, in fact, quite a controversial one, and such a relation is vigorously denied by mainstream Israeli politicians and scholars, who see Zionism as a 'unique' form of nationalism. However, there is powerful evidence for the effect of colonialism on the 'processes of legitimization employed by Zionists' and on the 'structure of Israeli society', as brought forward by some contemporary Jewish historians and thinkers in Israel, who are usually referred to as post-Zionist scholars. According to Gershon Shafir, for example, one of the first Israeli scholars to use the colonial method to interpret the nature of Zionist settlements, the fact that in the early Zionist discourse the land was represented as 'empty' indicates the presence of a colonialist view of 'the native population as being part and parcel of the environment that was to be subdued, tamed, and made hospitable for themselves'.[16] In a similar way, for Israeli historian Ilan Pappe, the state of Israel was created 'with the help of Western colonialism' and the dispossession of the Palestinians was justified on the basis of the 'uniqueness of Jewish history that derives from the Shoah'.[17] It is also stressed by Noam Chomsky, American Jewish scholar, that, as early as the 1920s, the Jewish settlers 'had contempt [for the Arabs] as an "uncivilized race", to whom some of them referred as "Red Indians" and others as "savages"'.[18] It is interesting to note that Statism, despite its elitist and chauvinistic nature, had sought to integrate Israel with other nations on terms of equality and mutual interest. However, this is not so surprising considering that those nations into which Israel intended to integrate were western nations, as opposed to eastern ones. Ben-Gurion is noted to have openly displayed his contempt even of Oriental Jews by describing them as having no 'trace of Jewish or human education'. As a matter of fact, what lies behind the Zionist project of turning Oriental Jews into true Ashkenazi Israelis is regarded by some as a Zionist distinction between the 'evil East' (the Muslim Arab) and the 'good East' (the Jewish Arab).[19] However, the failure of Statism in this programme of the westernization of Oriental Jews would result in the marginalization and exclusion of the latter. This process of marginalization and exclusion is, in effect, considered by Derrida and others to be 'endemic to Western thought and culture', in which a marginalized 'other' is required for one to define one's identity against.[20] Based on this consideration, the notion of superiority, too, both in its religious Jewish and secular Zionist form, can be seen as the result of the Jewish or Zionist self-definition 'as opposed to', and not 'in relation to', the other, namely the non-Jewish and the non-Zionist. While this does not apply to every Jewish or Zionist self-definition, in Israel it seems to have been the norm so far, in secular as well as in extremist religious–nationalist self-definitions.

To turn back to the Statist strategy, Statism, with its emphasis on integration into the West, retained the classical Zionist claim of being an outpost of western civilization in the Middle East, on the one hand, and that of making the Jewish people a normal people like others, by rendering them their own state, on the other. Accordingly, in relation to the Arab neighbours a sense of 'superiority' would be ascribed to Israel, and in relation to the West a sense of 'normality'. Statism, like the pre-state Zionist–socialist movement, also sought to distinguish itself from the Jewish past by negating the Diaspora and anything related to it. But what played an important role in the ideology of Statism were the nationalist symbols and values, rather than socialist ones. Traditional Jews were condemned, due to their religious-passive orientation; the extermination of European Jewry, on the other hand, was seen as a result of this passive attitude and part of a rejected Jewish past, and, therefore, was considered irrelevant to the image of the new secular Israeli Jew.[21]

It is important to mention here the shifting emphases in Israeli remembrance of the extermination of European Jewry as depicted at Yad Vashem, the Israeli Holocaust museum. During the 1950s, there had been an obvious emphasis on activism, and the two images at the entrance of the museum reflected a Statist contrast between martyrdom represented by Auschwitz and heroism displayed in Zionism. Again the 1960s were the years of the commemoration of heroism. The Statist indifference to the Holocaust was greatly related to the integrationist policy adopted by Israel back then, which placed an emphasis on the themes of normalcy and being part of the world, instead of victimhood and isolation. With the advent of the 1970s, however, the previous division between the Holocaust and heroism disappeared from Israeli consciousness. The emphasis shifted from heroism to an Israeli awareness of the Jews being one united group, and an empathy with the Holocaust victims was established among Israelis, a transformation which occurred partly as an outcome of the Eichmann trial, yet mostly arose in the wake of the Six Day and Yom Kippur wars. In fact, Ben-Gurion had displayed, not only after but also during the extermination of European Jewry, this early Zionist indifference to the fate of Jewry, by saying that instead of saving 'all the children in Germany by taking them to England', he would choose to save 'only half of the children by taking them to Eretz Israel'.[22] So, for Zionism, and later Statism, the establishment of a Jewish state in Palestine was the primary goal, while the fate of individual Jews was of secondary and instrumental importance. Accordingly, in these early years, the relation between the

Holocaust and the state of Israel was not understood in terms of suffering and redemption, as it was in the 1970s and 1980s. Instead, a disconnection between European Jews and Israelis was desired. The Holocaust was not the precursor of redemption; it was rather the punishment for European Jewry's indifference to Zionism and a justification for the Zionist claim that there was no future for Jews in Europe. Nevertheless, the creation of the state of Israel was still understood and presented, even back then, in terms of redemption, though with a more state-based emphasis. The state, as a secular epitome of the Jewish redemption, gained priority over the Jewish people and became a subject of worship and ultimate loyalty in the civil religion of Statism.

In fact, the traditional notions of messianism and mission, as mentioned earlier, would show the world Jewish superiority and the redemptive role undertaken by its people, as well as the necessity for a Jewish state in the middle of the Arab countries, the latter representing the barbaric East. In this way, the Jewish state would be presented as a light emanating from the Holy Land, as depicted in the Bible. As far as the civil religion of Statism is concerned, on the other hand, the rhetoric of the achievement of Jewish messianism would serve to establish the Zionist ideology of the founders of Israel as a civil religion. Statism thus translated the traditional Jewish notions of redemption, mission, and even chosenness, into the language of the modern secular nation-state, by applying the ultimate sanctity and loyalty to the Zionist state as well as to Jewish nationhood, sometimes even at the expense of the Jewish people, not to mention the non-Jewish population. So, despite the rhetoric of being a light unto the nations, which had an apparent moralist implication in prophetic language, Statism saw obedience to the Zionist state as an end in itself, in quasi-religious terms.

There is also religious–Zionism, a sincere yet problematic mixture of traditional Jewish and modern secular values and principles. This may be seen as a substitution of what has been understood, throughout Jewish history, as an eschatological and positive concept, namely the redemption of the Jewish people as well as all humankind, by power politics.[23] Extreme religious–Zionists, in particular, seem to hold to a rather particularist and ethnocentric interpretation of chosenness and redemption. It is interesting to note that there have been religious Jews right from the beginning, like the Mizrachi group, who saw Zionism as part of Jewish messianism, in terms of a Jewish return to, and re-establishment of the Jewish state in Zion. Nevertheless, religious–Zionism as a powerful entity in Israeli politics and an influential element in Israeli public life came into existence only in the aftermath of the Six Day and Yom Kippur wars. Religious–Zionism, as such, has been the ideology of Gush Emunim (Bloc of the Faithful), the Jewish fundamentalist group, which was founded in 1974 by the religious Jews trained in the Markaz Yeshiva of Rabbi Zvi Yehuda Kook. The emergence of a particularist and isolationist tendency in Israel, which led to the rise of Gush Emunim, is seen by many as the direct result of a 'legitimacy crisis' in Israeli politics after the Six Day War and a 'spiritual crisis' in Israeli society after the Yom Kippur War. At this point, the difference in the nature of the impacts that these two wars had on Israel, albeit both serving the same goal, is very important. The Six Day War, as a result of the rapid victory of the Israeli army and Israel's claim to newly acquired territory (the 'occupied territories'), provided Israel with enormous power and sudden security. In the face of this state of power and security on the part of Israel, a new form of legitimacy was required, one that could not be based on the rhetoric of being a light unto the nations any more. So, a new image of Israel as a vulnerable country was created, despite its obvious inconsistency with the above-mentioned reality. This new image, in turn, created a new problem of security, even survival, and caused alarm within Israeli society. In this development the anti-Israeli statements by Arab countries before the war also played an important role. The issue of survival, however, was presented in a new religious context, leading to the recognition of traditional Judaism and the use of Jewish religious symbols and values in Israeli politics. With this new religious symbolism, an association between Israelis and Diaspora Jews was also desired, religion being the most important tie between the two. In this way, Jewish people all over the world would begin to be understood as 'one people', who are in danger, and Israel could get Jewish support from other countries, especially from America.

As far as ordinary Israelis are concerned, however, the 1967 victory, which resulted in the Israeli appropriation of the West Bank area and East Jerusalem, was taken as a miraculous event and even strengthened the messianic expectations of the religious Jews.[24] In this way, the position of Israel before the war was interpreted by Israeli leaders as that of a country surrounded by enemies, and a parallel between the fate of Israelis and that of European Jewry in the Second World War was drawn. On the other hand, Israel's 'miraculous' victory in the 1967 war was ascribed to God's saving hand and, therefore, seen as divine approval of the existence of the state of Israel – the latter having been rejected by many religious Jews for being against God's will. Israel was thus given a religious, even messianic, meaning, being the epitome of redemption after persecution.

Nevertheless, as emphasized by many scholars, all these developments should be evaluated in the wake of the Yom Kippur War, which justified and escalated the atmosphere of isolation and the need to return to traditional Jewish symbols and ideas. Accordingly, the Yom Kippur War, with a near-defeat for the Israeli army, seemed an obvious negation of the secular Zionist claim that they were making the Jewish people into a normal people integrated in the world and, therefore, led to an atmosphere of isolation and victimhood in Israeli society. As far as messianic Jews were concerned, however, the insecurity created by the Yom Kippur War, after the miraculous Six Day War victory, was seen as a puzzle and appeared a step backwards. But different explanations were given to legitimate the war within a religious context. Gush Emunim interpreted it as the birth pangs of the Messiah. For some others, it was a warning to make the people undertake more responsibility in the process of redemption (activist interpretation) or, in contrast, to inform them that it was not the power and might of the people, but only God who, responding to the prayers of the people, could save the Jews (passivist interpretation).[25] In any case, the Yom Kippur War justified the notion of Israel as a people/state dwelling alone, furthering the feeling of alienation, and bringing secular and religious Jewish segments closer to each other. For the sense of alienation and isolation had been felt this time not only by secular but also by ultra-Orthodox Jews (*haredim*). The result was a growing association of Jewish nationalism with traditional Judaism, leading to the decline of Statism and the emergence of the New Civil Religion under the rule of Likud, the right-wing Zionist party.

The approach of New Civil Religion towards Jewish tradition and Jewish religious ideas was totally different from that of Statism. In the former, religious symbols and ideas, instead of being transformed or transvalued, were accepted as having positive values. Besides, New Civil Religion, with its emphasis on isolation and particularism, mobilized Israeli society around the symbols of peoplehood and religious roots, and not merely the symbol of the state. In this transformation, the problem of the integration of new immigrants into Israeli society also played an important role. They were mostly coming from Arab countries, and were to a great extent observant Jews who had had no contact with nationalist or secular tendencies. Thus what was needed for their integration into the society was an affirmative and religious (i.e. Jewish), and not a transformative and secular (i.e. Zionist), symbolism. It is interesting to note that, even before the rise of Likud, Gush Emunim had been supported by the Mapai government to a certain extent. This, in fact, indicates the existence of a legitimacy crisis and the following shift from a strict secular tendency in Israeli politics to a religious one already in the period of Statism. Nevertheless, the period that witnessed a full recognition of Gush Emunim in Israeli foreign policy and its enormous impact on Israeli society, began in 1977, when Likud won the elections. This period is extremely important in terms of Israeli understanding of the doctrines of chosenness and redemption, and the application of these to Israeli politics. In fact, the particularist-exclusivist interpretation of chosenness by Gush Emunim has been directly influential on Israeli–Arab relations as well as on Israeli self-conception. The elitist and ethnocentric orientation developed by Statism has thus been turned in New Civil Religion into a religiously particularist and ethnically exclusivist direction, with an emphasis not only on the 'uniqueness' but also on the 'abnormality' of the Jewish people.[26]

As pointed out by Liebman and Don-Yehiya, the basic principles of what is called New Civil Religion can be summarized as follows:

1   The acceptance of traditional religion as a positive value and the increasing exposition of Israeli society as well as Israeli politics to religious symbols as a basis of integration, legitimization and mobilization.
2   An emphasis on the Jewish people as one interrelated group and the reduction of God from being an active agent (traditional Jewish understanding) to a mere name.
3   The centrality of the Holocaust as the primary myth of Israeli society (covenant of fate) as well as the symbol of Israel's current condition (Esau hates Jacob) and that of legitimacy of its right to the land (God's promise to the Patriarchs).

4   A more particularist and exclusivist understanding of Jewishness in parallel to increasing isolationist tendencies.[27]

What seems most important among these developments is the emergence of the myth of the Holocaust and Redemption as a 'contemporary saga of exodus from enslavement to freedom and from subjugation to redemption',[28] which, as we have seen, greatly influenced American Jewry and established a three-fold, namely spiritual, political, and economic, connection between America and Israel. As regards the religious dimension of Israeli–American relations, Ian Lustick quotes Mordechai Nisan, a leading religious Gush intellectual, writing that 'America and Israel represent the "chosen" societies that carry the most noble dreams of civilization'.[29]

One of the most significant results of this myth of suffering (or innocence) and redemption is the Israeli application of a traditionally religious-messianic meaning and importance to the Jewish state. The state of Israel is thus understood not only as 'the state of the Jews', which has an ethnic connotation, but also as a 'Jewish state',[30] thus gaining more religious meaning. Israel was founded as a Jewish state in order to provide a shelter for Jews from all over the world, particularly for those who had escaped the Nazi genocide. However, Israel was also supposed to be a secular and democratic state as emphasized in the Declaration of Independence, which promised 'a complete equality of social and political rights to all its inhabitants irrespective of religion, race, or sex'. Moreover, in the declaration the main emphasis was placed on the historical, rather than on religious, connection between the Jewish people and Eretz Israel. However, as stated by Plaskow, this declaration did not have the force of law nor does Israel have a (secular) constitution that applies to all citizens. Besides, Arthur Hertzberg asserts that the state of Israel, despite its secular background, was 'created by Jews to be, and to remain, an essentially Jewish State, that is, to represent something more than a conventional, secular, political arrangement to serve the needs of its individual citizens of whatever condition or provenance'.[31] By so writing, Hertzberg indicates that there is a religious as well as an ethnic meaning attached to Israel right from the beginning. Indeed, Israel's Law of Return (1953) establishes Israel as a Jewish state, both ethnically and religiously, according to which every Jew from all over the world is entitled to settle there, whereas the non-Jewish inhabitants of the land are seen as foreign elements. On the other hand, for religious–Zionist groups, such as Gush Emunim, the existence of a Jewish state in Palestine is of a purely restorative meaning, namely the fulfilment of God's promise to Abraham. As put by one member of Gush Emunim, the Jews 'returned' to Israel not to seek shelter, but to take back the land which God had given them, as his chosen people.[32]

In this way, Israel, which was originally established as a secular state for the Jews (Statism), turned into a Jewish state (New Civil Religion). In this shift, the Western Wall with its clear religious image, instead of Mount Herzl, the symbol of secular Zionism, came to the fore. Again, the Yad Vashem museum began to attract more and more visitors than any other Zionist leader's memorial. It was later to become a great instrument of propaganda to publicize the unique nature of Jewish suffering and a means of justification for the existence of the state of Israel and for its policy of occupation. The aim behind those official visits to Yad Vashem, was to underline the idea that the 'temple of the Holocaust'[33] is, in effect, the sacred connection between the Holocaust and the state of Israel, based on two interrelated premises:

1   The Jewish state is compensation for unique Jewish suffering and therefore is a legal and just state.
2   All Jews, being unique and eternal victims of the Holocaust, are innocent; and so are Israelis.

In this context it is important to indicate an apparent difference between classical Zionist and religious–Zionist tendencies. As emphasized earlier, classical Zionism had an obvious optimistic and integrationist, albeit elitist and supremacist, character, when trying to end anti-Semitism by making Jews a 'normal' people within their own state and retaining the notion of a light unto the nations. Religious–Zionism, on the other hand, promoted particularist and isolationist rhetoric based on the 'abnormality' of the Jewish people and therefore the Jewish state. As rephrased by Ian Lustick, Harold Fisch, former rector of Bar-Ilan University and a member of Gush Emunim, claimed:

> Jews are not and cannot be a normal people; they are, in fact, irrevocably abnormal. The eternal uniqueness of the Jews is the result of the covenant God made with them at Mount Sinai – a real historical event with eternal and inescapable consequences for the entire world.[34]

In this way, statements like 'Esau hates Jacob' and 'a people who dwell alone' also predominated the new Israeli agenda. Moreover, New Civil Religion, with its isolationist rhetoric, encouraged intolerance towards non-Jews, as the strangers within the modern Jewish state. All non-Jews, especially the Arabs, as the epitome of Esau, were seen by extreme religious–Zionists as Jew-haters. Some rabbis would interpret the severe Arab opposition to Israel in terms of a desire to destroy all Jews, rather than the seeking of national redemption in their own land. In this way, Arab hostility towards Jews and Israel, which was mainly a political and, as such, a rational reaction, would be presented as part of a global and irrational anti-Semitism, and therefore a matter of theological and cosmic significance.[35] This, in turn, would give justification to the Jewish hatred of non-Jews on religious grounds. During the Lebanon War, Eleazar Waldman, a member of the Knesset, is quoted as saying that by fighting the Arabs Israel was carrying 'its mission to serve "as the heart of the world"' and that Arab hostility sprang, 'as does all anti-Semitism, from the world's recalcitrance in the face of Israel's mission to save it'. Thus, the cruelty of the Lebanon War should have been seen, for Waldman, 'as evidence of the advance of the redemption process'.[36]

   As we have seen, in the eyes of Rav Kook, the establishment of the state was considered as the beginning of redemption. Zvi Yehuda Kook, on the other hand, furthered his father's thesis by seeing Israel's victory in the Six Day War and the return of Judea and Samaria (the West Bank) to the Jews as clear signs of redemption. According to Zvi Yehuda Kook, while the Holocaust had demonstrated the wickedness and unreliability of the gentiles it had also paved the way to redemption in terms of the creation of the state of Israel and the subsequent victory of Israeli Defence Forces in the Six Day War. The emphasis on the role of the entire Jewish people, secular and religious, in the process of redemption was common to both Kooks's interpretations of redemption. However, despite a common view of Jewish solidarity, Zvi Yehuda Kook and the members of Gush Emunim, unlike Rav Kook, promoted a radically particularist and extremely intolerant approach to non-Jews. And what lay at the centre of such an approach was the extremist interpretation of the doctrine of the chosen people and the notion of the Promised Land. Rabbi Shlomo Goren, chief rabbi of Israel between 1973–83, declared, after the Six Day War, this religiously authorized, even sanctified, Jewish messianic task, promising that 'the hand of the clock will not move backwards again. The process of redemption will continue and will progress. No power on earth can exile us again and steal from us the land, promised to our fathers.'[37] A similar view was shared by Menachem Begin, too, Israeli Prime Minister at the time, who promised the permanent restoration of the whole land of Israel to the Jews.

For Zvi Yehuda Kook and other religious-messianic Jews, similar to Rav Kook's view, holiness was 'an unconditional attribute' of certain objects (i.e. the Holy Land) and certain beings (i.e. the Jewish people). Gush Emunim, as the representation of religious messianism and Jewish fundamentalism, held that since the Jews were living in a messianic age, the Jewish settlement in the occupied territories was a religious mandate and a very important stage in the coming of Jewish redemption. In this way, the Arab–Israeli wars, understood in terms of gentile–Jewish conflict, were given a religious interpretation and Jews, as the chosen people, were seen as duty-bound to take the land as a whole from the hands of the Arabs, the latter being equivalent to the ancient Canaanites. Moreover, what the redemption meant for those religious–Zionists was not only an eschatological-spiritual but also a this-worldly-political revival through which 'the Jews, aided by God, will thereafter triumph over the non-Jews and rule over them forever'. In this context, Israeli conquests in the Six Day War were seen as a transfer of the land from a satanic power to the divine sphere. It is also noted that, in these messianic efforts to conquer all the land, Joshua was naturally accepted as the figure to follow and the extermination of non-Jewish inhabitants of the land was encouraged.[38]

Coming to contemporary times, namely between the late 1980s and 1990s, it is possible to talk about approximately four different groups and four different stands they take on the questions of the state (Zionism), the land (redemption), and the people (chosenness). These groups include religious–Zionists, non-Zionists, anti-Zionists, and the advocates of a new orientation called post-Zionism, which mainly consists of secular Israeli scholars.

Religious–Zionists

The National Religious Party (NRP), along with Gush Emunim, constitutes the main religious–Zionist movement in Israel. The right-wing Likud party, too, has a similar orientation to religious–Zionists on many issues, such as territory and security. Liebman points to a process of toning down the messianic, though not nationalist, expectations of the Zionist *haredim*, who still retain their hawkish attitude in every aspect of Israeli policy. According to Liebman, this is a result of the development in which, parallel to the 'nationalization of the *haredim*', the 'haredization of the religious–Zionists' has taken place.[39] Again, Liebman in one of his later works maintains that 'a new form of religious radicalism' predominates within the majority of the Orthodox segment, 'a form of messianism which seeks the expansion of religious control over the entire society.'[40] This process creates a new type of religious–nationalist Jew, called *haredi–leumi*, drawing more and more Israelis from opposing camps, namely the nationalist and the Orthodox, closer to each other. So this provides a clear explanation as to why Orthodoxy, which represents an anti-universalist, anti-moralist, and anti-pluralist orientation in Israel, is the only officially accepted Jewish sect in the country.[41]

However, within the religious–Zionist camp there happen to be different groups, ranging from the most extreme to quite moderate. Liebman examines these groups under three main categories: expansionists, rejectionists, and pragmatists. Expansionists include the above-mentioned fundamentalist, nationalist, hawkish, and mostly Ashkenazi religious–Zionists, among whom can be found leading rabbis and religious leaders of Israel, including the chief rabbis. In this group, the biblical distinction between Jews and gentiles is understood, parallel to their expansionist understanding of chosenness, in rather extremist and supremacist terms. While the superiority of the Jews over other peoples is a common concept among this faction, as well as in some hasidic groups, such as Habad Hasidim, it is also argued by many that the gentiles are naturally cruel and bad.[42] For some rabbis such as Rabbi Yitzhak Ginsburgh, a member of Habad Hasidism, this genetic-based superiority 'invests Jewish life with greater value in the eyes of the Torah'. 'There is something', Ginsburgh asserts 'infinitely more holy and unique about Jewish life than non-Jewish life'.'[43] Among the Gush members, to be chosen is meant 'to be set apart and above the goyim', particularly the Arabs. As such, chosenness also conveys a sense of 'power' and 'supremacy'.[44] What is even more problematic, is the view voiced by another religious–Zionist rabbi according to whom only Jews are called human, whereas all non-Jews should be seen within the category of animals,[45] a view which brings to mind the distinction made by the Nazis between Aryan and non-Aryan nations.[46]

As a matter of fact, such an understanding of chosenness or holiness as a substantial reality of the Jewish people, as well as the notion of the superiority of the Jews, is not unknown in Jewish theology and in Jewish literature, as we have seen in previous chapters. However, what is to be emphasized here is the rise of such radical interpretations of chosenness in Israel since the 1970s. Besides, what makes the notion of Jewish superiority so unusually problematic is the fact that it does not represent just an abstract and marginal idea in the hands of religious–Zionists, as it did in the past but, on the contrary, it now determines Israel's foreign and domestic policies on many points, including the confiscation of lands from the Arabs for new Jewish settlements, and the refusal to comply with international law. The confiscation of Arab-owned land for subsequent Jewish settlements is considered by those religious Jews not to be an act of 'stealing', but rather an act of 'sanctification', according to which 'the land is redeemed by being transferred from the satanic to the divine sphere'.[47] It is also the rule derived from the Code of Maimonides and the Jewish law (*halakhah*) that non-Jews permitted to live in the land of Israel should suffer the 'humiliation of servitude'.[48] Thus, the religious–Zionist notion of Jewish superiority also serves to promote, and even justify, domination and hatred of non-Jews on a soil which is not only ruled, but also owned by the Jews. What is most interesting is the formula which is unanimously accepted by the Gush members, according to which

> whatever rights may be accorded to Arabs as individuals *in* the land (rights to own property, earn a livelihood, be treated respectfully, and so forth), no group, people, or nation may be recognized as having any rights *over* any portion of it.[49]

Such a statement comes as a reminder of what was stated by Count Stanislas Clermont-Tonnerre, in his address to the French National Assembly in 1789: 'The Jews should be denied everything as a nation, but granted everything as individuals'.[50]

Again, Rabbi Shlomo Aviner, one of the spiritual leaders of Gush Emunim, declares the alleged fundamentalist difference between Jews and non-Jews before the universal law by saying, '[w]hile God requires other normal nations to abide by abstract codes of justice and righteousness, such laws do not apply to Jews'.[51] Under this rule, the killing of a non-Jew, adult or child, is not considered a murder, not even a crime. In the same way, robbing a non-Jew is also permitted, as the Jews are regarded as exempt from human judgement. In the minds of such fundamentalist religious–Zionists, chosenness does not only refer to the spiritual superiority of the Jews, but also to their physical and genetic superiority, whereas redemption denotes an unconditional Jewish control over the land of Israel in its full biblical boundaries. As emphasized by Uriel Tal, Israeli scholar, what rules the ideology of political Jewish messianism in Israel is the priority of what is 'holy' over what is 'moral'[52] or good, which refers to an unconditional and uncontrolled interpretation and application of the Jewish notion of chosenness in Israeli socio-political life.

As for rejectionist religious–Zionists, they seem to adopt a position similar to non-Zionist religious Jews, such as Agudat Israel. As indicated by Liebman and Don-Yehiya, the rabbis who constitute the rejectionist religious–Zionist group, such as Rabbi Moshe Avigdor Amiel and Isaac Breuer, advocated a universalist and Torah-based understanding of Judaism in general and rejected Zionism as a new form of Judaism. Rabbi Amiel accused Zionists of forgetting that 'the God of Israel is God of the whole world'.[53] However, both rabbis sought to expand Jewish settlements and Jewish rights in the land of Israel. By so doing, Rabbi Amiel was prepared to cooperate with secular Zionists whereas Breuer first opposed any sort of cooperation with secular Zionists, but later agreed that secular Jews undertake a 'divinely set historical task'.[54] In general, they followed a line which is close to the policy adopted by Agudat Israel after the creation of the state of Israel. Agudat Israel, founded as an anti-Zionist organization (1912) to combat Zionism, gradually softened its opposition to Zionism and contributed to the Jewish settlements in Israel. The Agudat standing today is an acceptance of 'Jewish sovereignty over the holy land as a positive development' yet 'not a sign or a part of the process of redemption'.[55]

Pragmatist religious–Zionists, on the other hand, such as the Mizrachi, follow a middle path, rejecting Zionism as an alternative to Judaism, yet affirming it as a political movement alongside the Jewish religion. Lubavitcher Hasidism, a branch of Habad Hasidism, can also be classified under this grouping, as its members have been supporting Jewish settlements in Israel right from the beginning, despite their strict opposition to secular Zionism. Moreover, today, they represent more of an expansionist attitude, as they share many of the fundamentalist ideas of Gush Emunim and have a significant influence on the hawkish orientation of religious–Zionists.

Non-Zionists

It is difficult to speak of the existence of any clear non-Zionist orientation in Israel today. One can only mention individual Israelis, such as Yeshayahu Leibowitz, who accepts Zionism as a legitimate political movement, but rejects its authority as a civil religion. Although Liebman places Leibowitz under the category of pragmatist religious–Zionists, Leibowitz's understanding of Zionism seems closer to that of a non-Zionist, and in certain aspects even approaches an anti-Zionist orientation. For Leibowitz completely rejects the authority of anything other than God and his commandments over the Jewish people. In his thought, all cultural, historical, and spiritual aspects of Jewish identity should come from Judaism alone whereas Zionism can be understandable and acceptable only as a political movement driven from 'the desire of Jews for political independence in their own land'. So, in Leibowitz's thought, Zionism has nothing to do with religion or redemption. Therefore, he is severely critical of the Zionist sanctification of the state and the Israeli maltreatment of the Arabs in the name of the doctrine that 'nation and its welfare, the homeland and its security are sacred'.[56]

Leibowitz, in his article on 'The uniqueness of the Jewish people', puts forward a powerful argument on the questions of chosenness and holiness. He places the concept of a self-reflective mission against the substantialist interpretation of chosenness. Leibowitz argues that there is only one uniqueness/holiness which is absolute and it is the uniqueness/holiness of God. Accordingly, things that are created, unlike the Creator, cannot be holy; instead, holiness is demanded of them. Jews, Leibowitz maintains, 'are human beings like all others, and cannot be special or unique by nature, since by nature all of us, Jews and Gentiles alike, are the sons of the same Noah'.[57] Hence, the uniqueness attributed to the Jews 'is not a gift granted to the people as their everlasting property, but is instead a demand, a mission and a task imposed on the people, a goal towards which they must aspire eternally, with no guarantee that they will ever attain it'.[58] In the same way the Holy Land, for Leibowitz, is not sacred in itself; this can only be so in paganism, which Judaism came to combat. In true monotheism the land can only be sanctified, through the *mitzvot*, through the service of God. Here Leibowitz points to a fundamental distinction between the concept of sacred, which is the absolute 'quality' belonging to God alone, and the act of sanctification, which refers to the 'task' imposed on humankind. Moreover, an a priori sense of uniqueness in reference to the Jewish people or to the land, according to Leibowitz, is not only an idolatrous, but also a valueless, act. Because only an 'objective' can have a value, whereas a 'fact', as much as it is real, does not contain any value. The Jewish people, Leibowitz goes on,

> is not the chosen people; it is commanded to be the chosen people … The Jewish people is not endowed with uniqueness of essence; its uniqueness lies in the very demand made of it. It can respond to this demand or not; and therefore there is no guarantee of its fate.[59]

In fact, such an anti-substantialist interpretation of chosenness was supported in the past and still has its proponents today. However, this is not the dominant view in Israel where Zionism, despite its critics, remains, both in its secular and religious forms, the civil religion of the country and the most powerful determinant of Jewish identity.

Anti-Zionists

Those Israelis who are in the anti-Zionist camp completely reject and severely criticize Zionism and the state of Israel. They do so mainly on religious, but also on socialist and humanitarian, grounds as in the case of Mazpen, the radical Israeli socialist group, which came to prominence in the late 1960s and early 1970s with 'a position favorable to Palestinian rights', and an 'opposition to what it deemed "Israeli neo-colonialism"'.[60] The most important and most consistent religious anti-Zionist group that still exists today is the Neturei Karta (Guardians of the City), which first emerged as a subgroup among the Satmar Hasidim living in Israel and later became independent. They follow a traditional but also rather passive, faith-centred, and universalist version of Judaism. Their rejection of Zionism as an alternative false religion to Judaism places them in opposition primarily to secular Jews. According to Neturei Karta, the Zionist rhetoric is in complete contradiction with Judaism and with Jewish ideas and principles, among which are the doctrines of the chosen people and redemption.

G.J. Neuberger, a member of Neturei Karta, asserts that the Zionist leaders have been misleading many Jews by their 'misuse of names and symbols sacred in Judaism'.[61] Indeed, some of the most important propaganda instruments employed by secular Zionists, as we have seen, were, and still are, central traditional Jewish concepts and symbols, such as exile and redemption, as well as chosenness and mission; not to mention the name 'Israel' given to the Jewish state. Moreover, it was the political Zionism of the secular European Jews, not any messianic movement of the previous periods, that mobilized both secular and religious Jews around a premature redemption, through diplomatic, political and even military means. In other words, if it was not for secular Zionism, fundamentalist religious–Zionism would probably not exist or succeed.[62] As a matter of fact, in different periods in the history of the Jewish people, even as early as the first century, some messianic movements had occurred but none had the permanent success that political Zionism did. Those messianic attempts were considered to be part of pseudo-messianism and their failure confirmed the traditional Jewish belief that redemption would be brought about solely by the will and direct act of God when the Jewish people were properly repentant for their sins. Therefore, for the rabbis of Neturei Karta, the main problem is secular Zionism itself, not Jewish tradition. They assert that while the Zionists turn the Jews, a religious community, into a race, just like the Nazis did, the Zionist rhetoric completely ignores the universal and peace-centred message of Judaism. One of the main points on which Neturei Karta bases its criticism is related to the fact that where Judaism reveals a universal message with a notion of God as the father of and the sole object of worship for all humankind, Zionism proposes a quasi-religion for the Jews alone, a religion that is based on the worship of the Zionist state, even at the expense of peace with other peoples. By so doing, Zionists, according to Neturei Karta rabbis, use a twisted and unethical form of the traditional Jewish doctrine of the chosen people. The doctrine of chosenness, which means, for Neturei Karta members, obeying God and serving humankind, is also transformed in the hands of Zionists into a tool of domination, conquest and warfare. Neuberger declares the true meaning of being chosen by writing:

> The task for which the Jewish people were chosen is not to set an example of military superiority or technical achievements, but to seek perfection in moral behavior and spiritual purity. Of all the crimes of political Zionism, the worst and most basic ... is that from its beginning Zionism has sought to separate the Jewish people from their God, to render the divine covenant null and void, and to substitute a 'modern' statehood and fraudulent sovereignty for the lofty ideals of the Jewish people.[63]

As for the doctrine of the Promised Land, Rabbi David Weiss, another Neturei Karta member, writes,

> The Holy Land was a conditional Divine gift. It was a place set aside for God's worship.... The Bible foretold that if the 'children of Israel' should

fail in their spiritual task, they would be banished from the land and sent into exile. This exilic punishment will last until the Lord in His mercy, sees fit to end history as we know it, by ushering in the Messianic era – a time of universal brotherhood and peace.[64]

Apparently, the chosenness of the Jewish people, as understood by the Neturei Karta members, has nothing to do with a 'quality' rendering Jews with privilege or superiority. Instead, it is an eternal but positive 'duty' on the part of the Jewish people. On the other hand, the promise of the land is considered to be both essential and conditional: essential in relation to the redemption and conditional in relation to the Jews. In the same way, while the Jewish people are an important instrument for the redemption, its ultimate establishment is considered to belong to God. According to mainstream Jewish understanding, too, redemption will be established on earth by God's will, as a light emanating from Jerusalem, and its condition is the repentance of the Jews of their sins. Neturei Karta insists that the state of Israel, due to its irreligious character and its false claim to be the fulfilment of redemption, is the greatest obstacle to true redemption, which is to introduce a complete peace, the true worship of God, and justice, not only in the Holy Land, but also in the world.

Post-Zionists

The post-Zionist tendency, which emerged within the Israeli academia towards the end of the 1980s, is seen basically as a result of a widespread scepticism towards, and a disappointment in, the dominant historical narratives and social representations introduced by Zionism, which was conveying a 'mystical, monolithic, and idealized vision of Jewish history'. According to Silberstein, 'the 1967 War, the ensuing occupation of the captured territories, and the growing realization of social gaps and conflicts within Israeli society' were the main factors contributing to the growth of such tendency in Israeli academia.[65] Thus in the post-Zionist critique of Zionism and of the state of Israel, alongside and in parallel to the questions of the 'other', pluralism and democracy, which are also essential to Jewish feminist critique,[66] the term 'demythologization' takes the most important place. For the post-Zionist writers put into question the mainstream Zionist doctrines (or meta-narratives), among which are the nationhood of the Jews, the global nature of anti-Semitism, the uniqueness of the Holocaust, and the existence of a natural–historical tie between the people and the land. In this way, the post-Zionist critique undermines not only the central myths of Zionism but also the central doctrines of the Jewish religion, such as the chosenness of Israel and the Promised Land, upon which the Israeli-Jewish identity is built. What is thus suggested by most post Zionist scholars is the reshaping of Israeli identity with reference to democratic and pluralist premises, instead of Zionist and Jewish ones. What is suggested here is also the 'normalization' of the Jews (at least those who live in Israel), in the real sense of the term, namely with no reference to their uniqueness, even to their Jewishness. In this way, the post-Zionist movement appears to be a counter-movement to the mainstream Israeli–Jewish orientation in some important aspects. As far as its critics are concerned, however, post-Zionism is considered as tantamount to an attempt at suicide from the Jewish point of view.[67]

Perhaps it is possible to see this post-Zionist tendency in Israeli society in parallel to the process of the 'privatization of Jewishness' among American non-Orthodox Jewry. In the former case (Israeli experience) the discourse of Zionism and in the latter case (American experience) the ideology of affliction have proven ineffective in the wake of rising individualist and pluralist tendencies in both societies. In fact, this is considered quite a natural and healthy process by those who see 'identity' as a constant process of construction and transformation, namely as something created and dynamic rather than given and fixed.[68] Nevertheless, as far as the majority of Israeli Jews are concerned, a commitment to Jewish tradition, as well as to Zionism, still remains the determinant factor in shaping Israeli-Jewish identity today. What is called the 'religion of security', centred on the 'notion of a hostile world', should have played an important role in this commitment.[69] According to the findings of the Guttman Report in the early 1990s, a large number of Israelis stick to Jewish tradition, and this is primarily out of interest in the continuity of the Jewish peoplehood as a unique entity, that is for socio-political instead of religious reasons. In this context, it is important to note that half of the respondents to the Guttman Report affirm that the 'Jewish people was chosen among peoples';[70] this should be understood in terms of an ongoing Israeli commitment to the notion of uniqueness out of survivalist concerns, rather than an Israeli reception of the biblical notion of chosenness in a literal sense. For it is a clear fact that the Jewish religion has a negative connotation in the Israeli mind in contrast to an obvious traditional bent that has emerged in Israeli society. Moreover, there is an apparent parallel between the level of observance and the degree of attachment to Jewish peoplehood and Zionism. The more observant one is, the stronger one's feelings are for the Jewish people and Zionism.[71]

Yet, it is also emphasized by some that, despite such common concerns for Jewish identification, different groups in Israel relate to Jewish tradition in different and sometimes opposite ways, indicating the existence of cultural estrangement or even tension in Israeli society.[72] Apparently, the source for Jewish identification varies considerably from one camp to another. For those who describe themselves as 'strictly observant' the source is the 'authority of the *halakhah*', whereas for a great majority of Israelis, who can be called 'traditionalist', it is 'collective authority' while for others it is 'individual autonomy'. In the light of these remarks, it can be argued that survivalist concerns are too deeply embedded in Israeli consciousness to allow for the abandonment of Jewish tradition or with the notion of uniqueness. It seems to be that, just as American Jewish leaders need to hold onto the civil religion of the Holocaust and Redemption to guarantee Jewish collective continuity; Israeli Jewish leaders maintain their religion of security for quite the same reasons, the sense of uniqueness and the rhetoric of survival being embedded in both societies.

Conclusion

This book was an attempt to understand the nature of the Jewish insistence on 'chosenness' and the interaction between the idea of chosenness and the shape of Jewish religion as well as Jewish identity. I have tried to show that the idea of chosenness, as an essential element in Jewish theology and Jewish memory and an important constituent of Jewish identity, has been interpreted in divergent ways, not only in different Jewish movements or congregations, but also in different epochs. What has been common to all those various Jewish interpretations of chosenness, however, is a sense of 'uniqueness', as coupled most of the time with a feeling of 'superiority'.

Accordingly, I have argued that in the largely religious atmosphere of the pre-modern period, the idea of chosenness was accepted as an 'eternal-religious *truth*' by the then still traditional Jews. With the rationalist-universalist spirit of the early modern period, however, it turned into a 'universal-messianic *ideology*' in the hands of first liberal European and then American Reform Jews. In the wake of the Holocaust consciousness of a later period, on the other hand, chosenness served in terms of a '*policy* of survival' in both America and Israel. In other words, the traditional Jewish doctrine of the 'eternity of Israel' was transformed into what is called the 'survival of Israel'. In fact, such a shift took place in parallel to the process in which the 'supernatural revelation' that lies at the heart of the Jewish religion and of Jewish chosenness was replaced by first 'reason' and then 'experience'. Thus, the idea of chosenness originally referred to God's election of the people of Israel from all other peoples for the purpose of worshipping him alone. The Jews throughout the pre-modern period had a firm belief in being a people chosen by God and passionately awaited the day of redemption. This was so, notwithstanding the differing opinions on the nature of chosenness which led to the emergence of two main understandings of chosenness, namely substantial and relational ones. The modern period, however, witnessed the development of two different, even opposing, Jewish understandings of chosenness. In the wake of the Jewish Emancipation, modern Jewish thinkers redefined the doctrine of the chosen people in reference to a religious or spiritual genius of the Jewish people, instead of to a choosing God of the Israelites, which enabled the Jewish people to come up with the notions of monotheism and messianic monism. Later on, this rationalist-universalist atmosphere gave place to a particularist one when the deadly experience of the Jews in Auschwitz necessitated a focus on Jewish collective needs. Thus, the unique Jewish survival replaced the unique Jewish mission as the new consummation of chosenness.

I have maintained that, as a result, today fewer and fewer Jews speak of the truth, or the possibility of chosenness. What is at stake for many Jews, instead, is the function, or ever-changing meaning, of chosenness. It is not an 'absolute truth' or a 'religious doctrine' for many to believe in and to shape their life around. It is rather a 'myth' to make use of for either collective-survivalist (post-Holocaust) or individual-spiritual (post-modern) reasons. So, as Mordecai Kaplan proposed and even presupposed before the Second World War, what is at stake today for many Jews is Jewishness as a complex of spiritual, cultural, and ethnic elements rather than Judaism as a religious system. Indeed, this is the case for those Jews who endorse the Jewish doctrine of chosenness, despite their apparent indifference to the Jewish religion and to the biblical notion of God. In other words, they come to depend on chosenness not for any theological reasons. Instead, they do so in reference to some sort of spiritual, psychological, cultural, or socio-political reasons. In other words, the way that the Jews identify themselves with the notion of the chosen people varies in accordance with the way in which they relate to the Jewish religion. So, the more Jews come to see Jewish religion as merely part of Jewish tradition, the more they define their Jewishness in reference to the notions of community, identity, and belonging, instead of God, law, and covenant. Furthermore, it is claimed that the fundamentalist Jewish definition and use of 'chosenness', which displayed an apparent ascendance in Israel in parallel to the emergence of the rhetoric of survival, is not independent of this general tendency. Religious-Zionism, like many other fundamentalist religious groups, does not represent a pure religious system. Nor does it completely fit with the traditional Jewish outlook. It instead appears as a modern phenomenon which is highly intermingled with political, national, ethnic, and religious elements, and therefore belongs to the other extreme of the same spectrum.

On the other hand, I have also argued that the history of the idea of chosenness is tantamount to the story of the Jewish commitment to 'continuity'. Indeed, the main concern of most Jewish communities in all ages, particularly in modern times, has been related to Jewish existence and continuity, albeit from different perspectives, namely religious, cultural, and ethnic, and with varying emphases, that is universalist/integrationist or particularist/exclusivist, activist or passivist. However, the fact that in the modern period Jews began to take over pioneering roles in different and even opposing movements (such as universalism, nationalism, socialism, and liberalism) and in diverse areas, (such as science, politics, economics, arts, and the media), displays the apparent estrangement of the Jewish people from the traditional Jewish self-association with religion alone. Such an estrangement is related, apparently, to the fact that over the course of time, existence (Jewishness) – which was already embedded in the traditional Jewish doctrine of chosenness in terms of the election of a people in its physical collective entity – has come to take priority over essence (Judaism) for Jewish identity. So, for many Jews, being Jewish is the most important thing about them today and the way they relate to Judaism mainly depends on various cultural and ethnic dimensions. In other words, for those Jews, even maintaining the religious dimension of Jewishness serves some non-religious ends. So the question is more about preserving one's difference for its own sake. This is why, as long as one makes sure that they feel Jewish, they also feel free to adopt the dominant ideas and values of wherever they live. Thus it follows that Jewish memory takes precedence over Jewish faith for guaranteeing Jewish continuity, on the one hand, and for rendering Jewish existence with meaning, on the other, as it is best exemplified in the Jewish experience of the Holocaust.

I have also suggested that, in this process, the interaction of the Jewish people and Jewish religion with the Christian world, in relation to three great milestones in particular, that is the rise of Christianity, modernity, and the Holocaust, played an important role. In other words, the turning of the 'Jewish uniqueness' into the 'Jewish question' has been mainly the result of troublesome Jewish–Christian encounters throughout history. First of all, Christianity carried the notion of the 'other', which is embedded in Jewish tradition, into its own system and created its own Other, the Jew. It also provided the Jewish people with the privilege of an ongoing mysterious role in God's plan for the world, on the one hand, and the guilt of deicide, on the other, by applying an ambiguous character to Jewish being. In this way, Christianity's attitude towards the Jews has been a mixture of admiration and hatred. This early Jewish interaction with Christianity, in turn, caused the Jewish people to tighten their hold on the truth of chosenness as a reaction to the Christian rhetoric of the 'true Israel', and also provided them with a two-fold psychology, that is a 'covert superiority' on the one side, and an 'overt inferiority' on the other. Second, modernity, by placing an emphasis on what is rational and universal, gave a warm welcome to individual Jews (Emancipation), yet justified the ongoing Christian controversy with Judaism on completely different grounds, i.e. in reference to Jewishness. What was emphasized in this way is the ultimate 'otherness' of the Jews (anti-Semitism). So in the wake of these circumstances, some Jews got caught up in a total assimilation programme, while others chose to stick to tradition. An important number of Jews, on the other hand, came to the solution of universalizing their religion, doing so with reference to the notion of Jewish mission. This was, in fact, an attempt by the Enlightened Jews to overcome their otherness, by undertaking a positive mission and in this way justifying a separate, yet normal, Jewish identity on universally religious grounds. Even in the case of Jewish nationalism, particularly in the form of Zionism, which emerged as a response primarily to increasing anti-Semitism, the notion of mission and the rhetoric of normalization of the Jewish people ruled the movement at the beginning to a great extent. As for the impact that the image of the Holocaust had on Jewish identity, it turned out, in the wake of survivalist concerns both in America and Israel, to be a general Jewish acceptance, even endorsement, of otherness and a victimhood complex. What is meant by the rhetoric of survival is thus the reduction of chosenness to a mere Jewish difference and uniqueness (secular chosenness), and of Jewishness to a particularist and ethno-centric entity. However, what is important in this post-Holocaust Jewish identity is the fact that its essence, as well as its form, is based on negating what is non-Jewish rather than verifying what is Jewish. In other words, Jewishness and chosenness are redefined in reaction to the Holocaust, the ideology of affliction, rather than in continuity with the past, the doctrine of covenant. As a result of this, extreme animosity towards anything non-Jewish, in turn, results in radical and uncontrolled Jewish self-sanctification. This period thus witnesses the emergence of a new form of chosenness, with its religious and secular versions, as based on a uniqueness complex.

Recent years, however, witness the emergence of a more positive and individualist interpretation of chosenness, which stands alongside an ongoing rhetoric of survival. There is an obvious post-modern orientation within this novel understanding of Jewishness and chosenness, especially as experienced among American Jews. Accordingly, the new Jewish self-definition involves spirituality, personal memory and individual choice, and a rather eclectic and selective Jewish practice. It is not about totally submitting to a covenant relationship with God (pre-modern), or endorsing a complete universality at the expense of Jewish particularity (modern). Nor is it solely about adhering to the Jewish collectivity and Jewish survival without proposing something more positive (post-Holocaust). It is rather about fulfilling oneself as being Jewish; responding to the needs of the self, primarily, and those of the community, secondarily. The new Jewish covenant is not based on the address of God and the response of the people any more, but on the address of the self (American experience) or the community (Israeli experience) in terms of a search for meaning and one's response to this. So the idea of chosenness has been carried to present times as the Jewish right to choose one's own identity and the Jewish right to particularity. Thus the doctrine of the 'chosen' people, which is essentially religious in nature, is legitimized today by being transformed into the notion of the 'choosing' people, which is specifically cultural. On the whole, what is further suggested is that, as far as the mainstream approach to chosenness is concerned, it is not the sole or the absolute purpose of Jewish existence any more, as it was for both traditional and early modern Jews. On the contrary, chosenness is an effective cause for the Jewish survival in both physical and spiritual terms. In other words, the Jews are not so much a people shaped for chosenness, but rather chosenness is a useful instrument to keep the Jews together and alive (cultural chosenness). As for the nature of the next turn that the Jewish reinterpretation of chosenness will take, it depends to a large extent, I suspect, on the question of whether the Jews will find a happy place between existence and essence, between themselves and others, between particularity and universality, between suffering and surviving, and finally between fate and destiny – with better help from the Christian world this time.

Finally, it would be interesting for further research to engage in a serious discussion of whether Jewish chosenness, looking at the question from the perspective of globalization, has something to offer not only to the Jews, but also to the world. In fact, this book points to the capacity of the Jewish religion to convey its message to following generations that seek to retain their Jewishness in a global world. The question is whether the Jewish case could set a good example for other religions in contributing to globalization, without depriving themselves of their particularity, or whether this should be considered as yet another 'unique' Jewish phenomenon.

Notes

Introduction

1 For the relation between the notion of the chosen people and nationality, see S. Grosby, 'The chosen people of ancient Israel and the Occident: why does nationality exist and survive?' *Nations and Nationalism* 5/3 1999, 357–80.

2 Z. Falk, 'The mission of Israel: a view from within', *Immanuel* 12, September 1981, 102–9.

3 For a discussion of Jewish suffering from both Jewish and Christian perspectives, see I.I. Mattuck, 'The mystery of Israel (M. Maritain's philosophy of the Jews)', *Journal of Jewish Studies* 1/1, 1948–9, 55–60.

4 See, for example, R. Jospe, 'The concept of the chosen people: an interpretation', *Judaism* 43/2, 1994, 127–48.

5 For a discussion of the particularistic and universalistic aspects of chosenness, see S.H. Bergman, 'Israel and the *Oikoumené*', in R. Loewe (ed.), *Studies in Rationalism, Judaism and Universalism*, London: Routledge and Kegan Paul, 1966, pp. 47–66; F.W. Golka, 'Universalism and the election of the Jews', *Theology* 90, 1987, 273–80.

6 J. Neusner, *Torah through the Ages: A Short History of Judaism*, London: SCM, 1990, p. 14.

1 The biblical language of chosenness

1 This expression is seen as rather the product of later periods and is considered to be more in accord with the English language and the world of Christendom than the Hebrew language and Jewish culture. See A.M. Eisen, *The Chosen People in America: A Study in Jewish Religious Ideology*, Bloomington/Indianapolis: Indiana University Press, 1983, p. 167.

2 J. Hastings (ed.), *Dictionary of the Bible*, revised by F.C. Grant and H.H. Rowley, Edinburgh: T & T Clark, 1963, p. 387.

3 Unless otherwise indicated, all biblical citations are taken from the New Revised Standard Version of the Bible (NRSV).

4 Hastings, *Dictionary of the Bible*, p. 388.

5 D. Patrick, 'Election (Old Testament)', in D.N. Freedman (ed.), *Anchor Bible Dictionary*, New York: Doubleday, c1992, 2:438.

6 E.W. Nicholson, *Deuteronomy and Tradition*, Oxford: Basil Blackwell, 1967, p. 56. See also J. Cott, 'The biblical problem of election', *Journal of Ecumenical Studies* 21/2, 1984, 200.

7 R.H. Pfeiffer, *Introduction to the Old Testament*, London: Adam & Charles Black, 1952, p. 148.

8 Eisen, *Chosen People*, p. 169.

9 R. Clements, *God's Chosen People: A Theological Interpretation of the Book of Deuteronomy*, London: SCM, 1968, p. 32. Although there is no clear distinction between the future and the present in Hebrew as in the European languages, still the future tense here, unlike the present, indicates an uncompleted action or state.

10 Whereas the meaning of a possession that is 'acquired' can be observed in the term *segullah*, what is signified with the terms *heleq* and *nahala* is a property that is 'inherited'. See M.F. Unger and W. White (eds), *Nelson's Expository Dictionary of the Old Testament*, Nashville, TN: Nelson, 1980, p. 298; R.L. Harris, G.L. Archer, and B.K. Waltke (eds), *Theological Wordbook of the Old Testament*, Chicago, IL: Moody Press, 1980, p. 293.

11 NRSV translation reads as 'The Lord is my chosen portion'.

12 Cf. 'When the Most High apportioned the nations, when he divided the humankind, he fixed the boundaries of the peoples according to the number of the gods; the Lord's own portion was his people, Jacob his allotted share.' (NRSV translation).

13 See M.L. Margolis and A. Marx, *A History of the Jewish People*, New York: Atheneum, 1969, p. 91.

14 See R.G. Dentan, 'Religion and theology of the Old Testament', *Encyclopaedia Americana*, p. 683; 'Israel: God's covenanted people', in R.E. Brown, J.A. Fitzmyer, and R.E. Murphy (eds), *The New Jerome Biblical Commentary*, London: Geoffrey Chapman, 1990, p. 1297.

15 Other metaphors used for the relation between God and Israel include king and vassal, master and slave, shepherd and flock, mother and child, and groom and bride. See Lev. 25:55; Isa. 43:15; 49:15; 62:5; Ps. 23:1–3; 123:2.

16 See, for example, D.J. McCarthy, *Treaty and Covenant*, Rome: Pontifical Biblical Institute, 1963, pp. 173ff. For the centrality of 'grace' in Mosaic tradition, see also H.D. Hummel, 'Law and grace in Judaism and Lutheranism', in P. Opsahl and M.H. Tanenbaum (eds), *Speaking of God Today: Jews and Lutherans in Conversation*, Philadelphia, PA: Fortress, 1974, pp. 21f.; P.D. Hanson, *The People Called: The Growth of Community in the Bible*, San Francisco, CA: Harper & Row, 1987, pp. 24f.

17 W.J. Dumbrell, *Covenant and Creation: An Old Testament Covenantal Theology*, Exeter: Paternoster Books, 1984, pp. 117ff.

18 S.R. Driver, *Critical and Exegetical Commentary on Deuteronomy*, Edinburgh: T & T Clark, 1902, p. 100.

19 Rivkah Kluger points to the fact that in different English translations of the Hebrew Bible the word *bahar* is usually given the meanings of 'to love', 'to desire', and 'to take a joy'. See R.S. Kluger, *Psyche in Scripture: The Idea of the Chosen People and Other Essays*, Toronto: Inner City Books, 1995, pp. 12–14.

20 J.H. Tigay, *The JPS Torah Commentary: Deuteronomy*, Philadelphia, PA: JPS, 1996, p. xxviii.

21 For a detailed discussion of the concept of 'remnant', see H.H. Rowley, *The Biblical Doctrine of Election*, London: Lutterworth Press, 1950, pp. 72ff.

22 A form of religion in ancient Israel in which the existence of gods beside *YHWH* and their rule outside the land of Israel are acknowledged.

23 See J.M.P. Smith, 'The chosen people', *American Journal of Semitic Languages and Literatures* 45/2, 1929, 73f.

24 See B.S. Childs, *Exodus: A Commentary*, London: SCM, 1974, p. 221; L.L. Grabbe, *Judaic Religion in the Second Temple Period*, London: Routledge, 2000, pp. 212–15; cf. Y. Kaufmann, *The Religion of Israel: From Its Beginnings to the Babylonian Exile*, New York: Schocken, 1974, pp. 127f.

25 It is indicated that the correct translation of the passage in Genesis 12:33 is not 'in you shall all the families of the earth be blessed' but 'with you (or 'by means of you') shall all the families of the earth bless themselves.' Rowley points out that what is at stake in the passage is the 'honour of Abraham and his descendants', rather than 'any

sense of a mission to spread blessing among the nations'. See Rowley, *Biblical Doctrine of Election*, pp. 65f.

26 E.J. Kissane, *The Book of Isaiah*, Dublin: Browne & Nolan, 1943, 1:37.

27 Such particularistic tendency promoted by Ezra and Nehemiah is usually attributed to their former experience in Babylon where they had to isolate themselves from the surrounding community to preserve their faith and separateness. See, for example, M. Samuel, 'Race, nation, and people in the Jewish Bible', in A.L. Jamison (ed.), *Tradition and Change in Jewish Experience*, the B.G. Rudolph Lectures in Judaic Studies, New York: Syracuse University Press, 1978, p. 13. However, for some others like John Allegro, Ezra and Nehemiah did formulate 'the doctrine of the Chosen Race' for national–political reasons. See J.M. Allegro, *The Chosen People*, London: Hodder & Stoughton, 1971, p. 59.

28 L. Jacobs, *The Jewish Religion: A Companion*, New York/Oxford: Oxford University Press, 1995, p. 263. Cf. Kissane, *Book of Isaiah*, pp. 87f.

2 Ancient Jewish literature

1 For an alternative view, see D. Boyarin, *A Radical Jew: Paul and the Politics of Identity*, Berkeley: University of California Press, 1997.

2 N. de Lange, *Apocrypha: Jewish Literature of the Hellenistic Age*, New York: Viking Press, 1978, p. 1.

3 See, for example, W.D. Davies, *Paul and Rabbinic Judaism*, London: SPCK, 1962, p. 79.

4 E.P. Sanders, *Paul and Palestinian Judaism*, London: SCM, 1977, p. 368.

5 Those eternal laws consist of the commandments which 'govern man's behaviour to God', to the exclusion of those commandments which 'govern man's behaviour towards man'. Among the former are circumcision (Jub. 15:33–4) and Sabbath observance (23:19–23). See Sanders, *Paul and Palestinian Judaism*, pp. 364–6.

6 See Sanders, *Paul and Palestinian Judaism*, p. 374.

7 All citations of Qumran writings are taken from G. Vermes, *The Dead Sea Scrolls in English*, New York: Penguin, 1975.

8 For the absence of hope in the apocryphal writings for a future life for gentiles, see R.H. Charles, *Eschatology: The Doctrine of a Future Life*, introduction by G.W. Buchanan, New York: Schocken, 1970, pp. 297, 361.

9 All citations of Philo's works are taken from Philo Judaeus, *Philo*, with an English translation by F. Colson, Heinemann: Loeb, 1929–62.

10 Cf. Ex. 19. For the critique of Philo's translation of Israel as 'seeing God', see Philo Judaeus, *Legatio ad Gaium*, E.M. Smallwood (ed.), Leiden: Brill, 1961, pp. 153f.

11 The Greek word *ethnos*, usually translated as 'race', has various meanings, such as descendants of a common ancestor, family, nation/people, class/kind, etc., and Philo's usage of it (*Congr.* 51; *Post.* 92, etc.) is mostly associated with the meaning of class/kind. See W. Bauer, W.F. Arndt, and F.W. Gingrich (eds), *A Greek–English Lexicon of the New Testament and Other Early Christian Literature*, Chicago, IL: Chicago University Press, 1957, p. 156.

12 See, for example, M.E. Stone, *Jewish Writings of the Second Temple Period*, Philadelphia, PA: Fortress Press, 1984, p. 269. Cf. E.R. Goodenough, *By Light, Light: The Mystic Gospel of Hellenistic Judaism*, Amsterdam: Philo Press, 1969, pp. 136, 353.

13 See H.A. Wolfson, *Philo: Foundations of Religious Philosophy in Judaism, Christianity and Islam*, Cambridge, MA: Harvard University Press, 1947, 2:357–8.

14 See Wolfson, *Philo*, 2:51, 356–7.

15 Wolfson, *Philo*, 1:449–50.

16 Wolfson, *Philo*, 1:442.

17 Goodenough, *By Light*, p. 170.

18 Goodenough, *By Light*, p. 136.
19 E. Schürer, *The History of the Jewish People in the Age of Jesus Christ (175 BC–AD 135)*, Edinburgh: T & T Clark, c.1973, 2:817–18.
20 Schürer, *History of the Jewish People*, 2:888f.
21 M. Goodman, *Mission and Conversion*, Oxford: Clarendon Press, 1994, p. 53.
22 Wolfson, *Philo*, 2:356.
23 Goodenough maintains that if there was no ethnic concern involved in the royal representation of God, Judaism as a religion and nationhood would become pointless. See E.R. Goodenough, *The Politics of Philo Judaeus*, Hildesheim: Georg Olms Verlagsbuchhandlung, 1967, p. 114.
24 Davies, *Paul*, p. 67; A.F. Segal, *Paul the Convert*, New Haven, CT: Yale University Press, 1990, p. 124.
25 Sanders, *Paul and Palestinian Judaism*, pp. 147f. Cf. Boyarin, *Radical Jew*, p. 43.
26 K. Stendhal, *Paul among the Jews and Gentiles*, London: SCM, 1977, p. 13. This is what E.P. Sanders calls the 'third entity'; that is the united community in which there is only one path for salvation and which applies equally to Jews and non-Jews. See Sanders, *Paul, the Law, and the Jewish People*, London: SCM, 1983, p. 172.
27 J.M. Scott, 'Restoration of Israel', in G.F. Hawthorne and R.P. Martin (eds), *Dictionary of Paul and His Letters*, Leicester: Inter-Varsity Press, 1993, p. 799.
28 See Davies, *Paul*, pp. 68–9; Scott, 'Restoration of Israel', p. 799.
29 In Matthew, in a similar way, Jesus Christ is said to have instructed his disciples not to go near the gentiles but rather go to 'the lost sheep of the house of Israel' (Matt. 10:6). In the synoptic Gospels in general the main emphasis seems to be placed on the kingdom of God rather than on true Israel. In the Gospel of John, on the other hand, after Jews' rejection of his message, Jesus' address shifts to those outside Israel, as it is written: 'I have other sheep that do not belong to this fold. I must bring them also, and they will listen to my voice. So there will be one flock, one shepherd' (10:16). For more information on election in the New Testament, see B.S. Childs, *Biblical Theology of the Old and New Testaments: Theological Reflection on the Christian Bible*, Minneapolis, MN: Fortress Press, 1992, pp. 428–34.
30 For the interpretation of the expression 'all Israel', see W.L. Osbourne, 'The Old Testament background of Paul's "All Israel" in Romans 11:26a', *Asia Journal of Theology* 2, 1998, 282–93; D.G. Bloesch, '"All Israel will be saved": supersessionism and the biblical witness', *Interpretation* 43, 1989, 130–42. While in prophetic passages the physical Israel is regarded as a nation which will be a light to the nations making them recognize the glory of God (Isa. 51:4; Zech. 8:20–3), in Pauline theology, on the contrary, the gentiles become a means to bring Israel back to the acceptance of God's glory.
31 K. Barth, *A Shorter Commentary on Romans*, London: SCM, 1959, p. 115. See also E.E. Ellis, *Paul's Use of the Old Testament*, Edinburgh/London: Oliver & Boyd, 1957, p. 122.

3 Rabbinic literature

1 J. Neusner, *Torah through the Ages: A Short History of Judaism*, London: SCM, 1990, p. 50.
2 Neusner, *Torah*, pp. 12f.
3 Neusner, *Torah*, p. 60.
4 Among the late tannaitic midrashim, *Sifré Deuteronomy* includes passages on the question of Israel's chosenness which seem to be in line with later rabbinic writings. *Sifré to Numbers*, on the other hand, seems to adopt more of a mishnaic framework.
5 See Neusner, *Torah*, pp. 55ff. For a view that sees the impact of Christianity on the Jewish insistence on the doctrine of election as early as the beginning of the second

century BC, see B.W. Helfgott, *The Doctrine of Election in Tannaitic Literature*, New York: King's Crown Press, 1954. Helfgott mainly refers to the views of the Tannaim as quoted in late Rabbinic literature.

6 C.G. Montefiore and R. Loewe (eds), *A Rabbinic Anthology*, New York: Schocken, 1974, p. 116. See also J. Neusner, *The Theology of the Oral Torah*, Montreal: McGill University Press, 1999, p. 99.

7 See, for example, Neusner, *Oral Torah*, p. 96.

8 See Neusner, *Oral Torah*, p. 110.

9 See Neusner, *Oral Torah*, pp. 129f. Cf. E.P. Sanders, *Paul and Palestinian Judaism*, London: SCM, 1977, p. 209.

10 There is a rabbinic dispute on Psalm 9:17, 'The wicked shall return to Sheol, all the heathen that forget God.' Based on this R. Judah holds that 'None of the heathen has any share in the world to come.' R. Eliezer, however, disagrees by saying, 'since Scripture says: 'Who forget God', behold there must be righteous men among the heathen who have a share in the world to come.' See Sanh. 105a.

11 E.E. Urbach, *The Sages: Their Concepts and Beliefs*, trans. I. Abraham, Jerusalem: Hebrew University Press, 1973, p. 528. Cf. H. Tigay, *The JPS Torah Commentary: Deuteronomy*, Philadelphia, PA: JPS, 1996, p. 301.

12 See Urbach, *Sages*, p. 532.

13 See, for example, *Ex. R.* 47:3: 'If it were not for my Law which you accepted, I should not recognise you, and I should not regard you more than any of the idolatrous nations of the world.' See also *Dt. R.* 4:2; *Sifré Dt.* 36.

14 Sanders, *Paul and Palestinian Judaism*, p. 96. For the Jewish origin of the doctrine of grace, see also C. Rowland, *Christian Origins*, London: SPCK, 1985, pp. 26–7.

15 Sanders, *Paul and Palestinian Judaism*, pp. 147f. For the difference between the 'sinners' and 'apostates' of Israel, one referring to those who fail to obey the commandments and the other to those who formally reject the commandments, see S. Stern, *Jewish Identity in Early Rabbinic Writings*, Leiden/New York/Cologne: E.J. Brill, 1994, pp. 120ff.

16 'R. Samuel b. Nahmani said: Sometimes He does it for the sake of His people and His inheritance, and sometimes He does it for the sake of His Great Name. R. Ibbi said: When Israel merits it, [He does it] for the sake of His people and His inheritance, but when Israel does not merit it, for the sake of His Great Name. The Rabbis say: In the land of Israel [He does it] for the sake of His people and His inheritance; in the Diaspora, for the sake of His Great Name...' (*Ruth R.* 10:1; also Sanh. 97b).

17 Judah Halevi, *The Kuzari: An Argument for the Faith of Israel*, introduction by H. Slonimsky, trans. H. Hirschfeld, New York: Schocken, 1964, pp. 47ff., 64ff., 75f., 79f., 201ff.

18 For a discussion of the views of Halevi and Gersonides, see R. Eisen, *Gersonides on Providence, Covenant, and the Chosen People: A Study in Medieval Jewish Philosophy and Biblical Commentary*, New York: State University of New York Press, 1995. See also B. Frydman-Kohl, 'Covenant, conversion and chosenness: Maimonides and Halevi on "who is a Jew?"', *Judaism* 41/1, 1992, 64–79.

19 See G. Scholem, *Kabbalah*, New York: Meridian, 1974, pp. 156–7; L. Jacobs, *A Jewish Theology*, London: Darton, Longman & Todd, 1973, pp. 270–1.

20 *The Zohar*, Prologue 13a.

21 See M. Maimonides, 'Epistle of Yemen', and 'Helek: Sanhedrin, chapter ten', in I. Twersky (ed.), *A Maimonides Reader*, West Orange, NJ: Behrman House, 1972, pp. 439, 445f., 422; M. Maimonides, *Code of Law (Mishneh Torah): Book of Holiness*, Forbidden Intercourse 14:4, 5; *Book of Torts*, Murder 4:14; and *Book of Agriculture*, Gifts 10:3; Saadiah Gaon, *The Book of Beliefs and Opinions*, trans. S. Rosenblatt, New Haven, CT/London: Yale University Press, 1976, p. 158.

4 Universalistic Jewish philosophies: Spinoza and Mendelssohn

1 Y. Yovel, *Spinoza and Other Heretics: The Marrano of Reason*, Princeton, NJ: Princeton University Press, 1989, p. 177; R. Mason, *The God of Spinoza: A Philosophical Study*, Cambridge/New York: Cambridge University Press, 1997, p. 173.

2 Yovel, *Spinoza*, p. 194; Mason, *God of Spinoza*, p. 2.

3 Yovel, *Spinoza*, pp. 202f.

4 J.B. Agus, *The Evolution of Jewish Thought*, New York: Arno Press, 1973, p. 300. See also R. Misrahi, 'Spinoza and Christian thought: a challenge', in S. Hessing (ed.), *Speculum Spinozanum 1677–1977*, London: Routledge & Kegan Paul, 1977, p. 416.

5 Yovel, *Spinoza*, p. 177.

6 B. Spinoza, *Tractatus Theologico–Politicus*, trans. S. Shirley, Leiden/New York: E.J. Brill, 1989, p. 107. David Bidney points to a similarity between Spinoza and Maimonides, as both sought to 're-form the personal God of the Hebrews in order to exclude any human, finite attributes'. See D. Bidney, *The Psychology and Ethics of Spinoza*, New York: Russell & Russell, 1962, p. 359. For Maimonides' rejection of God's corporeality and essential attributes, see also J.S. Minkin, *The Teachings of Maimonides*, Northvale, NJ: Jason Aronson, 1993, pp. 170ff.

7 B. Spinoza, *Ethic*, trans. W.H. White, New York/Oxford: Oxford University Press, 1930, pp. 1, 19.

8 See D. Garrett (ed.), *The Cambridge Companion to Spinoza*, Cambridge: Cambridge University Press, 1996, p. 1.

9 Yovel, *Spinoza*, p. 175. Cf. Garrett, *Cambridge Companion to Spinoza*, pp. 356f.

10 Spinoza, *Tractatus*, p. 103. For Spinoza's understanding of the origin of religion, in general, and of Judaism, in particular, in terms of human fears of nature and the need for self-preservation, see A. Arkush, 'Judaism as egoism: from Spinoza to Feuerbach to Marx', *Modern Judaism* 11/1, 1991, 212f.

11 Spinoza, *Tractatus*, p. 89.

12 Spinoza, *Tractatus*, p. 107.

13 Spinoza, *Tractatus*, p. 86. Spinoza explicitly asserts that 'it is only in respect of religion – i.e., in respect of the universal divine law – that Scripture can properly be called the Word of God' (p. 211).

14 Spinoza, *Tractatus*, p. 91.

15 D. Novak, *The Election of Israel: The Idea of the Chosen People*, Cambridge, MA: Cambridge University Press, 1995, p. 24; Yovel, *Spinoza*, pp. 190f.

16 Spinoza, *Tractatus*, p. 89.

17 See Novak, *Election of Israel*, pp. 23f.

18 Spinoza, *Tractatus*, p. 90.

19 Spinoza, *Tractatus*, p. 88.

20 Spinoza, *Tractatus*, p. 90.

21 Spinoza, *Tractatus*, p. 96.

22 See Arkush, 'Judaism as egoism', p. 212.

23 Spinoza, *Tractatus*, p. 98.

24 Spinoza, *Tractatus*, p. 107.

25 Spinoza, *Tractatus*, pp. 92, 112.

26 Spinoza, *Tractatus*, p. 91.

27 Spinoza, *Tractatus*, p. 104. This is, in fact, one of the main themes of the book of Deuteronomy, as it is written: 'You shall love the Lord, your God' (6:4; 11:1; 30:6).

28 Spinoza, *Tractatus*, p. 99.

29 Spinoza, *Tractatus*, p. 94.

30 Spinoza, *Tractatus*, pp. 98f.

31 Spinoza, *Tractatus*, p. 205.

32 See Misrahi, 'Spinoza and Christian thought', p. 411.

33 Spinoza, *Tractatus*, p. 108.
34 Spinoza, *Tractatus*, p. 64.
35 Spinoza, *Tractatus*, pp. 113f. See also Matt. 5:17.
36 Misrahi, 'Spinoza and Christian thought', p. 414. Cf. Spinoza, *Tractatus*, p. 215.
37 'For Christ is the end of law so that there may be righteousness for everyone who believes' (Rom. 10:4).
38 Spinoza, *Tractatus*, p. 114.
39 Spinoza, *Tractatus*, p. 97.
40 Spinoza, *Tractatus*, p. 108. 'And so, brothers and sisters, I could not speak to you as spiritual people, but rather as people of the flesh, as infants in Christ. I fed you with milk, not solid food, for you were not ready for solid food' (1 Cor. 3:1–2).
41 Spinoza, *Tractatus*, p. 108.
42 Misrahi, 'Spinoza and Christian thought', p. 416.
43 Spinoza, *Tractatus*, pp. 109, 111.
44 Spinoza, *Tractatus*, p. 97. See also Rom. 3:1, 2.
45 M. Mendelssohn, *Jerusalem: Or on Religious Power and Judaism*, trans. A. Arkush, Hanover, CA/London: University Press of New England, 1983, p. 97.
46 Mendelssohn, *Jerusalem*, pp. 126ff.
47 Mendelssohn, *Jerusalem*, p. 134. Cf. Acts 24:14; 1 Cor. 7:17–18.
48 This is why Spinoza uses the term Hebrew to separate the Jewishness as an ethnic status from Jewishness as a national religion. He was a Hebrew ethnically and a Dutch nationally, there was no room for Jewishness which was the nation-religion of the ancient Israelites.
49 W.Z. Harvey, response to 'Philosophy and religious values in modern Jewish thought' by M. Fox, in J. Katz (ed.), *The Role of Religion in Modern Jewish History*, Cambridge, MS: Association for Jewish Studies, 1975, p. 88.
50 Mendelssohn, *Jerusalem*, p. 99.
51 See Harvey, response to 'Philosophy and religious values', p. 89.
52 According to Marvin Fox, this is the most important point that differentiates Mendelssohn's theology from that of Maimonides, who gave a higher place to the prophet over the philosopher and excluded all moral principles from the sphere of reason. See M. Fox, 'Philosophy and religious values in modern Jewish thought', in Katz, *Religion in Modern Jewish History*, pp. 73f.
53 Agus, *Jewish Thought*, p. 378.
54 Mendelssohn, *Jerusalem*, p. 97. Cf. Agus, *Jewish Thought*, pp. 377–8.
55 Agus, *Jewish Thought*, p. 376.
56 Agus, *Jewish Thought*, p. 379.
57 Mendelssohn, *Jerusalem*, p. 118.
58 For Franz Rosenzweig's critique of Mendelssohn, see P. Mendes-Flohr, 'Mendelssohn and Rosenzweig', *Journal of Jewish Studies* 23/2, 1987, 204.

5 Jewish emancipation and modern Jewish movements in Germany

1 See D. Rudavsky, *Modern Jewish Religious Movements: A History of Emancipation and Adjustment*, rev. edn, New York: Behrman House, 1979, p. 198.
2 For a discussion of the concept of 'other' in relation to Jews in both Jewish and Christians traditions, see Z. Bauman, 'Allosemitism: premodern, modern, and post-modern', in B. Cheyette and L. Marcus (eds), *Modernity, Culture, and "The Jew"*, Stanford, CA: Stanford University Press, 1998, pp. 143–56.
3 For detailed information, see M.A. Meyer, *Response to Modernity: A History of the Reform Movement in Judaism*, Detroit, IL: Wayne State University Press, 1988; R.M. Seltzer, *The Jewish People, The Jewish Thought: The Jewish Experience in History*, New York/London: Collier-MacMillan, 1980; and Rudavsky, *Modern Jewish Religious Movements*.

4 M.A. Meyer, 'Universalism and Jewish unity in the thought of Abraham Geiger', in J. Katz (ed.), *The Role of Religion in Modern Jewish History*, Cambridge, MA: Association for Jewish Studies, 1975, p. 92.

5 M.A. Meyer, 'Abraham Geiger's historical Judaism', in J.J. Petuchowski (ed.), *New Perspectives on Abraham Geiger*, New York: Ktav, 1975, p. 7.

6 Abraham Geiger, *Abraham Geiger and Liberal Judaism: The Challenge of the Nineteenth Century*, compiled with a biographical introduction by M. Wiener, trans. E.J. Schlochauer, Cincinnati, OH: Hebrew Union College Press, 1981, p. 84.

7 See Meyer, *Response to Modernity*, p. 97.

8 *Abraham Geiger*, pp. 86, 247.

9 *Abraham Geiger*, pp. 87, 88.

10 *Abraham Geiger*, p. 289.

11 *Abraham Geiger*, p. 181.

12 *Abraham Geiger*, p. 183.

13 A. Geiger, *Judaism and Its History in Two Parts*, Boston, MA: University Press of America, 1985, pp. 159f.

14 *Abraham Geiger*, p. 151.

15 *Abraham Geiger*, p. 152.

16 See Meyer, *Response to Modernity*, pp. 99, 97.

17 The *Aleinu* prayer is recited as a daily prayer in Orthodox synagogues and as a concluding prayer for Sabbath services in Reform synagogues.

18 For both texts, see J.J. Petuchowski, *Prayerbook Reform in Europe: The Liturgy of European Liberal and Reform Judaism*, New York: World Union for Progressive Judaism, 1968, pp. 302, 303.

19 For the text of *Aleinu* prayer in different editions, see Petuchowski, *Prayerbook Reform*, pp. 301–5.

20 See Petuchowski, *Prayerbook Reform*, p. 306.

21 *Authorised Daily Prayer Book* of the United Hebrew Congregations of the British Commonwealth of Nations, trans. S. Singer, Eyre: Spottiswoode, 1962, p. 221.

22 See Meyer, *Response to Modernity*, p. 206.

23 M. Fox, 'Philosophy and religious values in modern Jewish thought', in Katz, *Religion in Modern Jewish History*, p. 81.

24 S.H. Bergman, *Faith and Reason: Modern Jewish Thought*, New York: Schocken, 1966, p. 30.

25 See Bergman, *Faith and Reason*, p. 31.

26 See Bergman, *Faith and Reason*, p. 29.

27 See W.S. Dietrich, 'The function of the idea of messianic mankind in Hermann Cohen's later thought', *JAAR* 48/2, 1980, 246ff.

28 H. Cohen, *Religion of Reason: Out of the Sources of Judaism*, 2nd edn, translated with an introduction by S. Kaplan, Atlanta, GA: Scholars Press, 1995, p. 253.

29 Cohen, *Religion of Reason*, pp. 259, 239, 268.

30 See Dietrich, 'The idea of messianic mankind', p. 249.

31 Cohen, *Religion of Reason*, p. 338.

32 See Bergman, *Faith and Reason*, p. 31; D. Novak, *The Election of Israel: The Idea of the Chosen People*, Cambridge: Cambridge University Press, 1995, pp. 65ff.

33 Novak, *Election of Israel*, p. 74.

34 W.Z. Harvey, response to 'Philosophy and religious values in modern Jewish thought' by M. Fox, in Katz, *Religion in Modern Jewish History*, pp. 88f.

35 M. Gopin, 'An Orthodox embrace of gentiles? interfaith tolerance in the thought of S.D. Luzzatto and E. Benamozegh', *Modern Judaism* 18/2, 1998, 192.

36 For a detailed discussion, see Gopin, 'An Orthodox embrace of gentiles?' pp. 177–88.

37 Fox, 'Philosophy and Religious Values', p. 79. Cf. Maimonides' view of reason as a means of attaining truth. It was believed by many, including Mendelssohn, that Maimonides did not expand salvation to those gentiles who attain truth out of their

'own rational considerations'. For a detailed discussion, see Harvey, response to 'Philosophy and religious values', p. 90; E. Korn, 'The gentiles, the world to come, and Judaism: the odyssey of a rabbinic text', *Modern Judaism* 14, 1994, 265–87.

38 S.R. Hirsch, *The Nineteen Letters on Judaism*, New York: Feldheim, 1969, p. 54.

39 S.R. Hirsch, *Horeb*, London: Soncino Press, 1997, pp. 32–3.

40 Rudavsky, *Jewish Religious Movements*, p. 232.

41 Hirsch, *Nineteen Letters*, p. 54.

42 Rudavsky, *Jewish Religious Movements*, p. 233.

43 Hirsch, *Nineteen Letters*, p. 55.

44 The same passage is translated in The Soncino Chumash in a similar way to Hirsch's translation: 'Yea, He loveth the peoples, And His holy ones – they are in Thy hand.' In RSV, however, it reads: 'Yea, he loved his people; all those consecrated to him were in his hand.'

45 Hirsch, *Nineteen Letters*, p. 56; see also *Horeb*, p. 461.

46 Fox, 'Philosophy and religious values', p. 83.

47 P. Mendes-Flohr, 'Mendelssohn and Rosenzweig', *Journal of Jewish Studies* 23/2, 1987, 207.

48 N.N. Glatzer (ed.), *Essays in Jewish Thought*, Alabama: University of Alabama Press, c.1978, p. 240.

49 See Bergman, *Faith and Reason*, p. 64. See also F. Rosenzweig, *The Star of Redemption*, trans. W.W. Hallo, London: University of Notre Dame Press, 1985, pp. 407f.; *Franz Rosenzweig: His Life and Thought*, presented by N.N. Glatzer, New York: Schocken, 1972, pp. 396, 342.

50 Rosenzweig, *Star of Redemption*, pp. 396, 397, 407.

51 Rosenzweig, *Star of Redemption*, pp. 404f.

52 See Bergman, *Faith and Reason*, pp. 70f.

53 See Seltzer, *Jewish People*, p. 738.

54 See Glatzer, *Franz Rosenzweig*, pp. 242f.

55 Rosenzweig, *Star of Redemption*, pp. 405ff.

56 Rosenzweig, *Star of Redemption*, pp. 415–16; see also Bergman, *Faith and Reason*, p. 64.

57 Rosenzweig, *Star of Redemption*, pp. 341, 342.

58 Bergman, *Faith and Reason*, p. 65.

59 Rosenzweig, *Star of Redemption*, pp. 331, 370.

60 Glatzer, *Franz Rosenzweig*, p. 234; see also Bergman, *Faith and Reason*, p. 59.

61 See Bergman, *Faith and Reason*, pp. 61, 62; N. Glatzer, forward to *Star of Redemption* by Rosenzweig, p. xii.

62 See Bergman, *Faith and Reason*, pp. 67f; Rosenzweig, *Star of Redemption*, pp. 312–13.

63 Novak, *Election of Israel*, p. 103.

64 Novak, *Election of Israel*, p. 105f.

65 See Rosenzweig, *Star of Redemption*, p. 218; N.M. Samuelson, *A User's Guide to Franz Rosenzweig's* Star of Redemption, Surrey: Curzon, 1999, p. 180.

66 See E. Luz, 'Buber's hermeneutics: the road to the revival of the collective memory and religious faith', *Modern Judaism* 15/1, 1995, 69f.

67 M. Buber, 'I and Thou', in E.N. Dorff and L.E. Newman (eds), *Contemporary Jewish Theology: A Reader*, New York/Oxford: Oxford University Press, 1999, p. 62.

68 Buber, 'I and Thou', p. 64.

69 M. Buber, 'Judaism and civilization and thought on Jewish existence', in N.N. Glatzer (ed.), *Modern Jewish Thought: A Source Reader*, New York: Schocken, 1977, p. 133. Israel's greatness as the people who stood and talked with God face to face at Sinai is an essential biblical, and particularly deuteronomic, notion, which has been greatly emphasized in Jewish tradition. See Dt. 4:32f.; *Sifré Dt.* 33, 59; Ber. 2:2; Ab. 29f.; Philo, *Post.*, 91–2; *Congr.* 51; *Som.* ii, 173; *Legat.* 4.

70 Buber, 'I and Thou', p. 62.

71 M. Buber, *On the Bible: Eighteen Studies*, N.N. Glatzer (ed.), New York: Schocken, 1982, pp. 81–2; M. Buber, *Biblical Humanism: Eighteen Studies by Martin Buber*, N.N. Glatzer (ed.), London: McDonald, 1968, p. 82. See also B.B. 79a.
72 Buber, *On the Bible*, pp. 86–7.
73 Glatzer, *Franz Rosenzweig*, p. 216.
74 M. Buber, *On Judaism*, New York: Schocken, 1967, p. 111.
75 Buber, *On Judaism*, pp. 181f.
76 Bergman, *Faith and Reason*, p. 64.
77 P. Vermes, *Buber on God and the Perfect Man*, London/Washington, DC: Littman Library of Civilization, 1994, pp. 41f.

6 Modern Jewish congregations in America

1 C. Gleason, 'The chosen people of God: Mary Rowlandson's captivity narrative', *Hanover Historical Review* 4, Spring 1996.
2 A.M. Eisen, *The Chosen People in America: A Study in Jewish Religious Ideology*, Bloomington/Indianapolis: Indiana University Press, 1983, p. 51.
3 M.A. Meyer, *Response to Modernity: A History of the Reform Movement in Judaism*, Detroit, IL: Wayne State University Press, 1988, p. 274.
4 S.D. Temkin, *Creating American Reform Judaism: The Life and Times of Isaac Mayer Wise*, London/Portland, OR: Littman Library of Jewish Civilization, 1998, p. 157.
5 Meyer, *Response to Modernity*, p. 239.
6 Cited in Meyer, *Response to Modernity*, p. 246.
7 Ibid.
8 I.M. Wise, *Judaism: Its Doctrines and Duties*, Cincinnati, OH: Office of the Israelite, 1872, p. 34.
9 Wise, *Judaism*, p. 37.
10 Temkin, *American Reform Judaism*, pp. 81, 142.
11 Meyer, *Response to Modernity*, p. 249.
12 See Meyer, *Response to Modernity*, p. 248.
13 K. Kohler, *Jewish Theology: Systematically and Historically Considered*, introduction by J.L. Blau, New York: Ktav, 1968, p. 325.
14 Meyer, *Response to Modernity*, p. 287.
15 E. Mendelsohn, *On Modern Jewish Politics*, New York/Oxford: Oxford University Press, 1993, p. 97.
16 N. Glazer, *American Judaism*, 2nd edn, Chicago, IL: University of Chicago Press, 1972, p. 137.
17 Glazer, *American Judaism*, pp. 138f. See also S.M. Cohen, *Religious Stability and Ethnic Decline: Emerging Patterns of Jewish Identity in the United States*, New York: Jewish Community Centers Association, 1998, p. 19.
18 Cited in Meyer, *Response to Modernity*, p. 294.
19 Ibid.
20 Cited in Meyer, *Response to Modernity*, p. 295.
21 Eisen, *Chosen People*, p. 68.
22 Cited in Meyer, *Response to Modernity*, p. 274.
23 S.S. Cohon, *Jewish Theology: A Historical and Systematic Interpretation of Judaism and Its Foundations*, Assen, Netherlands: Royal Vangorcum, 1971, p. 81.
24 Cited in Meyer, *Response to Modernity*, pp. 329f. See also A.H. Silver, *Where Judaism Differed: An Inquiry into the Distinctiveness of Judaism*, London: Collier-MacMillan, 1956, p. 19.
25 Eisen, *Chosen People*, p. 42ff.
26 Cited in Eisen, *Chosen People*, p. 54.
27 Cited in Eisen, *Chosen People*, p. 43.

28 Eisen, *Chosen People*, p. 44.
29 Silver, *Where Judaism Differed*, p. 10.
30 Cohon, *Jewish Theology*, p. 78.
31 Eisen, *Chosen People*, pp. 63f.
32 Meyer, *Response to Modernity*, p. 317.
33 Paraphrased in Meyer, *Response to Modernity*, pp. 336f. For Baeck's emphasis on the 'world-historic mission of Israel', see L. Baeck, *The Essence of Judaism*, New York: Schocken, 1961 (*c*.1948), pp. 66f.
34 S. Schechter, *Some Aspects of Rabbinic Theology*, New York: The MacMillan Company, 1910, p. viii.
35 L. Jacobs, *The Jewish Religion: A Companion*, New York/Oxford: Oxford University Press, 1995, pp. 172–3.
36 A. Cohen, *The Natural and the Supernatural Jew: A Historical and Theological Introduction*, London: Vallentine Mitchell, 1967, p. 285.
37 Schechter, *Rabbinic Theology*, p. 61.
38 Schechter, *Rabbinic Theology*, pp. 51f. See also Ex. 32:5; Dt. 7:7; Isa. 61:9; *Sifré Dt.* 73b; *Lev. R.* 10:2; *Ex. R.* 32:2.
39 Schechter, *Rabbinic Theology*, p. 57.
40 Schechter, *Rabbinic Theology*, p. 48.
41 D. Novak, *The Election of Israel: The Idea of the Chosen People*, Cambridge: Cambridge University Press, 1995, p. 246.
42 Schechter, *Rabbinic Theology*, p. 168.
43 S. Schechter, *Studies in Judaism: Essays on Persons, Concepts, and Movements of Thought in Jewish Tradition*, New York: Atheneum, 1970, p. 83.
44 Schechter, *Rabbinic Theology*, pp. 86, 88.
45 S. Schechter, 'Zionism: a statement', excerpted in A. Hertzberg (ed.), *The Zionist Idea: A Historical Analysis and Reader*, Philadelphia, PA: JPS, 1997, p. 512.
46 Here the term Israel is based on the distinction that Norbert Samuelson makes between 'Jews' as a national group and 'Israel' as a religious entity. According to Schechter, Israel, not Jews, should be considered as the chosen people. See N.M. Samuelson, 'Response to Menachem Kellner', in D.H. Frank (ed.), *A People Apart: Chosenness and Ritual in Jewish Philosophical Thought*, Albany: State University of New York Press, 1993, p. 79.
47 Cited in D. Cohn-Sherbok, *Modern Judaism*, London: Macmillan, 1996, p. 128.
48 Eisen, *Chosen People*, p. 113.
49 Eisen, *Chosen People*, p. 109.
50 Eisen, *Chosen People*, p. 107.
51 Eisen, *Chosen People*, p. 117.
52 See Eisen, *Chosen People*, p. 109.
53 See Eisen, *Chosen People*, pp. 77, 78.
54 Cohn-Sherbok, *Modern Judaism*, p. 140.
55 M.M. Kaplan, *Judaism as a Civilization: Toward a Reconstruction of American-Jewish Life*, Philadelphia: JPS, 1981, p. 43.
56 M.M. Kaplan, *The Meaning of God in Modern Jewish Religion*, New York: Reconstructionist Press, 1962, pp. 90, 53–4.
57 Kaplan, *Judaism*, pp. 22–3; *Meaning of God*, p. 94.
58 Kaplan, *Judaism*, p. 43.
59 Jacobs, *Jewish Religion*, p. 120. See also Kaplan, *Meaning of God*, pp. 97–9.
60 Kaplan, *Meaning of God*, p. 84.
61 Kaplan, *Meaning of God*, p. 100.
62 Kaplan, *Meaning of God*, p. 96.
63 Kaplan, *Meaning of God*, p. 102.
64 Eisen, *Chosen People*, p. 86.
65 A. Hertzberg, introduction to *Judaism as a Civilisation* by Kaplan, p. xxxii.

7 Zionist understanding

1 J.L. Blau, *Modern Varieties of Judaism*, New York: Columbia University Press, 1966, pp. 128f.
2 Y. Kaufmann, 'The pangs of redemption', in A.A. Cohen *Arguments and Doctrines: A Reader of Jewish Thinking in the Aftermath of the Holocaust*, Philadelphia, PA: JPS, 1970, p. 495.
3 For Abraham Geiger's severe critique of Moses Hess's nationalist ideas as they first appeared in his *Rome and Jerusalem* (1865), see M.I. Urofsky, introduction to *The Revival of Israel: Rome and Jerusalem* by M. Hess, Lincoln/London: University of Nebraska Press, 1995, p. xv.
4 See M. Sicker, *Judaism, Nationalism and the Land of Israel*, Boulder, CO: Westview Press, 1992, p. 142.
5 For Orthodox Rabbis' opposition to Zionism, see A. Ravitzky, *Messianism, Zionism, and Jewish Religious Radicalism*, trans. M. Swirsky and J. Chipman, Chicago, IL: University of Chicago Press, 1996, pp. 13ff.
6 A. Hertzberg (ed.), *The Zionist Idea: A Historical Analysis and Reader*, Philadelphia, PA and Jerusalem: JPS, 1997, p. 15.
7 See E. Aminov, 'Redefining Zionism: rebuilding the ghetto walls', Society of St Yves-Catholic Legal Resource and Human Rights Center, Jerusalem/Bethlehem, 15 September 1996 (Online).
8 See Y. Gorny, 'Thoughts on Zionism as a utopian ideology', *Modern Judaism* 18/3, 1998, 246.
9 See L.J. Silberstein, *The Postzionism Debates: Knowledge and Power in Israeli Culture*, New York and London: Routledge, 1999, p. 25.
10 Hertzberg, *Zionist Idea*, p. 18.
11 See, for example, M. Nordau, 'Speech to the first Zionist congress', excerpted in Hertzberg, *Zionist Idea*, pp. 236f.
12 Ravitzky, *Messianism*, p. 10; M.A. Meyer, *Jewish Identity in the Modern World*, Seattle/London: University of Washington Press, 1990, p. 69.
13 See Hertzberg, *Zionist Idea*, pp. 18f.
14 E. Mendelsohn, *On Modern Jewish Politics*, New York/Oxford: Oxford University Press, 1993, p. 97.
15 R.D. McKinzie, 'Oral history interview with Edwin M. Wright', 1977 (Online). Here it is also stated that 'Zionists and Christian Fundamentalists have frequently used the Hebrew *Bible* as an authority for justifying a Jewish State'.
16 T. Herzl, 'The Jewish state' (1896), excerpted in Hertzberg, *Zionist Idea*, p. 222. For the similarity between Zionist colonization in Palestine and the European settler ideology in general, see N. Finkelstein, 'A comparison between native Americans and the Palestinians', *The Link*, December 1999 and E.W. Said, *Culture and Imperialism*, London: Vintage, 1993, p. 8.
17 T. Herzl, *The Jewish State*, New York: Dover, 1988, p. 19.
18 T. Herzl, 'A solution of the Jewish question' (1896), excerpted in P.R. Mendes-Flohr and J. Reinharz (eds), *The Jew in the Modern World: A Documentary History*, New York/Oxford: Oxford University Press, p. 535.
19 Herzl, *Jewish State*, p. 146.
20 Herzl, 'Jewish question', p. 533.
21 Herzl, 'Jewish state', p. 621.
22 Herzl, *Jewish State*, p. 157.
23 Nordau, 'First Zionist congress', pp. 238f.
24 Meyer, *Jewish Identity*, p. 67.
25 M. Nordau, 'Jewry of muscle' (1903), excerpted in Mendes-Flohr and Reinharz, *Jew in the Modern World*, p. 547.
26 Nordau, 'Speech to the first Zionist congress', p. 241.

27 Cited in J.J. Zogby, *Zionism and the Problem of Palestinian Human Rights*, Association of Arab–American University Graduates, Information paper no. 20, October 1976, 6.
28 L. Pinsker, 'The auto-Emancipation: an appeal to his people by a Russian Jew' (1882), excerpted in Hertzberg, *Zionist Idea*, p. 187.
29 Meyer, *Jewish Identity*, p. 67.
30 Pinsker, 'Auto-emancipation', p. 190.
31 Pinsker, 'Auto-emancipation', pp. 185f.
32 Herzl, 'Jewish question', p. 534.
33 J. Klatzkin, 'Boundaries' (1914–21), excerpted in Hertzberg, *Zionist Idea*, p. 317, 319.
34 Klatzkin, 'Boundaries', p. 317.
35 Hertzberg, *Zionist Idea*, p. 315.
36 Klatzkin, 'Boundaries', p. 327.
37 Ahad Ha-Am, 'The Jewish state and the Jewish problem' (1897), excerpted in Hertzberg, *Zionist Idea*, p. 266.
38 Ahad Ha-Am, 'The first Zionist congress' (1897), excerpted in Mendes-Flohr and Reinharz, *Jew in the Modern World*, pp. 541f.
39 Ahad Ha-Am, 'On nationalism and religion' (1910), excerpted in Hertzberg, *Zionist Idea*, p. 262.
40 Cited in R.M. Seltzer, *The Jewish People, The Jewish Thought: The Jewish Experience in History*, New York/London: Collier-MacMillan, 1980, p. 699.
41 M.M. Kaplan, *Judaism as a Civilization: Toward a Reconstruction of American-Jewish Life*, Philadelphia, PA: JPS, 1981, p. 182.
42 Seltzer, *Jewish People*, p. 698.
43 Ibid. See also Ahad Ha-Am, 'Jewish state and Jewish problem', p. 267.
44 Ahad Ha-Am, 'Flesh and spirit' (1904), excerpted in Hertzberg, *Zionist Idea*, p. 259.
45 Ahad Ha-Am, 'Flesh and spirit', p. 257.
46 Seltzer, *Jewish People*, p. 700.
47 A.M. Eisen, *The Chosen People in America: A Study in Jewish Religious Ideology*, Bloomington/Indianapolis: Indiana University Press, 1983, p. 89.
48 Ahad Ha-Am, 'Jewish state and Jewish problem', p. 267.
49 Kaplan, *Judaism*, pp. 43–4.
50 Eisen, *Chosen People*, pp. 76f.
51 D. Greene, 'A chosen people in a pluralist nation: Horace Kallen and the Jewish-American experience', *Religion and American Culture: A Journal of Interpretation* 16/2, 2006, 169.
52 Hertzberg, *Zionist Idea*, pp. 525–6.
53 Y. Gorny, *The State of Israel in Jewish Public Thought: The Quest for Collective Identity*, London: Macmillan, 1994, p. 79.
54 H.M. Kallen, 'Zionism and liberalism' (1919), excerpted in Hertzberg, *Zionist Idea*, p. 530.
55 Eisen, *Chosen People*, p. 46.
56 Eisen, *Chosen People*, p. 47.
57 H.M. Kallen, 'In the hope of Zion', *International Journal of Ethics* 29/2, 1919, 147.
58 Kallen, 'In the hope of Zion', p. 150.
59 Kallen, 'In the hope of Zion', p. 152f.
60 Urofsky, introduction to *Rome and Jerusalem*, p. xiv.
61 Urofsky, introduction to *Rome and Jerusalem*, p. xiii.
62 M. Hess, 'Rome and Jerusalem' (1862), excerpted in Hertzberg, *Zionist Idea*, p. 128.
63 Hess, 'Rome and Jerusalem', p. 134.
64 See Seltzer, *Jewish People*, p. 707.
65 N. Syrkin, 'The Jewish problem and the socialist–Jewish state' (1898), excerpted in Hertzberg, *Zionist Idea*, pp. 334f.
66 Syrkin, 'Jewish problem and the socialist-Jewish state', p. 350.
67 Ibid.

68 Dt. 7:7; 4:6. See also Isa. 41:15f.: 'I will make of you a threshing sledge, sharp, new, and having teeth; you shall thresh the mountains and crush them, etc'.

69 L.D. Brandeis, 'The Jewish problem and how to solve it' (1915), excerpted in Hertzberg, *Zionist Idea*, p. 520.

70 Brandeis, 'Jewish problem and how to solve it', p. 517.

71 Meyer, *Jewish Identity*, p. 69.

72 M.J. Berdichevski, 'Wrecking and building' (1900–3), excerpted in Hertzberg, *Zionist Idea*, p. 294.

73 M.J. Berdichevski, 'The question of culture' (1900–3), and 'On sanctity' (1899), excerpted in Hertzberg, *Zionist Idea*, pp. 297, 301.

74 Seltzer, *Jewish People*, p. 705.

75 M.J. Berdichevski, 'In two directions' (1900–3), excerpted in Hertzberg, *Zionist Idea*, p. 296.

76 A.D. Gordon, 'Our tasks ahead' (1920), excerpted in Hertzberg, *Zionist Idea*, p. 381.

77 See, for example, Isa. 55:3f.; Jer. 31:31f.; 32:37f.; Ezk. 18:30–1, etc.

78 C.S. Liebman, 'Religion and modernity: *the special case of Israel*', in C.S. Liebman and E. Katz (eds), *The Jewishness of Israelis: Responses to the Guttman Report*, New York: State University of New York Press, 1997, p. 90.

79 Gordon, 'Our tasks ahead', p. 3.

80 J.H. Brenner, 'Self-criticism' (1914), excerpted in Hertzberg, *Zionist Idea*, p. 310.

81 Brenner, 'Self-criticism', p. 308.

82 C.S. Liebman and E. Don-Yehiya, *Civil Religion in Israel: Traditional Judaism and Polifical Culture in the Jewish State*, Berkeley: University of California, 1983, p. 39. Cf. Jer. 31:31f.: 'I will make a new covenant with the house of Israel and the house of Judah' and Ezek. 36:26: 'A new heart I will give you, and a new spirit I will put within you'.

83 Liebman and Don-Yehiya, *Civil Religion*, p. 33. Cf. Dt. 4:39: 'you would acknowledge that the Lord is God; there is no other besides him'.

84 Liebman and Don-Yehiya, *Civil Religion*, p. 60.

85 P. Beyer, *Religion and Globalization*, London: Sage, 1994, p. 189.

86 Liebman and Don-Yehiya, *Civil Religion*, p. 66.

87 See V. Jabotinsky, 'What the Zionist–Revisionists want' (1926), excerpted in Mendes-Flohr and Reinharz, *Jew in the Modern World*, p. 594.

88 Liebman and Don-Yehiya, *Civil Religion*, p. 61.

89 V. Jabotinsky, 'Evidence submitted to the Palestine Royal Commission' (1937), excerpted in Hertzberg, *Zionist Idea*, p. 561.

90 Liebman and Don-Yehiya, *Civil Religion*, p. 65.

91 Jabotinsky, 'Palestine Royal Commission', p. 562. See also Jabotinsky, 'What the Zionist-Revisionists want', pp. 594–6.

92 Beyer, *Religion*, p. 192.

93 Liebman and Don-Yehiya, *Civil Religion*, p. 67.

94 Ravitzky, *Messianism*, p. 27.

95 Ibid. See also E. Meir, 'Judaism: people or religion?: some positions in modern Jewish thought', *Sidic* 25/1, 1992, 21.

96 E. Schweid, 'Jewish messianism: metaphors of an idea', *Jerusalem Quarterly* 36, Summer 1985, 71f.

97 As regards the usage of the 'three oaths' ('that Israel not ascend the wall' from exile, 'that they not rebel against the nations of the world', and that 'they not force the End' – *Cant. R.* 2:7; Ket. 111a) and the relation between the passive and active tendencies, see Ravitzky, *Messianism*, p. 23.

98 Hertzberg, *Zionist Idea*, p. 103.

99 S. Avineri, *The Making of Modern Zionism: The Intellectual Origins of the Jewish State*, London: Weidenfeld and Nicolson, 1981, p. 51.

100 Ravitzky, *Messianism*, p. 30.

101 Z.H. Kalischer, 'Seeking Zion' (1862), excerpted in Hertzberg, *Zionist Idea*, p. 114.
102 For the distinction made between the messianic age, which is to be established on earth, and the world to come, following the earthly kingdom, see Sanh. 99a; also C.G. Montefiore and R. Loewe (eds), *A Rabbinic Anthology*, New York: Schocken, 1974, p. 581.
103 See H. Rabinowicz, *Hasidism and the State of Israel*, London/Toronto: Associated University Press, 1982, p. 213.
104 See Rabinowicz, *Hasidism*, p. 108.
105 Rabinowicz, *Hasidism*, p. 120.
106 M. Bar-Ilan, 'What kind of life should we create in Eretz Israel?' (1922), excerpted in Hertzberg, *Zionist Idea*, p. 549.
107 Y.M. Pines, 'Jewish nationalism cannot be secular' (1895), excerpted in Hertzberg, *Zionist Idea*, p. 412.
108 See Rabinowicz, *Hasidism*, p. 91.
109 'Manifesto' (1902) by Mizrachi, excerpted in Mendes-Flohr and Reinharz, *Jew in the Modern World*, p. 546.
110 H.N. Bialik, 'At the inauguration of the Hebrew University Jerusalem, January 4, 1925', excerpted in Hertzberg, *Zionist Idea*, p. 288.
111 A.I. Kook, *Abraham Isaac Kook: The Lights of Penitence, the Moral Principles, Lights of Holiness: Essays, Letters, and Poems*, trans. and introduction by B.Z. Bokser, London: SPCK, 1979, p. 289.
112 Kook, *Lights of Penitence*, p. 279.
113 A.I. Kook, 'Lights for rebirth' (1910–30), excerpted in Hertzberg, *Zionist Idea*, p. 430.
114 M. Gurfinkiel, 'The Jewish state: the next fifty years', *Azure*, Winter 5759/1999 (Online).
115 Ravitzky, *Messianism*, p. 94.
116 L. Kaplan, 'Rabbi Abraham I. Kook, Rabbi Joseph B. Soloveitchik and Dr Isaac Breuer on Jewish identity and the Jewish national revival', in C. Selengut (ed.), *Jewish identity in the Postmodern Age: Scholarly and Personal Reflections*, Minnesota: Paragon House, 1999, p. 49.
117 Liebman and Don-Yehiya, *Civil Religion*, p. 196.
118 Kook, 'Lights for rebirth', p. 430.
119 Liebman and Don-Yehiya, *Civil Religion*, p. 195.
120 A.I. Kook, 'The rebirth of Israel' (1910–30), and 'Lights for rebirth', excerpted in Hertzberg, *Zionist Idea*, pp. 425, 429.
121 Avineri, *Modern Zionism*, p. 195.
122 Ibid.
123 Ibid.
124 J.L. Magnes, 'Like all the nations?' (1930), excerpted in Hertzberg, *Zionist Idea*, p. 444.
125 Ibid.
126 Magnes, 'Like all the nations?' p. 447.

It is our duty to praise the Lord of all things ... since he has not made us like the nations of other lands, and has not placed us like other families of the earth, since he has not assigned unto us a portion as unto them, nor a lot as unto all their multitudes...

See *Authorised Daily Prayer Book*, of the United Hebrew Congregations of the British Commonwealth of Nations, trans. S. Singer, Eyre: Spottiswoode, 1962, p. 163.
127 Magnes, 'Like all the nations?' p. 449.
128 M. Buber, 'Hebrew humanism' (1942), excerpted in Hertzberg, *Zionist Idea*, p. 459.
129 See M. Buber and H. Cohen, 'A debate on Zionism and Messianism' (1916), excerpted in Mendes-Flohr and Reinharz, *Jew in the Modern World*, pp. 571ff.
130 M. Buber, 'The Jew in the world' (1934), excerpted in Hertzberg, *Zionist Idea*, p. 454.

131 M. Buber, 'Judaism and civilization and thought on Jewish existence', in N.N. Glatzer (ed.), *Modern Jewish Thought*, New York: Schocken, 1977, p. 131.
132 Buber, 'Hebrew humanism', p. 461.
133 For a distinction made by Buber between what he calls 'overt' and 'covert' histories, see E. Luz, 'Buber's hermeneutics: the road to the revival of the collective memory and religious faith, *Modern Judaism* 15/1, 1995, 76. For a similar view of Rosenzweig's, see also *Franz Rosenzweig: His Life and Thought*, presented by N.N. Glatzer, New York: Schocken, 1972, p. 292.
134 Luz, 'Buber's hermeneutics', pp. 77–8.
135 M. Buber, 'From an open letter to Mahatma Gandhi' (1939), excerpted in Hertzberg, *Zionist Idea*, p. 465.
136 L. Jacobs, *A Jewish Theology*, London: Darton, Longman & Todd, 1973, p. 280.

8 The discourse of 'Holocaust and Redemption'

1 J. Neusner, 'American Judaism of Holocaust and Redemption', in *Judaism in Modern Times: An Introduction and Reader*, Cambridge, MA: Blackwell, 1995, p. 6 and *Stranger at Home: 'The Holocaust', Zionism, and American Judaism*, Atlanta, GA: Scholars Press, 1997, pp. 61f. This is also what Marc Ellis refers to as the myth of 'Innocence and Redemption'. See M.H. Ellis, *Beyond Innocence and Redemption: Confronting the Holocaust and Israeli Power*, New York: Harper & Row, 1990.
2 For all this, see N. Glazer, *American Judaism*, 2nd edn, Chicago, IL/London: University of Chicago Press, 1972, pp. 155–6.
3 D. Marmur, *Beyond Survival: Reflections on the Future of Judaism*, London: Darton, Longman & Todd, 1982, p. 53.
4 A.M. Eisen, *The Chosen People in America: A Study in Jewish Religious Ideology*, Bloomington/Indianapolis: Indiana University Press, 1983, p. 127f. In relation to the emergence of a new theology particularly among Reform Jewry, which is characterized by its attention to the biblical concept of 'covenant', see also M.A. Meyer, *Response to Modernity: A History of the Reform Movement in Judaism*, Detroit, IL: Wayne State University Press, 1988, p. 360.
5 See, for example, F.A. Doppelt, 'Are the Jews a chosen people?', *Liberal Judaism* 9/6, 1942, 6–9; J.L. Halevi, 'Clashing concepts: chosen people versus master race', *Liberal Judaism* 12/11, 1945, 28–32.
6 Y. Gorny, *The State of Israel in Jewish Public Thought: The Quest for Collective Identity*, London: Macmillan, 1994, p. 79.
7 Ibid.
8 P. Novick, *The Holocaust and Collective Memory: The American Experience*, London: Bloomsbury, 2001, p. 113. See also Neusner, 'Holocaust and Redemption', p. 210.
9 See E. Shapiro, 'Liberal politics and American Jewish identity', *Judaism* 47/4, 1998, 428; Meyer, *Response to Modernity*, 365; Glazer, *American Judaism*, p. 167; B. Susser and C.S. Liebman, *Choosing Survival: Strategies for a Jewish Future*, New York/Oxford: Oxford University Press, 1999, p. 73.
10 Glazer, *American Judaism*, pp. 181f.
11 Glazer, *American Judaism*, p. 172. See also Gorny, *State of Israel*, p. 80. Novick, *Holocaust*, p. 102; C.E. Silberman, *A Certain People: American Jews and Their Lives Today*, New York: Summit Books, 1985, p. 183.
12 See *The Condition of Jewish Belief: A Symposium Compiled by the Editors of* Commentary *Magazine*, New York: Macmillan Company; London: Collier-MacMillan Ltd., 1966.
13 See also J.L. Hellig, 'The myth of Jewish chosenness in the modern world', *Dialogue and Alliance* 3, Fall 1989, 7; Eisen, *Chosen People*, p. 149.

14 Novick, *Holocaust*, pp. 184f., 188f.; Neusner, 'Holocaust and Redemption', pp. 218f.; Meyer, *Response to Modernity*, pp. 365. Cf. Glazer, *American Judaism*, p. 171.

15 M. Polner and A. Simms, 'When Israel is wrong, Christians shouldn't be afraid to say so', *Commonweal* 129/17, 2002, 19–20.

16 Eisen, *Chosen People*, p. 128.

17 Novick maintains that, although this was not the understanding of American Jews, 'President Lyndon Johnson's intelligence experts debated whether it would take a week or ten days for Israel to demolish its enemies' (*Holocaust*, p. 148).

18 For the feeling of isolation among Israelis prior to the Six Day War, see, for example, Silberman, *Certain People*, pp. 181–5.

19 Novick, *Holocaust*, p. 3.

20 Novick, *Holocaust*, pp. 3, 83.

21 Novick, *Holocaust*, pp. 115–16; Neusner, *Stranger at Home*, pp. 78, 84.

22 N.G. Finkelstein, *The Holocaust Industry: Reflections on the Exploitation of Jewish Suffering*, London/New York: Verso, 2000, pp. 54f. For the post-war focus on brotherhood and other universal ideals, see also M. Mart, 'Constructing a universal ideal: anti-Semitism, American Jews, and the founding of Israel', *Modern Judaism* 20/2, 2000, 181ff.

23 L.A. Coser (ed. and trans.) *Maurice Halbwachs on Collective Memory*, Chicago, IL: University of Chicago Press, 1992, p. 25.

24 Coser, *Maurice Halbwachs*, p. 34.

25 J. Plaskow, *Standing Again at Sinai: Judaism from a Feminist Perspective*, New York: HarperCollins, 1991, p. 75.

26 Novick, *Holocaust*, pp. 3f. For a similar understanding as regards the nature of collective memory, see L.J. Silberstein, 'Cultural criticism, ideology, and the interpretation of Zionism: toward a post-Zionist discourse', in S. Kepnes (ed.), *Interpreting Judaism in a Postmodern Age*, New York/London: New York University Press, 1996, p. 339.

27 The term 'myth' here is used not in the sense of false story but rather as an unconditionally accepted sacred truth. To make a distinction between two different usages of the extermination of European Jewry by the Nazis, namely one as an 'historical event' and the other as a 'myth', some scholars refer to the former as 'holocaust' and to the latter as 'the Holocaust'. See, for example, Neusner, *Stranger at Home*, p. 86.

28 Novick, *Holocaust*, pp. 6f.

29 Novick, *Holocaust*, p. 166; see also Finkelstein, *Holocaust Industry*, pp. 31f.

30 M.H. Ellis, *O, Jerusalem: The Contested Future of the Jewish Covenant*, Minneapolis, MN: Fortress Press, 1999, p. 26.

31 T. Segev, *The Seventh Million: The Israelis and the Holocaust*, trans. H. Watzman, New York: Henry Holt and Company, 1991, p. 97.

32 M.A. Meyer, *Jewish Identity in the Modern World*, Seattle/London: University of Washington Press, 1990, p. 57.

33 Novick, *Holocaust*, p. 7.

34 Meyer, *Jewish Identity*, p. 56.

35 Susser and Liebman, *Choosing Survival*, p. 55. See also Neusner, 'Holocaust and Redemption', p. 206.

36 For a substantial analysis of those reasons, see Novick, *Holocaust*, pp. 85–123.

37 For the usage of the term 'the Holocaust', see I. Schorsch, 'The Holocaust and Jewish survival', *Midstream*, January 1981, 38.

38 Meyer, *Jewish Identity*, p. 75.

39 Neusner, *Stranger at Home*, p. 86.

40 See L. Rubinoff, 'Auschwitz and the theology of the Holocaust', in P. Opsahl and M.H. Tanenbaum (eds), *Speaking of God Today: Jews and Lutherans in Conversation*, Philadelphia, PA: Fortress, 1974, p. 127.

41 A.H. Foxman, 'God's chosen', excerpted in *Journal of Historical Review* 14/2,

1994, 41. The identification of the enemies of Israel with the enemies of God appears as a common theme in Jewish tradition. See C.G. Montefiore and R. Loewe (eds), *A Rabbinic Anthology*, New York: Schocken, 1974, p. 562.

42 E. Wiesel, 'Talking and writing and keeping silent', in F.H. Little and H.G. Locke (eds), *The German Church Struggle and the Holocaust*, San Francisco, CA: Mellen Research University Press, 1990, p. 274.

43 S. Freedman and I. Greenberg, *Living in the Image of God*, conversations with Rabbi I. Greenberg, Northvale, NJ: Jason Aronson, 1998, p. 81. For a similar view, see also Y.K. Halevi, 'Survival', in A. Cohen and P. Mendes-Flohr (eds), *Contemporary Jewish Religious Thought: Original Essays on Critical Concepts, Movements, and Beliefs*, London/New York: Collier-MacMillan, 1987, p. 948.

44 For the critics of the doctrine of the uniqueness of the Holocaust, such as David Stannard, while Jewish suffering in Auschwitz was indeed unique in certain ways and only as much as any other people's suffering can be, the conviction of the uniqueness of Jewish suffering 'is itself an outgrowth not of true scholarly analysis but of straightforward religious dogma'. See D.E. Stannard, 'Uniqueness as denial: the politics of genocide scholarship', in A.S. Rosenbaum (ed.), *Is the Holocaust Unique?* Oxford: Westview Press, 1998, pp. 169.

45 Silberman, *Certain People*, p. 78.

46 Finkelstein, *Holocaust Industry*, p. 48.

47 See J.M. Cuddihy, 'The Holocaust: the latent issue in the uniqueness debate', in P.E. Gallagher (ed.), *Christians, Jews and Other Worlds: Patterns of Conflict and Accommodation*, New York/London: University Press of America, 1988, p. 67; Stannard, 'Uniqueness as denial', pp. 192f. For an opposite view that regards the killing of the Jews as essentially 'incidental', see A.J. Mayer's thesis as reviewed in D. Michman, ' "The Holocaust" in the eyes of historians: the problem of conceptualization, periodization, and explanation', *Modern Judaism* 15, 1995, 252–3, 255.

48 Stannard, 'Uniqueness as denial', p. 188; M. Goldberg, *Why Should Jews Survive? Looking Past the Holocaust toward a Jewish Future*, New York/Oxford: Oxford University Press, 1995, p. 46. See also Marmur, *Beyond Survival*, p. 30.

49 Cited in Eisen, *Chosen People*, p. 136.

50 E.B. Borowitz, *Renewing the Covenant: A Theology for the Postmodern Jews*, Philadelphia, PA: JPS, 1991, p. 199. Cf. Freedman and Greenberg, *Living*, p. 81.

51 D. Novak, *The Election of Israel: The Idea of the Chosen People*, Cambridge: Cambridge University Press, 1995, p. 19.

52 Cited in Finkelstein, *Holocaust Industry*, p. 49.

53 Schorsch, 'Holocaust and Jewish survival', p. 39.

54 For a parallel drawn between 'Euro-American ideology of white supremacy' and the Jewish 'exclusivist idea' of the Holocaust uniqueness, see Stannard, 'Uniqueness as denial', pp. 167, 171, 176, 197; I. Hancock, 'Responses to the Porrajmos: the Romani Holocaust', in Rosenbaum, *Is the Holocaust Unique?*, pp. 46f.

55 Silberman, *Certain People*, p. 79.

56 Cuddihy, 'The Holocaust', pp. 68f.

57 'Battle for the Holocaust', Channel 4 (UK), 27 January 2001.

58 Cited in Silberman, *Certain People*, p. 81.

59 Silberman, *Certain People*, p. 78.

60 C.S. Liebman and E. Don-Yehiya (eds), *Civil Religion in Israel: Traditional Judaism and Political Culture in the Jewish State*, Berkeley: University of California Press, 1983, p. 125.

61 See, for example, Schorsch, 'Holocaust and Jewish survival', p. 39.

62 Goldberg, *Why Should Jews Survive?* p. 48. Cf. Dt. 5:8f.

63 See Novick, *Holocaust*, p. 219.

64 Neusner, *Stranger at Home*, p. 61.

65 J. Neusner, *Judaism Transcends Catastrophe: God, Torah, and Israel Beyond the Holocaust – God Commands*, Macon, GA: Mercer University Press, 1995, p. 10.

66 See, for example, R.A. Miller, *Rejoice O Youth!: An Integrated Jewish Ideology*, New York: Balshon Printing and Offset, 1962. For a similar view, see also 'Where was the merciful Almighty during the Holocaust?', in M. Sternbuch, *Rav Moshe Speaks: An Anthology of Talks*, Y. Rosenes (ed.) Jerusalem: Jewish Writers Guild, 1988.

67 For Zionism-related arguments, see J. Sacks, *Crisis and Covenant: Jewish Thought after the Holocaust*, Manchester/New York: Manchester University Press, 1992, pp. 29–31.

68 E. Berkovits, *Faith after the Holocaust*, New York: Ktav, 1973, pp. 89, 105–6.

69 The term historicism here is used as a particular theological approach, which evaluates the biblical relationship between God and Israel not in accordance with the eternal truth of the Torah, but instead, in the light of historical changes. See S.T. Katz, *Historicism, the Holocaust, and Zionism: Critical Studies in Modern Jewish Thought and History*, New York: New York University Press, 1992, pp. 3.

70 Neusner, *God Commands*, p. 8.

71 Sacks, *Crisis and Covenant*, p. 28; See also Freedman and Greenberg, *Living*, p. 52.

72 M. Gifter, 'A path through the ashes: some thoughts on teaching the Holocaust', in N. Wolpin (ed.), *A Path through the Ashes: Penetrating Analysis and Inspiring Stories of the Holocaust from a Torah Perspective*, New York: Mesorah in conjunction with Agudath Israel of America, 1996, p. 62.

73 Gifter, 'Path through the ashes', p. 59.

74 Berkovits, *Faith*, p. 130. In rabbinic literature the problem of suffering is mainly tackled in terms of individual suffering. While the rabbis seek to justify or normalize national disasters by attributing them to certain reasons such as punishment for sins, innocent suffering, etc., they see individual suffering as being far too complicated to explain away.

75 Berkovits, *Faith*, p. 89f.

76 M. Wyschogrod, 'Faith and the Holocaust', *Judaism* 20, 1971, 294.

77 It is a view widely accepted by the ultra-Orthodox Jews that no matter what happens to the Jewish people, Judaism still remains the same.

78 M. Wyschogrod, *The Body of Faith: God in the People of Israel*, San Francisco, CA/New York: Harper & Row, 1989, pp. 59–60.

79 D. Novak, *Jewish Social Ethics*, Oxford/New York: Oxford University Press, 1992, p. 7.

80 E.L. Fackenheim, *The Jewish Return into History*, New York: Schocken, 1978, p. 21. See also Rubinoff, 'Auschwitz and the theology of the Holocaust', pp. 122–3.

81 Cited in Katz, *Historicism*, p. 237. See also Freedman and Greenberg, *Living*, pp. 53, 55–7, 80f.

82 I. Greenberg, *The Jewish Way: Living the Holidays*, New York: Touchstone Books/Simon and Schuster, 1993, p. 19. For the Reconstructionist endorsement of an active Jewish involvement in survival and the redemption of the world, see D. Cohn-Sherbok, 'Post-messianic Judaism in modern times', *Theology* 101, 1998, 278–84.

83 Katz, *Historicism*, pp. 234f.

84 See Rubinoff, 'Auschwitz and the theology of the Holocaust', p. 130.

85 See O. Leaman, *Evil and Suffering in Jewish Philosophy*, Cambridge/New York: Cambridge University Press, 1995, pp. 186, 209.

86 R.L. Rubenstein, *After Auschwitz: Radical Theology and Contemporary Judaism*, New York: The Bobbs-Merrill Company, 1966, pp. 293ff.

87 Leaman, *Evil and Suffering*, p. 187.

88 Neusner, *Stranger at Home*, p. 86.

89 See Ellis, *O Jerusalem*, p. 27.

90 Novick, *Holocaust*, pp. 69–70.
91 I. Greenberg, 'Cloud of smoke, pillar of fire: Judaism, Christianity, and Modernity after the Holocaust', in E.N. Dorff and L.E. Newman (eds), *Contemporary Jewish Theology: A Reader*, New York/Oxford: Oxford University Press, 1999, pp. 404–5. See also Freedman and Greenberg, *Living*, p. 57.
92 Fackenheim, *Jewish Return*, p. 29.
93 This is a theology that is mostly shared by religious Jews, especially the ultra-Orthodox, as well as some Christians such as the Dean Grüber. See Rubenstein, *After Auschwitz*, pp. 52f.
94 See Dt. 28:47–9, 58–9, 63, 64.
95 Rubenstein, 'After Auschwitz', in Dorff and Newman, *Contemporary Jewish Theology*, p. 58.
96 R.L. Rubenstein, 'Some perspectives on religious faith after Auschwitz', in Little and Locke, *German Church Struggle and the Holocaust*, p. 263.
97 For a detailed discussion of the problem of theodicy in relation to the Holocaust, see F. Sherman, 'Speaking of God after Auschwitz', in Opsahl and Tanenbaum, *Speaking of God Today*, pp. 144–59; M. Sarot, 'Auschwitz, morality and the suffering of God', *Modern Theology* 7/2, 1991, 135–52.
98 See also *Ex. R.* 1:1; *Dt. R.* 3:2, etc.
99 In all these passages (e.g., Ps. 44, Jer. 12:1, Hab. 1:13) God is criticized for hiding his face by forsaking and punishing Israel despite its obedience, and the story of Job which again presents, via Job's mouth, a severe critique of God's punishment of the innocent. Regarding the book of Job, in particular, some rabbis urged either to completely ignore the problematic passages or to prohibit the study of the book in the first place. See Ber. 10b; Sot. 31a, etc.
100 Berkovits, *Faith*, pp. 98ff.
101 See D.C. Kraemer, *Responses to Suffering in Classical Rabbinic Literature*, New York/Oxford: Oxford University Press, 1995, p. 221.
102 See Yoma 9b.
103 'Battle for the Holocaust'.
104 Schorsch, 'Holocaust and Jewish survival', p. 40.
105 Cited in Novick, *Holocaust*, pp. 198–9. For the instrumentalist use of the uniqueness argument in American Jewish and Israeli politics, see also Stannard, 'Uniqueness as denial', p. 194.
106 Stannard, 'Uniqueness as denial', p. 194.
107 Schorsch, 'Holocaust and Jewish survival', p. 40.
108 Novick, *Holocaust*, p. 181.
109 Meyer, *Jewish Identity*, p. 76.
110 For the theme of diselection, see R.C. Heard, *Dynamics of Diselection: Ambiguity in Genesis 12 36 and Ethnic Boundaries in Post-Exilic Judah*, Atlanta, GA: Society of Biblical Literature, 2001.
111 Marmur, *Beyond Survival*, p. 10. The word *vayishakehu* ('he kissed him') in Genesis 33:4 is read by Jewish commentators as *vayishakhehu* ('he bit him'). See *Gen. R.* 78:12.
112 See Michman, '"The Holocaust" in the eyes of historians', p. 256.
113 C. Ozick, 'All the world wants the Jews dead', *Esquire*, November 1974, 104. Cf. 1 Mac. 5:10: 'The gentiles around us have gathered together against us to destroy us'.
114 Novick, *Holocaust*, p. 152.
115 Coser, *Maurice Halbwachs*, p. 4.
116 Plaskow, *Standing at Sinai*, p. 75.
117 See Fackenheim, *Jewish Return*, p. 31.
118 See Ex. 13:3; Dt. 11:2; 16:3; 24:22.
119 Goldberg, *Why Should Jews Survive?*, p. 5.
120 Ibid.

121 E.L. Fackenheim, *What is Judaism?*, New York: Collier, 1987, pp. 121ff.

122 See, for example, A.A. Cohen, *The Natural and the Supernatural Jew: A Historical and Theological Introduction*, London: Vallentine Mitchell, 1967.

123 It should suffice to look at the association, made in rabbinic literature, between the terms *sinai*, which exemplified God's covenantal relationship with Israel, and *sinah* which referred to the 'hatred' of the Jews on the part of other nations, on the basis of the former being the people of God (Sab. 89b; *Num. R.* 1:8).

124 Schorsch, 'Holocaust and Jewish survival', p. 41.

125 See I. Shahak and N. Mezvinsky, *Jewish Fundamentalism in Israel*, London: Pluto Press, 1999, p. 58; M. Friedman, 'What is the cause of antisemitism?' (Online).

126 For Baudrillard's description of post-modernity as 'the immense process of the destruction of meaning', see D. Kellner, 'Postmodernism as social theory: some challenges and problems', *Theory, Culture and Society* 5/2–3, 1988, 246. 'The postmodern world', Kellner maintains, 'is devoid of meaning; it is a universe of nihilism.... Meaning requires depth, a hidden dimension, an unseen substratum; in postmodern society, however, everything is visible, explicit, transparent, obscene'.

127 See D. Singer, 'Change and continuity in American Judaism: the case of Nathan Glazer', in R.S. Wistrich (ed.), *Terms of Survival: The Jewish World Since 1945*, London/New York: Routledge, 1995, pp. 329f.

128 See, for example, W. Herberg, 'The "chosenness" of Israel and the Jew of today', in A.A. Cohen (ed.), *Arguments and Doctrines: A Reader of Jewish Thinking in the Aftermath of the Holocaust*, Philadelphia, PA: JPS, 1970, pp. 270–83.

129 For the Christian imagery attached to the myth of the Holocaust, see Novick, *Holocaust*, pp. 236f.

130 L.A. Olan, 'The doctrine of the chosen people reaffirmed', *Judaism* 29/116, 1980, 466.

131 Schorsch, 'The Holocaust and Jewish survival', p. 39.

132 Goldberg, *Why Should Jews Survive?*, p. 49.

9 The American experience

1 *The Condition of Jewish Belief: A Symposium Compiled by the Editors of* Commentary *Magazine*, New York: The MacMillan Company; London: Collier-MacMillan, 1966, pp. 34, 36.

2 *Gates of Prayer: The New Union Prayerbook*, New York: Central Conference of American Rabbis, 1975, p. 615.

3 *The Authorised Daily Prayer Book* of the United Hebrew Congregations of the British Commonwealth of Nations, trans. S. Singer, Eyre: Spottiswoode, 1962, p. 221.

4 *Forms of Prayer for Jewish Worship*, the Assembly of Rabbis of the Reform Synagogues of Great Britain, 7th edn, Cambridge: Cambridge University Press, 1977, p. 167. Cf. '... who has chosen us from all peoples, and has given us your Law' (*Authorised Daily Prayer Book*, p. 197).

5 See, for example, B.H. Block, 'The problem with the Aleinu-Adoration', 12 January 1996 (Online).

6 *Gates of Prayer*, p. 322.

7 N. Glazer, *American Judaism*, 2nd edn, Chicago, IL: University of Chicago Press, 1972, pp. 150. See also A.M. Eisen, *The Chosen People in America: A Study in Jewish Religious Ideology*, Bloomington/Indianapolis: Indiana University Press, 1983, p. 162.

8 M.H. Danzger, *Returning to Tradition: The Contemporary Revival of Orthodox Judaism*, New Haven, CT/London: Yale University Press, 1989, p. 327.

9 S.S. Cohon, 'The theology of the Union Prayer Book', in J.L. Blau (ed.), *Reform Judaism: A Historical Perspective – Essays from the Yearbook of the Central Conference of American Rabbis*, New York: Ktav, 1973. p. 275.

10 Cited in Eisen, *Chosen People*, p. 161.
11 E.B. Borowitz, 'The chosen people concept as it affects Jewish life in the diaspora', *Journal of Ecumenical Studies* 12, 1975, 566. See also E.B. Borowitz, 'The autonomous Jewish self', *Modern Judaism* 4/1, 1984, 42f.
12 E.B. Borowitz, 'The dialectic of Jewish particularity', *Journal of Ecumenical Studies* 8/3, 1971, 567–8.
13 Borowitz, 'The chosen people concept', p. 553ff.
14 M.A. Meyer, *Response to Modernity: A History of the Reform Movement in Judaism*, Detroit, IL: Wayne State University Press, 1988, p. 368; Glazer, *American Judaism*, p. 150.
15 B. Susser and C.S. Liebman, *Choosing Survival: Strategies for a Jewish Future*, New York/Oxford: Oxford University Press, 1999, p. 44.
16 P. Novick, *The Holocaust and Collective Memory: The American Experience*, London: Bloomsbury, 2001, p. 181.
17 Eisen, *Chosen People*, p. 161.
18 W.G. Plaut, *The Case for the Chosen People*, New York: Doubleday, 1965, pp. 111–12.
19 Eisen, *Chosen People*, pp. 160ff.
20 A.A. Cohen, *The Natural and the Supernatural Jew: A Historical and Theological Introduction*, London: Vallentine Mitchell, 1967, p. 6.
21 Cohen, *Natural*, p. 53, fn. 3.
22 Cohen, *Natural*, p. 278.
23 Cohen, *Natural*, p. 282.
24 See Eisen, *Chosen People*, p. 156.
25 W. Herberg, 'Jewish existence and survival: a theological view', *Judaism*, July 1952, 26.
26 W. Herberg, 'The "chosenness" of Israel and the Jew of today', in A.A. Cohen (ed.), *Arguments and Doctrines: A Reader of Jewish Thinking in the Aftermath of the Holocaust*, Philadelphia: JPS, 1970, pp. 272, 273.
27 Herberg, 'The "chosenness" of Israel', pp. 282, 283.
28 Susser and Liebman, *Choosing Survival*, pp. 72ff.
29 L. Fein, 'American pluralism and Jewish interests', in A. Hirt-Manheimer (ed.), *The Jewish Condition: Essays on Contemporary Judaism Honoring Rabbi Alexander M. Schindler*, New York: UAHC Press, 1995, p. 66.
30 Susser and Liebman, *Choosing Survival*, p. 70. See also S.M. Cohen and A.M. Eisen, *The Jew Within: Self, Family, and Community in America*, Bloomington/Indianapolis: Indiana University Press, 2000, pp. 187f.
31 S.M. Cohen, *Religious Stability and Ethnic Decline: Emerging Patterns of Jewish Identity in the United States*, New York: Jewish Community Centers Association, 1998, pp. 3–4.
32 See Susser and Liebman, *Choosing Survival*, p. 72.
33 T. Bayfield, 'Mission: a Jewish perspective', *Theology* 96, 1993, 184.
34 Susser and Liebman, *Choosing Survival*, pp. 84f.
35 Eisen, *Chosen People*, pp. 157, 158.
36 Cited in Susser and Liebman, *Choosing Survival*, p. 81.
37 Susser and Liebman, *Choosing Survival*, p. 80. For the contemporary emphasis on choosing, see Y.K. Greenberg, 'The choosing, not the chosen people', in C. Selengut (ed.), *Jewish Identity in the Postmodern Age: Scholarly and Personal Reflections*, St Paul, MN: Paragon House, 1999, pp. 13–23.
38 Susser and Liebman, *Choosing Survival*, p. 70.
39 T. Zahavy, 'The predicament of the postmodern American Jew', in Selengut, *Jewish Identity*, p. 247. For the importance of personal experiences in this new Jewish self-understanding and taken-for-granted Jewishness, see also Cohen and Eisen, *Jew Within*, pp. 13–16, 187.
40 Susser and Liebman, *Choosing Survival*, p. 7.
41 See J. Wertheimer, 'Judaism without limits', *Commentary* 104, July 1997, 27.

42 E. Shapiro, 'Liberal politics and American Jewish identity', *Judaism*, 47/4, 1998, 425–36.

43 'What do American Jews believe? a symposium', *Commentary*, August 1996 (Online).

44 E.H. Yoffie, Keynote Lecture in RSGB Conference, Nottingham University, 1 July 2000 (Online).

45 E.B. Borowitz, *Renewing the Covenant: A Theology for the Postmodern Jew*, Philadelphia, PA: JPS, 1991, p. 222.

46 Borowitz, *Renewing the Covenant*, p. 223.

47 D. Novak, 'The Jewish theology', *Modern Judaism* 10/3, 1990, 316f.

48 E.B. Borowitz, *Judaism after Modernity: Papers from a Decade of Fruition*, Lanham, MD: University Press of America, 1999, p. 210.

49 L. Finkelstein, 'The Jewish religion: its beliefs and practices', in L. Finkelstein (ed.), *The Jews: Their Religion and Their Culture*, 4th edn, New York: Schocken, 1973, p. 484.

50 S. Siegel, 'Election and the people of God', in P. Opsahl and M.H. Tanenbaum (eds), *Speaking of God Today: Jews and Lutherans in Conversation*, Philadelphia, PA: Fortress, 1974, p. 45.

51 Siegel, 'Election and the people of God', p. 53.

52 Siegel, 'Election and the people of God', p. 52. See also *The Condition of Jewish Belief*, pp. 225–7.

53 R. Gordis, *Understanding Conservative Judaism*, New York: Rabbinical Assembly, 1978, p. 106.

54 L. Jacobs, *The Jewish Religion: A Companion*, New York/Oxford: Oxford University Press, 1995, p. 274.

55 Gordis, *Conservative Judaism*, p. 144.

56 Gordis, *Conservative Judaism*, p. 145.

57 According to Arthur S. Harrow, Senior Vice-President of the Temple Beth-El, the distinction made here between Israel and other nations refers to an acknowledgement of 'Israel's distinct character among the nations of the earth, premised on Israel's acceptance of the One Universal God'. Available at www.uscj.org/seabd/richmotb/articles/shabbatsvcs.html (accessed January 2001). Orley Denman, a Masorti rabbi, on the other hand, interpreted it in relation to the second part of the prayer, namely as an expression of Jewish hope for a more united, tolerant world in which all peoples cherish one another's humanity: 'Therefore, we put our hope in you, the Lord our God, that we may soon see Your mighty splendour…. On that day, God will be One and His Name will be One.' Available at www.masorti.org.uk/11–03–00.htm (accessed January 2001).

58 *Condition of Jewish Belief*, p. 90.

59 A. Hertzberg (ed.), *Judaism*, New York: George Braziller, 1962, p. 14.

60 Hertzberg, *Judaism*, p. 19.

61 *Condition of Jewish Belief*, pp. 90–1.

62 D. Singer, review on *Jews: The Essence and Character of a People* by A. Hertzberg and A. Hirt-Manheimer (San Francisco, CA: HarperSanFrancisco, 1998), *Commentary*, July 1998 (Online).

63 See Hertzberg, *Judaism*, p. 12; Hertzberg and Hirt-Manheimer, *Jews*, p. 30.

64 A.J. Heschel, *God in Search of Man: A Philosophy of Judaism*, New York: Octagon, 1976, p. 426.

65 A.J. Heschel, *Israel: An Echo of Eternity*, Woodstock, VT: Jewish Lights Publishing, 1997, p. 130.

66 Heschel, *God in Search of Man*, p. 425.

67 Heschel, *God in Search of Man*, p. 424.

68 L. Jacobs, *A Jewish Theology*, London: Darton, Longman & Todd, 1973, p. 271, 273.

69 *Condition of Jewish Belief*, p. 14.

70 *Condition of Jewish Belief*, p. 13.
71 *Condition of Jewish Belief*, pp. 218–19.
72 M. Sklare, *An American Religious Movement: Conservative Judaism*, Lanham, MD/London: University Press of America, 1985, p. 134.
73 For Maimonides's recognition, see J.S. Minkin, *The Teachings of Maimonides*, Northvale, NJ: Jason Aronson, 1993, pp. 318–19, 374–5.
74 'What do American Jews believe?'.
75 Susser and Liebman, *Choosing Survival*, p. 73.
76 I. Schorsch, 'The sacred cluster: the core values of Conservative Judaism', 1995 (Online).
77 Ibid.
78 D. Novak, *The Election of Israel: The Idea of the Chosen People*, Cambridge: Cambridge University Press, 1995, pp. 116–17.
79 Novak, *Election of Israel*, pp. 213ff.
80 Novak, *Election of Israel*, pp. 115ff.
81 Novak, *Election of Israel*, p. 163ff.
82 Novak, *Election of Israel*, p. 169. See also Est. 9:27.
83 Novak, *Election of Israel*, p. 117.
84 Novak, *Election of Israel*, p. 247.
85 Novak, *Election of Israel*, pp. 244–5.
86 Novak, *Election of Israel*, p. 77.
87 Novak, *Election of Israel*, p. 248f.
88 Novak, *Election of Israel*, p. 249ff.
89 D. Novak, *Jewish Social Ethics*, Oxford/New York: Oxford University Press, 1992, p. 9.
90 Susser and Liebman, *Choosing Survival*, pp. 140f.; Eisen, *Chosen People*, p. 165.
91 M.S. Berger, '*U-Vikashtem Mi-Sham*: Rabbi Joseph B. Soloveitchik's response to Martin Buber's religious existentialism', *Modern Judaism* 18, 1998, 109.
92 Ibid.
93 *Condition of Jewish Belief*, pp. 63–4, 106.
94 *Condition of Jewish Belief*, pp. 111, 134–5, 239–40.
95 *Condition of Jewish Belief*, p. 126.
96 M. Gifter, 'A path through the ashes: some thoughts on teaching the Holocaust', in N. Wolpin (ed.), *A Path through the Ashes: Penetrating Analysis and Inspiring Stories of the Holocaust from a Torah Perspective*, New York: Mesorah in conjunction with Agudath Israel of America, 1986, p. 62.
97 See, for example, Y. Hutner, '"Holocaust": a Rosh Yeshiva's response', in Wolpin, *Path through the Ashes*, pp. 43.
98 L. Davidman, 'Accommodation and resistance to modernity: a comparison of two contemporary Orthodox Jewish groups', *Sociological Analysis* 51/1, 1990, 35–52.
99 See Eisen, *Chosen People*, p. 140.
100 J.B. Soloveitchik, *Fate and Destiny: From the Holocaust to the State of Israel*, New York: Ktav, 2002, pp. 2ff.
101 Soloveitchik, *Fate and Destiny*, p. 6.
102 Berger, '*U-Vikashtem Mi-Sham*', p. 98.
103 D. Hartman, *A Living Covenant: The Innovative Spirit in Traditional Judaism*, New York: Free Press; London: Collier-MacMillan, 1985, p. 3.
104 D. Singer, 'The new Orthodox theology', *Modern Judaism* 9/1, 1989, 40.
105 D. Hartman, 'Suffering', in A.A. Cohen and P. Mendes-Flohr (eds) *Contemporary Jewish Religious Thought: Original Essays on Critical Concepts, Movements, and Beliefs*, London/New York: Collier-MacMillan, 1987, p. 940.
106 Hartman, 'Suffering', p. 946.
107 See Singer, 'New Orthodox theology', p. 42.
108 See Singer, 'New Orthodox theology', pp. 44f.; J.A. Rapaport, 'Worshipping

Mammon: the pursuit of affluence and the assimilation of modern Orthodox Jewry', in Selengut, *Jewish Identity*, p. 142.

109 S. Freedman and I. Greenberg, *Living in the Image of God: Jewish Teachings to Perfect the World*, conversations with Rabbi I. Greenberg, Northvale, NJ: Jason Aronson, 1998, p. 79.
110 Freedman and Greenberg, *Living*, p. 80.
111 D. Novak, 'The Jewish theology', *Modern Judaism* 10/3, 1990, 318.
112 Singer, 'New Orthodox theology', p. 45.
113 M. Wyschogrod, *The Body of Faith: God in the People of Israel*, San Francisco, CA/New York: Harper & Row, 1989, p. 177.
114 'What do American Jews believe?'.
115 See C.E. Librach, 'The fragmented faith of American Jews', *First Things* 70, February 1997, 19.
116 See C. Poll 'The Jewish community in America: it is the safest of times and the most dangerous of times', in Selengut, *Jewish Identity*, p. 25.
117 Rapaport, 'Worshipping Mammon', p. 143.
118 Rapaport, 'Worshipping Mammon', pp. 145, 147. See also E. Shapiro, 'Modern Orthodoxy in crisis: a test case', *Judaism* 51/3, 2002, 347–61.
119 See S. Zalman, *Tanya: Likutei Amarim*, chs 1–2 (Online). See also I. Shahak and N. Mezvinsky, *Jewish Fundamentalism in Israel*, London: Pluto Press, 1999, p. 60; C. Liebman, 'Religious trends among American and Israeli Jews', in R.S. Wistrich (ed.), *Terms of Survival: The Jewish World since 1945*, London/New York: Routledge, 1995, p. 318, fn. 24.
120 See D.S. Ariel, *What Do Jews Believe? The Jewish Faith Examined*, London: Rider, 1995, pp. 117–18.
121 Cf. Philo's emphasis on the name 'Israel', meaning 'seeing God'.
122 R.L. Kremnizer, 'Lech Lecha – finding oneself', in *The Curtain Parted: Glimpsing the Week Ahead* (Online).
123 Cited in Davidman, 'Accommodation and resistance', p. 45.
124 Gifter, 'Path through the ashes', p. 59.
125 Shahak and Mezvinsky, *Jewish Fundamentalism*, p. 60.
126 M. Friedman, 'What is the cause of antisemitism?' (Online).

10 The Israeli experience

1 See L.J. Silberstein, 'Cultural criticism, ideology, and the interpretation of Zionism: toward a post-Zionist discourse', in S. Kepnes (ed.), *Interpreting Judaism in a Postmodern Age*, New York/London: New York University Press, 1996, pp. 336–7.
2 C.S. Liebman and E. Don-Yehiya (eds), *Civil Religion in Israel: Traditional Judaism and Political Culture in the Jewish State*, Berkeley: University of California Press, 1983, p. 86.
3 See D.H. Harrison, 'Skirball examines Truman, "the American Cyrus",' *San Diego Jewish Press Heritage*, 1 May 1998 (Online).
4 R.D. McKinzie, 'Oral history interview with Edwin M. Wright', 1977 (Online).
5 According to 1987 survey results, more than half of the American Protestants and one third of the American Catholics see the creation of the state of Israel in terms of 'a prophetic interpretation'. See R.O. Smith, 'Between restoration and liberation: theopolitical contributions and responses to U.S. foreign policy in Israel/Palestine', *Journal of Church and State* 46/4 2004, 838.
6 E. Cohen, 'Israel as a post-Zionist society', in R. Wistrich and D. Ohana (eds), *The Shaping of Israeli Identity: Myths, Memories and Trauma*, London: Frank Cass, 1995, p. 203.
7 Y. Leibowitz, 'The religious and moral significance of the redemption of Israel', in

E.N. Dorff and L.E. Newman (eds), *Contemporary Jewish Theology: A Reader*, New York/Oxford: Oxford University Press, 1999, p. 454.

8 Liebman and Don-Yehiya, *Civil Religion*, p. 87.

9 Y. Leibowitz, 'The uniqueness of the Jewish people', *Jerusalem Quarterly* 19, Spring 1981, p. 53.

10 J. Plaskow, *Standing Again at Sinai: Judaism from a Feminist Perspective*, New York: HarperCollins, 1991, p. 96. For rabbinic evidence on the hierarchical nature of the people of Israel, see *Ex. R.* 37:4; Hor. 3:8.

11 Ex. 12:42; Lev. 18:26; Num. 15:15; Dt. 5:12–15.

12 See Lev. 21; Num. 5:2–3; 18; Dt. 12:16; 14:21. In some respect 'proselytes', 'women', and 'slaves' are presented as constituting of a separate category in rabbinic literature, alongside what are called the Israelites, which apparently refers to ordinary, i.e., non-priest and non-Levite, male Israelites. See, for example, *Num. R.* 11: 8; Men. 43a.

13 See, for example, *Ex. R.* 30:9; *Num. R.* 1:8; 2:13; 10:2; *Dt. R.* 7: 3.

14 See B.Z. Kahane, 'There are no innocent Midyanites', 1993 (Online).

15 For the relation between Zionism and western colonialism, see, for example, M. Rodinson, *Israel: A Colonial-settler State?* New York: Anchor Foundation, 1973.

16 Cited in L.J. Silberstein, *The Postzionism Debates: Knowledge and Power in Israeli Culture*, New York/London: Routledge, 1999, pp. 106. See also A.M. Lilienthal, *The Zionist Connection: What Price Peace?*, New York: Dodd, Mead & Company, 1978, p. 147; N. Chomsky, *The Fateful Triangle: The United States, Israel and the Palestinians*. London/Sydney: Pluto Press, 1983, p. 51; Y. Kaufmann, 'The pangs of redemption', in A.A. Cohen, *Arguments and Doctrines: A Reader of Jewish Thinking in the Aftermath of the Holocaust*, Philadelphia, PA: JPS, 1970, p. 488.

17 Cited in Silberstein, *Postzionism Debates*, p. 117.

18 Chomsky, *Fateful Triangle*, p. 61.

19 L. Levidow, 'Zionist anti-Semitism', *Return*, December 1990 (Online).

20 Silberstein, 'Cultural criticism, ideology, and the interpretation of Zionism', p. 336.

21 See Liebman and Don-Yehiya, *Civil Religion*, pp. 87–8, 93–4, 100–7.

22 Cited in T. Wise, 'Reflections on Zionism from a dissident Jew', 2001 (Online). See also T. Segev, *The Seventh Million: The Israelis and the Holocaust*, trans. H. Watzman, New York: Henry Holt and Company, 1991, pp. 101f.

23 In Jewish tradition there have been two opposing views regarding the nature of the messianic world. One view presupposes the disappearance of all national, ethnic, and religious boundaries and the Judaization of the entire world, whereas the other accepts an ongoing difference between Jews and non-Jews, and a world totally dominated by the former. See M. Kellner, 'Messianic postures in Israel today', *Modern Judaism* 6/2, 1986, 200–1.

24 S. Sharot, *Messianism, Mysticism, and Magic: A Sociological Analysis of Jewish Religious Movements*, Chapel Hill: University of North Carolina Press, 1982, p. 236.

25 C.S. Liebman, 'Paradigms sometimes fit: the Haredi response to the Yom Kippur War', in Wistrich and Ohana, *Shaping of Israeli Identity*, p. 175.

26 See I. Shahak and N. Mezvinsky, *Jewish Fundamentalism in Israel*, London: Pluto Press, 1999, pp. 70–1; Liebman and Don-Yehiya, *Civil Religion*, p. 201.

27 See Liebman and Don-Yehiya, *Civil Religion*, pp. 135ff.

28 E. Schweid, 'Judaism in Israeli culture', in D. Urian and E. Karsh (eds), *In Search of Identity: Jewish Aspects in Israeli Culture*, London/Portland, OR: Frank Cass, 1999, p. 18.

29 I.S. Lustick, *For the Land and the Lord: Jewish Fundamentalism in Israel*, New York: Council on Foreign Relations, 1988, p. 130. For America's political, financial, and military support of Israel, see also Chomsky, *Fateful Triangle*; M.H. Ellis, *Beyond Innocence and Redemption: Confronting the Holocaust and Israeli Power*, New York: Harper & Row, 1990.

30 Schweid, 'Judaism in Israeli culture', p. 20.
31 A. Hertzberg, 'Judaism and the land of Israel', in J. Neusner (ed.), *Understanding Jewish Theology: Classical Issues and Modern Perspectives*, New York: Ktav, 1973, p. 75.
32 See E. Cantarow, 'Gush Emunim: the twilight of Zionism?' 2001 (Online).
33 For this usage, see G. Shaked, 'Israeli society and secular-Jewish culture', in C.S. Liebman and E. Katz (eds), *The Jewishness of Israelis: Responses to the Guttman Report*, New York: State University of New York Press, 1997, p. 162.
34 Lustick, *For the Land*, p. 75.
35 See Liebman, 'Religion, democracy and Israeli society', p. 85; Lustick, *For the Land*, pp. 77ff.
36 See Lustick, *For the Land*, p. 77.
37 Cited in Liebman and Don-Yehiya, *Civil Religion*, p. 201.
38 Shahak and Mezvinsky, *Jewish Fundamentalism*, pp. 64ff. See also Plaskow, *Standing at Sinai*, p. 115; Chomsky, *Fateful Triangle*, p. 151.
39 C.S. Liebman, 'Jewish fundamentalism', in M.E. Marty and R.S. Appleby (eds), *Fundamentalisms and the State: Remaking Polities, Economies, and Militance*, Chicago/London: University of Chicago Press, 1993, p. 72.
40 C.S. Liebman, 'Religious trends among American and Israeli Jews', in R.S. Wistrich (ed.), *Terms of Survival: The Jewish World since 1945*, London/New York: Routledge, 1995, pp. 309f.
41 For fundamental differences between American and Israeli Judaisms in general, and American and Israeli Orthodoxies in particular, see C.S. Liebman and S.M. Cohen, *Two Worlds of Judaism: The Israeli and American Experiences*, New Haven, CT: Yale University Press, 1990.
42 See B.Z. Kahane, 'There is no placing trust [in] the gentile', 1992 and 'Everything you wanted to know about Ishmael', 1997 (Online). See also Liebman and Cohen, *Two Worlds of Judaism*, pp. 60f.
43 Cited in Shahak and Mezvinsky, *Jewish Fundamentalism*, p. 62.
44 See Cantarow, 'Gush Emunim'.
45 See Liebman, 'Religious trends among American and Israeli Jews', p. 318, fn. 24.
46 See Shahak and Mezvinsky, *Jewish Fundamentalism*, pp. 62, 65.
47 Shahak and Mezvinsky, *Jewish Fundamentalism*, p. 67.
48 Shahak and Mezvinsky, *Jewish Fundamentalism*, p. 74.
49 See Lustick, *For the Land*, p. 79.
50 See 'Debate on the eligibility of Jews for citizenship' (1789), excerpted in P. Mendes-Flohr and J. Reinharz (eds), *The Jew in the Modern World: A Documentary History*, New York/Oxford: Oxford University Press, 1995, p. 115.
51 Cited in Shahak and Mezvinsky, *Jewish Fundamentalism*, p. 71. See also U. Tal, 'Foundations of a political messianic trend in Israel', *Jerusalem Quarterly* 35, Spring 1985, 42f.
52 Tal, 'Political messianic trend in Israel', p. 43.
53 Liebman and Don-Yehiya, *Civil Religion*, p. 190.
54 L. Kaplan, 'Rabbi Abraham I. Kook, Rabbi Joseph B. Soloveitchik and Dr Isaac Breuer on Jewish identity and the Jewish national revival', in Selengut, *Jewish Identity in the Postmodern Age*, p. 60.
55 Sharot, *Messianism*, p. 229.
56 Liebman, and Don-Yehiya, *Civil Religion*, p. 193.
57 Leibowitz, 'Uniqueness of the Jewish people', p. 48.
58 Leibowitz, 'Uniqueness of the Jewish people', p. 53.
59 Leibowitz, 'Uniqueness of the Jewish people', p. 54.
60 S. Rotbart, 'Who is afraid of the post Zionists?', 30 April 2001 (Online). See also Silberstein, *Postzionism Debates*, pp. 84f.
61 G.J. Neuberger, 'The great gulf between Zionism and Judaism', 2000 (Online).
62 For the existence of both traditional and modern elements in Gush Emunim, see

S. Sharot, 'Traditional, modern or postmodern? recent religious developments among Jews in Israel', in K. Flanagan and P.C. Jupp (eds), *Postmodernity, Sociology and Religion*, London: Macmillan, 1996, pp. 128–9.

63 Neuberger, 'The great gulf between Zionism and Judaism'.

64 D. Weiss, 'Perspective Judaism: an alternative to Zionism', 2001 (Online).

65 Silberstein, *Postzionism Debates*, p. 93.

66 See, for example, M. Oppenheim, 'Feminism, Jewish philosophy, and religious pluralism', *Modern Judaism* 16, 1996, 147–60.

67 M. Gurfinkiel, 'The Jewish state: the next fifty years', *Azure*, Winter 5759/1999 (Online).

68 Silberstein, 'Cultural criticism, ideology, and the interpretation of Zionism', pp. 338ff.

69 Liebman, 'Cultural conflict in Israeli society', in Liebman and Katz, *Jewishness of Israelis*, p. 106.

70 Liebman and Katz, *Jewishness of Israelis*, p. 25.

71 C.S. Liebman, 'Religion and modernity: *The Special Case of Israel*', in Liebman and Katz, *Jewishness of Israelis*, p. 97.

72 See E. Schweid, 'Is there really no alienation or polarization?', in Liebman and Katz, *Jewishness of Israelis*, p. 151; cf. Liebman, 'Religion and modernity', p. 96.

Bibliography

Agus, J.B., *The Evolution of Jewish Thought*, New York: Arno Press, 1973.

Ahad Ha-Am, 'On nationalism and religion' (1910), excerpted in A. Hertzberg (ed.), *The Zionist Idea: A Historical Analysis and Reader*, Philadelphia, PA/Jerusalem: JPS, 1997, pp. 261–2.

—— 'Flesh and spirit' (1904), excerpted in Hertzberg, *The Zionist Idea*, pp. 256–9.

—— 'The first Zionist congress' (1897), excerpted in P. Mendes-Flohr and J. Reinharz (eds), *The Jew in the Modern World: A Documentary History*, 2nd edn, New York/Oxford: Oxford University Press, 1995, pp. 541–3.

—— 'The Jewish state and the Jewish problem' (1897), excerpted in Hertzberg, *Zionist Idea*, pp. 262–9.

Allegro, J.M., *The Chosen People*, London: Hodder & Stoughton, 1971.

Aminov, E., 'Redefining Zionism: rebuilding the ghetto walls', Society of St Yves-Catholic Legal Resource and Human Rights Center, Jerusalem/Bethlehem, 15 September 1996. Available at http://servus.christusrex.org/www2/news/9-96/sy9-15-96.html (accessed 24 October 2001).

Ariel, D.S., *What Do Jews Believe? The Jewish Faith Examined*, London: Rider, 1995.

Arkush, A., 'Judaism as egoism: from Spinoza to Feuerbach to Marx', *Modern Judaism* 11/1, 1991, 211–23.

The Authorised Daily Prayer Book of the United Hebrew Congregations of the British Commonwealth of Nations, trans. S. Singer, Eyre: Spottiswoode, 1962.

Avineri, S., *The Making of Modern Zionism: The Intellectual Origins of the Jewish State*, London: Weidenfeld and Nicolson, 1981.

The Babylonian Talmud, trans. I. Epstein, London: Soncino Press, 1961 (18 vols).

Baeck, L., *The Essence of Judaism*, New York: Schocken, 1948.

Bar-Ilan, M., 'What kind of life should we create in Eretz Israel?' (1922), excerpted in Hertzberg, *Zionist Idea*, pp. 548–55.

Barth, K., *A Shorter Commentary on Romans*, London: SCM, 1959.

'Battle for the Holocaust', Channel 4 (UK), 27 January 2001.

Bauer, W., Arndt, W.F., and Gingrich, F.W. (eds), *A Greek–English Lexicon of the New Testament and Other Early Christian Literature*, Chicago, IL: Chicago University Press, 1957.

Bauman, Z., 'Allosemitism: premodern, modern, and postmodern', in B. Cheyette and L. Marcus (eds), *Modernity, Culture, and 'The Jew'*, foreword by H. Bhabha, Stanford, CA: Stanford University Press, 1998, pp. 143–56.

Bayfield, T., 'Mission: a Jewish perspective', *Theology* 96, 1993, 180–90.

Berdichevski, M.J., 'In two directions' (1900–3), excerpted in Hertzberg, *Zionist Idea*, pp. 295–7.

—— 'The question of culture' (1900–3), excerpted in Hertzberg, *Zionist Idea*, pp. 299–301.

—— 'Wrecking and building' (1900–3), excerpted in Hertzberg, *Zionist Idea*, pp. 293–5.

—— 'On sanctity' (1899), excerpted in Hertzberg, *Zionist Idea*, pp. 301–2.

Berger, M.S., '*U-Vikashtem Mi-Sham*: Rabbi Joseph B. Soloveitchik's response to Martin Buber's religious existentialism', *Modern Judaism* 18, 1998, 93–118.

Bergman, S.H., *Faith and Reason: Modern Jewish Thought*, New York: Schocken, 1966.

—— 'Israel and the *Oikoumené*', in R. Loewe (ed.), *Studies in Rationalism, Judaism and Universalism*, London: Routledge and Kegan Paul, 1966, pp. 47–66.

Berkovits, E., *Faith after the Holocaust*, New York: Ktav, 1973.

Beyer, P., *Religion and Globalization*, London: Sage, 1994.

Bialik, H.N., 'At the inauguration of the Hebrew University Jerusalem, January 4, 1925', excerpted in Hertzberg, *Zionist Idea*, pp. 281–8.

Bidney, D., *The Psychology and Ethics of Spinoza*, New York: Russell & Russell, 1962.

Blau, J.L., *Modern Varieties of Judaism*, New York: Columbia University Press, 1966.

Block, B.H., 'The problem with the Aleinu-Adoration', 12 January 1996. Available at www.beth-elsa.org/be_s0112.htm (accessed 4 September 2001).

Bloesch, D.G., '"All Israel will be saved": supersessionism and the biblical witness', *Interpretation* 43, 1989, 130–42.

Borowitz, E.B., *Judaism after Modernity: Papers from a Decade of Fruition*, Lanham, MD: University Press of America, 1999.

—— *Renewing the Covenant: A Theology for the Postmodern Jew*, Philadelphia, PA: JPS, 1991.

—— 'The autonomous Jewish self', *Modern Judaism* 4/1, 1984, 39–56.

—— 'The chosen people concept as it affects life in the diaspora', *Journal of Ecumenical Studies* 12, 1975, 553–68.

—— 'The dialectic of Jewish particularity', *Journal of Ecumenical Studies* 8/3, 1971, 560–74.

Boyarin, D., *A Radical Jew: Paul and the Politics of Identity*, Berkeley/Los Angeles/London: University of California Press, 1997.

Brandeis, L.D., 'The Jewish problem and how to solve it' (1915), excerpted in Hertzberg, *Zionist Idea*, pp. 517–23.

Brenner, J.H., 'Self-criticism' (1914), excerpted in Hertzberg, *Zionist Idea*, pp. 307–12.

Brown, R.E., Fitzmyer, J.A., and Murphy, R.E. (eds), *The New Jerome Biblical Commentary*, 2nd edn, London: Geoffrey Chapman, 1990.

Buber, M., 'Hebrew humanism' (1942), excerpted in Hertzberg, *Zionist Idea*, pp. 457–63.

—— 'From an open letter to Mahatma Gandhi' (1939), excerpted in Hertzberg, *Zionist Idea*, pp. 463–6.

—— 'I and Thou', in E.N. Dorff and L.E. Newman (eds), *Contemporary Jewish Theology: A Reader*, New York/Oxford: Oxford University Press, 1999, pp. 60–4.

—— 'The Jew in the world' (1934), excerpted in Hertzberg, *Zionist Idea*, pp. 450–3.

—— *On the Bible: Eighteen Studies*, N.N. Glatzer (ed.), New York: Schocken, 1982.

—— 'Judaism and civilization and thought on Jewish existence', in N.N. Glatzer (ed.), *Modern Jewish Thought: A Source Reader*, New York: Schocken, 1977, pp. 131–9.

—— *Biblical Humanism: Eighteen Studies by Martin Buber*, N.N. Glatzer (ed.), London: McDonald, 1968.

—— *On Judaism*, N.N. Glatzer (ed.), New York: Schocken, 1967.

Buber, M. and Cohen, H., 'A debate on Zionism and Messianism' (1916), excerpted in Mendes-Flohr and Reinharz, *Jew in the Modern World*, pp. 571–7.

Cantarow, E., 'Gush Emunim: the twilight of Zionism?' 2001. Available at www.media-monitors.net/cantarow1.html (accessed 10 December 2007).

Charles, R.H., *Eschatology: The Doctrine of a Future Life*, introduction by G.W. Buchanan, New York: Schocken, 1970.

Childs, B.S., *Biblical Theology of the Old and New Testaments: Theological Reflection on the Christian Bible*, Minneapolis, MN: Fortress Press, 1992.

—— *Exodus: A Commentary*. London: SCM, 1974.

Chomsky, N., *The Fateful Triangle: The United States, Israel and the Palestinians*, London/Sydney: Pluto Press, 1983.

Clements, R., *God's Chosen People: A Theological Interpretation of the Book of Deuteronomy*, London: SCM, 1968.

Cohen, A.A., *The Natural and the Supernatural Jew: A Historical and Theological Introduction*, London: Vallentine Mitchell, 1967.

Cohen, E., 'Israel as a post-Zionist society', in R. Wistrich and D. Ohana (eds), *The Shaping of Israeli Identity: Myths, Memory, and Trauma*, London: Frank Cass, 1995, pp. 203–13.

Cohen, H., *Religion of Reason: Out of the Sources of Judaism*, 2nd edn, trans. with an introduction by S. Kaplan, Atlanta, GA: Scholars Press, 1995.

Cohen, S.M., *Religious Stability and Ethnic Decline: Emerging Patterns of Jewish Identity in the United States*, New York: Jewish Community Centers Association, 1998.

Cohen, S.M. and Eisen, A.M., *The Jew Within: Self, Family, and Community in America*, Bloomington/Indianapolis: Indiana University Press, 2000.

Cohn-Sherbok, D., 'Post-messianic Judaism in modern times', *Theology* 101, 1998, 278–84.

—— *Modern Judaism*, London: Macmillan, 1996.

Cohon, S.S., 'The theology of the Union Prayer Book', in J.L. Blau (ed.), *Reform Judaism: A Historical Perspective – Essays from the Yearbook of the Central Conference of American Rabbis*, New York: Ktav, 1973, pp. 257–84.

—— *Jewish Theology: A Historical and Systematic Interpretation of Judaism and Its Foundations*, Assen, Netherlands: Royal Vangorcum, 1971.

The Condition of Jewish Belief: A Symposium Compiled by the Editors of Commentary *Magazine*, New York: The MacMillan Company; London: Collier-MacMillan, 1966.

Coser, L.A., *Maurice Halbwachs on Collective Memory*, ed., trans. and with an introduction by L.A. Coser, Chicago, IL: University of Chicago Press, 1992.

Cott, J., 'The biblical problem of election', *Journal of Ecumenical Studies* 21/2, 1984, 200.

Cuddihy, J.M., 'The Holocaust: the latent issue in the uniqueness debate', in P.E. Gallagher (ed.), *Christians, Jews and Other Worlds: Patterns of Conflict and Accommodation*, New York/London: University Press of America, 1988, pp. 62–79.

Dahl, N.A., 'Election and the people of God: some comments', in P. Opsahl and M.H. Tanenbaum (eds), *Speaking of God Today: Jews and Lutherans in Conversation*, Philadelphia, PA: Fortress, 1974, pp. 31–8.

Danzger, M.H., *Returning to Tradition: The Contemporary Revival of Orthodox Judaism*, New Haven, CT/London: Yale University Press, 1989.

Davidman, L., 'Accommodation and resistance to modernity: a comparison of two contemporary Orthodox Jewish groups', *Sociological Analysis* 51/1, 1990, 35–52.

Davies, W.D., *Paul and Rabbinic Judaism*, London: SPCK, 1962.

Davis, M., *The Emergence of Conservative Judaism: The Historical School in 19th Century America*, Westport, CT: Greenwood Press, 1977 (*c.*1963).

'Debate on the eligibility of Jews for citizenship' (French National Assembly, 1789), excerpted in Mendes-Flohr and Reinharz, *Jew in the Modern World*, pp. 114–16.

Dentan, R.G., 'Religion and theology of the Old Testament', *Encyclopedia Americana*, 3: 683.

Dietrich, W.S., 'The function of the idea of messianic mankind in Hermann Cohen's later thought', *JAAR* 48/2, 1980, 245–58.

Doppelt, F.A., 'Are the Jews a chosen people?', *Liberal Judaism* 9/6, 1942, 6–9.

Douglas, M., 'The stranger in the Bible', *Archives Europeenas de Sociologie* 35, 1994, 283–98.

Driver, S.R., *An Introduction to the Literature of the Old Testament*, 9th edn, Edinburgh: T & T Clark, 1950.

—— *Critical and Exegetical Commentary on Deuteronomy*, Edinburgh: T & T Clark, 1902.

Dumbrell, W.J., *Covenant and Creation: An Old Testament Covenantal Theology*, Exeter: Paternoster Books, 1984.

Eisen, A.M., *The Chosen People in America: A Study in Jewish Religious Ideology*, Bloomington/Indianapolis: Indiana University Press, 1983.

Eisen, R., *Gersonides on Providence, Covenant, and the Chosen People: A Study in Medieval Jewish Philosophy and Biblical Commentary*, New York: State University of New York Press, 1995.

Ellis, E.E., *Paul's Use of the Old Testament*, Edinburgh/London: Oliver & Boyd, 1957.

Ellis, M.H., *O, Jerusalem: The Contested Future of the Jewish Covenant*, Minneapolis, MN: Fortress Press, 1999.

—— *Beyond Innocence and Redemption: Confronting the Holocaust and Israeli Power*, New York: Harper & Row, 1990.

Fackenheim, E.L., *What Is Judaism?*, New York: Collier, 1987.

—— *The Jewish Return into History*, New York: Schocken, 1978.

Falk, Z., 'The mission of Israel: a view from within', *Immanuel* 12, September 1981, 102–9.

Featherstone, M., 'In pursuit of the postmodern: an introduction', *Theory, Culture and Society* 5/2–3, 1988, 195–215.

Fein, L., 'American pluralism and Jewish interests', in A. Hirt-Manheimer (ed.), *The Jewish Condition: Essays on Contemporary Judaism Honoring Rabbi Alexander M. Schindler*, New York: UAHC Press, 1995, pp. 63–76.

Finkelstein, L. (ed.), *The Jews: Their Role in Civilization*, New York: Schocken, 1974.

—— (ed.), *The Jews: Their Religion and Culture*, 4th edn, New York: Schocken, 1973.

Finkelstein, N.G., *The Holocaust Industry: Reflections on the Exploitation of Jewish Suffering*. London/New York: Verso, 2000.

—— 'A comparison between native Americans and the Palestinians', *The Link*, December 1999.

Forms of Prayer for Jewish Worship: Daily, Sabbath and Occasional Prayers the Assembly of Rabbis of the Reform Synagogues of Great Britain, 7th edn, Cambridge: Cambridge University Press, 1977.

Fox, M., 'Philosophy and religious values in modern Jewish thought', in J. Katz (ed.), *The Role of Religion in Modern Jewish History: Proceedings of Regional Conferences of the Association for Jewish Studies*, Cambridge, MA: Association for Jewish Studies, 1975, pp. 69–85.

Foxman, A.H., 'God's chosen', excerpted in *Journal of Historical Review* 14/2, 1994, 41.

Freedman, S. and Greenberg, I., *Living in the Image of God: Jewish Teachings to Perfect the World*, foreword by R.J. Telushkin, Northvale, NJ: Jason Aronson, 1998.

Friedman, M., 'What is the cause of antisemitism?' Available at www.chabad.org/library/article_cdo/aid/2902/jewish/What-Is-the-Cause-of-Antisemitism.htm (accessed 10 December 2007).

Frydman-Kohl, B., 'Covenant, conversion and chosenness: Maimonides and Halevi on "who is a Jew?"', *Judaism* 41/1, 1992, 64–79.

Garrett, D. (ed.), *The Cambridge Companion to Spinoza*, Cambridge: Cambridge University Press, 1996.

Gates of Prayer: The New Union Prayerbook, New York: Central Conference of American Rabbis, 1975.

Geiger, A., *Judaism and Its History in Two Parts*, Boston, MA: University Press of America, 1985.

—— *Abraham Geiger and Liberal Judaism: The Challenge of the Nineteenth Century*, compiled with a biographical introduction by M. Wiener, trans. E.J. Schlochauer, Cincinnati, OH: Hebrew Union College Press, 1981.

Gifter, M., 'A path through the ashes: some thoughts on teaching the Holocaust', in N. Wolpin (ed.), *A Path through the Ashes: Penetrating Analysis and Inspiring Stories of the Holocaust from a Torah Perspective*, New York: Mesorah in conjunction with Agudath Israel of America, 1986, pp. 56–63.

Ginzberg, L., *The Legends of the Jews*, trans. H. Szold, Philadelphia, PA: JPS, 1910–38 (7 vols).

Glatzer, N.N. (ed.), *Essays in Jewish Thought*, Alabama: University of Alabama Press, c1978.

—— *Franz Rosenzweig: His Life and Thought*, 2nd rev. edn, presented by N.N. Glatzer, New York: Schocken, 1972.

Glazer, N., *American Judaism*, 2nd edn, Chicago, IL: University of Chicago Press, 1972.

Gleason, C., 'The chosen people of God: Mary Rowlandson's captivity narrative', *Hanover Historical Review* 4, Spring 1996. Available at http://history.hanover.edu/hhr/hhr4–2.html (accessed 26 February 2002).

Goldberg, M., *Why Should Jews Survive? Looking Past the Holocaust toward a Jewish Future*, New York/Oxford: Oxford University Press, 1995.

Golka, F.W., 'Universalism and the election of the Jews', *Theology* 90, 1987, 273–80.

Goodenough, E.R., *By Light, Light: The Mystic Gospel of Hellenistic Judaism*, Amsterdam: Philo Press, 1969.

—— *The Politics of Philo Judaeus*, Hildesheim: Georg Olms Verlagsbuchhandlung, 1967.

Goodman, M., *Mission and Conversion*, Oxford: Clarendon Press, 1994.

Gopin, M., 'An Orthodox embrace of gentiles? interfaith tolerance in the thought of S.D. Luzzatto and E. Benamozegh', *Modern Judaism* 18/2, 1998, 173–96.

Gordis, R., *Understanding Conservative Judaism*, New York: Rabbinical Assembly, 1978.

Gordon, A.D., 'Our tasks ahead' (1920), excerpted in Hertzberg, *Zionist Idea*, pp. 119–33.

Gorny, Y., 'Thoughts on Zionism as a utopian ideology', *Modern Judaism* 18/3, 1998, 241–51.

Gorny, Y., *The State of Israel in Jewish Public Thought: The Quest for Collective Identity*, London: Macmillan, 1994.

Grabbe, L.L., *Judaic Religion in the Second Temple Period*, London: Routledge, 2000.

Greenberg, I., *The Jewish Way: Living the Holidays*, New York: Touchstone Books/Simon and Schuster, 1993.

—— 'Cloud of smoke, pillar of fire: Judaism, Christianity, and modernity after the Holocaust', in Dorff and Newman, *Contemporary Jewish Theology*, pp. 396–416.

Greenberg, Y.K., 'The choosing, not the chosen people', in C. Selengut (ed.), *Jewish Identity in the Postmodern Age: Scholarly and Personal Reflections*, St Paul, MN: Paragon House, 1999, pp. 13–23.

Greene, D., 'A chosen people in a pluralist nation: Horace Kallen and the Jewish-American experience', *Religion and American Culture: A Journal of Interpretation* 16/2, 2006, 169–93.

Grosby, S., 'The chosen people of ancient Israel and the Occident: why does nationality exist and survive?', *Nations and Nationalism* 5/3, 1999, 357–80.

Gurfinkiel, M., 'The Jewish state: the next fifty years', *Azure*, Winter 5759/1999. Available at www.jafi.org.il/education/azure/6/6-gurfinkel.html (accessed 10 December 2007).

Halevi, J., *The Kuzari (Kitab al-Khazari): An Argument for the Faith of Israel*, introduction by H. Slonimsky, trans. H. Hirschfeld, London: Schocken, 1964.

Halevi, J.L., 'Clashing concepts: chosen people versus master race', *Liberal Judaism* 12/11, 1945, 28–32.

Halevi, Y.K., 'Survival', in A. Cohen and P. Mendes-Flohr (eds), *Contemporary Jewish Religious Thought: Original Essays on Critical Concepts, Movements, and Beliefs*, London/New York: Collier-MacMillan, 1987, pp. 947–52.

Hals, R.M., 'The promise and the land', in Opsahl and Tanenbaum, *Speaking of God Today*, pp. 57–72.

Hancock, I., 'Responses to the Porrajmos: the Romani holocaust', in A.S. Rosenbaum (ed.), *Is the Holocaust Unique? Perspectives on Comparative Genocide*, with a foreword by I.W. Charny, Oxford: Westview Press, 1998, pp. 39–64.

Hanson, P.D., *The People Called: The Growth of Community in the Bible*, San Francisco, CA: Harper & Row, 1987.

Harris, R.L., Archer, G.L. and Waltke, B.K. (eds), *Theological Wordbook of the Old Testament*, Chicago, IL: Moody Press, 1980.

Harrison, D.H., 'Skirball examines Truman, "the American Cyrus"', *San Diego Jewish Press Heritage*, 1 May 1998. Available at http://sandiegojewishworld.com/usa/missouri/independence/truman_library/19980501-truman_israel.htm top (accessed 10 December 2007).

Hartman, D., 'Suffering', in Cohen and Mendes-Flohr, *Contemporary Jewish Religious Thought*, pp. 939–46.

—— *A Living Covenant: The Innovative Spirit in Traditional Judaism*, New York: Free Press; London: Collier-MacMillan, 1985.

Harvey, W.Z., response to 'Philosophy and religious values in modern Jewish thought' by M. Fox, in Katz, *Religion in Modern Jewish History*, pp. 86–90.

Hastings, J. (ed.), *Dictionary of the Bible*, 2nd edn, revised by F.C. Grant and H.H. Rowley, Edinburgh: T & T Clark, 1963.

Heard, R.C., *Dynamics of Diselection: Ambiguity in Genesis 12–36 and Ethnic Boundaries in Post-Exilic Judah*, Atlanta, GA: Society of Biblical Literature, 2001.

Helfgott, B.W., *The Doctrine of Election in Tannaitic Literature*, New York: King's Crown Press, 1954.

Hellig, J.L., 'The myth of Jewish chosenness in the modern world', *Dialogue and Alliance* 3, Fall 1989, 5–16.

Herberg, W., *Judaism and Modern Man: An Interpretation of Jewish Religion*, New York: Atheneum, 1980.

—— 'The "chosenness" of Israel, and the Jew of today', in A.A. Cohen (ed.), *Arguments and Doctrines: A Reader of Jewish Thinking in the Aftermath of the Holocaust*, Philadelphia, PA: JPS, 1970, pp. 270–83.

—— 'Jewish existence and survival: a theological view', *Judaism*, July 1952, 19–26.

Hertzberg, A. (ed.), *The Zionist Idea: A Historical Analysis and Reader*, Philadelphia, PA and Jerusalem: JPS, 1997.

—— 'Judaism and the land of Israel', in J. Neusner (ed.), *Understanding Jewish Theology: Classical Issues and Modern Perspectives*, New York: Ktav, 1973, pp. 75–88.

—— (ed.), *Judaism*, New York: George Braziller, 1962.

Hertzberg, A. and Hirt-Manheimer, A., *Jews: The Essence and Character of a People*, San Francisco, CA: HarperSanFrancisco, 1998.

Herzl, T., 'The Jewish state' (1896), excerpted in Hertzberg, *Zionist Idea*, pp. 119–33.

—— 'A solution of the Jewish question' (1896), excerpted in Mendes-Flohr and Reinharz, *Jew in the Modern World*, pp. 533–8.

—— *The Jewish State*, New York: Dover, 1988.

Heschel, A.J., *Israel: An Echo of Eternity*, Woodstock, VT: Jewish Lights Publishing, 1997.

—— *God in Search of Man: A Philosophy of Judaism*, New York: Octagon, 1976.

Hess, M., *The Revival of Israel: Rome and Jerusalem, The Last Nationalist Question*, trans. with introduction and notes by M. Waxman, introduction to the Bison Book Edition by M.I. Urofsky, Lincoln/London: University of Nebraska Press, 1995.

—— 'Rome and Jerusalem' (1862), excerpted in Hertzberg, *Zionist Idea*, pp. 119–33.

Hirsch, S.R., *Horeb*, London: Soncino, 1997.

—— *The Nineteen Letters on Judaism*, New York: Feldheim, 1969.

Hummel, H.D., 'Law and grace in Judaism and Lutheranism', in Opsahl and Tanenbaum, *Speaking of God Today*, pp. 15–30.

Hutner, Y., ' "Holocaust": a Rosh Yeshiva's response', in Wolpin, *Path through the Ashes*, pp. 39–55.

Jabotinsky, V., 'Evidence submitted to the Palestine Royal Commission' (1937), excerpted in Hertzberg, *Zionist Idea*, pp. 559–70.

—— 'What the Zionist-Revisionists want' (1926), excerpted in Mendes-Flohr and Reinharz, *Jew in the Modern World*, pp. 594–7.

Jacobs, L., *The Jewish Religion: A Companion*, Oxford/New York: Oxford University Press, 1995.

—— *A Jewish Theology*, London: Darton, Longman & Todd, 1973.

Jospe, R., 'The concept of the chosen people: an interpretation', *Judaism* 43/2, 1994, 127–48.

Kahane, B.Z., 'There are no innocent Midyanites' 1993. Available at www.kahane.org/parsha/41.html (accessed 17 January 2002).

—— 'Everything you wanted to know about Ishmael', 1997 and 'There is no placing trust [in] the gentile', 1992. Available at www.kahane.org/parsha/5.html (accessed 17 January 2002).

Kalischer, Z.H., 'Seeking Zion' (1862), excerpted in Hertzberg, *Zionist Idea*, pp. 111–14.

Kallen, H.M., 'In the hope of Zion', *International Journal of Ethics* 29/2, 1919, 145–73.

—— 'Zionism and liberalism' (1919), excerpted in Hertzberg, *Zionist Idea*, pp. 528–31.

Kaplan, L., 'Rabbi Abraham I. Kook, Rabbi Joseph B. Soloveitchik and Dr Isaac Breuer on Jewish identity and the Jewish national revival', in Selengut, *Jewish Identity*, pp. 47–66.

Kaplan, M.M., *Judaism as a Civilization: Toward a Reconstruction of American-Jewish Life*, Philadelphia, PA: JPS, 1981.

—— *The Meaning of God in Modern Jewish Religion*, New York: Reconstructionist Press, 1962.

Katz, S.T., *Historicism, the Holocaust, and Zionism: Critical Studies in Modern Jewish Thought and History*, New York: New York University Press, 1992.

Kaufmann, Y., 'On the faith and survival of the Jews', in N.N. Glatzer (ed.), *Modern Jewish Thought: A Source Reader*, New York: Schocken, 1977, pp. 100–8.

—— 'The pangs of redemption', in Cohen, *Arguments and Doctrines*, pp. 473–500.

—— *The Religion of Israel: From Its Beginnings to the Babylonian Exile*, trans. and abbreviated by M. Greenberg, New York: Schocken, 1974 (*c*.1960).

Kellner, D., 'Postmodernism as social theory: some challenges and problems', *Theory, Culture and Society* 5/2–3, 1988, 239–69.

Kellner, M., 'Messianic postures in Israel today', *Modern Judaism* 6/2, 1986, 197–209.

Kissane, E.J., *The Book of Isaiah*, trans. with commentary E.J. Kissane, Dublin: Browne & Nolan, 1943 (2 vols).

Klatzkin, J., 'Boundaries' (1914–21), excerpted in Hertzberg, *Zionist Idea*, pp. 316–27.

Kluger, R.S., *Psyche in Scripture: The Idea of the Chosen People and Other Essays*, Toronto: Inner City Books, 1995.

Kohler, K., *Jewish Theology: Systematically and Historically Considered*, introduction by J.L. Blau, New York: Ktav, 1968.

Kook, A.I., 'Lights for rebirth' (1910–30), excerpted in Hertzberg, *Zionist Idea*, pp. 427–31.

—— 'The rebirth of Israel' (1910–30), excerpted in Hertzberg, *Zionist Idea*, pp. 424–7.

—— *Abraham Isaac Kook: The Lights of Penitence, the Moral Principles, Lights of Holiness, Essays, Letters and Poems*, trans. and introduction by B.Z. Bokser, preface by J. Agus and R. Schatz, London: SPCK, 1979.

Korn, E., 'The gentiles, the world to come, and Judaism: the odyssey of a rabbinic text', *Modern Judaism* 14, 1994, 265–87.

Kraemer, D.C., *Responses to Suffering in Classical Rabbinic Literature*, New York/Oxford: Oxford University Press, 1995.

Kremnizer, R.L., 'Lech Lecha – finding oneself', in *The Curtain Parted: Glimpsing the Week Ahead*. Available at www.sichosinenglish.org/books/the-curtain-parted/03.htm (accessed 10 December 2007).

de Lange, N., *Apocrypha: Jewish Literature of the Hellenistic Age*, New York: Viking Press, 1978.

Leaman, O., *Evil and Suffering in Jewish Philosophy*, Cambridge/New York: Cambridge University Press, 1995.

Leibowitz, Y., 'The religious and moral significance of the redemption of Israel', in Dorff and Newman, *Contemporary Jewish Theology*, pp. 453–64.

—— 'The uniqueness of the Jewish people', *Jerusalem Quarterly* 19, 1981, 47–55.

Levidow, L., 'Zionist anti-Semitism', *Return*, December 1990. Available at www.iahushua.com/Zion/zionrac12.html (accessed 10 December 2007).

Librach, C.E., 'The fragmented faith of American Jews', *First Things* 70, February 1997, 19–21.

Liebman, C.S., 'Cultural conflict in Israeli society', in C.S. Liebman and E. Katz (eds), *The Jewishness of Israelis: Responses to the Guttman Report*, New York: State University of New York Press, 1997, pp. 103–18.

—— *Religion, Democracy and Israeli Society*, Amsterdam: Harwood Academic Publishers, 1997.

—— 'Religion and modernity: *the special case of Israel*', in Liebman and Katz, *Jewishness of Israelis*, pp. 85–102.

—— 'Paradigms sometimes fit: the Haredi response to the Yom Kippur War', in Wistrich and Ohana, *Shaping of Israeli Identity*, pp. 171–84.

—— 'Religious trends among American and Israeli Jews', in R.S. Wistrich (ed.), *Terms of Survival: The Jewish World since 1945*, London/New York: Routledge, 1995, pp. 299–319.

—— 'Jewish fundamentalism and the Israeli polity', in M.E. Marty and R.S. Appleby (eds), *Fundamentalisms and the State: Remaking Polities, Economies, and Militance*, Chicago, IL/London: University of Chicago Press, 1993, pp. 68–87.

Liebman, C.S. and Cohen, S.M., *Two Worlds of Judaism: The Israeli and American Experiences*, New Haven, CT: Yale University Press, 1990.

Liebman, C.S. and Don-Yehiya, E. (eds), *Civil Religion in Israel: Traditional Judaism and Political Culture in the Jewish State*, Berkeley: University of California Press, 1983.

Liebman, C.S. and Katz, E. (eds), *The Jewishness of Israelis: Responses to the Guttman Report*, New York: State University of New York Press, 1997.

Liebman, C.S. and Susser, B., 'The forgotten center: traditional Jewishness in Israel', *Modern Judaism* 17, 1997, 211–20.

Lilienthal, A.M., *The Zionist Connection: What Price Peace?*, New York: Dodd, Mead & Company, 1978.

Lustick, I.S., *For the Land and the Lord: Jewish Fundamentalism in Israel*, New York: Council on Foreign Relations, 1988.

Luz, E., 'Buber's hermeneutics: the road to the revival of the collective memory and religious faith', *Modern Judaism* 15/1, 1995, 69–94.

Magnes, J.L., 'Like all the nations?' (1930), excerpted in Hertzberg, *Zionist Idea*, pp. 443–8.

Maimonides, M., *Code of Law (Mishneh Torah): Book of Torts*, ed. J. Obermann, trans. H. Klein, New Haven, CT: Yale University Press, 1982.

—— *Code of Law (Mishneh Torah): Book of Agriculture*, ed. L. Nemoy, J. Goldin and S. Lieberman, trans. I. Klein, New Haven, CT: Yale University Press, 1979.

—— *Code of Law (Mishneh Torah): Book of Holiness*, ed. L. Nemoy, S. Lieberman, and H.A. Wolfson, trans. L.I. Rabinowitz and P. Grossman, New Haven, CT: Yale University Press, 1965.

'Manifesto' (1902) by Mizrachi, excerpted in Mendes-Flohr and Reinharz, *Jew in the Modern World*, p. 546.

Margolis, M.L. and Marx, A., *A History of the Jewish People*, New York: Atheneum, 1969.

Marmur, D., *Beyond Survival: Reflections on the Future of Judaism*, London: Darton, Longman & Todd, 1982.

Mart, M., 'Constructing a universal ideal: anti-Semitism, American Jews, and the founding of Israel', *Modern Judaism* 20/2, 2000, 181–202.

Mason, R., *The God of Spinoza: A Philosophical Study*, Cambridge/New York: Cambridge University Press, 1997.

Mattuck, I.I., 'The mystery of Israel (M. Maritain's philosophy of the Jews)', *Journal of Jewish Studies* 1/1, 1948–9, 55–60.

McCarthy, D.J., *Treaty and Covenant*, Rome: Pontifical Biblical Institute, 1963.

McKinzie, R.D., 'Oral history interview with Edwin M. Wright', 1977. Available at www.trumanlibrary.org/oralhist/wright.htm (accessed 10 December 2007).

Meir, E., 'Judaism: people or religion? some positions in modern Jewish thought', *Sidic* 25/1, 1992, 20–6.

Mekilta de-Rabbi Ishmael, trans. J.Z. Lauterbach, Philadelphia, PA: JPS, 1961 (3 vols).

Mendelsohn, E., *On Modern Jewish Politics*, New York/Oxford: Oxford University Press, 1993.

Mendelssohn, M., *Jerusalem: Or on Religious Power and Judaism*, trans. A. Arkush, introduction and commentary by A. Altman, Hanover, CT: University Press of New England, 1983.

Mendes-Flohr, P., 'Mendelssohn and Rosenzweig', *Journal of Jewish Studies* 23/2, 1987, 204–11.

Mendes-Flohr, P.R. and Reinharz, J. (eds), *The Jew in the Modern World: A Documentary History*, New York/Oxford: Oxford University Press.

Meyer, M.A., *Jewish Identity in the Modern World*, Seattle/London: University of Washington Press, 1990.

—— 'Modernity as a crisis for the Jews', *Modern Judaism* 9/2, 1989, 151–64.

—— *Response to Modernity: A History of the Reform Movement in Judaism*, Detroit, IL: Wayne State University Press, 1988.

—— 'Abraham Geiger's historical Judaism', in J.J. Petuchowski (ed.), *New Perspectives on Abraham Geiger: An HUC-JIR Symposium*, Cincinnati, OH: HUC-Jewish Institute of Religion, New York: Ktav, 1975, pp. 3–16.

—— 'Universalism and Jewish unity in the thought of Abraham Geiger', in Katz, *Role of Religion in Modern Jewish History*, pp. 91–104.

Michman, D., 'The Holocaust in the eyes of historians: the problem of conceptualization, periodization, and explanation', *Modern Judaism* 15, 1995, 253–64.

Midrash Rabbah, translated under the editorship of H. Freedman and M. Simon, foreword by I. Epstein, London: Soncino Press, 1939 (10 vols).

Miller, R.A., *Rejoice O Youth!: An Integrated Jewish Ideology*, New York: Balshon Printing and Offset, 1962.

Minkin, J.S., *The Teachings of Maimonides*, Northvale, NJ: Jason Aronson, 1993.

The Mishnah, trans. H. Danby, London: Oxford University Press, 1944 (1933).

Misrahi, R., 'Spinoza and Christian thought: a challenge', in S. Hessing (ed.), *Speculum Spinozanum 1677–1977*, London: Routledge & Kegan Paul, 1977, pp. 387–417.

Montefiore, C.G. and Loewe, R. (eds), *A Rabbinic Anthology*, New York: Schocken, 1974.

Neuberger, G.J., 'The great gulf between Zionism and Judaism', 2000. Available at www.nkusa.org/AboutUs/Zionism/greatgulf.cfm (accessed 15 January 2002).

Neusner, J. (ed.), *The Theology of the Oral Torah*, Montreal: McGill University Press, 1999.

—— *Stranger at Home: 'The Holocaust', Zionism, and American Judaism*, Atlanta, GA: Scholars Press, 1997.

—— *Judaism in Modern Times: An Introduction and Reader*, Cambridge, MA: Blackwell, 1995.

—— (ed.), *Judaism Transcends Catastrophe: God, Torah, and Israel beyond the Holocaust – God Commands*, Macon, GA: Mercer University Press, 1995.

—— *Torah through the Ages: A Short History of Judaism*, London: SCM, 1990.

—— *Understanding Rabbinic Judaism: From Talmudic to Modern Times*, New York: Ktav, 1974.

Nicholson, E.W., *Deuteronomy and Tradition*, Oxford: Basil Blackwell, 1967.

Nordau, M., 'Jewry of muscle' (1903), excerpted in Mendes-Flohr and Reinharz, *Jew in the Modern World*, pp. 547–8.

—— 'Speech to the first Zionist congress' (1897), excerpted in Hertzberg, *Zionist Idea*, pp. 235–42.

Novak, D., *The Election of Israel: The Idea of the Chosen People*, Cambridge: Cambridge University Press, 1995.

—— *Jewish Social Ethics*, Oxford/New York: Oxford University Press, 1992.

—— 'The Jewish theology', *Modern Judaism* 10/3, 1990, 311–23.

Novick, P., *The Holocaust and Collective Memory: The American Experience*, London: Bloomsbury, 2001.

Olan, L.A., 'The doctrine of the chosen people reaffirmed', *Judaism* 29/116, 1980, 461–8.

Oppenheim, M., 'Feminism, Jewish philosophy, and religious pluralism', *Modern Judaism* 16, 1996, 147–60.

Opsahl, P. and Tanenbaum, M.H. (ed.), *Speaking of God Today: Jews and Lutherans in Conversation*, Philadelphia, PA: Fortress, 1974.

Osbourne, W.L., 'The Old Testament background of Paul's "all Israel" in Romans 11:26a', *Asia Journal of Theology* 2, 1998, 282–93.

Ozick, C., 'All the world wants the Jews dead', *Esquire*, November 1974, 103.

Patrick, D., 'Election (Old Testament)', in D.N. Freedman (ed.), *Anchor Bible Dictionary*, New York: Doubleday, c.1992.

Pesikta de-Rab Kahana, trans. W.G. Braude and I.J. Kapstein, Philadelphia, PA: JPS, 2002.

Petuchowski, J.J., *Prayerbook Reform in Europe: The Liturgy of European Liberal and Reform Judaism*, New York: World Union for Progressive Judaism, 1968.

Pfeiffer, R.H., *Introduction to the Old Testament*, London: Adam & Charles Black, 1952.

Philo Judaeus, *Legatio ad Gaium*, ed., intro. trans., and commentary by E.M. Smallwood, Leiden: Brill, 1961.

—— *Philo*, with an English translation by F. Colson, Heinemann: Loeb, 1929–62.

Pines, Y.M., 'Jewish nationalism cannot be secular' (1895), excerpted in Hertzberg, *Zionist Idea*, pp. 411–12.

Pinsker, L., 'The auto-Emancipation: an appeal to his people by a Russian Jew' (1882), excerpted in Hertzberg, *Zionist Idea*, pp. 181–97.

Plaskow, J., *Standing Again at Sinai: Judaism from a Feminist Perspective*, New York: HarperCollins, 1991.

Plaut, W.G., *The Case for the Chosen People*, New York: Doubleday, 1965.

Poll, C., 'The Jewish community in America: it is the safest of times and the most dangerous of times', in Selengut, *Jewish Identity*, pp. 25–39.

Polner, M. and Simms, A., 'When Israel is wrong, Christians shouldn't be afraid to say so', *Commonweal* 129/17, 2002, 19–21.

Rabinowicz, H., *Hasidism and the State of Israel*, London/Toronto: Associated University Press, 1982.

Rapaport, J.A., 'Worshipping Mammon: the pursuit of affluence and the assimilation of modern Orthodox Jewry', in Selengut, *Jewish Identity*, pp. 127–50.

Ravitzky, A., *Messianism, Zionism, and Jewish Religious Radicalism*, trans. M. Swirsky and J. Chipman, Chicago, IL/London: University of Chicago Press, 1996.

Rodinson, M., *Israel: A Colonial-settler State?*, New York: Anchor Foundation, 1973.

Rosenbaum, A.S. (ed.), *Is the Holocaust Unique?* Oxford: Westview Press, 1998.

Rosenzweig, F., *The Star of Redemption*, trans. W.W. Hallo, London: University of Notre Dame Press, 1985.

Rotbart, S., 'Who is afraid of the post Zionists?', 30 April 2001. Available at www.hagshama.org.il/en/resources/view.asp?id=5&subject=189 (accessed 28 February 2002).

Rowland, C., *Christian Origins*, London: SPCK, 1985.

Rowley, H.H., *The Biblical Doctrine of Election*, London: Lutterworth Press, 1950.

Rubenstein, R., 'After Auschwitz', in Dorff and Newman, *Contemporary Jewish Theology*, pp. 374–84.

—— 'Some perspectives on religious faith after Auschwitz', in F.H. Little and H.G. Locke (eds), *The German Church Struggle and the Holocaust*, San Francisco, CA: Mellen Research University Press, 1990, pp. 256–68.

—— *After Auschwitz: Radical Theology and Contemporary Judaism*, New York: The Bobbs-Merrill Company, 1966.

Rubinoff, L., 'Auschwitz and the theology of the Holocaust', in Opsahl and Tanenbaum, *Speaking of God Today*, pp. 121–43.

Rudavsky, D., *Modern Jewish Religious Movements: A History of Emancipation and Adjustment*, rev. edn, New York: Behrman House, 1979.

Saadiah Gaon, *The Book of Beliefs and Opinions*, trans. S. Rosenblatt, New Haven, CT/London: Yale University Press, 1976.

Sacks, J., *Crisis and Covenant: Jewish Thought after the Holocaust*, Manchester/New York: Manchester University Press, 1992.

Said, E., *Culture and Imperialism*, London: Vintage, 1993.

Samuel, M., 'Race, nation, and people in the Jewish Bible', in A.L. Jamison (ed.), *Tradition and Change in Jewish Experience*, the B.G. Rudolph Lectures in Judaic Studies, New York: Syracuse University Press, 1978, pp. 26–45.

Samuelson, N.M., *A User's Guide to Franz Rosenzweig's* Star of Redemption, Surrey: Curzon, 1999.

—— 'Response to Menachem Kellner', in D.H. Frank (ed.), *A People Apart: Chosenness and Ritual in Jewish Philosophical Thought*, Albany: State University of New York Press, 1993, pp. 77–83.

Sanders, E.P., *Paul, the Law, and the Jewish People*, London: SCM, 1983.

—— *Paul and Palestinian Judaism*, London: SCM, 1977.

Sarot, M., 'Auschwitz, morality and the suffering of God', *Modern Theology* 7/2, 1991, 135–52.

Schechter, S., *Studies in Judaism: Essays on Persons, Concepts, and Movements of Thought in Jewish Tradition*, New York: Atheneum, 1970.

—— *Some Aspects of Rabbinic Theology*, New York: The MacMillan Company, 1910.

——'Zionism: a statement' (1906), excerpted in Hertzberg, *Zionist Idea*, pp. 504–13.

Scholem, G., *Kabbalah*, New York: Meridian, 1974.

Schorsch, I., 'The sacred cluster: the core values of Conservative Judaism', 1995. Available at http://a2vigil.org/cjcorevalues.htm (accessed 10 December 2007).

—— 'The Holocaust and Jewish survival', *Midstream*, January 1981, 38–42.

Schürer, E., *The History of the Jewish People in the Age of Jesus Christ (175 B.C.–A.D. 135)*, Edinburgh: T & T Clark, *c.*1973.

Schwarz, L.W., *Great Ages and Ideas of the Jewish People*, New York: Modern Library, 1956.

Schweid, E., 'Judaism in Israeli Culture', in D. Urian and E. Karsh (eds), *In Search of Identity: Jewish Aspects in Israeli Culture*, London/Portland, OR: Frank Cass, 1999, pp. 9–28.

—— 'Is there really no alienation or polarization?' in Liebman and Katz, *Jewishness of Israelis*, pp. 151–8.

—— 'Jewish messianism: metaphors of an idea', *Jerusalem Quarterly* 36, Summer 1985, 63–78.

Scott, J.M., 'Restoration of Israel', in G.F. Hawthorne and R.P. Martin (eds), *Dictionary of Paul and His Letters*, Leicester: Inter-Varsity Press, 1993.

Segal, A.F., *Paul the Convert*, New Haven, CT: Yale University Press, 1990.

Segev, T., *The Seventh Million: The Israelis and the Holocaust*, trans. H. Watzman, New York: Henry Holt and Company, 1991.

Selengut, C. (ed.), *Jewish identity in the Postmodern Age: Scholarly and Personal Reflections*, Minnesota: Paragon House, 1999.

Seltzer, R.M., *The Jewish People, The Jewish Thought: The Jewish Experience in History*, New York/London: Collier-MacMillan, 1980.

Shahak, I. and Mezvinsky, N., *Jewish Fundamentalism in Israel*, London: Pluto Press, 1999.

Shaked, G., 'Israeli society and secular-Jewish culture', in Liebman and Katz, *Jewishness of Israelis*, pp. 159–65.

Shapiro, E., 'Modern Orthodoxy in crisis: a test case', *Judaism* 51/3, 2002, 347–61.

—— 'Liberal politics and American Jewish identity', *Judaism* 47/4, 1998, 425–36.

Sharot, S., 'Traditional, modern or postmodern? recent religious developments among Jews in Israel', in K. Flanagan and P.C. Jupp (eds), *Postmodernity, Sociology and Religion*, London: Macmillan, 1996, pp. 118–33.

—— *Messianism, Mysticism, and Magic: A Sociological Analysis of Jewish Religious Movements*, Chapel Hill: University of North Carolina Press, 1982.

Sherman, F., 'Speaking of God after Auschwitz', in Opsahl and Tanenbaum, *Speaking of God Today*, pp. 144–59.

Sicker, M., *Judaism, Nationalism and the Land of Israel*, Boulder, CO: Westview Press, 1992.

Siegel, S., 'Election and the people of God', in Opsahl and Tanenbaum, *Speaking of God Today*, pp. 39–53.

Sifré: A Tannaitic Commentary on the Book of Deuteronomy, trans. R. Hammer, New Haven, CT: Yale University Press, 1986.

Silberman, C.E., *A Certain People: American Jews and Their Lives Today*, New York: Summit Books, 1985.

Silberstein, J.L., *The Postzionism Debates: Knowledge and Power in Israeli Culture*, New York/London: Routledge, 1999.

—— 'Cultural criticism, ideology, and the interpretation of Zionism: toward a post-Zionist discourse', in S. Kepnes (ed.), *Interpreting Judaism in a Postmodern Age*, New York/London: New York University Press, 1996, pp. 325–58.

Silver, A.H., *Where Judaism Differed: An Inquiry into the Distinctiveness of Judaism*, London: Collier-MacMillan, 1956.

Singer, D., review on *Jews: The Essence and Character of a People* by A. Hertzberg and A. Hirt-Manheimer, *Commentary*, July 1998. Available at www.commentarymagazine.com/viewarticle.cfm/Jews-by-Arthur-Hertzberg-and-Aron-HirtManheimer-8900 (accessed 10 December 2007).

—— 'Change and continuity in American Judaism: the case of Nathan Glazer', in Wistrich, *Terms of Survival*, pp. 320–31.

—— 'The new Orthodox theology', *Modern Judaism* 9/1, 1989, 35–54.

Sklare, M., *An American Religious Movement: Conservative Judaism*, Lanham, MD: University Press of America, 1985.

Smith, J.M.P., 'The chosen people', *American Journal of Semitic Languages and Literatures* 45/2, 1929, 73–82.

Smith, R.O., 'Between restoration and liberation: theopolitical contributions and responses to U.S. foreign policy in Israel/Palestine', *Journal of Church and State* 46/4, 2004, 833–60.

Soloveitchik, J.B., *Fate and Destiny: From the Holocaust to the State of Israel*, New York: Ktav, 2002.

Spinoza, B., *Tractatus Theologico–Politicus*, trans. S. Shirley, Leiden/New York: E.J. Brill, 1989.

—— *Ethic*, trans. W.H. White, Oxford: Oxford University Press, 1930.

Stannard, D.E., 'Uniqueness as denial: the politics of genocide scholarship', in Rosenbaum, *Is the Holocaust Unique?*, pp. 163–208.

Stendhal, K., *Paul among the Jews and Gentiles*, London: SCM, 1977.

Stern, S., *Jewish Identity in Early Rabbinic Writings*, Leiden/New York/Cologne: E.J. Brill, 1994.

Sternbuch, M., *Rav Moshe Speaks: An Anthology of Talks*, Y. Rosenes (ed.), Jerusalem: Jewish Writers Guild, 1988.

Stone, M.E., *Jewish Writings of the Second Temple Period*, Philadelphia, PA: Fortress, 1984.

Susser, B. and Liebman, C.S., *Choosing Survival: Strategies for a Jewish Future*, New York/Oxford: Oxford University Press, 1999.

Syrkin, N., 'The Jewish problem and the socialist-Jewish state' (1898), excerpted in Hertzberg, *Zionist Idea*, pp. 333–50.

Tal, U., 'Foundations of a political messianic trend in Israel', *Jerusalem Quarterly* 35, Spring 1985, 42–5.

Temkin, S.D., *Creating American Reform Judaism: The Life and Times of Isaac Mayer Wise*, London/Portland, OR: Littman Library of Jewish Civilization, 1998.

Tigay, J.H., *The JPS Torah Commentary: Deuteronomy*, Philadelphia, PA: JPS, 1996.

Twersky, I. (ed.), *A Maimonides Reader*, West Orange, NJ: Behrman House, 1972.

Unger, M.F. and White, W. (eds), *Nelson's Expository Dictionary of the Old Testament*, Nashville, TN: Nelson, 1980.

Urbach, E.E., *The Sages: Their Concepts and Beliefs*, trans. I. Abraham, Jerusalem: Hebrew University, 1973.

Urofsky, M.I., introduction to *The Revival of Israel*, by M. Hess, pp. i–xvii.

Vermes, G., *The Dead Sea Scrolls in English*, New York: Penguin, 1975.

Vermes, P., *Buber on God and the Perfect Man*, London/Washington, DC: Littman Library of Civilization, 1994.

Weiss, D., 'Judaism: an alternative to Zionism', 2001. Available at www.mediamonitors.net/rabbidavidweiss1.html (accessed 6 September 2001).

Werblowsky, Z., 'The people and the land', in Opsahl and Tanenbaum, *Speaking of God Today*, pp. 73–98.

Wertheimer, J. 'Judaism without limits', *Commentary* 104, July 1997, 24–7.

'What do American Jews believe? a symposium', *Commentary*, August 1996. Available at www.commentarymagazine.com/viewarticle.cfm/What-Do-American-Jews-Believe-8600 (accessed 27 November 2001).

Wiesel, E., 'Talking and writing and keeping silent', in Little and Locke, *German Church Struggle and the Holocaust*, pp. 269–77.

Wise, I.M., *Judaism: Its Doctrines and Duties*, Cincinnati, OH: Office of the Israelite, 1872.

Wise, T., 'Reflections on Zionism from a dissident Jew', 2001. Available at www.zmag.org/sustainers/content/2001–09/05wise.htm (accessed 10 December 2007).

Wistrich, R.S. (ed.), *Terms of Survival: The Jewish World since 1945*, London/New York: Routledge, 1995.

Wolfson, H.A., *Philo: Foundations of Religious Philosophy in Judaism, Christianity and Islam*, Cambridge, MA: Harvard University Press, 1947.

Wyschogrod, M., *The Body of Faith: God in the People of Israel*, San Francisco, CA/New York: Harper & Row, 1989.

—— 'Faith and the Holocaust', *Judaism* 20, 1971, 286–94.

Yoffie, E.H., Keynote Lecture in RSGB Conference, Nottingham University, 1 July 2000. Available at www.refsyn.org.uk (accessed 3 September 2001).

Yovel, Y., *Spinoza and Other Heretics: The Marrano of Reason*, Princeton, NJ: Princeton University Press, 1989.

Zahavy, T., 'The predicament of the postmodern American Jew', in Selengut, *Jewish Identity*, pp. 235–48.

Zalman, S., *Tanya: Likutei Amarim*. Available at www.chabad.org/library/article_cdo/aid/6239/jewish/Likutei-Amarim.htm (accessed 10 December 2007).

Zogby, J., *Zionism and the Problem of Palestinian Human Rights*, Association of Arab-American University Graduates, Information paper no. 20, October 1976.

The Zohar, trans. H. Sperling and M. Simon, introduction by J. Abelson, London/New York: Soncino Press, 1984 (5 vols).

Index of ancient sources

Index of names and subjects

Abba bar Zavda, Rabbi 38
Abraham 29; descendants of 16, 31, 43,
  155; election of 14, 155, 156, 175; faith
  in God 14; seeking God 28
aggadah 34
Agudat Israel 106, 179, 180
Agus, Jacob 49, 57, 85, 117, 153
Ahad Ha-Am 93, 97–8, 101, 111
Akiba, Rabbi 38
Aleinu prayer 63–4, 85, 88, 109, 139–40,
  151, 197n7, 204n126, 212n57
Alkalai, Rabbi Yehudah 104–6, 109
Alter, Rabbi Avraham Mordechai 107
American Jewry 115, 146; emphasis on
  social justice 78, 79, 80; fear of
  assimilation 75, 117, 119, 120, 136, 142,
  147; and identity 117, 120; and the state
  of Israel 117, 120, 138, 167
Amiel, Rabbi Moshe Avigdor 179, 180
anti-Semitism 69, 77, 79, 90, 92, 94, 95,
  109, 117, 132, 145, 148, 149, 176, 183,
  187
Apocrypha 4, 192n8
Arabs 111; identified with Canaanites 177;
  identified with Esau 176; in Israel 169,
  176, 177, 179, 180; of Palestine 91, 104,
  109; Zionists' contempt of 170, 172,
  175
Arad, Gulie Ne'eman 123, 132
Ashkenazi Jews 47, 106, 124, 169, 170,
  178
Auschwitz 134; compared to Sinai 126,
  127, 131, 135, 166; memory of 132; *see
  also* Holocaust
Aviner, Rabbi Shlomo 179
Avineri, Shlomo 108

Baeck, Leo 82
Balfour Declaration 78, 106

Bamberger, Bernard 80
Bar-ilan, Rabbi Meir 106
Barth, Karl 32
Baudrillard, J. 210n126
Bayfield, Tony 146
Begin, Menachem 177
Ben-Gurion, David 120, 168, 169, 170,
  171
Benamozegh, Elijah 67
Berdichevski, Micha 92, 101
Berger, David 163
Berger, Michael 161
Bergman, Samuel 64, 71
Berkovits, Eliezer 125–6, 131
Berman, Saul 163
Bettelheim, Bruno 118
Beyer, Peter 104
Bialik, Hayyim 106
Bidney, D. 195n6
Borowitz, Eugene 123, 138, 140, 147–9,
  161, 163; *Judaism after Modernity* 149;
  Renewing the Covenant 148
Brandeis, Louis 100–1
Breger, Marshall 163
Brenner, Joseph 92, 102–3
Buber, Martin 60, 69, 70, 72–4, 82, 93,
  109–10; 'I–Thou' 73, 149

Carter, Jimmy 167
Chomsky, Noam 170
chosen people, concept of 65, 94, 146,
  159, 165, 181; in the book of
  Deuteronomy 10; and chauvinism 78,
  153, 169; Christian notion of 99;
  Commentary magazine's survey on
  117–18, 138, 148, 151, 153–4, 159,
  163–4; essential to Judaism 151; as an
  expression 9, 190n1; and hierarchical
  differentiation 169, 215n12; and